VERA LEX HISTORIAE?

Before you start to read this book, take this moment to think about making a donation to punctum books, an independent non-profit press,

@ https://punctumbooks.com/support/

If you're reading the e-book, you can click on the image below to go directly to our donations site. Any amount, no matter the size, is appreciated and will help us to keep our ship of fools afloat. Contributions from dedicated readers will also help us to keep our commons open and to cultivate new work that can't find a welcoming port elsewhere. Our adventure is not possible without your support.

Vive la Open Access.

Fig. 1. Detail from Hieronymus Bosch, *Ship of Fools* (1490–1500)

VERA LEX HISTORIAE? CONSTRUCTIONS OF TRUTH IN MEDIEVAL HISTORICAL NARRATIVE. Copyright © 2022 by the authors and editors. This work carries a Creative Commons BY-NC-SA 4.0 International license, which means that you are free to copy and redistribute the material in any medium or format, and you may also remix, transform and build upon the material, as long as you clearly attribute the work to the authors (but not in a way that suggests the authors or punctum books endorses you and your work), you do not use this work for commercial gain in any form whatsoever, and that for any remixing and transformation, you distribute your rebuild under the same license. http://creativecommons.org/licenses/by-nc-sa/4.0/

First published in 2022 by Gracchi Books, Binghamton, NY,
an imprint of punctum books, Earth, Milky Way.
https://punctumbooks.com

ISBN-13: 978-1-68571-030-9 (print)
ISBN-13: 978-1-68571-031-6 (ePDF)

DOI: 10.53288/0369.1.00

LCCN: 2022944329
Library of Congress Cataloging Data is available from the Library of Congress

Book design: Vincent W.J. van Gerven Oei
Cover image: Peter Heelas, St. Paul's Monastery, Jarrow, Sept. 17, 2019.

spontaneous acts of scholarly combustion

"Too many echoes, not enough voices."
— Cornel West

Catalin Taranu &
Michael J. Kelly (eds.)

Vera Lex Historiae?
Constructions of Truth in Medieval Historical Narrative

Contents

Preface: Truth & Anti-History   13
Michael J. Kelly

Introduction: *Vera Lex Historiae?*   35
Catalin Taranu & Ralph O'Connor

The Shoemaker and the Troubadour Knight, and Other
Stories: Historicity and the Truth of Fiction in Medieval
Castilian Literature   83
Kim Bergqvist

How the Barking Nuns Forgot Their Abbesses   113
Cynthia Turner Camp

Alternative Histories: Phantom Truths in Stone   141
Catherine E. Karkov

Narratio Probabilis in Early Medieval Historiography:
A Reconsideration   177
Justin Lake

The Literary Imaginary of the Past as the Truth of the
Present: Occasional Literature in Twelfth-Century
Constantinople   213
Ingela Nilsson

Romance, Legend, and the Remote Past: Historical
Frameing in Late Medieval Icelandic Sagas 251
Ralph O'Connor

"Truth is the trickiest": Vernacular Theories of Truth and
Strategies of Truth-making in Old English Verse 307
Catalin Taranu

Contributors 357

Index 361

Editors' Acknowledgments

For Efrat.
— Michael J. Kelly

This collective volume has been long in the making, taking twists and turns that had not been planned, and it will keep being alive, in the making, for as long as it will have readers. It would be impossible to mention all the people and contexts that contributed to what it came to be, but a few names have to be named: the people at the University of Leeds and beyond taking part in the *Philosophies of History* seminar series (2013–2016), brought together by Michael J. Kelly et co. — the ideas for this project grew out of many conversations with Michael over cheese and wine; Alaric Hall and Jay Paul Gates, for essential help with this project; Oana Cojocaru, for her friendship and inspiration; Adrian Haret, for many invigorating discussions; my parents, Gabriela and Octavian, for keeping me fed in my times of academic precariat; all of the above, and many other friends (Hervin Fernández Aceves, Otávio Luiz Vieira Pinto, Mike Burrows, to mention only a few) for providing couches for sleeping in times of need.
— Catalin Taranu

Preface:
Truth & Anti-History

Michael J. Kelly

> *"The only writer of history with the gift of setting alight the sparks of hope in the past, is the one who is convinced of this: that not even the dead will be safe from the enemy, if he is victorious. And this enemy has not ceased to be victorious."*
> — Walter Benjamin, *On the Concept of History*

Writing history must begin with the acceptance that there are no "objective" facts out there waiting to be discovered and compiled together into a story. History is a narrative method that engenders what we call the facts, the details that seem to contain in themselves the actual basis of the historical tale, what the historian reveals as a reality. Facts are the product of this process of factuality and, with that, also historical truth. So, to begin historical research with the aim of finding the historical "truth" is a circular endeavor unless one admits that it is itself a product of historiography. As a result of discourse, the announced historical truth, in order to have effect, must be understandable to those encountering it, must be within the boundaries of what is believable and also reconcilable, even if unconsciously, with the Real (and the anti-History truth event, as explained below). As this book shows, a number of early medieval writers, although perhaps not proto-Foucauldians or proto-Lacanians, grasped well this historical truth procedure.

As Kim Bergqvist explains in his chapter, "The Shoemaker and the Troubadour Knight, and Other Stories: Historicity and the Truth of Fiction in Medieval Castilian Literature," "Fictional texts in the Middle Ages could definitively have, or be thought to have, a *plausibility* that separated them further from purely imaginary fiction than from referential historical texts. Both history and fiction had to be credible representations of plausible events, or something like it. That is, histories were fictionally embellished or developed in order to be plausible representations of the lived and experienced past (for example, dialogues invented, gaps filled in between the accepted facts, etc.), whereas fictional discourse also had to meet standards of plausibility, in order not to be disregarded as *fabulae*. Consequently, plausibility characterizes medieval history writing as well as medieval fiction, and does not help us distinguish or delineate boundaries between them (or identify a medieval distinction between the two)." For earlier medieval Iberian writers, history was also plausible narration, that is, the conscious/unconscious encounter with the *epistēmē* and the Real was an endemic aspect of presenting the past as fact.[1] Yet, as Bergqvist shows, centuries later we find this relationship, via the vortex plausibility, a lesser or even unreliable element in determining history from fiction.

---

1 For Isidore of Seville, *historia est narratio*, and it is *argumentum*, a term which implies narrative deception and can be translated as "riddle," "trick," "sinister argument," or "plausible narration." (Isid., *Etymologies*, 1.41.1 and 1.44.5). This was a view common at the time, as seen in a letter between a monk Mauricius and the metropolitan bishop of Narbonne in the early 610s in which "history" is equated with narration (*Epistolae Wisigothicae*, 18 [*Epistolae Merovingici et Karolini aevi*, ed. Wilhem Gundlach, Monumenta Germaniae Historica, Epistolarum 3 (Berlin: Weidmann, 1892), 687]: "Hos namque et alios quam plurimos Dei notatos electione multum sacra narrat historia, quos nec tempori nec loci coarctat necessitas per ordinem replicare."). For more on Isidore's history writing see chapter 3 of Michael J. Kelly, *Isidore of Seville and the "Liber Iudiciorum": The Struggle for the Past in the Visigothic Kingdom*, The Medieval and Early Modern Iberian World 80 (Boston and Leiden: Brill, 2021).

Slavoj Žižek rethinks Jacques Lacan's Real into that which exposes the perspectival gap (and so we'll turn to negative dialectics in a moment), as opposed to harboring the permanent, which is what it may have done for Visigothic authors and audiences but not for those later ones that Bergqvist explores.[2] For them, historical truth is a moveable object — along a methodological plausibility spectrum — and because of this motion it is, we can say, a sort of Kantian antinomy, i.e., a phenomenon occupying varying viewer-dependent space. What does this mean then for understanding early medieval and medieval historical truth? At the very least, it means that throughout the Iberian Middle Ages the Real, as a determining factor in historical truth, went from being ontologically monistic to being a multiplicity, or Lacanian–Žižekian to Deleuzian.

What is the precise relation though between the constructed historical truth and the latent materialist immanence, the universal truth, the truth of the anti-History event, and so of the possibilities for a *vera lex historiae* as laid out and potentially grasped by medieval authors? In Alain Badiou's theory of the subject, which drove the conception of this volume, a truth is both always universal and always unpredictable, unable to be forced, arriving unannounced via one of four truth procedures (art, love, politics, or science).[3] But our historical truth is a construction. And so, it is more properly speaking a belief, a fidelity fueling a partisan subjectivity. It is closer, then, to a religious or political ideology built — by the historian, the faithful subject — around a universal truth which the historian as prophet announced had arrived. The theological nature of history should be no surprise given the origins of divine truth in explanations

---

2   See Slavoj Žižek, *The Parallax View* (Cambridge: MIT Press, 2006). In this book, to which, amongst others, I am theoretically indebted, Žižek also explains how it is the object, that which is actualized by a truth event, an anti-History event as I call it, which moves History, which, as he says, tickles the subject.
3   See Alain Badiou, *Theory of the Subject,* trans. Bruno Bosteels (New York: Continuum, 2009), passim. For an introduction to Badiou's philosophy, see Michael J. Kelly, *Alain Badiou: A Graphic Guide* (London: Icon Book, 2004).

of what happened at some previous moment. It also means though that our historical truth is — and here the Platonism of Badiou is evident and unavoidable — a shadow or a representation of what is figured to be faithful to a (past) truth event.

Yet also, once a truth is subjectivized or actualized as a particular discourse — as here through the historical process — it is on a trajectory towards nomination, and with that the death of the subjective moment, the ultimate turning of that truth into dogma. In other words, the historical truth de-universalizes (or actualizes, to sound less sinister) the original un- or anti-historical truth event which ripped a hole in existing knowledge and had the historian announce it as a new truth and build a faith around it. As such, historical truth is effectively not quite teleological but certainly on a potential (arborescent, non-rhizomatic) path towards some end, or, nomination. Once the Christ Event, for instance, was nominated as Catholic, it was (despite the meaning of the word catholic) made a partisan, historical discourse. This is what history does. And so this theory of history transcends Badiou's, built on Theodor Adorno's negative dialectic — the anti- as the originary — in that historical truths emerge when we realize not only the limits of knowledge and Real but that they have been breached by an anti-History event.

But is this a *vera lex historiae* akin at all to the theological and religious thinking of Bede and other medieval authors? Did it help them and can it help us to "delineate the boundaries" between history and fiction in the Middle Ages, i.e., that the former, alone of the two, is grounded in a truth event and the subsequent process of subjectivity? That is, that although plausibility is a truth-procedure common denominator of both medieval history and medieval fiction, and so cannot be relied upon to distinguish them, what can be relied upon is the distinct revelatory nature of history, by structure and intent meant to enlighten and convince the would-be subject to become a partisan of the new truth. Was this distinction evident to medieval authors?

Michel de Certeau maintained that once you put something in a museum you destroy its potential for action, as it is no longer significant in the present world, no longer part of it, is removed from being a being in time to an object out of time. Badiou decries any writing of the history of philosophy for this reason.[4] Once philosophy becomes a discourse about the past of philosophy it has been removed from the realm of political potential in the present, it becomes an object in a museum, or an icon frozen in and out of time. Historians likewise put universal, anti-history truth events into a virtual museum when we build for them an edifice for display, like the universality of the God truth, the Word nominated and de-universalized when put inside the Ark of the Covenant, itself a museum of a once radical, anti-historical, knowledge-shattering truth replaced by a singular, ultimately dogmatic historical truth, or rather, belief system. Is this what medieval authors meant when thinking of a *vera lex historiae,* or just of historical truth, and does it demonstrate a persistent desire — even if unstable — for a monist Real? Yes and no.

What Bergqvist calls "*reality elements* in some of his (Juan Manuel) texts, that is, referential or pseudo-referential elements such as historical figures or episodes included therein" are similar to what Jouni-Matti Kukkanen calls in his "postnarrative history" the *kernels* of truth. They are dormant truths brought to life through a new historical process, the writing of a text which endows these truths, the "reality elements," with historical meaning, makes them into "facts," and from that projects authority, or even authenticity, onto the rest of the narrative. But, what does this figural truth indicate about the historicity of the text built around such "reality elements"? As Michel

---

4 I reference this from Badiou via my first (yet unpublished) interview with him in Amsterdam in 2013, but one can also find the idea in Alain Badiou, *The Rebirth of History: Times of Riots and Uprisings,* trans. Gregory Elliott (New York: Verso, 2012). Despite the name of the book, Badiou simply repeats — and here I mean it in the Deleuzian sense, see note below — his theory of the subject which, as it is constituted — before my continual reworking of it — is not yet a philosophy or theory of history.

Foucault contends, the "figure of man" reveals the human to be fundamentally a historical subject, that is, we could say, a man is always a product of contingent choices (contingency as *the* Absolute Truth?), of fidelity to a truth, never a truth in himself, insofar as conscious choices were made.[5]

The unconscious actions of the pre-figured person, a person's being, could elicit a truth event, but the figuration of man uncovers their subjectivity. And so the "reality elements" present historical belief (otherwise called "truth") and from belief then lessons or revelations (the "let me tell you what *really* happened, what you should *really* think"), and that is their didactic aim, as we see, I contend, in Bergqvist's chapter. And furthermore, as he shows, Juan Manuel imagined these historical "truths," for example, figurations of past characters, as able in themselves to deliver universal truths through their partisan or religious subjectivity, that is, their narrative conditioning. As Bergqvist notes: "Juan Manuel's strategic use of reality elements […] suggests that the truth present in the narratives is exterior and prior to the composition of the work, and that this truth is thus not created by its author, but merely revealed to its audience."[6]

So, whether it's "Charlemagne in the *Chanson de Roland*" or Napoleon in Leo Tolstoy's *War and Peace,* or Vlad the Impaler in David Foster Wallace's *The Broom of the System,* the figuration of the man endows the character with historical and fic-

---

5 As a process of figuration, History reveals the human to be always a historical subject, on which see Michel Foucault, *The Order of Things: An Archaeology of the Human Sciences* (New York: Routledge, 2005), 406 (but 400–407 more widely). Or, as the self-proclaimed anti-Christ LaVache Beadsman tells his sister Lenore, we cannot think ourselves thinking and "that means that we ourselves are things that can't think themselves, and so are the proper objects for our thought; we fulfill the game's condition, we are ourselves Others. So, if we can think ourselves, we can't; and if we can't, we can." We ourselves, therefore, are our own Other, this gap allowing the unconscious us to be a truth event. For the quote see David Foster Wallace, *The Broom of the System* (New York: Penguin, 2004), 248. For Kuukkanen's philosophy of history see Jouni-Matti Kuukkanen, *Postnarrativist Philosophy of Historiography* (New York: Palgrave MacMillan, 2015).

6 John of Salisbury, she suggests, would appear to have felt the same way about historical truth.

tive subjectivity, endowed with a certain fidelity, a narrative or poetic strategy, and requiring one to suspend disbelief (and embrace the figure as real). Thus, the structural uniqueness of such historical writing is its intent at subjective revelation, the building of a faith around an external-made-apparent truth. (It is no wonder then that the modern founders of the profession imagined this universal potential as an "objective" site discoverable by the emergent religion, science).

In Badiou's theory of the subject there are three possible reactions to a truth event: one can either become a partisan of the new truth (i.e., a faithful subject, a historian), a reactionary to it (i.e., the fetishist of the present, of the current world, that is, historical discourse, who says an event happened but that it is a false one), or deny it (i.e., the occultist hiding the truth). The faithful subject is the historian type that we have discussed so far, the one Juan Manuel understood, who builds from some external truth a plausible narration that also portends to reveal the *reality* of the event and its universal importance. In "How the Barking Nuns Forgot Their Abbesses," Cynthia Turner Camp turns our attention to medieval England and specifically to the liturgy of Barking Abbey, about which she says that "By exercising careful control over the precise rites through which they prayed for their early abbesses' souls, the nuns of Barking engaged in the historiographic dialectic of remembering and forgetting to craft a decidedly, almost exclusively, female heritage that negotiates the achievements of individual abbesses with a singular nunnery identity."

Such a performative historical process that presents and sustains historical truths through the actions of the body, by the habitus of nuns, in particular the truth of the Christ Event, is echoed in Martin Buber: "[…] the last (even the tiniest) thing in the world is worthy that through it God should reveal Himself to the man who truly seeks Him; for no thing can exist without a divine spark (truth event), and each person can uncover and redeem this spark at each time and through each action, even the most ordinary, if only he performs it in purity, wholly directed to God and concentrated in Him. Therefore, it will not do to serve God only in isolated hours and with set words and gestures. One must serve God with one's whole life, with the whole of the everyday, with the whole of reality. The salvation of man does not lie in his holding himself far removed from the worldly, but in consecrating it to the holy, to divine meaning: his work and his food, his rest and his wandering, the structure of the family and the structure of society."[7]

This dedication to the divine truth was evident in the actions of the nuns, but theirs was also, as Camp shows, a fidelity to a historical truth that they constructed to promote the female figures of their (the logics of their) world, and to exclude others. "Bringing together these holy women within the liturgical year," Camp contends, "the [Barking] *Ordinal* enables a supratemporal recognition of female accomplishment, associating significant women across the centuries and bringing them into focus in the modern nuns' devotions." This is effectively the historical process that Bergqvist shows of Juan Manuel, although it may seem endowed with another feature: *damnatio memoriae*, the purposed forgetting, or negating, at the root of historiography.[8] In

---

7 Martin Buber, *Hasidism and Modern Man*, intro. David Biale (Princeton: Princeton University Press, 2016), 17–18.

8 The concept of *damnatio memoriae* is a Roman one, found across material and written culture and especially popular in late-Roman and post-Roman ("vulgar") legal codification. The use of *damnatio memoriae*, in which the condemned person is written-out of textual records or the texts containing their name and signature are destroyed, can be found, for example, throughout Justinian's *Corpus Iuris Civilis*, in laws that deal with political, social, and religious infamy: in *Codex*, 1.3.23, Eutyches is condemned by a Catholic council for impiety, while *Dig.*, 28.3.6.11 demands the condemnation of a person's memory because of treason or other similar offence. The most interesting case is perhaps *Inst.*, 3.1.5, which explains the damnation of memory as a way of blocking the heirs of the condemned. (This could have been particularly pertinent to the aims of the Barking nuns.) The Roman phrase for such erasure from the records was, to be precise, *memoria damnata* (but see also *Codex*, 1.5.4.4, 7.2.2 and 9.8.6, *Dig.*, 28.3.6.11 and 31.76.9, *Inst.*, 3.1.5 and 4.18.3). *Damnatio memoriae* is, to be precise, an early modern term, first appearing in scholarship in 1689 as the title of a PhD dissertation by Christopher Schreiter, *Iuridicam de Damnatione Memoriae, Praescitu Superiorum*. For a short discussion see Peter Stewart, "The Destruction of Statues in Late Antiquity," in *Constructing Identity in Late*

Camp's words, "Forgetting (or,) — more properly, the judicious privileging of some events over others — is a necessary historiographic operation, for it is impossible to emplot *everything* into a coherent presentation of a meaningful past." In other words, what seems like a deviance or additional narrative act here is part and parcel of this historical process, that is, the construction of a historical truth by the faithful subject. Badiou's theory of the subject as grounding for our ontology of History — which I argue always begins at the anti-History moment, or something like Badiou's truth event — is an ontology that fits so far also that of the medieval historian. But let's continue.

Catherine Karkov, in her chapter, "Alternative Histories: Phantom Truths in Stone," while interrogating stone and its place in the formation of historical truth, introduces us to, via Donna Haraway and Karen Barad, the term "intra-action," which is effectively a type of post-Hegelian, Deleuzian-rhizomatic "dialectic" (we'll say) in which indiscrete non-entities oscillate and entangle without the influencing expectations of interaction. This seems to negate the need for the absolute truth of contingency (i.e., an absolute beyond subjectivity). As such, it works well for imagining stone as the space of the Real, while still allowing that historical truths demand a process grounded

---

Antiquity, ed. Richard Miles (London: Routledge, 1999), 184, n. 3, and for a view of the general subject from a non-literary point of view, see Eric R. Varner, *Mutilation and Transformation: "Damnatio Memoriae" and Roman Imperial Portraiture* (Boston and Leiden: Brill, 2004). The use of *damnatio memoriae* continued on well past late-imperial Rome, for example, by Jordanes in his politically expedient constructions of the past concerning the Goths and Romans in broader Byzantium. For Jordanes's *damnatio memoriae* see Walter Goffart, *The Narrators of Barbarian History (AD 550–800): Jordanes, Gregory of Tours, Bede and Paul the Deacon* (Princeton: Princeton University Press, 1988), 97–111, and for its employment by Carolingian writers see, Yitzhak Hen, *Roman Barbarians: The Royal Court and Culture in the Early Medieval West* (New York: Palgrave MacMillan, 2007), and by the Anglo-Saxon writers, Tom Shippey, "The Merov(ich)ingian Again: damnatio memoriae and the *usus scholarum*," in *Latin Learning and English Lore: Studies in Anglo-Saxon Literature for Michael Lapidge*, vol. 1, ed. Katherine O'Brien O'Keeffe and Andy Orchard (Toronto: University of Toronto Press, 2005), 389–406.

absolutely in contingency. The ontological understanding that figures the concept of "intra-action" may be slightly away from the modified object-oriented-ontological theory of history that I have expressed so far, but the subjective, fidelity process of historical truth is the same, particularly when "intra-action" refers to the epistemological conditions of stone. As Karkov notes, "Of course, it is impossible not to rely in some measure on the written sources as they provide information on dates, patrons, the historical contexts in which stone buildings were constructed, and sometimes even the sources of the stone. This chapter is an attempt to begin to put those sources in dialogue with the stone itself."

As such, we have historical truths constructed via the factuality process that finds the universal somewhere in the realm of the intra-action dialogue of stone, stone being the source of the truth event. In referring to stone as presenting a "deeper history," it offers not another form of historical truth but rather a truth point around which to create an endless procession of historical fidelities and faithful subjects. Truth events are egalitarian in their unconscious, unanticipated arrival, hence the lack of any necessary humanness to figure the human subject, to "write" history. As Karkov argues, "Equally important, however, is the ability of things, in this case of stone as object and material, to subvert the linear histories or narratives they are asked to construct," as "stone can expose the frailties and failures" of written narratives, can short circuit the prevailing logic of the world, its epistemic reality; "the ruined and crumbling settlements and buildings of the wall [...] were the foundation of human stories." In this sense yes, stone is precisely the truth event.

This is evident, Karkov shows, with the Anglian cross at Bewcastle which, as a new form of the polytheistic obelisk, demonstrates well how the stone itself was the transhistorical referent, or Real, able to be perpetually re-actualized as (made into) an external fact inside an endless possibility of histories; it could serve as the foundation of subjective historical truths for those "historians" engaging with the stone over and over again, the same performance of a universal truth from a truth event, as with the communist idea for Badiou, able to be made historical over and over again, with each historical discourse ultimately reaching nomination and so death, fading back into the non-actualized, latent side of the universal truth helix.[9]

Justin Lake, with his mid-volume historical-historiographical chapter, "*Narratio Probabilis* in Early Medieval Historiography: A Reconsideration," offers the reader a near short circuit. In adding evidence to the thesis of the narrativity of historical truth in the Middle Ages, Lake makes it also clear that historiography was an evolving genre with historians debating the merits of rhetoric and the proper modes for representing the past. This is, I think, a crucial breaker — food also for thought about philosophy of history today, driven so often not even by historians — to offer us a way to "brush history against the grain," to look beyond the prevailing practices of medieval historiography and into the competing voices. There was, it becomes clear, a belief by some medieval writers in objective facts and the danger of presenting them alongside fiction, as seen in the prologue to the mid-eleventh-century *Encomium Emmae Reginae*, even if there was an intended or accidental ironic element to the presentation of such an idea of objective facts.

Nevertheless, Lake contends, that even though amongst early medieval historians we "cannot, therefore, assume that the beliefs about the interrelationship of history and rhetoric expounded by Cicero in the first century BCE and appreciated anew by the *litterati* of the twelfth century (the great age of Latin historiography) were widely shared during the intervening centuries," "there can be little doubt that by this time (the twelfth century) the Ciceronian view of history as literature that worked through '*exaedificatio* [...] in rebus et verbis' had become generally accepted by the literary elite of the Latin West." On the other hand, "early medieval historians reinvented the genre of histo-

---

9 Didn't think a cow, a horse, a goat, or a pig could have historical agency? Guess again. The cows that provide the vellum combine these historical, subjective activities of historiography, performance, and material object, serving as the ultimate historians or at least aesthetic repeaters of much of the Middle Ages. Karkov's thesis is a solid reminder of this.

riography as they went, picking and choosing between classical and late antique models, while incorporating vernacular traditions as well, and in many cases puzzling modern readers with finished products that depart from more familiar classical genre distinctions [...]," so that it is only "with Richer (Richer of Saint-Remi, d. after 998) [that] we have, for the first time, incontrovertible evidence of a medieval historian writing in accordance with the Ciceronian rules for *narratio probabilis*."

It is discussed above how plausibility is indeed *a* but not *a unique* feature of medieval history writing, as it is shared with fiction. As such, a revelatory aspect of the former is offered to distinguish them, that is, the intention to create the faithful subject as being the unique feature between genres that share modes of representation. Lake's chapter reminds us though that even plausibility as a component of medieval history writing was a contested historical truth until it became hegemonic, until enough faith was established in this historical mode amongst historians, that is, until the subject faithful to this discourse had been established. In contrasting historiographical forms, whether classical, medieval or other, we can also take from Lake a reminder of the crucial gap between historicism's lack of a theoretical framework and compiling "facts" upon themselves to fill up time vs. historical materialism's announcing of the truth event of a past and the subjective constructive process.

Ingela Nilsson, in "The Literary Imaginary of the Past as the Truth of the Present," analyzes the "occasional literature" of the twelfth-century Byzantine author Constantine Manasses, which, she argues, attempts to connect the real with the imagined, to entangle "poetry with life," "placing itself in a position between the fictional and the factual." This literature, Nilsson notes, is "'occasioned' by specific events and/or needs to express a certain message of an often ideological character. In so doing, it "creates a link between the fictional imaginary of the past and the occasion at hand." The added element here to our theory of historical subjectivity, and a powerful one, is the emphasis on a prevailing imaginary about a past object, the product of an already revealed truth event and so that source of an existing historical discourse. This makes this literature a powerful emotional device, one that has the appearance of being historical — in that it would seem to be a historian reaching back to a truth event and constructing from it alternative, original historical truths — but which is only a simulacrum. Instead of breaking with an historical situation through original fidelity to the universality of the revealed truth event, the void, this literature is defined by an existing one. As such, it has the appearance of being a historical process, but in fact reinforces the present. It is a fidelity to a prevailing historical ideology (particularism), not a fidelity to a (universal) truth event revealed by a historian. It is as such not only a powerful rhetorical and political device, but also a useful demonstration of what is perhaps the vast majority of "history writing," echoes of the present, aesthetics over historical construction. Yet, although "my own understanding of occasional literature includes both commissioned works and self-promotional works produced in the hope of future commissions," Nilsson contends, "that, in my view, both the occasional situation and writing on command privilege originality and encourage the challenging of conventions." But in what sense?

With the rise of the Komnenos imperial family in the twelfth century, Nilsson argues, came also the need for "an intellectual elite that could write occasional literature of different kinds — poems to celebrate a new-born prince or orations to announce and praise the victories of the emperor — for the new aristocracy that now had a central place next to the imperial court and acted as both patrons and audience of the rhetorical production" and "a need for constant confirmation of one's own identity as Roman, Greek (in the cultural sense), and orthodox Christian." As Badiou argues, identity, as a closed (ontological and epistemological) set, an existing referential body or historical discourse, is precisely what the simulacrum form advances, and it does so through an aesthetics of fetishizing the past instead of constructing new truths from it.[10] Where we see

---

10 Alain Badiou, *Ethics: An Essay on the Understanding of Evil*, trans. and intro. Peter Hallward (New York: Verso, 2001), 74 (but also the rest of the chapter

the originality is not in the realm of the historical but rather of the aesthetic. Constantine Manasses as the "model author" who "projected himself in his texts, using a voice that was recognizable to his audience," in complement to the previous chapter and the inaesthetics of, for instance, Juan Manuel, provides instead of a brushing against the grain an aesthetic canvassing, in a Henri Marrou-Jacques Fontaine type of way, expressing the dominant culture through the represented image.[11]

In interrogating the commissioned occasional literature and the meaning of patronage it relies on, Nilsson follows the "anthropological-semiotic model" of Claudio Annibaldi "which focuses on the product (whether music or text) as an expression of a cultural and semiotic relationship rather than a factual relationship between people," and so "the performance of the text, along with the text itself (its functions and form), demonstrate the 'artistic sensibility and connoisseurship' of the patron. Iin Byzantine terms it demonstrates their *paideia*." Thus, in its occasioning, its performance for the patron, the commissioned text "offered a connection between that 'real' event (i.e., the present) and its hypotextual reality (the past)" and instead of announcing a truth event inserted the patron as a historical object, a truth of the past — as simulacrum, as false truth — into an established epistemological set "in order to present the narrator and his addressee in a convincing and historically grounded manner."

Nilsson concludes that "The study of occasional literature also displays how the line between the fictional and the factual never is straightforward in literary compositions. The question is not so much about genre (as in historiography vs. novel), but rather about immediate as well as wider, socio-cultural func-

---

"Simulacrum and Terror"), and generally Alain Badiou, *Handbook of Inaesthetics*, trans. Alberto Toscano (Stanford: Stanford University Press, 2005).

11 See Henri-Irénée Marrou, *St. Augustin et la fin de la culture antique* (Paris: E. Boccard, 1958); Jacques Fontaine, *Isidore de Séville et la culture classique dans l'Espagne Wisigothique*, 2 vols. (Paris: Études Augustiniennes, 1959); and Charles Cochrane, *Christianity and Classical Culture: A Study of Thought and Action from Augustus to Augustine* (Oxford: Oxford University Press, 1940).

tions." In other words, we see in the occasional literature of twelfth-century Constantinople the entanglement of aesthetics and (as) function, the production of original performances over the construction of original historical truths, as well as another crucial reminder both that literary genres overlapped and that establishing a text's generic relationship with genre is beside the point in seeking how genuine historical truths were constructed, especially as what see in Manasses is not a genuine or authentic historian but the painter adding to the canvas.

The "anti-History" theory of history (what I elsewhere call speculative objectivity) allows any object, whether animate or inanimate, human or otherwise, to initiate the historical process, the road toward constructing historical truths, and I think this matches at least some medieval thinking on history writing. And yet, it is also a limiting definition — as is the nature of definitions — in that although historical subjectivity is radically opened up it is opened up only to the radical. The historian is only who or what grounds the universality of a past object, through a revealed event, into historical truths that emancipate the subject from the existing world.

In Ralph O'Connor's "Romance, Legend, and the Remote Past: Historical Framing in Late Medieval Icelandic Sagas," we see how in medieval Icelandic sagas "invention was not limited to flights of fancy or anecdotal interludes," but "dominates the whole story" and "invited audiences to treat their (sagas') contents as historical." Moreover, he contends, "the attitude that a saga was expected at some level to communicate true stories about the past seems to have remained surprisingly constant, despite considerable variation in its expression." Even the "sagas' formulaic and implausible nature, with their dastardly raiders, knowledgeable princesses and shape-shifting wizards [...] are part of the stories' claim to be believable accounts of distant times and places." In this, O'Connor elicits and explicitly notes the important issue of audience trust in the construction of historical truths in the sagas, that is, the faith that is projected by the fideliitous subject (historian) needs to be returned by the receiver for the truth to be "real." As O'Connor explains, "there were ways of enjoying and learning from these sagas without any strong *investment* in their veracity. But there is no evidence that they were generally assumed to be made up."

Ultimately from this investigation of the medieval Icelandic sagas and their application of plausible narration and the revelation of supposed distant, eternal truths, O'Connor calls on scholars to expand the scope of the historiographical genre, in particular to be more open to the possibility of adding to it romance literature. In this sense, O'Connor, while interrogating medieval conceptions of historical truth, specifically how Icelandic sagas "were framed as history by the people who wrote and transmitted them in the Middle Ages," continues the advocacy of the other authors in this volume for scholars to reconsider the boundaries of history writing and re-examine the constructive process in terms of the relationship between the "historian," a truth event and past object, and the development of a partisan discourse via invention, plausibility, and narration.

In Catalin Taranu's chapter, "'Truth is the trickiest': Vernacular Theories of Truth and Strategies of Truth-making in Old English Verse," our analyses of truth making in the Middle Ages come to a seemingly — or plausibly? — paradoxical end-beginning via a Deleuzian-approved, Umberto-Eco-type conclusion about the openness truth procedure of *Beowulf*.[12] In other [maybe less philosophically obnoxious] words, Taranu concludes that the decision on what was true or not was left open for audiences of *Beowulf* to determine for themselves, it allowed them to take up the mantle of ultimately producing historical facts. As Taranu says, "the truth of the matter is left suspended, unresolved, for the audiences (both the Danes in the poem and the early medieval English hearing or reading it) to ruminate on and judge for themselves or collectively." That is, "The poem is interested not in establishing but in allowing the procedures of

---

[12] See especially the opening chapters of Gilles Deleuze and Felix Guattari, *A Thousand Plateaus: Capitalism and Schizophrenia*, trans. Brian Massumi (Minneapolis: University of Minnesota Press, 2003). Also, Umberto Eco, *The Open Work*, trans. Anna Cancogni (Cambridge: Harvard University Press, 1989).

generating truth to unfold." Thus, *Beowulf* may be the ultimate historiographical text, eliciting the writing of history and, in this way, itself being an anti-historical truth event. And yet, as Taranu maintains, these "constellative dynamics of *collaboratio* [...] are married to the conventionality of *traditio*" which presents false truths or rather repetitive (in a non-differential sense[13]) or additive knowledge to existing historical discourse. And so the openness maintains its power of openness only insofar as it is limited by form and knowledge, *epistēmē*, and discourse.

But what exactly is this *traditio,* and its contrast, as Taranu relates, with *auctoritas*? *Traditio* is like the aestheticist painter of historical facts vs. the *auctoritas* of the historian, or, in Taranu's words, "*traditio* as truth-making strategy is based on a theory of truth that is coherence-based (i.e., truth as what is formally coherent with a corpus of knowledge)." In this framework, "New truths (e.g., novel experiences, events, insights) have to be made understandable in the extant cultural horizon, hence they have to be formulated in extant poetic or narrative forms; rather than signifying stagnation, it is this insistence on faithfulness to traditional forms that ensures that new truths are understandable within mental frameworks already in place." Yet, "While *Beowulf* predominantly relies on truth procedures other than *auctoritas*, the latter is indeed present in its inclusion of Christian narratives which many early scholars found so incongruous." This presents then the convincingness or plausibility of accepted narrative procedures for creating/revealing truths vs. the use of one's authority, or the authority of the source, e.g., the Bible, to command fidelity to the constructed truth. Thus, what we have must be something akin to a limited openness, or the limits of interpretation, that Umberto Eco stresses grounds all literary works,[14] and for us more broadly for this volume, we find here

---

13 See Gilles Deleuze, *Difference and Repetition*, trans. Paul Patton (New York: Columbia University Press, 1994).
14 See Umberto Eco, *The Limits of Interpretation* (Bloomington: Indiana University Press, 1991).

the limits then of subjectivity, the limits of the potentiality for genuine historical truths, moments, and historians.

If objectivity would be all that were allowable to history, a historian could never present a new historical truth, could never break the logic of the world to announce a revelatory fact via an anti-history event. Subjectivity makes possible the historical truth procedure, which my theory of speculative objectivity attempts to prove in the speculative reliance on contingency at the point of the void actualized, the anti-history moment and the historian's logic derived from the illogical, presented via a radical discourse. This means that actual historical truths, and historians, are rare or at least are not a given, tending to be more like the inauthentic Heideggerian *Dasein* than the genuine *Dasein* who is a being-in-the-world able to stare into the abyss and create from it alternative truths.[15] *Beowulf* poses then a powerful anti-historical, historiographical text which continues pushing us to reevaluate history-writing in the Middle Ages, a primary aim of this volume.

---

15 I have argued elsewhere, including in my Jerusalem course lectures at The Hebrew University and my earlier graduate essay there, about the influence of Heidegger's *Dasein*, read in this way, on Alain Badiou's ontology. But, I only present here for reference Martin Heidegger, *Being and Time*, trans. John Macquarrie and Edward Robinson (New York: Harper Perennial, 2008), particularly section 60 in Division 2, Part 2, titled "The Existential Structure of the Authentic Potentiality-for-Being which is Attested in the Conscience."

Bibliography

Primary

Epistolae Wisigothicae. In *Epistolae Merovingici et Karolini aevi*, edited by Wilhelm Gundlach, 658–90. Monumenta Germaniae Historica, Epistolarum 3. Berlin: Weidmann, 1892.

Isidore of Seville. *Etymologies*. Edition: *Isidori Hispalensis Episcopi Etymologiarum sive Originum Libri XX*. Edited by W. M. Lindsay, Oxford, 1911; *Etymologies IX*. Edited by Marc Reydellet. Paris: Les Belles Lettres, 1984. Translation: *The "Etymologies" of Isidore of Seville*. Translated by Stephen A. Barney, W.J. Lewish, J.A. Beach, and Oliver Berghof. Cambridge: Cambridge University Press, 2006.

Secondary

Badiou, Alain. *Ethics: An Essay on the Understanding of Evil*. Translated and introduced by Peter Hallward. New York: Verso, 2001.

———. *Handbook of Inaesthetics*. Translated by Alberto Toscano. Stanford: Stanford University Press, 2005.

———. *Theory of the Subject*. Translated by Bruno Bosteels. New York: Continuum, 2009.

———. *The Rebirth of History: Times of Riots and Uprisings*. Translated by Gregory Elliott. New York: Verso, 2012.

Buber, Martin. *Hasidism and Modern Man*. Introduction by David Biale. Princeton: Princeton University Press, 2016. DOI: 10.1515/9781400874095.

Cochrane, Charles. *Christianity and Classical Culture: A Study of Thought and Action from Augustus to Augustine*. Oxford: Oxford University Press, 1940.

Deleuze, Gilles. *Difference and Repetition*. Translated by Paul Patton. New York: Columbia University Press, 1994.

Deleuze, Gilles, and Félix Guattari. *A Thousand Plateaus: Capitalism and Schizophrenia*. Translated by Brian Massumi. Minneapolis: University of Minnesota Press, 2003.

Eco, Umberto. *The Limits of Interpretation*. Bloomington: Indiana University Press, 1991.

———. *The Open Work*. Translated by Anna Cancogni. Cambridge: Harvard University Press, 1989.

Fontaine, Jacques. *Isidore de Séville et la Culture Classique dans l'Espagne Wisigothique*. 2 volumes. Paris: Études Augustiniennes, 1959.

Foucault, Michel. *The Order of Things: An Archaeology of the Human Sciences*. New York: Routledge, 2005. DOI: 10.4324/9780203996645.

Goffart, Walter. *The Narrators of Barbarian History (AD 550–800): Jordanes, Gregory of Tours, Bede and Paul the Deacon*. Princeton: Princeton University Press, 1988.

Heidegger, Martin. *Being and Time*. Translated by John Macquarrie and Edward Robinson. New York: Harper Perennial, 2008.

Hen, Yitzhak. *Roman Barbarians: The Royal Court and Culture in the Early Medieval West*. New York: Palgrave MacMillan, 2007. DOI: 10.1057/9780230593640.

Kelly, Michael J. *Alain Badiou: A Graphic Guide*. London: Icon Book, 2004.

———. *Isidore of Seville and the "Liber Iudiciorum": The Struggle for the Past in the Visigothic Kingdom*. The Medieval and Early Modern Iberian World 80. Boston and Leiden: Brill, 2021.

Kuukkanen, Jouni-Matti. *Postnarrativist Philosophy of Historiography*. New York: Palgrave MacMillan, 2015. DOI: 10.1057/9781137409874.

Marrou, Henri-Irénée. *St. Augustin et la fin de la culture antique*. Paris: E. Boccard, 1958.

Shippey, Tom. "The Merov(ich)ingian Again: *damnatio memoriae* and the *usus scholarum*." In *Latin Learning and English Lore: Studies in Anglo-Saxon Literature for Michael Lapidge*, Vol. 1, edited by Katherine O'Brien O'Keeffe and Andy Orchard, 389–406. Toronto: University of Toronto Press, 2005. DOI: 10.3138/9781442676589-021.

Stewart, Peter. "The Destruction of Statues in Late Antiquity." In *Constructing Identity in Late Antiquity*, edited by Richard Miles, 159–89. London: Routledge, 1999.

Varner, Eric R. *Mutilation and Transformation: "Damnatio Memoriae" and Roman Imperial Portraiture.* Boston and Leiden: Brill, 2004.

Wallace, David Foster. *The Broom of the System.* New York: Penguin, 2004.

Žižek, Slavoj. *The Parallax View.* Cambridge: MIT Press, 2006. DOI: 10.7551/mitpress/5231.001.0001.

Introduction: *Vera Lex Historiae*?

Catalin Taranu & Ralph O'Connor

All historians profess to tell the truth. What exactly this means is hard to agree upon. Writing circa 730, Bede promises in the introduction to his *Historia Ecclesiastica Gentis Anglorum* that he will write his account of the past of the English as a *verax historicus*, following only *vera lex historiae*. As we shall see below, Bede's notion of truthfulness does not quite match ours. Short of accusing Bede of consciously lying, then, one would need to understand how his notion of "truth" is constituted.[1]

Indeed, those who tell stories about the past generally claim their narratives are true — this includes grandpa's war-time stories, scholarly monographs written by professional, academically trained historians, and oral epics singing the life and deeds of a community's hero a little bit differently in each performance. Sometimes, all these histories weave together different narra-

---

1 All quotations from Bede are from *The Ecclesiastical History of the English People*, ed. Bertram Colgrave and R.A.B. Mynors, OMT (Oxford: Oxford University Press, 1969): here, the preface is on 6–7. Note regarding references: Icelandic authors' names are cited (and alphabetized in the bibliography) with the first name taking priority, as is customary in Iceland where few people have surnames. Ralph O'Connor thanks the Leverhulme Trust for their financial support.

tives about the same events. So, either they are not all true, in which case one might devise a method by which one can select the hard grain of truth from the chaff of invention — the positivistic approach prevalent until recently in (and still largely identified with) modern, professional, academic history-writing. Or, if they are all considered on their own terms and recognized as true by at least some of their audiences, then it would be necessary to determine whether the truth of these different accounts of the same events resides in the narrative itself, in its relationship to the events or to its intended audience, or perhaps somewhere else.

This collection of essays is dedicated to grappling with some of the questions that lie at the heart of this conundrum: what does it mean to claim a narrative about the past is true? Where does this truthfulness reside in a historical account — in its formal qualities, in its relationship to an anticipated audience (or perhaps its reception and reuse by an unanticipated one), in its adherence to a narrative or poetic tradition, in its subsequent appraisal by modern academically trained scholars? And how is a narrative constructed so that it can be recognized and assessed as true by its intended audience?

The authors of these essays are medievalists, which means that the scope of this volume is focused on the Middle Ages, specifically on narratives from this period that claim to be historical. Their historicity is to be broadly understood. This means that we do not privilege the canonical historiography in Latin written by the likes of Bede or Dudo as the only shape that historical narrative could take. Rather, beside it, we also consider epics, sagas, romances, stones, and heroic poems as forms of historical representation, when understood on their own terms rather than by reference to much later standards of historiographical professional accuracy. Beyond their medieval focus, however, the topics treated in this volume speak to broader problems in academic fields beyond medieval studies (philosophy of history or narratology, for example) and indeed beyond academia. This project is especially timely in a much-lamented post-truth era—but have we ever talked about the same thing when we talked about truth?

We begin this introduction by tracing a history of previous approaches to the topic, which will then serve as a springboard for explaining how our methods differ from them, starting with their underlying assumptions. Previous conversations on truth, veracity, and realism in pre-modern historical narrative have often revolved around a distinction between historicity and fictionality, the interplay of which was used (it has been often argued) in increasingly self-conscious and complex ways especially in the central and later Middle Ages.

This volume takes a different route. We suggest that it is the notion of "truth" itself (whether understood as narrative truthfulness or as an extra-textual historical reality to which a narrative refers) that needs to be historicized. If we do not do this, then using these conceptual categories in relation to pre-modern texts assumes that (however sophisticated and alien their configurations in these narratives may be) they are based on a universal human notion of what is true and what is not—that, for instance, dragons do not exist and saints cannot fly through the air, but that winter is a cold season and people need food to live. When medieval authors profess the former to be true, it appears to follow that they are playing with fictionality. In other words, although they could feign truthfulness or deploy its tropes creatively, and although their audiences could be complicit in bending the truth or taken in by the ruse, deep down both audience and author presumably knew just as well as we do today how to define truth. Many perceptive discussions of medieval *historia* as potentially including self-conscious fictionality, some of which are surveyed below, thus reinforce these terms as ontologically distinct, thereby reinscribing on them the implicit theory of truth shared by modern scholars, but not necessarily by the medieval creators and audiences in play. In scholarship that takes this approach, then, the issue is never that medieval people might have had a different notion of truth from ours, but that they were simply used to different patterns of employing and presenting it.

Rather than considering such a common-sense notion of "truth" as the barometer against which to measure fictionality and historicity, the editors and contributors of this volume are more interested in understanding how the barometer itself is put together, and indeed in showing that there are many ways to build such a barometer. This volume intends to bring to light the ways in which truth itself is not so much a quality inherent in the narrative stuff, or a relationship between a story and a reality it is supposed to represent. Rather, we see it more as a process that involves the cultural and linguistic norms by which a true account is constructed and which ensure that its veracity is recognized by an audience. These norms include the emotional life of a community: truth is, in part, a measure of the socio-emotional fitness of a historical account in relation to culturally embedded patterns of affective expression and structural expectation. "Truth" will thus be revealed to be as much a socio-cultural and emotionally charged process of emergence as a set of rhetorical weights and measures against which a narrative is assessed.

***

We can gain an especially clear sense of the theoretical presuppositions implicit in previous approaches to these matters if we begin at the beginning and consider medieval narratives about a remote past: origin-legends, legendary histories, epic narratives about ancestral figures, and chivalric romance. Here the role of the creative imagination in constructing a past is hardest to ignore. Scholarly assumptions about the boundary between history and fiction are most clearly revealed when attempts are made to describe and explain how self-consciously fictional writing emerged from imaginative forms of history-writing set in the distant past. Legendary history, notably Geoffrey of Monmouth's *History of the Kings of Britain,* is often thought to have stimulated experiments with more fictional modes, with the first tentative steps taken in vernacular histories such as Wace's

Roman de Brut (adapting Geoffrey) and in the hybrid form of the *romans d'antiquité* (adapting Classical narratives), then in the fully fictional courtly romances of Chrétien de Troyes and his successors, after which there was no looking back: the seeds of the modern novel had been sown.[2] Vernacular history and saga-writing in the Gaelic and Norse-Icelandic cultural zones is generally assumed to have followed a similar path, beginning as a kind of (pseudo-)history but evolving in a more fictional direction, often equated with a more "literary" direction. Indeed, the Gaelic case — typified by the mass of genealogical, dynastic and heroic legend surviving from the seventh century onwards in Old and Middle Irish — predates the twelfth-century Renaissance and the birth of romance by several centuries. Yet accounts of this precocious development are underpinned by very similar literary-historical assumptions about the nature and relationship between "history" and "literature," expressed most memorably by the late Donnchadh Ó Corráin. As writing about the past developed, "the imaginative re-creation of that past [...] produces a literature which, in time, frees itself from the historical matrix in which it is formed and becomes progressively an autonomous work of art, responding not to any one narrow historical situation but to broader and increasingly universal human situations [...]."[3] This is one of the master-narratives of European literary history. In all these accounts, the movement away from historical truth is viewed as a liberating,

---

2 See, for example, Geoffrey T. Shepherd, "The Emancipation of Story in the Twelfth Century," in *Medieval Narrative: A Symposium*, ed. Hans Bekker-Nielsen et al. (Odense: Odense University, 1979), 44–57; Dennis H. Green, *The Beginnings of Medieval Romance: Fact and Fiction, 1150–1220* (Cambridge: Cambridge University Press, 2002), esp. 176–80; Peter Ainsworth, "Legendary History: *historia* and *fabula*," in *Historiography in the Middle Ages*, ed. Deborah Mauskopf Deliyannis (Boston and Leiden: Brill, 2003), 387–416.

3 Donnchadh Ó Corráin, "Irish Origin Legends and Genealogy: Recurrent Aetiologies," in *History and Heroic Tale: A Symposium*, ed. Tore Nyberg et al. (Odense: Odense University Press, 1985), 51–96, at 85–86.

emancipatory move, part of an "adventure of fiction" on which bolder spirits embarked as time went by.[4]

There is no doubt that, as the Middle Ages progressed, the resources available to (at least some) writers of narrative became more numerous and varied, and some authors were inclined to test the limits of the genres in which they wrote, indulging more in literary play as their respective traditions gained in status and maturity. This kind of experimentation was fueled in part by the rise of secular patronage, and subsequently secular literacy, which lent increasing importance to the entertainment-function of narrative about the past.

Fiction may look like the natural result of these trends, and some individual romances, epics or sagas may be justifiably described as such. But was this the general rule? Did the freer use of techniques we associate with fiction really constitute a departure from history? Or was that freedom, instead, a sign that the limits of truthfulness in historical writing were potentially much broader than is generally assumed?

Here it is necessary to touch on how recent theories of fictional and historical writing apply to medieval literature. Narratologists and philosophers of narrative generally have no problem distinguishing between narratives intended as history and those intended as fiction, but this is because they almost always focus on texts written after the mid-eighteenth century, a period which saw a sharp divergence between the main narrative conventions of historical and novelistic writing.

Many features that we associate unproblematically with modern fiction — focalization through a character's viewpoint, description of characters' thoughts or experiences, artful play on the temporal pace of narration — might make it easy to distinguish in practice between history and (most) historical fiction

---

[4] The phrase is Emmanuèle Baumgartner's, in *De l'histoire de Troie au livre du Graal: le temps, le récit (XIIe–XIIIe siècles)* (Orléans: Paradigme, 1994), 2, translated by Ainsworth, "Legendary History," 399. More recently, the short lived nature of this "adventure" has become clearer, at least in the case of Continental romance: see Green, *Beginnings*, 200.

today,[5] but are found in all kinds of medieval and early modern history-writing, making them false indicators of fictional purpose before the Enlightenment.

Medievalists may therefore be tempted to draw on the late Hayden White's contrary view that no distinction exists between historical and fictional narrative at a purely formal level.[6] Yet it must be remembered that in making such statements, White was quite deliberately excluding matters of authorial intention and audience reception. White's interest was in structural continuities, not in claims to veracity; but intention and reception are crucial to any understanding of narrative truth-value.

A different approach was taken by Suzanne Fleischman in a landmark study published more than thirty years ago.[7] Fleischman's analysis of features internal to the texts (narrative organization and narratorial presence) found that self-conscious narrators and structured narratives, while lacking in some historical texts (notably annalistic chronicles), are found in some others and provide no basis for a history-fiction distinction. Under the criterion of "social function," she assessed the common claim that chronicles commemorate whereas romances exemplify, and found that chronicles are full of *exempla* and romances generally claim to commemorate. Finally, she turned to reception, here drifting away from romance but showing that epics were often treated by medieval chroniclers as historical testimony.

Fleischman's conclusion was that the history-fiction distinction in the Middle Ages did exist, but that it shifted depending on each audience's expectations and beliefs. Formal or functional distinctions do not help us place a text in one or the other category: historical narrative in the Middle Ages was any narra-

---

5 For example, Dorrit Cohn, "Signposts of Fictionality: A Narratological Perspective," *Poetics Today* 11, no. 4 (1990): 775–804.
6 See, for example, Hayden White, *The Content of the Form: Narrative Discourse and Historical Representation* (Baltimore: Johns Hopkins University Press, 2009).
7 Suzanne Fleischman, "On the Representation of History and Fiction in the Middle Ages," *History and Theory* 22, no. 3 (1983): 278–310.

tive willingly believed,⁸ and the limits of belief were set by the resources and attitudes of each audience. In this way Fleischman extended into a wider range of literary forms and periods some of the conclusions reached by Nancy Partner in her trailblazing study of literary techniques in medieval history-writing.⁹

Partner's and Fleischman's studies have been followed by a growing body of scholarship analyzing literary strategies in medieval history-writing. But, with a few notable exceptions, that scholarly tradition continues, often without even realizing it, to define history in terms of the same few genres: national histories, dynastic or institutional histories, chronicles, and (when they are thought of) (auto)biography and hagiography. Other genres of writing about the past which claimed veracity, such as epics, Biblical narratives and many romances, are generally excluded from the category of history-writing by definition — even when it is acknowledged that some of these texts claim to tell truthful stories about the past.¹⁰

Some scholars, such as Robert M. Stein and Gabrielle Spiegel, have explored the exchanges which took place between history and romance; but this approach, too, is usually predicated on an irreconcilable difference in implied veracity between the two kinds of narrative.¹¹ After all, the insights that romancers

---

8   Compare here C.S. Lewis, *The Discarded Image: An Introduction to Medieval and Renaissance Literature* (Cambridge: Cambridge University Press, 1964), 181.
9   Nancy F. Partner, *Serious Entertainments: The Writing of History in Twelfth-Century England* (Chicago: University of Chicago Press, 1977).
10 On the scholarly tendency to exclude Biblical narrative from the domain of history, focusing on an anachronistic critical "linkage of history writing to documentation," see Meir Sternberg, *The Poetics of Biblical Narrative: Ideological Literature and the Drama of Reading* (Bloomington: Indiana University Press, 1984), 26, 32.
11 Robert M. Stein, *Reality Fictions: Romance, History, and Governmental Authority, 1025–1180* (Notre Dame: University of Notre Dame Press, 2006); Gabrielle M. Spiegel, *Romancing the Past: The Rise of Vernacular Prose Historiography in Thirteenth-Century France* (Berkeley: University of California Press, 1993), 63. An important exception to this trend is Ruth Morse, *Truth and Convention in the Middle Ages: Rhetoric, Representation, and Reality* (Cambridge: Cambridge University Press, 1991).

engaged with issues also treated in history-writing, or that some historians used literary modes associated with romance, would seem less striking if romances themselves were a variety of history-writing.

Conversely, most literary scholarship on romance, epic, and saga continues to use the mainstream genres of history-writing as a foil against which their own more "imaginative" corpus stands out. A still-powerful strand in scholarship on chivalric romance, typified by the work of Paul Zumthor and Michel Zink, holds that these texts' storylines focus primarily on personal relationships, solitary adventures and states of mind, not on political or social realities, and thus turn in on themselves, becoming fiction.[12] This inward-looking interpretation has been challenged, for instance in Stein's *Reality Fictions* and (applied to *lais*) in R. Howard Bloch's *The Anonymous Marie de France*.[13] But even here, the underlying distinction in referentiality remains intact and frequently gravitates around the question of chronology. Historians observe the same line of demarcation: for Peter Ainsworth, historiography's referential claims are embodied in its being structured around external (i.e., universal or sacred) chronology, whereas romances lack interest in external chronology as a means of ensuring overall narrative coherence, and sometimes even leave their internal chronology hazy too. Instead, their coherence is provided at a thematic level.[14]

As it happens, external chronology is used as a structuring device only in a narrow subset of history-writing, namely chronicles — and even chroniclers did not always show consis-

---

12 Paul Zumthor, *Langue, texte, énigme* (Paris: Seuil, 1975), 245–48; Michel Zink, *Medieval French Literature: An Introduction*, trans. Jeff Rider (Binghamton: Medieval & Renaissance Texts & Studies, 1995), 53–55; Baumgartner, *De l'histoire de Troie*, 3. Zumthor's rather compressed formulations are elucidated and developed further by Ainsworth, "Legendary History," 390–96.
13 Stein, *Reality Fictions*; R. Howard Bloch, *The Anonymous Marie de France* (Chicago: University of Chicago Press, 2003).
14 Ainsworth, "Legendary History," 402–3.

tent interest in this device.¹⁵ National histories, by contrast, were often structured around internal (national) rather than external (world) chronology, and dates are rare. Saxo Grammaticus, for example, built most of the vast timespan of his *History of the Danes* around the reigns of Danish rulers and commonly known events in Scandinavian history. The same is true of Geoffrey of Monmouth's *History of the Kings of Britain*: almost no dates are included, and an initial scattering of universal-history synchronisms peters out after Julius Caesar's invasion.¹⁶

That said, Ainsworth is quite right that many romancers show strikingly little interest in any explicit chronological framework, whether national or universal. The same is true of many epics and sagas. The question is, does this necessarily translate into a lack of interest in writing history? Ainsworth sees no reason to challenge Baumgartner's view that the opening of Chrétien's *Erec et Enide* "brutally wrenches Arthurian space and time away from the chronological and historical time in which Geoffrey of Monmouth and later Wace had inscribed their narratives, doing away with any temporal or even spatial point of anchorage [...]. The first lines postulate without any apology and as so many 'attested facts': Arthur, his kingdom, his knights and their occupation."¹⁷

According to this line of argument, Chrétien's provision of such a minimal setting amounts to a denial of historicity: romance storylines play out in a timeless world which never really existed. Yet, for a romance's audience, those initial allusions to Arthur would have been sufficient to anchor the narrative in historical time and space, had that audience wished to receive

---

15 Aengus Ward, *History and Chronicles in Late Medieval Iberia: Representations of Wamba in Late Medieval Narrative Histories* (Boston and Leiden: Brill, 2011), 187–89.
16 Saxo Grammaticus, *"Gesta Danorum": The History of the Danes,* ed. Karsten Friis-Jensen, trans. Peter Fisher, 2 vols. (Oxford: Clarendon Press, 2015), vol. 1, 19–20, n. 1.
17 Baumgartner, *De l'histoire de Troie*, 3, translated in Ainsworth, "Legendary History," 397.

the narrative as historical. There is, at the very least, room for further debate.

Not all romances are inward-looking in their storylines. Rosalind Field has emphasized the "conscious historicity" implicit in the style and narratorial stance of a number of Anglo-Norman and Middle English "family romances."[18] But their formal differences from more established genres of historical writing have kept these, too, beyond the *cordon sanitaire*. The suggestion that such romances might have a historical purpose has been smartly put down by Peter Damian-Grint solely because their "romantic" tone and "folklore" motifs make them look more like romances or lais than like chronicles or national histories.[19] The assumption is that the stylistic and structural features of the larger-scale forms of history-writing, such as synchronisms and a "dry factual tone,"[20] are non-negotiable components of any medieval history-writing, and that any narrative lacking these must not have been intended as history at all. For Damian-Grint, Wace's *Brut* and comparable vernacular histories of the twelfth century engage with the romance mode and even flirt with it, but they resist the temptation to plunge into it.

Even in the case of the *chansons de geste,* which repeatedly claim to be true stories, a still-influential school of thought denies real historical intention to these epic narratives because they tell the story so dramatically, using the historic present and various other techniques of immediacy to make the event present again in performance. These techniques weaken the sense of chronological progression so that, as Paul Zumthor put it, "history [*l'histoire*] remains, but abolishes itself as historicity" and reinvents itself as "a timeless fiction."[21] In other words, dramatized or popular history is not history at all if it does not follow

---

18 Rosalind Field, "Romance as History, History as Romance," in *Romance in Medieval England*, ed. Maldwyn Mills et al. (Cambridge: D.S. Brewer, 1991), 163–73, at 173.
19 Peter Damian-Grint, *The New Historians of the Twelfth-Century Renaissance* (Woodbridge: Boydell Press, 1999), 177–78.
20 Ibid., 177.
21 Zumthor, *Langue, texte, énigme*, 239, our translation.

the ordering principles of a chronicle.²² As a result of fetishizing the chronicle, the forest has been lost from sight in examining the trees: the whole point of commemoration was that the event commemorated was believed to have happened.

Despite the increasing adoption of literary approaches within historical studies, then, and despite the renewed attention paid to large-scale historical writings within literary studies, the wall between these disciplines has proved robust in terms of how the genres and functions of history are conceptualized. Building on recent work on *Beowulf* and other heroic poetry as a form of "poetic history," we would like to suggest that chronicles and national histories should not be treated as the sole representatives of medieval history-writing, but can be more productively situated within a broader ecology of narrative genres that attempt to represent the past. As well as chronicles and national histories, these genres also included romances, *lais,* heroic poems, sagas, Biblical vernacular epic (such as the Old English *Genesis* or *Judith* and the Old Saxon *Heliand*), and a significant proportion of *exempla*.²³ It has often been noted that *historia* did not constitute a single genre at any point in the Middle Ages, and that great rhetorical and imaginative latitude was allowed to (and exercised by) medieval historians.²⁴ This of course makes their writings less reliable or transparent as source-material for the modern historian, but all the more revealing of the attitudes of their authors and the needs of their patrons and audiences. Yet even

---

22 The most forceful attempts to assert the historical intentions of the *chansons de geste* have, until very recently, formed part of an oral-traditional line of argument, typified by Joseph J. Duggan, "Medieval Epic as Popular Historiography: Appropriation of Historical Knowledge in the Vernacular Epic," in *La Littérature historiographique des origines à 1500,* ed. Hans Ulrich Gumbrecht et al., 2 vols. (Heidelberg: Carl Winter Universitätsverlag, 1986), 285–311.
23 Catalin Taranu, *The Bard and the Rag-Picker: Vernacular Verse Histories in Early Medieval England and Francia* (London: Routledge, 2021).
24 Bert Roest, "Mediaeval Historiography: About Generic Constraints and Scholarly Constructions," in *Aspects of Genre and Type in Pre-Modern Literary Culture,* ed. Bert Roest and Herman Vanstiphout (Groningen: Styx, 1995), 15–31.

the most revisionist scholars of medieval history-writing have shown little enthusiasm for the idea of opening the front gates and letting unashamedly imaginative genres such as epic and romance take their place as modes of historical writing. They are seen as the property of a different academic department.

If we extend the scope of what counts as "history" to include narrative categories like these, that would have been recognized as historical by their creators and their audiences (even though we might not), we are better situated to tease out the different modes of constructing historical truth, narrative authority, and what might be called "realism" at work in them. White's insight that "the possible modes of historiography are the same as the possible modes of speculative philosophy of history" opens up some interesting possibilities.[25] White saw these different modes as "formalizations of poetic insights that analytically precede them and that sanction the particular theories used to give historical accounts the aspect of an 'explanation.'"[26]

Thus, going beyond the "fact vs. fiction" paradigm, there emerges the possibility to see as many visions of history as there are genres of narrative claiming identification as history — that is, if we follow the contract set up between their creators and their audiences, rather than privileging the formal attributes of one mode of history-writing (whether Classical Latinate or modern post-Rankean).[27] Thus, epics, sagas and other non-canonical forms of historical representation can be treated not as "imperfect histories," but rather as "particular products of possible conceptions of historical reality, conceptions that are alternatives to, rather than failed anticipations of, the fully realized historical discourse that modern history is supposed to embody."[28]

---

[25] Keith Jenkins, *On 'What Is History?'* (London: Routledge, 1995), 147.

[26] Ibid., 147. Hayden White, *Metahistory: The Historical Imagination in Nineteenth-Century Europe* (Baltimore: Johns Hopkins University Press, 1973), xi–xii.

[27] Taranu, *The Bard and the Rag-Picker*.

[28] Hayden White, "The Value of Narrativity in the Representation of Reality," *Critical Inquiry* 7, no. 1 (1980): 5–27, at 10.

One of the criteria for distinguishing between history and fiction which Fleischman mentioned, but barely discussed, was that of authenticity as opposed to invention. Perhaps echoing White's impatience with intentionality, Fleischman diverted her discussion of this point into a consideration of how the narratives were received by medieval audiences. That is a crucial aspect of any discussion of fictionality, but intention is relevant too: the extent to which a writer invented an account or passed on something he or she trusted as authentic or deserving consideration as authentic.

This is important, because many scholars make no distinction between fiction on the one hand and pseudohistory or fabricated history on the other. Geoffrey of Monmouth's *History of the Kings of Britain* is viewed by many as "fiction" because it contains a lot of invention. Some scholars even assert that Geoffrey did not want his work to be received as history and that it "had no pretensions to being 'historical.'"[29] But Geoffrey's *History* contains no signals of fictionality. From title-rubric to conclusion, in Vulgate and Variant versions, this work claims to be history, even if its author made a lot of it up. And this is how it was received: most medieval historians accepted its main outlines as true and built their own work on it, and even his bitterest critics engaged head-on with his claim to be writing history (even though they thought it was false history).[30]

Despite White's efforts, it is not easy to dislodge the intuitive assumption that the more made-up a narrative is, the more fic-

---

29 Ainsworth, "Legendary History," 394; Stein, *Reality Fictions*, 105–25.
30 The clearest case against the fictionality of Geoffrey's work is Green, *Beginnings*, 169–76, with further references. On Geoffrey's reception, see also Ad Putter, "Latin Historiography after Geoffrey of Monmouth," in *The Arthur of Medieval Latin Literature: The Development and Dissemination of the Arthurian Legend in Medieval Latin*, ed. Siân Echard (Cardiff: University of Wales Press, 2011), 85–108. Monika Otter, *"Inventiones": Fiction and Referentiality in Twelfth-Century English Historical Writing* (Chapel Hill: University of North Carolina Press, 1996), offers some intriguing reflections on the same matter from a different perspective. See also Monika Otter, "Functions of Fiction in Historical Writing," in *Writing Medieval History*, ed. Nancy Partner (London: Hodder Arnold, 2005), 109–30, at 119–21.

tional it is. Rather than White's effacing of the whole history-fiction distinction, a more helpful theoretical lodestone here is the notion, developed influentially by Paul Ricœur, of an implicit or explicit contract between narrator and audience which any narrative sets up. A fictional narrative does not invite belief in its historicity as a whole, even if it happens to include real events. It implies a contract of make-believe: the audience is invited to imagine that everything narrated took place, while knowing that much or all of it did not. History, on the other hand, claims to be referential: it invites its audience to accept that what is narrated really, or probably, happened.[31] Invented history might be bad history in our eyes, but that does not make it fiction.

At first glance, this dichotomy resembles Isidore of Seville's much-quoted Ciceronian distinction between *historia* (narrating true things, *res verae*, which were done, *factae*) and *fabula* (narrating events which could not and did not happen because they were contrary to nature). But there is a middle term in Isidore's typology, *argumentum*, which narrated things which were not done, but could be done: plausible invention.[32] Today we would call this realistic fiction, and Isidore's refusal to include it within *historia* might seem to suggest that medieval historians were not supposed to have any truck with invention. But rhetoric, and thus invention, were fundamental to medieval history-writing. That point was, in fact, emphasized by the Ciceronian manuals which underpinned Isidore's formulation: Cicero's own *De inventione* and *De oratore*, and the pseudo-Ciceronian *Rhetorica ad Herennium*.

A word about Isidore is in order at this point. Because of his unquestioned influence in other areas of medieval European literary activity, and because his formulation is so neat and tidy, Isidore's tripartite classification of narrative still enjoys an unmerited centrality in modern scholarly discussions of truth, fic-

---

31 Paul Ricœur, *Memory, History, Forgetting*, trans. Kathleen Blamey and David Pellauer (Chicago: University of Chicago Press, 2010), 261.
32 Isidore of Seville, *Etymologiarum sive Originum libri XX*, ed. Wallace M. Lindsay, 2 vols. (Oxford: Clarendon Press, 1911), 1:unpaginated (I.xliv.5).

tion, and falsehood in medieval narrative. Yet the assumption that Isidore's schema was used as a practical standard for anyone before the twelfth-century revival of the Latin tradition of history-writing is very much in doubt. Bede's own *vera lex historiae* or "true law of history" was, as Roger Ray has shown, a direct challenge to Isidore's pronouncements.[33]

Even in the twelfth century and later, Isidore's schema and other Ciceronian prescriptions only provided old means to conceptualize and shape new ideas of narrative representation, rather than a handbook method to be scrupulously followed.[34] As Justin Lake convincingly argues in this volume, the Isidorian view of the history-writing had virtually no impact in the Early Middle Ages (with the exception of a group of tenth-century authors that includes Dudo and Richer), and that indeed to a certain extent, "early medieval historians reinvented the genre of historiography as they went [...] picking and choosing between classical and late-antique models, and in many cases puzzling modern readers with finished products that depart from more familiar classical genre distinctions"[35]

Thus, even in the case of medieval narratives written in Latin that apparently follow Classical traditions more closely, the implicit theories of truth at work in them still need to be explicated on their own terms and cannot be simply assumed to be reducible to Cicero or Isidore. In some cases, they do not coincide with their own authors' theoretical discussions of history-writing, truth, and narrative.

To return to the thorny problem of "invented history": when we turn from Isidore's arid summaries to the more practical medieval articulations of Ciceronian rhetorical theory, plausible invention turns out to be not only allowed to historians, but also

---

33 Roger Ray, "Bede's *Vera Lex Historiae*," *Speculum* 55, no. 1 (1980): 1–21, esp. 15–17.

34 Päivi Mehtonen, *Old Concepts and New Poetics: "historia," "argumentum," and "fabula" in the Twelfth- and Early Thirteenth-Century Latin Poetics of Fiction*, Commentationes Humanarum Litterarum 108 (Helsinki: Societas Scientarum Fennica, 1996), 16; Otter, "Functions of Fiction," 113.

35 See Justin Lake's contribution in this volume.

required of them in order to make their histories convincing. The English word "plausible" hints at fraud, but Latin *probabilis* more often referred to the probable, the credible, that which could be believed.[36] Credible invention, narrated as *res gestae*, was particularly necessary in histories of remote times: these would otherwise be limited to skeletal lists of the kind Isidore called *annales*, the only species of *historia* he allowed to represent the distant past.[37] Fortunately for us, most medieval writers ignored Isidore, rolled up their sleeves and practiced their inventive skills to turn bare facts into convincing narratives. This is why medieval accounts of the remote past have an especially high degree of social or behavioral stereotyping, exemplary narrative, lively dialogue, speeches and romantic episodes, telescoping or amplifying events known from other sources, and artfully shaped storylines borrowed from other literary models or from relatively unauthorized sources such as popular legends and fairytales.

These imaginative passages in history-writing have been seen by some critics as "fictions" floating momentarily free of literal, historical truth-claims.[38] Examples from Geoffrey of Monmouth's history might include the episode of superhuman, nation-making warfare between invading humans and indigenous giants such as Gogmagog, or the brief anecdote about King Bladud's messy death in an aviation accident. Some later historians, wishing to incorporate the most important parts of Geoffrey's work into their own, often much more condensed accounts of universal history, were ruthless with their pruning, but still saw fit to retain improbable or fantastic episodes like these two. Both are included, for instance, in the Icelandic universal-

---

36 Morse, *Truth and Convention*; Justin Lake, "Truth, Plausibility, and the Virtues of Narrative at the Millennium," *Journal of Medieval History* 35, no. 3 (2009): 221–38. For a detailed account of what was involved in the composition of credible history, see Matthew Kempshall, *Rhetoric and the Writing of History, 400–1500* (Manchester: Manchester University Press, 2011), 265–427.
37 Isidore, *Etymologiarum*, vol. 1, unpaginated (I.xliv.1–4).
38 Otter, *Inventiones*.

history compilation surviving in the fourteenth-century manuscript AM 764 4to (in Reykjavik's Stofnun Árna Magnússonar).[39]
Rhetorical inventiveness need not mean a lack of intended veracity: what made these marvels remarkable, and worth including in a history, was surely the fact that they were supposed to have happened. They were "strange but true." The appeal to the audience's sense of wonder does imply a different kind of audience engagement from accounts of more mundane events, but this need not be pigeonholed as "fictive."[40] Even where their authors expressed skepticism or uncertainty about such episodes, they did so in terms of displaying doubts about a tradition handed down, rather than admitting or hinting at fabrication. When the prologue to the S-redaction of Oddr Snorrason's *Óláfs saga Tryggvasonar* (*The Saga of Óláfr Tryggvason*), written in late twelfth-century Iceland, acknowledges that "it can often happen that the false is mixed with the true" (*opt kan þat at beraz at fals er blandit sonno*), the point is to request the skeptical reader or listener to provide corrections or simply to believe or not as seems best to them, and to refrain from calling the whole saga a lie.[41] Bede's reservations about popular opinion are of

---

39 Svanhildur Óskarsdóttir, "Universal History in Fourteenth-Century Iceland: Studies in AM 764 4to" (PhD diss., University College London, 2000), 161–62; part of the Gogmagog episode is quoted from AM 764 4to in Stefanie Würth, "The Common Transmission of *Trójumanna saga* and *Breta sögur*," in *Beatus Vir: Studies in Early English and Norse Manuscripts in Memory of Phillip Pulsiano*, ed. A.N. Doane and Kirsten Wolf (Tempe: Arizona Center for Medieval and Renaissance Studies, 2006), 297–327, at 320.

40 Otter, *Inventiones*, presents a valuable sequence of case studies of such quasi-fictional moments in purportedly historical writing, as also in her "Functions of Fiction." On the claim that these episodes make no claim to literal truthfulness, compare Anthony Kemp, Review of Monika Otter, *Inventiones*, *Speculum* 74, no. 1 (1999): 235–37, and Justin Lake, "Current Approaches to Medieval Historiography," *History Compass* 13 (2015): 89–109, at 91.

41 *Saga Óláfs Tryggvasonar af Oddr Snorrason munk*, ed. Finnur Jónsson (Copenhagen: Gad, 1932), 2. On this passage, see Carl Phelpstead, "Fantasy and History: The Limits of Plausibility in Oddr Snorrason's *Óláfs saga Tryggvasonar*," *Saga-Book of the Viking Society* 36 (2012): 27–42. On similar passages in Norse-Icelandic sagas, see Ralph O'Connor, "History or Fiction? Truth-Claims and Defensive Narrators in Icelandic Romance-Sagas," *Mediaeval Scandinavia* 15 (2005): 1–69.

the same kind: they are, in part, a defensive measure. Episodes of this kind might invite a looser or more provisional form of credence, but they were still included within a historical rather than a fictional project. They were part of truthful narration, not its opposite, and using the word "fiction" to describe these passages risks sidelining that overarching intention even though it does full justice to the inventive capacities of the historian.

Reflecting on both Geoffrey's work and Scandinavian historians writing in Latin, Lars Boje Mortensen has called this process not fiction or fabrication but "mythopoiesis": socially and politically authorized mythmaking.[42] Mortensen's focus has been on national histories by named high-status authors, but anonymous vernacular narratives can also be seen as forms of imaginative historiography, in this case bearing the authority of tradition itself rather than of a named author. The same relative frequency of imaginative techniques, stylistic heightening and stereotyping seen in the first nine (prehistoric) books of Saxo Grammaticus's *Gesta Danorum* can be found in epics, romances and sagas — which is hardly surprising given the nature of much of Saxo's source-material.

To sum up these reflections on the borderlands between history and fiction: history today is expected to tell what really or probably happened, but historical narratives in the Middle Ages were expected to tell what really, probably or (especially concerning the distant past) possibly happened. Much effort was spent on explaining how the apparently fabulous could be true, so histories of the remote past could blend *historia, argumentum* and what looks to us like *fabula,* while still claiming in all honesty to be *historia*: true stories about a past too distant to be comprehended in any detail except through invention.

In regard to veracity, perhaps the closest modern analogue is not the historical novel sometimes invoked, but the kind of

---

42 Lars Boje Mortensen, "The Status of the 'Mythical' Past in Nordic Latin Historiography (c. 1170–1220)," in *Medieval Narratives between History and Fiction: From the Centre to the Periphery of Europe, c. 1100–1400,* ed. Panagiotis A. Agapitos and Lars Boje Mortensen (Copenhagen: Museum Tusculanum, 2012), 103–39, at 133.

popular science-writing which presents speculations in narrative form about the early history of the universe or of our planet. In such books, bursts of imaginative writing which bring that unwitnessed past vividly before the reader's mind's eye — often using plenty of dramatic and poetic license — are not intended to be taken as self-conscious fictions. They are intended to represent what really, probably or possibly happened to the best of the author's knowledge, or rather, that of the author's sources (in this respect also resembling legendary history). They invite the reader or viewer, not to participate in a game of make-believe, but to give those representations the benefit of the doubt as reflections of real past events, even though they are acknowledged to be based partly on imagination.[43] Of course, the epistemology underpinning modern popular science is different from that of medieval historiography: such concepts as objectivity and "fact" have no precise equivalent in the earlier period. But the underlying challenge of narrating an irrecoverable past has remained constant, and so have some of the rhetorical devices developed to meet that challenge.

***

Yet the cognitive dissonance between these many ways to truth remains and troubles us. How are we to parse the many underlying conceptualizations of veracity? If we approach how the notion of truth itself is constituted in narratives about the past via a straightforward dichotomy of historicity vs. fictionality, we are bound to be restricted to the ways in which these texts deploy these (otherwise modern) genre categories rather than going to the heart of the matter: what did people really *believe* about them? When considered by present-day researchers working with pre-modern or non-Western sources, the issue of the truth-value of improbable narratives such as the ones quoted

---

43 On the origins of much of this kind of writing, see Ralph O'Connor, *The Earth on Show: Fossils and the Poetics of Popular Science, 1802–1856* (Chicago: University of Chicago Press, 2007).

above is typically whisked away by a methodological sleight of hand: it is the cultural, social, or political functions fulfilled by such fictions that are supposed to interest us, not whether they were believed to be true.

In an astute indictment of received notions of medieval belief, Steven Justice lists several such "functionalist" explanations current in scholarship that discount the act of belief itself (and hence the truth value of miracle-narratives as perceived by the people involved in this act):

> Margery Kempe claimed her visions in order to secure in her corporal experience an authority that a woman like herself never could acquire by office; John of Gaunt supported John Wyclif's disendowment program because it gave the crown theological warrant for appropriating church property; Bonaventure created the image of the pacific and stigmatized St. Francis in order to pacify and mainstream Francis's followers; Gregory of Nazianzus humbly refused ecclesiastical office so that office would be forced upon him and he could combine episcopal power with saintly authority. What gives such assertions the look of hardheaded realism they ostentatiously sport is their insistence on cutting straight from utterance or action to some form of institutional or cultural capital (sometimes literal capital) it is thought to acquire: no mucking about with anything so immaterial and treacherous as thought. And so we do not ask whether John of Gaunt believed that Wyclif was right, whether Bonaventure thought that his idea of Francis was true to the saint's idea of himself, whether Margery Kempe actually saw her visions.[44]

As Justice argues with regard to miracle-stories, this narrowly functionalist or rhetoricist approach impoverishes (indeed, hinders) our understanding of the cognitive processes involved in belief and the authorization of truth in medieval discourses.

---

44 Steven Justice, "Did the Middle Ages Believe in Their Miracles?," *Representations* 103, no. 1 (2008): 1–29, at 11.

As he puts it, if we leave aside the question of function, there can be only two answers to the questions above: medieval people narrating visions and miracles "must speak either in a cynical and nearly sociopathic detachment from the truth-content of their words, or in a nearly delusional bondage to interests they do not even recognize as the source of those words."[45] Put more plainly, "the cultural account of religion views belief as either an ideological mask or communal delusion."[46]

This is not an issue only in accounts of religious belief. It is also vexing for anthropologists working on non-Western cultures. For instance, as Rane Willerslev has expressed it, some Victorian scholars might have said that while hunters in "animistic" cultures claiming to turn into animals were not actually lying, they must be "suffering from delusions of some sort and would be incapable of telling fact from fantasy, or reality from dreams"; but more recent anthropologists might "accept the hunter's story by adding an 'as if' to his account — so instead of talking nonsense, the hunter is deemed to be speaking in metaphors, constructing figurative parallels between the two separate domains of nature and culture."[47] Yet both the Victorian positivist and the more recent and "enlightened" metaphorical paradigms discount the literalness of such insider accounts by reassuringly (for the scholar) affirming the primacy of Western metaphysics over indigenous understandings of the world — a

---

45 Ibid., 11.
46 Hussein Fancy, *The Mercenary Mediterranean: Sovereignty, Religion, and Violence in the Medieval Crown of Aragon* (Chicago: University of Chicago Press, 2016), 148.
47 Rane Willerslev, *Soul Hunters: Hunting, Animism, and Personhood among the Siberian Yukaghirs* (Berkeley: University of California Press, 2007), 2–3. For instances of Victorian positivistic constructions of "animism," see Edward Burnett Tylor, *Primitive Culture*, 2 vols., vol. 1 (1871; rpt. London: John Murray, 1929), 477 and James George Frazer, "On Certain Burial Customs as Illustrative of the Primitive Theory of the Soul," *Journal of the Anthropological Institute of Great Britain and Ireland* 15 (1886): 63–104, at 66, discussed in George W. Stocking, *After Tylor: British Social Anthropology, 1888-1951* (London: Athlone, 1996), 131.

perspective forever incapable of understanding the act of belief from the inside out.[48]

From this impasse arises a need for asking different questions from our sources: not only whether these improbable accounts were believed or meant to be believed as true (one is about reception, the other about authorial intent), but also *how* they were believed. This new way of asking the questions bypasses the binary true/false and points to the possibility that even for the same person different narratives can coexist with different epistemological statuses. As Willerslev's work on the Siberian Yukaghir shows, these people live in the world of ordinary objects where elk are animals one kills for food, but in particular contexts, elk are also endowed with personhood.[49] Different epistemologies for different contexts — just as we might hold grandpa's improbable war stories and a book about World War II written by a professional historian to different standards of truth.

Still, well-meaning but reductionist accounts of medieval credulity as inherent in predominantly oral cultures persist to this day.[50] Such teleological arguments implicitly value the moments of skepticism sometimes encountered in medieval sources as forerunners of an inevitable rise of reason and thus as more akin to modern attitudes than are such extraordinary claims as miracles, visions, or ominous dragons in the sky. But skepticism is more than mere unwillingness to believe something improbable. As Justice deftly argues, skepticism was part and parcel of the process of belief, which medieval thinkers knew to be a constant struggle of the mind against itself. What Justice calls "deflationary strategies," such as narrators of miracles avowing their initial disbelief in such supernatural phenomena, are essential to the act of belief (and, adapting it to our argument here, to strategies of truth-making) because they reassure the readers

---

48 Willerslev, *Soul Hunters*, 184.
49 Ibid., 8.
50 Keagan Brewer, *Wonder and Skepticism in the Middle Ages* (New York: Routledge, 2016), 10.

of such accounts that the events depicted are indeed incredible, while their truth is attested by the narrator undergoing a process of conviction documented in the account.[51] And when the latter is not available, narrators rely on various narrative, poetic, rhetorical strategies that cast an improbable event into a narrative form that marks it as true.[52]

Thus, belief in miracles is by no means some special cognitive state peculiar to medieval states of mind (and thus inaccessible to post-Enlightenment people). It is based neither on credulity nor on ignorance of the (social, political, economic) "reality" of the miraculous narrative. Instead, it is a dynamic process of (self-)conviction in which the truth of the supernatural event is probed. The process of producing belief does not take place in ignorance of the truth-value of the narrative under discussion, but rather places this very truth at the center, validating it through what we may call strategies of truth-making — a phrase which is preferable to "theories of truth," as it better conveys the dynamic nature of the process. It is only the strategy by which this is done that is unfamiliar to us, not the insistence on truth.

The process of enjoining belief as described by Justice is only one of a variety of ways by which narratives of improbable events are authenticated as being true. This variety is due to the different strategies of truth-making that are specific to different socio-cultural horizons, textual genres, and orders of discourse. Thus, the question is not whether some people in Late Antiquity and the Middle Ages believed dragon stories to be true, but how the specific truth-making strategy at work in these narratives differed from that pertaining to (say) belief in the Christian God — and how both of these might differ from the truth-mak-

---

51 Justice, "Did the Middle Ages Believe in Their Miracles?," 12–14, 17–18.
52 This runs counter to Otter's view (e.g., "Functions of Fiction," 118–19) that medieval historians' expressions of skepticism towards improbable events they are about to narrate were intended to signal a retreat from literal historical truthfulness and a temporary move into a self-consciously fictional narrative mode. For Justice, the expression of skepticism strengthens the declared intention of narrating a literally true account, even though it engages with the audience's as well as the author's potential doubts.

ing strategies current in judicial contexts or in daily life (gossip, bed-time stories).

So far, this discussion has dealt with theoretical understandings of belief. This may appear as a detour, but only if one fails to consider that belief (including the ways in which it is enjoined, justified, and verified and the forms in which it propagates via institutions and via organic socio-cultural channels) is a fundamental component in the construction of truth. To suggest that truth depends on belief might appear ridiculously relativist to many among the educated Western(ized) individuals who probably form the bulk of this book's readership, who have been taught to conceptualize truth as a correspondence between a "real" fact in the world and an utterance about it.[53] As such, truth is independent of belief: the Planck constant is $6.62607015 \times 10^{-34}$ $J \cdot Hz^{-1}$ even if there is no consciousness in the world able to recognize it, let alone believe it. As one recent philosopher puts it, "the truth of a belief depends on how things are; not on how I or anyone else might wish them to be."[54]

Yet, even if we restrict our parameters to philosophical discourse in the modern Western tradition, the correspondence theory of truth is but one of at least five main families of theories of truth extant in philosophical scholarly discourse (the other families are, roughly, the pragmatist, deflationary, pluralist, and coherence theories) and just one of roughly 500 vernacular definitions of truth that non-academics formulated on request in an intriguing sociological-philosophical study conducted by Arne Næss in the 1930s.[55] Næss concluded that, contrary to expectations, there is no one "common-sense" theory of truth that the "man on the Clapham omnibus" (city bus) holds, and that the

---

53 For the landmark critique of the bias of most sociological research towards the WEIRD (Western, Educated, Industrialized, Rich, and Democratic) societies and individuals who are the majority of its subjects, see Joseph Henrich, Steven J. Heine, and Ara Norenzayan, "The Weirdest People in the World?," *Behavioral and Brain Sciences* 33, nos. 2–3 (2010): 61–83.
54 Michael P. Lynch, *Truth as One and Many* (Oxford: Oxford University Press, 2009), 8.
55 Arne Næss, "Common Sense and Truth," *Theoria* 4, no. 1 (1938): 39–58.

bewildering multitude of theories of truth developed by philosophers corresponds to the variety and complexity of opinion that people outside academia have on such a common notion as truth.

For instance, pragmatist definitions of truth view it "as a function of the practices people engage in, and the commitments people make," and some of them point to the broader practical and performative dimensions of truth: "true statements might be those that are useful to believe."[56] Meanwhile, pluralist theories of truth point out that "different statements can be all true without being true in the same way," and that there is no single theory of truth applicable to all domains: truth can mean something quite different in justice, in science, and in theology. This being so, "one needs a different theory of truth for each domain, and that is precisely what ordinary humans employ in their daily lives."[57]

These alternative theories of truth may appear counterintuitive to mental habits that consider a fact or an utterance as either true or false and nothing in between. According to these theories, truth can be something that is constructed *post factum*, the result of a process of social, political, or cultural negotiation, not as a relationship existing *a priori* between things in the world and things in the mind. We suggest that a similar variety of theories of truth existed in medieval (and indeed, all human) societies, and consequently that the cognitive dissonance between medieval reports of supernatural or fantastic events and our intuitive notions of how the world works is rooted in the

---

[56] John Capps, "The Pragmatic Theory of Truth," in *The Stanford Encyclopedia of Philosophy* (Summer 2019 Edition), ed. Edward N. Zalta, https://plato.stanford.edu/archives/sum2019/entries/truth-pragmatic.

[57] Eric A. Kreuter and Kenneth M. Moltner, *Treatment and Management of Maladaptive Schemas* (New York: Springer, 2014), 49 (quoting Piero Scaruffi). See also Nikolaj Jang Lee Linding Pedersen and Cory Wright, "Pluralist Theories of Truth," in *The Stanford Encyclopedia of Philosophy* (Winter 2018 Edition), ed. Edward N. Zalta, https://plato.stanford.edu/archives/win2018/entries/truth-pluralist.

different theories of truth according to which narratives come to be considered to be true.

We do not presume there is a clearly defined limit (temporal, social, or geographical) separating "people now" and "people back then" or "people out there" in this respect. Rather, we suggest that different theories of truth, or strategies of truth-making, are part of discursive practices implicitly shared by different socio-cultural communities both in modern Western(ized) and in pre-modern or non-Western societies. These practices may be shared in non-uniform ways: there are always dissenters and people sharing only some of the elements of a conceptualization schema. They are emergent rather than static, arising, stabilizing, and changing via a myriad of socio-cultural and political negotiations between individuals, communities, and institutions. They are dynamic, being poised between, on the one hand, the coagulating tendency of socio-political institutions to install one of them as the only valid one and, on the other hand, the centrifugal impulse of individuals and communities to create new lines of flight. These implicit conceptualizations of truth are always in flux, although stable configurations occur at points of emergent or manufactured consensus.[58]

This "constructivist" approach to truth is inspired by Foucault's notion of a "regime of truth," adjusted to the medieval socio-political contexts to which the sources we investigate belong. It also draws on cognitive linguist Farzad Sharifian's account of how cultural conceptualizations emerge through more organic and less institutional processes than Foucault (with his predominant focus on early modern and industrial-era institutions) allows for. As Foucault put it:

---

[58] Compare Foucault's account of discursive practices in Michel Foucault, "Discourse on Language," in *The Archaeology of Knowledge and the Discourse on Language*, trans. A.M. Sheridan Smith (New York: Pantheon, 1972), 215–16, and Farzad Sharifian's account of cultural conceptualizations, in *Cultural Conceptualizations and Language: Theoretical Framework and Applications* (Amsterdam: John Benjamins, 2011).

Each society has its regime of truth, its general politics of truth: that is, the types of discourse which it accepts and makes function as true; the mechanisms and instances which enable one to distinguish true and false statements, the means by which each is sanctioned, the techniques and procedures accorded value in the acquisition of truth, the status of those who are charged with saying what counts as true.[59]

This notion of a "regime of truth" is totalizing: it is based on the assumption that a hegemonic regime is sustainably enforceable in any society. This would not be the case in a society lacking many of the modern state institutions involved in the production of knowledge and power on which Foucault focuses most of his work. This is why we continue to use the notion of "strategy of truth-making" (understood as the socio-cultural, political, and rhetorical/narrative/poetic processes by which truth is legitimized, enjoined, and sanctioned, as explained above), and occasionally also "truth theory," this being the heuristic reconstruction of the implicit conceptualizations produced via such truth-making strategies.

A case in point is Bede's introduction to the *Historia Ecclesiastica Gentis Anglorum* and the famous *vera lex historiae* which provides the title of this volume. Much discussion has revolved around the following passage in Bede's preface:

I humbly implore the reader that he not impute it to me if in what I have written he finds anything other than the truth. For, in accordance with *a true law of history*, I have tried to set down in a simple style what I have collected from common report, for the instruction of posterity.[60]

---

59 Michel Foucault, "Truth and Power," in *Power/Knowledge: Selected Interviews and Other Writings by Michel Foucault, 1972–1977*, ed. Colin Gordon (Brighton: Harvester, 1980), 109–33, at 131.

60 The original Latin in Bede, *Ecclesiastical History*, preface, 6: "Lectoremque suppliciter obsecro ut, siqua in his quae scripsimus aliter quam se ueritas habet posita reppererit, non hoc nobis imputet, qui, quod uera lex historiae est, simpliciter ea quae fama uulgante collegimus ad instructionem posteri-

As Roger Ray explains, the preface itself is "a skillful web of long-standing commonplaces, and they all function in the traditional way," and thus it does not explicitly contain much theorizing on truth and history-writing, although his unusually long explanations for the variety of his sources point to a vexing issue for Bede.[61] It may be suggested that both the absence of a clear, explicit theory of truth and the length of Bede's explanations about his sources may result from a tension between two theories of historical truth at work in Bede's own text.

Following Ray, we argue that this opposition arises between what Bede sees as the superior truth of theology (only discernible to a minority of elite readers) and *vera lex historiae*. By that last phrase, as both Ray and Walter Goffart have pointed out, Bede did not mean any definitive and universal "law of history" in an anachronistic Hegelian or Marxian sense, but instead intended to make a humble concession to the role of *fama vulgans* (public opinion), however wrong, when writing a certain type of historically truthful narrative.[62] Thus, ironically (more so to us than to him), Bede's self-declared adherence to *vera lex historiae* means not that he holds himself to any quasi-modern standard of objective truth, but rather the reverse — that in the *Historia Ecclesiastica* he is compelled to write the narrative as it was known by a more public audience whose opinion already had a definite shape.

In a half-apologetic, half-defensive passage later in the *Historia Ecclesiastica,* Bede employs a quite different theory of truth, according to which the *verax historicus* (true historian) must relate only good things of good men. In this light, Bede acknowledges that his reader might be surprised to find, in his account of the admirable bishop Aidan of Lindisfarne, direct criticism of Aidan's adherence to a flawed method of calculating the date of Easter, a serious shortcoming in Bede's eyes. Bede escapes from

---

tatis litteris mandare studuimus." We have used Roger Ray's translation, in Ray, "Bede's *Vera Lex Historiae*," 12–13.

61 Ibid., 11.
62 Ibid., 11; Walter Goffart, "Bede's *uera lex historiae* Explained," *Anglo-Saxon England* 34 (2005): 111–16, at 114.

this difficulty by emphasizing that Aidan's chief motivation for holding to his error was pure and, in that sense, admirable.⁶³

The tension between the theories of truth cited by Bede in these two passages — the *vera lex historiae* which gives popular report a place in historical narrative, and that of the *verax historicus* who tells only good things of good men — is only sharpened by Bede's suggestion that Aidan might have been swayed, in his adherence to error, by "the force of public opinion." It is only in, for instance, *The Life of Cuthbert* that he can strip down the "(woefully) historical […] picturesque irrelevancies" of the *Anonymous Life of St Cuthbert* which he reworked to unravel the spiritual significance of the saint's life via a theological mode of narration meant to reveal the superior truth (however unrealistic from a merely human perspective) for a different audience that was not particularly interested in the accidents of Cuthbert's material-historical existence.⁶⁴ Similarly, it is only in his *Letter to Ecgbert* that he can complain about the problematic proliferation of Northumbrian *Eigenkirchen*, whereas he appears content with this development in the *Historia Ecclesiastica*.⁶⁵

Even in the classicizing Latinate tradition of history-writing that Bede is carrying forward, there are at least three truth-making strategies, described in the *Historia Ecclesiastica* in very different terms. The strategy of the *verax historicus*, mentioned in connection with Aidan, is based on a pragmatist (albeit strongly idealizing) theory of truth in which the choice of content is dictated entirely by its potential to edify audiences in a particular moral or spiritual direction. The other two strategies are both cited in Bede's preface. One is based either on trustworthy oral informants, some of which he names (such as Abbot Albinus of Canterbury for the southern material) or on information handed down through a faithful line of bearers of an oral tradition (designated explicitly as *traditio seniorum, traditio priorum,*

---

63 Ray, "Bede's *Vera Lex Historiae*," 18–20.
64 The quoted words are from Goffart, "Bede's *uera lex historiae* Explained," 110.
65 Ibid., 116.

traditio majorum, and only in the preface as *fama vulgans*).[66] The other rests on the spiritual and documentary authority of written sources: for example, a priest of London named Nothelm, under the guidance of Albinus, had gone abroad to search the papal archives for Roman sources relevant to Augustine's mission, while for the *Life of St. Cuthbert,* Bede writes that he "partly took and faithfully copied" from the authorized Lindisfarne *vita.*[67]

Bede clearly gives the latter strategy priority. As Ray argues, he uses vera lex historiae as an apology for using so much oral information, "the factual quality of which he was himself in a poor position to judge."[68] But while he does not fully trust it, he is compelled to use it, and thus feels a duty to explain his temporary and partial adherence to a different theory of truth, one based on *fama vulgans,* the opinions of the public. This is a different form of pragmatist theory of truth whereby truth is whatever has been agreed upon by a community remembering their past (whether a monastic community telling the story of their foundation, or Kentish elites narrating the coming of their ancestors on the island), however diffident Bede may be in private about the truth of these narratives (hence his protestations about potential untruthful reports, and removing all doubts — "occasionem dubitandi subtraham").

Bede sets this theory of truth against the truth of Scripture and, generally, of the written word (be it papal records, hagiography, or theology), which is a more correspondence-based theory of truth whereby only what is written down is faithful to the

---

66 These tradition-bearers are also implied in Bede's use of verbs and phrases such as *fertur, perhibentur,* and *ut aiunt.*
67 Ray, "Bede's *Vera Lex Historiae,*" 17–18 for oral informants and 12 for written sources. On the role of orality in Bede's work, see Catherine Cubitt, "Folklore and Historiography: Oral Stories and the Writing of Anglo-Saxon History," in *Narrative and History in the Early Medieval West,* ed. Elizabeth M. Tyler and Ross Balzaretti (Turnhout: Brepols, 2006), 189–221 (especially 209–11) and John McNamara, "Bede's Role in Circulating Legend in the *Historia Ecclesiastica*," *Anglo-Saxon Studies in Archaeology and History* 7 (1994): 61–69.
68 Ray, "Bede's *Vera Lex Historiae,*" 12–13.

truth of the matter. Even when it comes to oral informants, part of Albinus's authority comes from the fact that he is an authority (*auctor*) and a man "most learned in all things" ("reverentissimus vir per omnia doctissimus exstitit"), and not necessarily because he is the last link in an oral chain of tradition. Bede also implies that his faithfully copying the Lindisfarne *Life of Cuthbert* makes his report incontrovertibly true ("assumsi, simpliciter fidem historiae, quam legebam"). He does not designate as *historia* any of the oral traditions that he uses, nor does he call any of his informants an *auctor*: these terms are employed only in relation to the more prestigious written sources.[69]

A full survey of the use of these words in Bede is unnecessary here and would require a separate study, so we provide only one example here. In book 4 chapter 19 of the *Historia Ecclesiastica*, he feels compelled to assure his audience of the fact that queen Æthelthryth preserved her virginity even though she had been married for twelve years to Tondberct, king of the South Gyrwas, and then to Ecgfrith of Northumbria, since some doubted this ("sicut mihimet sciscitanti, cum hoc an ita esset, quibusdam venisset in dubium").[70] He provides this assurance by quoting his oral informant, bishop Wilfrid, as an undoubted witness of her virginity ("testem integritatis ejus esse certissimum"). But, in order to strengthen this personal testimony, since he feels some might still doubt that such things could happen in that age ("nec diffidendum est nostra etiam aetate fieri potuisse"), he states: "true histories tell us they happened several times in former ages" ("quod aevo praecedente aliquoties factum fideles historiae narrant") through God's assistance.[71]

The "true histories" Bede mentions can be none other than the hagiographies narrating the lives of previous saintly virgins and Scripture itself, which tells of the archetype of them all, the Virgin Mary — all written sources containing divinely inspired narratives. They are the true histories that Bede credits more

---

69 Bede, *Ecclesiastical History*, preface, 6.
70 Ibid.
71 Ibid.

than even his most trustworthy informants, since in this passage he feels the need to appeal to their authority to establish the truth of an unlikely event for which he had already quoted the oral testimony of an important bishop.

Interestingly, here, too, we have a confirmation of the dynamics between belief and skepticism described by Justice. Bede acknowledges that Æthelthryth's virginity is an improbable fact, and he twice admits that people have expressed doubt — even after his initial citation of testimony, he acknowledges that some would still doubt it — but, as an *auctor* himself, he guides his audience with a sure hand from their natural skepticism to belief in a divinely facilitated truth that is improbable, even impossible, for mere humanity.

In Bede's preface we have, *in nuce*, two truth-making strategies which can be called *traditio* (community-dependent and socially useful truth via oral tradition) and *auctoritas* (spiritual or simply factual truth via Scripture or trustworthy written sources such as canonical authors). This heuristic is at work in diverse narrative embodiments in all early medieval sources under scrutiny in this book, regardless of their belonging to very different traditions. Both of these conceptualizations are very different from the correspondence theory of truth that we are drawn to. Medieval texts, as Norris Lacy has put it, "are often authenticated neither by the reality or factual truth of their content, nor by their own authors' narrative acts, but by their association with other texts and their participation in a larger narrative tradition."[72]

Jan Ziolkowski has argued that *auctoritas* had a strongly juridical and political connotation in Classical antiquity, whereas in the Middle Ages it moved from residing in "the people of authority" to being identified with the texts themselves. This mimetic rhetoric was fetishized to such a degree as a procedure of veracity that it often coexisted (especially after the twelfth century) with either vague invocations of authority such as "the authorities say […]," or citations of fictitious authors (or fictitious

---

72 Norris J. Lacy, *Reading Fabliaux* (London: Garland, 1993), 103.

citations of real authors) which simultaneously evinced "a deep faith in *auctores* and a willingness to tamper with the authenticity of those *auctores*."[73] This need not be paradoxical. In the model presented here, *auctoritas* is a truth-making strategy, but it does not produce a strictly correspondence-based truth, but rather one that is partly pragmatist (truth equated with conformity to authority, whether cultural, political, or theological, or all three) and partly coherence-based (whereby the truth conditions of a proposition consist, not in objective features of the world, but in other propositions that together make up an internally consistent system of beliefs).[74]

So, rather than reflecting only "the self-consciousness about fictionality that intensified during the same period," as Ziolkowski assumes, this apparently cavalier attitude to truth and to authorities may also be due to the fact that the implicit theory of truth underlying *auctoritas* simply does not coincide with ours.[75] It is quite possible that not all medieval authors citing fictitious authorities were deliberately making things up: some of them, at least, may have really believed they were telling the truth, but that the only way to legitimize this truth was to cite *auctoritas*.

In other words, the fictionality of a source need not imply the self-conscious fictionality of the narrative it was used to warrant. It is not that Bede believed he was telling lies when he felt compelled to give a voice to *fama vulgans* when telling his story; it is merely that he was skeptical about the ability of popular opinion via oral tradition to contain the entire truth of the matter. This skepticism in itself cannot be presumed to be characteristic of even all Classically educated Latinate authors of the Middle Ages.

---

73 Jan M. Ziolkowski, "Cultures of Authority in the Long Twelfth Century," *Journal of English and Germanic Philology* 108 (2009): 421–44, at 439.
74 James Young, "The Coherence Theory of Truth," in *The Stanford Encyclopedia of Philosophy* (Fall 2018 Edition), ed. Edward N. Zalta, https://plato.stanford.edu/archives/fall2018/entries/truth-coherence.
75 Ziolkowski, "Cultures of Authority," 438.

Bede's *Historia Ecclesiastica* shows us only some of the many truth-making strategies and their underlying theories of truth which are at work in the medieval historical narratives explored in this volume. What the essays in this volume show is the variety of strategies to claim, legitimize, and assess the truthfulness of a narrative about the past.

The editors and contributors to this volume also hope to move conversations around truth, fictionality, and historicity in pre-modern narrative beyond the "fact vs. fiction" dichotomy by revealing the rootedness of historical production and truth-making in the life of emotions and in social relations. In the context of history-writing, truth is not a legal procedure or a purely logical operation, but a function of the culturally determined socio-emotional appropriateness of a narrative. As Elizabeth Tonkin (working on West African oral history) suggests, realism is a "culture-bound judgment of likelihood," which involves an audience's assessment of "whether the linguistic and genre patterns, as well as the content of the discourse, are appropriate for its representation" of a reality. Thus, truth ("that elusive historical goal") "lie[s] in the intersection of narrator and discourse, where we have to see how accounts are authorised," an endeavor that "varies generically and politically and culturally, as does the kind of truth claimed, expected or accepted." Indeed, in Tonkin's view, a "genre of discourse can carry with it a claim to a particular kind of truth."[76]

Our title's reference to "constructing truth" aims to do more than vaguely point to the classic relativistic argument for the unknowability of the past. Building on Hayden White's often misunderstood point, it aims to state that the truth never comes to us as such (i.e., truth is never an intrinsic quality of a narrative), but within a linguistic (and sometimes also narrative) construction whose parameters belong to a cultural horizon of expectation and to a certain textual tradition. In other words, the truth of a narrative is a process — a negotiation between people,

---

[76] Elizabeth Tonkin, *Narrating Our Pasts: The Social Construction of Oral History* (Cambridge: Cambridge University Press, 1990), 8.

between text and a textual tradition, and between people and their cultural matrix.

Our task here is to investigate how historical truthfulness — that is, the collective understanding that a particular narration of the past was true — emerged out of myriad interactions between agents inside a society. Hence, the construction of truth need not always be understood as a process of self-conscious deliberation when telling a story about the past, but also as a negotiation already existent in the fabric of the narrative, and in the society or community for which that narrative emerges as true. If "truth is a matter of interpretation of accounts, and in order to judge their veracity, one must first understand their construction," the contributions in this volume aim to do just that.[77]

***

Kim Bergqvist's chapter examines certain "reality elements" in the fictional and historical tales of the fourteenth-century Castilian frame-tale collection of *exempla El Conde Lucanor* (*Tales of Count Lucanor,* 1335) and other works of its author Don Juan Manuel. It focuses on the use of autofiction and the insertion of historical figures in a fictional setting or their use in such a mode. This topic is approached through wider discussions about the distinction between allegorical and historical truth in Juan Manuel's work, the discursive common ground between medieval history and fiction in terms of their plausibility, and the notion of the purported self-referentiality of fiction. Bergqvist argues that autofictional and other reality elements do not so much attempt to verify or authenticate otherwise fictional narratives, as they consciously play with the common ground of the historical and the fictional mode. As such, these features are part of a cohesive didactic strategy on the part of the author in question, interconnected with his social and political position in fourteenth-century Castile.

---

77 Ibid., 113.

Cynthia Turner Camp's essay investigates the historiographic process of forgetting, or rather the judicious privileging of some events over others, in the later medieval nunnery of Barking Abbey. Following the lead of Margot Fassler and others, the essay considers liturgical rites, in this instance the recording of obits and performance of masses for the revered dead, as an embodied historiographic practice through which monasteries and nunneries would develop somatic relationships with their institutional past. While the celebration of feast-days and obits at any monastic institution would cement a particular vision of the institution's identity, at Barking these liturgical rites established the nunnery's identity as founded on and sustained by women. Additionally, as the later medieval nuns simplified their anniversary masses for the nunnery's earlier abbesses, they engage in a deliberate "forgetting" of those abbesses' distinctive personalities; this simplification homogenizes the nunnery's identity through the rhetorical trope of the "timeless nun" while simultaneously preserving those abbesses' positions as institutional foremothers.

Catherine Karkov's chapter explores the use of stone for architectural purposes in seventh- and eighth-century England and its agency throughout its troubled history amongst modern scholars who study the period. In this endeavor, stone and building with stone are considered as forms of record-making that are just as rich and multivalent as graphical forms of inscription and history-making. Rather than prioritizing written histories, this chapter interrogates the stone itself in order to reach the deeper history of specific sites in early medieval England. The ability of stone to relate stories and to create or remember histories has been exploited by conquerors and colonizers across the globe for centuries, and Karkov employs thinking about the use of stone in the Incan Andes and in medieval India to stimulate useful new ways of thinking differently about the use and reuse of stone in early medieval England, and about its peoples' relationship with both land and history. Rather than drawing comparisons amongst three very different postcolonial situations, this essay focuses specifically on what the use of stone in these cultures might have to contribute to our understanding of the use and reuse of stone along the Hadrian's Wall frontier and of what stone had to say to the inhabitants of early medieval England as well as what it has to say to us today.

Justin Lake's chapter focuses on the rhetorical doctrine of *narratio probabilis* (plausible narrative), which according to the Ciceronian tradition was used to impart verisimilitude to narrative—written history included—through the use of plausible, but not necessarily true, details. Lake argues that earlier medieval authors did not adopt this view of history-writing, and that there is little evidence narratio probabilis played any significant role in the writing of history until the late tenth century, when a trio of authors writing in northern France all produced historical works that manifested a new relationship with Classical rhetoric. This style of history, characterized by fictional set-piece orations and descriptive passages, arose out of a close engagement with Ciceronian rhetorical doctrines as practiced by innovative schoolmasters such as Gerbert of Aurillac and Abbo of Fleury and presaged the more literarily ambitious style of historiography that flowered in the twelfth century.

Ingela Nilsson's chapter explores the concept of occasional literature as a fruitful way of defining and understanding twelfth-century Byzantine literature. Such literature, Nilsson argues, inscribes itself as a link between the past and the present, placing itself in a position between the fictional and the factual. Such procedures presume an intellectual and cultural tradition that extends backwards in time, making the connection to the past relevant to present society, along with a political and social system based on patronage that offers social and professional advancement as a reward for texts or other cultural expressions. For an author working in such a system, self-fashioning and self-promotion become important factors in gaining the attention and appreciation of patrons. Therefore, Nilsson's chapter demonstrates that stylistically speaking, occasional literature demanded a strong individualized voice, as in the case of the textual production of Constantine Manasses, a teacher and writer on command who remained in the service of several different patrons in Constantinople for at least thirty years.

Ralph O'Connor's chapter explores to what extent Norse-Icelandic sagas were framed as history by the people who wrote and transmitted them in the Middle Ages. Because sagas straddle the assumed boundary between historical and imaginative writing, they provide a useful corpus with which to re-examine that boundary and expand the range of literary genres which could be historical. By focusing on framing devices primarily in sagas commonly viewed as fictional, O'Connor finds evidence of historical intent in the passages of historical information (*fræði*) placed at sagas' beginnings and endings to provide a context, outside the story proper, from which the narrative is seen to emerge. These historical anchorage-points appear not only in sagas conventionally pigeonholed as (pseudo)historical, but also in those seen as fictional, which means that increasing inventiveness did not necessarily imply decreasing veracity for their authors and redactors, most of whom framed their sagas in ways which invited audiences to treat their contents as historical. By making this argument, O'Connor dismantles a common grand narrative according to which sagas can be placed on a spectrum of intended veracity corresponding to their date of composition, corresponding to a "rise of fiction" as a kind of upward escalator. This chapter argues that the freer use of imaginative and entertaining techniques in certain sagas did not necessarily constitute a departure from history in their terms. Rather, the creative freedom enjoyed by saga-writers indicates that the limits of truthfulness in historical writing were often broader than we assume, especially in histories of the remote past.

And finally, Catalin Taranu's chapter investigates the issues of truthfulness, veracity, and realism. It starts from the oft-remarked-upon presence of apparently incongruously fabulous elements in otherwise "realistic" medieval narratives, which it explains by proposing the existence of a variety of underlying theories of truth and narrative representation governed by different expectations, patterns of eventuality, and social functions that are at work in different types of discourse and modes of historical production. Focusing on a variety of Old English sources, ranging from heroic verse to elegies and maxims, the chapter traces three main truth-constructing strategies (i.e., the ways in which truth is asserted, assessed, and recognized in a type of discourse) throughout this corpus: *auctoritas* (the dominant mode in theological and later medieval narrative, whereby truth is based on a written record and on the religious authority and/or narrative prestige of a named author), *traditio* (truth is procedural, guaranteed by following a certain traditional process, such as composing oral verse in the right way or fulfilling the formalities of judicial process), and *collaboratio* (truth is in abeyance, waiting to be assessed and pieced together by a knowing audience, thus establishing it is a collective enterprise which often has an agonistic, polemical dimension).

Bibliography

Primary

Bede's Ecclesiastical History of the English People. Edited by Bertram Colgrave and R.A.B. Mynors. Oxford Medieval Texts. Oxford: Oxford University Press, 1969.

Isidore of Seville. *Etymologiarum sive Originum libri XX.* Edited by Wallace M. Lindsay. 2 volumes. Oxford: Clarendon Press, 1911.

Saga Óláfs Tryggvasonar af Oddr Snorrason munk. Edited by Finnur Jónsson. Copenhagen: Gad, 1932.

Saxo Grammaticus. *Gesta Danorum: The History of the Danes.* Edited by Karsten Friis-Jensen. Translated by Peter Fisher. 2 volumes. Oxford: Clarendon Press, 2015.

Secondary

Ainsworth, Peter. "Legendary History: *historia* and *fabula*." In *Historiography in the Middle Ages*, edited by Deborah Mauskopf Deliyannis, 387–416. Boston and Leiden: Brill, 2003.

Baumgartner, Emmanuèle. *De l'histoire de Troie au livre du Graal: le temps, le récit (XIIe–XIIIe siècles).* Orléans: Paradigme, 1994.

Bloch, R. Howard. *The Anonymous Marie de France.* Chicago: University of Chicago Press, 2003. DOI: 10.7208/chicago/9780226059693.001.0001.

Brewer, Keagan. *Wonder and Skepticism in the Middle Ages.* New York: Routledge, 2016. DOI: 10.4324/9781315691510.

Capps, John. "The Pragmatic Theory of Truth." In *The Stanford Encyclopedia of Philosophy* (Summer 2019 Edition), edited by Edward N. Zalta. https://plato.stanford.edu/archives/sum2019/entries/truth-pragmatic.

Cohn, Dorrit. "Signposts of Fictionality: A Narratological Perspective." *Poetics Today* 11, no. 4 (1990): 775–804. DOI: 10.2307/1773077.

Cubitt, Catherine. "Folklore and Historiography: Oral Stories and the Writing of Anglo-Saxon History." In *Narrative and History in the Early Medieval West,* edited by Elizabeth M.

Tyler and Ross Balzaretti, 189–221. Turnhout: Brepols, 2006. DOI: 10.1484/M.SEM-EB.3.3768.

Damian-Grint, Peter. *The New Historians of the Twelfth-Century Renaissance*. Woodbridge: Boydell Press, 1999.

David, Marian. "The Correspondence Theory of Truth." In *The Stanford Encyclopedia of Philosophy* (Fall 2016 Edition), edited by Edward N. Zalta. https://plato.stanford.edu/archives/fall2016/entries/truth-correspondence.

Duggan, Joseph J. "Medieval Epic as Popular Historiography: Appropriation of Historical Knowledge in the Vernacular Epic." In *La Littérature historiographique des origines à 1500*, edited by Hans Ulrich Gumbrecht et al., 285–311. Heidelberg: Carl Winter Universitätsverlag, 1986.

Fancy, Hussein. *The Mercenary Mediterranean: Sovereignty, Religion, and Violence in the Medieval Crown of Aragon*. Chicago: University of Chicago Press, 2016. DOI: 10.7208/chicago/9780226329789.001.0001.

Field, Rosalind. "Romance as History, History as Romance." In *Romance in Medieval England*, edited by Maldwyn Mills et al., 163–73. Cambridge: D.S. Brewer, 1991.

Fleischman, Suzanne. "On the Representation of History and Fiction in the Middle Ages." *History and Theory* 22, no. 3 (1983): 278–310. DOI: 10.2307/2504985.

Foucault, Michel. *The Archaeology of Knowledge and the Discourse on Language*. Translated by A.M. Sheridan Smith. New York: Pantheon, 1972.

———. "Truth and Power." In *Power/Knowledge: Selected Interviews and Other Writings by Michel Foucault, 1972–1977*, edited by Colin Gordon, 109–33. Brighton: Harvester, 1980.

Frazer, James George. "On Certain Burial Customs as Illustrative of the Primitive Theory of the Soul." *Journal of the Anthropological Institute of Great Britain and Ireland* 15 (1886): 63–104. DOI: 10.2307/2841908.

Goffart, Walter. "Bede's *uera lex historiae* Explained." *Anglo-Saxon England* 34 (2005): 111–16. DOI: 10.1017/S0263675105000049.

Green, Dennis H. *The Beginnings of Medieval Romance: Fact and Fiction, 1150–1220*. Cambridge: Cambridge University Press, 2002. DOI: 10.1017/CBO9780511485787.

Henrich, Joseph, Steven J. Heine, and Ara Norenzayan. "The Weirdest People in the World?" *Behavioral and Brain Sciences* 33, nos. 2–3 (2010): 61–83. DOI: 10.1017/S0140525X0999152X.

Jenkins, Keith. *On "What Is History?"* London: Routledge, 1995.

Justice, Steven. "Did the Middle Ages Believe in Their Miracles?" *Representations* 103, no. 1 (2008): 1–29. DOI: 10.1525/rep.2008.103.1.1.

Kemp, Anthony. Review of Monika Otter, *Inventiones*. *Speculum* 74, no. 1 (1999): 235–37. DOI: 10.2307/2887340.

Kempshall, Matthew. *Rhetoric and the Writing of History, 400–1500*. Manchester: Manchester University Press, 2011.

Kreuter, Eric A., and Kenneth M. Moltner. *Treatment and Management of Maladaptive Schemas*. New York: Springer, 2014. DOI: 10.1007/978-3-319-06817-6.

Lacy, Norris J. *Reading Fabliaux*. London: Garland, 1993.

Lake, Justin. "Current Approaches to Medieval Historiography." *History Compass* 13, no. 3 (2015): 89–109. DOI: 10.1111/hic3.12222.

———. "Truth, Plausibility, and the Virtues of Narrative at the Millennium." *Journal of Medieval History* 35, no. 3 (2009): 221–38. DOI: 10.1016/j.jmedhist.2009.05.003.

Lewis, C.S. *The Discarded Image: An Introduction to Medieval and Renaissance Literature*. Cambridge: Cambridge University Press, 1964.

Lynch, Michael P. *Truth as One and Many*. Oxford: Oxford University Press. 2009. DOI: 10.1093/acprof:oso/9780199218738.001.0001.

McNamara, John. "Bede's Role in Circulating Legend in the *Historia Ecclesiastica*." *Anglo-Saxon Studies in Archaeology and History* 7 (1994): 61–69.

Mehtonen, Päivi. *Old Concepts and New Poetics: "historia," "argumentum," and "fabula" in the Twelfth- and Early Thirteenth-Century Latin Poetics of Fiction*. Commentationes Humanarum Litterarum 108. Helsinki: Societas Scientiarum Fennica, 1996.

Morse, Ruth. *Truth and Convention in the Middle Ages: Rhetoric, Representation, and Reality.* Cambridge: Cambridge University Press, 1991.

Mortensen, Lars Boje. "The Status of the 'Mythical' Past in Nordic Latin Historiography (c. 1170–1220)." In *Medieval Narratives between History and Fiction: From the Centre to the Periphery of Europe, c. 1100–1400,* edited by Panagiotis A. Agapitos and Lars Boje Mortensen, 103–39. Copenhagen: Museum Tusculanum, 2012.

Næss, Arne. "Common Sense and Truth." *Theoria* 4, no. 1 (1938): 39–58. DOI: 10.1111/j.1755-2567.1938.tb00438.x.

Ó Corráin, Donnchadh. "Irish Origin Legends and Genealogy: Recurrent Aetiologies." In *History and Heroic Tale: A Symposium,* edited by Tore Nyberg et al., 51–96. Odense: Odense University Press, 1985.

O'Connor, Ralph. "History or Fiction? Truth-Claims and Defensive Narrators in Icelandic Romance-Sagas." *Mediaeval Scandinavia* 15 (2005): 1–69.

———. *The Earth on Show: Fossils and the Poetics of Popular Science, 1802–1856.* Chicago: University of Chicago Press, 2007.

Otter, Monika, "Functions of Fiction in Historical Writing." In *Writing Medieval History,* edited by Nancy Partner, 109–30. London: Hodder Arnold, 2005.

———. *"Inventiones": Fiction and Referentiality in Twelfth-Century English Historical Writing.* Chapel Hill: University of North Carolina Press, 1996.

Partner, Nancy F. *Serious Entertainments: The Writing of History in Twelfth-Century England.* Chicago: University of Chicago Press, 1977.

Pedersen, Nikolaj Jang Lee Linding, and Cory Wright. "Pluralist Theories of Truth." In *The Stanford Encyclopedia of Philosophy* (Winter 2018 Edition), edited by Edward N. Zalta. https://plato.stanford.edu/archives/win2018/entries/truth-pluralist.

Phelpstead, Carl. "Fantasy and History: The Limits of Plausibility in Oddr Snorrason's *Óláfs saga Tryggvasonar*." *Saga-Book of the Viking Society* 36 (2012): 27–42. https://www.jstor.org/stable/48611886.

Putter, Ad. "Latin Historiography after Geoffrey of Monmouth." In *The Arthur of Medieval Latin Literature: The Development and Dissemination of the Arthurian Legend in Medieval Latin*, edited by Siân Echard, 85–108. Cardiff: University of Wales Press, 2011.

Ray, Roger. "Bede's *Vera Lex Historiae*." *Speculum* 55, no. 1 (1980): 1–21. DOI: 10.2307/2855707.

Ricœur, Paul. *Memory, History, Forgetting*. Translated by Kathleen Blamey and David Pellauer. Chicago: University of Chicago Press, 2010.

Roest, Bert. "Mediaeval Historiography: About Generic Constraints and Scholarly Constructions." In *Aspects of Genre and Type in Pre-Modern Literary Culture*, edited by Bert Roest and Herman Vanstiphout, 15–31. Groningen: Styx, 1995.

Sharifian, Farzad. *Cultural Conceptualizations and Language: Theoretical Framework and Applications*. Amsterdam: John Benjamins, 2011. DOI: 10.1075/clscc.1.

Shepherd, Geoffrey T. "The Emancipation of Story in the Twelfth Century." In *Medieval Narrative: A Symposium*, edited by Hans Bekker-Nielsen et al., 44–57. Odense: Odense University, 1979.

Spiegel, Gabrielle M. *Romancing the Past: The Rise of Vernacular Prose Historiography in Thirteenth-Century France*. Berkeley: University of California Press, 1993. DOI: 10.1525/9780520915565.

Stein, Robert M. *Reality Fictions: Romance, History, and Governmental Authority, 1025–1180*. Notre Dame: University of Notre Dame Press, 2006.

Sternberg, Meir. *The Poetics of Biblical Narrative: Ideological Literature and the Drama of Reading*. Bloomington: Indiana University Press, 1984.

Stocking, George W. *After Tylor: British Social Anthropology, 1888–1951*. London: Athlone, 1996.

Stoljar, Daniel, and Nic Damnjanovic. "The Deflationary Theory of Truth." In *The Stanford Encyclopedia of Philosophy* (Fall 2014 Edition), edited by Edward N. Zalta. https://plato.stanford.edu/archives/fall2014/entries/truth-deflationary.

Svanhildur Óskarsdóttir. "Universal History in Fourteenth-Century Iceland: Studies in AM 764 4to." PhD diss., University College London, 2000.

Taranu, Catalin. *The Bard and the Rag-Picker: Vernacular Verse Histories in Early Medieval England and Francia.* London: Routledge, 2021.

Tonkin, Elizabeth. *Narrating Our Pasts: The Social Construction of Oral History.* Cambridge: Cambridge University Press, 1990.

Tylor, Edward Burnett. *Primitive Culture.* 2 volumes. 1871; rpt. London: John Murray, 1929.

Ward, Aengus. *History and Chronicles in Late Medieval Iberia: Representations of Wamba in Late Medieval Narrative Histories.* Boston and Leiden: Brill, 2011. DOI: 10.1163/ej.9789004202726.i-220.

White, Hayden. *Metahistory: The Historical Imagination in Nineteenth-century Europe.* Baltimore: Johns Hopkins University Press, 1973.

———. *The Content of the Form: Narrative Discourse and Historical Representation.* Baltimore: Johns Hopkins University Press, 2009.

———. "The Value of Narrativity in the Representation of Reality." *Critical Inquiry* 7, no 1 (1980): 5–27. DOI: 10.1086/448086.

Willerslev, Rane. *Soul Hunters: Hunting, Animism, and Personhood among the Siberian Yukaghirs.* Berkeley: University of California Press, 2007. DOI: 10.1525/9780520941007.

Würth, Stefanie. "The Common Transmission of *Trójumanna saga* and *Breta sögur.*" In *Beatus Vir: Studies in Early English and Norse Manuscripts in Memory of Phillip Pulsiano*, edited by A.N. Doane and Kirsten Wolf, 297–327. Tempe: Arizona Center for Medieval and Renaissance Studies, 2006.

Young, James O. "The Coherence Theory of Truth." In *The Stanford Encyclopedia of Philosophy* (Fall 2018 Edition), edited by Edward N. Zalta. https://plato.stanford.edu/archives/fall2018/entries/truth-coherence.

Zink, Michel. *Medieval French Literature: An Introduction.* Translated by Jeff Rider. Binghamton: Medieval & Renaissance Texts & Studies, 1995.

Ziolkowski, Jan M. "Cultures of Authority in the Long Twelfth Century." *Journal of English and Germanic Philology* 108, no. 4 (2009): 421–44. DOI: DOI.org/10.1353/egp.0.0071.

Zumthor, Paul. *Langue, texte, énigme*. Paris: Seuil, 1975.

1

The Shoemaker and the Troubadour Knight, and Other Stories: Historicity and the Truth of Fiction in Medieval Castilian Literature

Kim Bergqvist

And thus I have told you how it happened and how I knew about these three things of which you asked me. And because the words are many and I heard them from many people, it could well be that there were a few words more or less, or they are changed in some way; but believe me, surely, that the justice and the sentiment and the intention and the truth were as it is written here.
— Don Juan Manuel, "Libro de las armas o Libro de las tres razones"[1]

---

1 "Y así vos he contado cómo passó y cómo yo sope estas tres cosas que me preguntastes. Y porque las palabras son muchas [y] oílas a muchas personas, non podría ser que non oviese ý algunas palabras más o menos, o mudadas en alguna manera; mas cred por cierto que la justicia y la sentencia y la entención y la verdat así passó como es aquí escrito." Juan Manuel, *Obras completas*, ed. Carlos Alvar and Sarah Finci (Valencia: Proyecto Parnaseo de la Universitat de València, 2014), 757. All translations into English are mine unless otherwise credited.

The general prologue composed by Don Juan Manuel (1282–1348 CE) to introduce readers to his collected works opens with a narrative about a shoemaker and a noble troubadour. There was once a knight in Perpignan who was a great troubadour. He composed a song that was so brilliant and popular that everyone wanted to sing and hear that song and none other, and this pleased the knight greatly. Riding down the street one day, the knight hears a cobbler singing his song, disastrously erring in words and sound, so that whoever heard the song for the first time would consider it very poorly written. Consumed by rage, the knight descends from his mount, hears the shoemaker garbling his creation, thereupon snatches up a pair of scissors and goes to work cutting and destroying the fruits of the cobbler's labor. Their dispute is taken before the king, who understands the reasoning behind the knight's actions, pays the damages to the shoemaker and forbids him to sing that song in future.

This prologue to the works of the Castilian fourteenth-century *litterateur* Don Juan Manuel, that metaphorically imagines what happens to an author's works when copied into new manuscripts by less than competent scribes, recounts a story that has a similar structure to much older retellings, but one that is recast in significant ways here, in the MS 6376 of the Biblioteca Nacional de España in Madrid (fol. 1ʳ–1ᵛ). As Leonardo Funes reminds us, the story the author narrates in his prologue, though a tale known from folklore, is assigned to a very specific time and place in Juan Manuel's version: in this case, the city of Perpignan, then under the dominion of the Kingdom of Majorca, ruled by King Jaume II (r. 1276–1311).[2] The Majorcan king, who was actually the father-in-law of Juan Manuel, even makes an appearance in the story. According to Funes, Juan Manuel used this strategy to transform a traditional anecdote into the semblance of a historical event, giving it an air of verisimili-

---

[2] Leonardo Funes, *Investigación literaria de textos medievales: Objeto y práctica* (Buenos Aires: Miño y Dávila, 2009), 130–32; Ralph Steele Boggs, *Index of Spanish Folktales* (Helsinki: Suomalainen Tiedeakatemia, Academia Scientiarum Fennica, 1930), 139 (1695 A).

tude and defending the veracity of the tale.³ We should bear in mind, though, that according to Suzanne Fleischmann, Funes and Chris Given-Wilson historical truth did not imply authenticity of events in the Middle Ages, but rather plausibility and familiarity, "what was willingly believed" or commonly held to be true.⁴

Setting a fictional narrative — whether folklore or original invention — in a historical setting was a common way of conferring plausibility to imaginative stories. The prologue to the contemporaneous *Libro del caualiero Zifar* (*Book of the Knight Zifar*; c. 1300), a didactic, epic, and chivalric narrative ostensibly translated from Arabic, which allegorically recounts the legend of Saint Eustace, similarly places the story within a specified historical context, namely the jubilee celebrated by Pope Boniface VIII in Rome in the year 1300. A certain Ferrand Martínez, archdeacon of Madrid — who is charged with transferring the body of the deceased, prior archbishop of Toledo, cardinal Gonzalo García (Pérez) Gudiel, to Toledo — is also introduced, and has been identified as the author of the work.⁵ Apart from the plausibility effect, I would like to argue in the following that there is something more at work here, in Juan Manuel's didactic fiction, than the authentication of this tale, and others in his literary output, through its historical mode of writing. The complex interactions between the historical and fictional modes in Juan Manuel's work will be addressed through an analysis of what I will call *reality elements* in some of his texts, that is, referential or pseudo-referential elements such as historical figures or epi-

---

3   Funes, *Investigación literaria de textos medievales*, 131.
4   Suzanne Fleischmann, "On the Representation of History and Fiction in the Middle Ages," *History and Theory* 22, no. 3 (1983): 305 (quote); Leonardo Funes, *El modelo historiográfico alfonsí: Una caracterización* (London: Department of Hispanic Studies, Queen Mary, University of London, 1997), 27; and Chris Given-Wilson, *Chronicles: The Writing of History in Medieval England* (London: Hambledon and London, 2004), 3.
5   On the prologues to the Zifar, see Fernando Gómez Redondo, *Historia de la prosa medieval castellana II: El desarrollo de los géneros. La ficción caballeresca y el orden religioso* (Madrid: Cátedra, 1999), 1380–92. Cf. Hugo O. Bizzarri, *La otra mirada: El "exemplum" histórico* (Vienna: Lit, 2019).

sodes included therein. This is of interest in the context of the present volume since we are concerned with the meanings and significance of historical truth in different textual communities and discursive practices.

Don Juan Manuel has often been credited with introducing literary fiction into Castilian prose, building on the translated and original works of his uncle, King Alfonso X of Castile-León (r. 1252–1284), in a number of genres.[6] Among Juan Manuel's early works are an abbreviated version of the Alfonsine *Estoria de Espanna* (*History of Spain*) entitled *Crónica abreviada* (*Abridged Chronicle*), and a book on hunting (*Libro de la caza*), closely modeled on previous exemplars, whereas his later production includes more sophisticated and idiosyncratic texts, didactic and fictional.[7] The first extensive works of fiction produced in medieval Castile were translations from Arabic, undertaken during the reign of Fernando III (r. 1217–1252), in part by his son, the then *infante* Alfonso. According to Francisco Márquez Villanueva, the mature Alfonso X came to regard purely fictional narratives as unprofitable, discourses from which no important lessons could be gleaned.[8] That conception was definitely not shared by his nephew, who considered stories of very diverse character and origin as salutary lessons, as evidenced by the type of narrative he included in his well-known collection of *exempla, El Conde Lucanor* (1335). This frametale collection includes fifty stories of varied origin — from animal fables to stories about real historical figures — which are all related explicitly to the situation of the fictional nobleman Lucanor and his councilor, Patronio, who offers them as advice

---

6   See Fernando Gómez Redondo, "Géneros literarios en don Juan Manuel," *Cahiers de linguistique hispanique médiévale* 17 (1992): 87–125.
7   See, for example, Diego Catalán, "Don Juan Manuel ante el modelo alfonsí: El testimonio de la *Cronica abreviada*," in *Juan Manuel Studies,* ed. Ian Macpherson (London: Tamesis, 1977), 50–51, and Olivier Biaggini, "Stratégies du paratexte dans les œuvres de don Juan Manuel," *Cahiers d'études hispaniques médiévales* 35 (2012): 195–232.
8   Francisco Márquez Villanueva, *El concepto cultural alfonsí,* 2nd edn. (Barcelona: Edicions Bellaterra, 2004), 130–31.

to solve certain issues the count encounters. According to Peter Dunn, the selection is based on "didactic usefulness in explicating a dilemma — which is verified within the book itself. None of the *exemplos* would have gained a place in it if they had not been 'found to be' true in the experience of the young Count."[9]

What will be discussed in the following is, above all, fictional texts that were perceived as "true" in the Castilian Middle Ages — and I shall return below to the question of truth-claims in medieval literature and how truth should be understood in this context. The analysis is concerned mostly with brief exemplary, didactic fictions with some historical content or written in a historical mode. The texts under scrutiny offer a means to understand how the past was represented so as to create a semblance of historical truth, in order to attain certain narrative and ideological aims.

Three main lines of argument will concern us here. The first is a discussion of the discursive common ground between history and fiction in the Middle Ages, based on the notion of plausibility as a foundational aspect. The second is a reflection about the function of historical figures, authorial or otherwise, or other reality elements in fictional texts, and their significance for the question of the autonomy and self-referentiality of fiction. Does the introduction of such characters signify added truth-value and authentication or is it a game of fiction, a way of upsetting the fiction and displacing the narrative voice?[10] Do these reality elements within fiction typically raise or deconstruct the status of fictional texts? That is, are they meant to introduce an aspect of truth to fiction? In doing so, are they (consciously) playing with the discursive common ground between fiction and history in the Middle Ages? Third, a discussion of Juan Manuel's

---

9   Peter N. Dunn, "The Structure of Didacticism: Private Myths and Public Fictions," in *Juan Manuel Studies,* ed. Ian McPherson (London: Tamesis, 1977), 63–64.
10 Cf. Wim Verbaal, "How the West Was Won by Fiction: The Appearance of Fictional Narrative and Leisurely Reading in Western Literature (11th and 12th century)," in *True Lies Worldwide: Fictionality in Global Contexts,* ed. Anders Cullhed and Lena Rydholm (Berlin: de Gruyter, 2014), 196–98.

work and its notions of historical and figural truth will be offered in relation to this concept of reality elements.

It is reasonable to assume that exemplary narratives, primarily intended as didactic literature, were held to be true. They were not necessarily accounts of actual historical events, but they often used historical settings to transmit general truths and wisdom, some kind of *sensus moralis*. The truth-value of didactic fictions is well-attested in medieval theories of fiction and relates closely to the integumentum theory, according to which one may transmit "a true meaning enclosed in an invented tale" (Bernardus Silvestris: "Integumentum vero est oratio sub fabulosa narratione verum claudens intellectum").[11] Even so, they were largely fictional and used various narrative devices. Our question here is, what function did the historical characters and settings of some of these didactic fictions serve?

Plausibility and Utility in Medieval History and Fiction

Fictional texts in the Middle Ages could definitely have, or be thought to have, a *plausibility* that separated them further from purely imaginary fiction than from referential historical texts. Both history and fiction had to be credible representations of plausible events, or something like it. That is, histories were fictionally embellished or developed in order to be plausible representations of the lived and experienced past (for example, dialogues invented, gaps filled in between the accepted facts, etc.),[12] whereas fictional discourse also had to meet standards

---

11 Walter Haug, *Vernacular Literary Theory in the Middle Ages: The German Tradition, 800–1300, in Its European Context,* trans. Joanna M. Catling (Cambridge: Cambridge University Press, 1997), 230. Quote from Édouard Jeauneau, "Note sur l'École de Chartres," *Mémoires de la Société archéologique d'Eure-et-Loir* 23 (1964–68): 36.

12 Ruth Morse, *Truth and Convention in the Middle Ages: Rhetoric, Representation, and Reality* (Cambridge: Cambridge University Press, 1991), 231, and Fritz Peter Knapp, "Historicity and Fictionality in Medieval Narrative," in *True Lies Worldwide: Fictionality in Global Contexts,* ed. Anders Cullhed and Lena Rydholm (Berlin: de Gruyter, 2014), 181.

of plausibility in order not to be disregarded as *fabulae*.[13] Consequently, plausibility characterizes medieval history-writing as well as medieval fiction, and it does not help us distinguish or delineate boundaries between them (or identify a medieval distinction between the two). In other words, there was a discursive common ground shared between historically grounded "fiction" and historiography as such.[14] Even such authors as Isidore of Seville (c. 560–636), who might seem at first to present history and fiction (*fabulae*) as entirely distinct — since the latter are "made up" (*fictae*) — do present more nuance at closer inspection. According to Martin Irvine, Isidore's definition is close to Priscian's rhetorical doctrine in the *Praeexercitamina*, stating that "a fable is a fictional statement resembling true life and showing an image of truth in its structure" ("fabula est oratio verisimili dispositione imaginem exhibens veritatis").[15] Truth was not exclusive to historical discourse, and fictional discourse was neither wholly untruthful nor necessarily less plausible or verisimilar than history.

These plausible fictions, then, were narratives which were deemed to treat events that *could* have happened. This corresponds very well to what Else Mundal, writing on medieval Icelandic literature, characterizes as the "broad sense" of historical truth, in contrast to a narrow sense, meaning true accounts of actual events.[16] In relation to Old Norse saga literature (of the

---

13   Mark Chinca, *History, Fiction, Verisimilitude: Studies in the Poetics of Gottfried's "Tristan"* (London: The Modern Humanities Research Association for The Institute of Germanic Studies, University of London, 1993), 100ff.

14   I wish to acknowledge my intellectual debt to Simon Gaunt, whose lecture "Romancing the Truth: Vernacular History and the Origin of Fiction" at Maison Française of New York University on November 22, 2016 aided me in developing my incipient ideas on this topic.

15   Martin Irvine, *The Making of Textual Culture: "Grammatica" and Literary Theory, 350–1100* (Cambridge: Cambridge University Press, 1994), 239.

16   Else Mundal, "The Growth of Consciousness of Fiction in Old Norse Culture," in *Medieval Narratives between History and Fiction: From the Centre to the Periphery of Europe, c. 1100–1400*, ed. Panagiotis A. Agapitos and Lars B. Mortensen (Copenhagen: Museum Tusculanum Press, University of Copenhagen, 2012), 169–75.

classical period), it has been suggested that stories that were blatantly untrue did not appeal to audiences, who preferred to hear about things that "could have happened."[17] This holds true for a range of medieval European literatures. According to Dennis H. Green, fictionality arose out of a complicity between the author and his audience to engage in a game of make-believe, to accept accounts that would otherwise have been regarded as untrue. This hinges on the ability of the recipient of the discourse to "adopt a fictive stance," and thus makes the attitude of the audience crucial, allowing for the same text to be interpreted as historical, fabricated, or fictional depending on how it was received.[18] Green also recognizes that fictional writing derived from historical writing, and for a long time lived side by side with this genre.[19]

For Juan Manuel, in a manner similar to that of the Middle-High German poet Thomasin von Zirclaere (c. 1186–c. 1235), the didactic function of his writing always took center stage, and so a historical or fictional "stance" would not have been essential to the reception of his work. The utility of good stories — albeit clothed in beautiful falsehoods — lies in their store of virtuous examples:

> I am not criticizing adventure stories — even though the message of adventures leads us to distort the truth — because they depict courtesy and reality: truth is [simply] cloaked in fabrications. [...] Even if the stories are not [strictly] true, they can nevertheless indicate what a man should do if he wishes to lead a good and virtuous life. Therefore, I wish to thank those who have rendered many stories into the German language for us. A good story enhances good behavior. However, I would have thanked them even more if they had

---

17 Ibid., 175.
18 Dennis H. Green, *The Beginnings of Medieval Romance, Fact and Fiction, 1150–1220* (Cambridge: Cambridge University Press, 2002), 4, 12–13 (quote on 12).
19 Ibid., 201.

composed tales completely devoid of lies: they would have derived even more honor from that.[20]

This quote indicates the existence of a demarcation between truth and lies, yet also of untrue stories bearing a deeper truth, cloaked in lies, that could be profitable. The fact is that the same kinds of stories could be perceived as pure entertainment — even a sign of depravity — or as instruments of moral instruction and edification, depending on the context. That is, both historical and fictional narratives could further the moral edification of readers or hearers of those discourses.[21] For Juan Manuel, the didactic function of the *exemplum* needed to be married to the narrative mode; and so, more than a historical or fictive stance in the reader, the text needed an exemplary mode of articulation.[22] He did not display a fear of or anxiety about fiction. On the contrary, he used it to the best of his ability to further his didactic purposes:

> If it happens one night that he cannot sleep when he goes to bed, or that after having slept for a while he wakes up and cannot return to sleep, he should take care to do those things that aid and save his soul, and increase his honor, and his

---

20 Thomasin von Zirclaere, *Der Welsche Gast (The Italian Guest)*, trans. Marion Gibbs and Winder McConnell (Kalamazoo: Medieval Institute Publications, 2009), 69. The edition of the Middle High German text reads: "[I]ch schilt die âventiure niht,|swie uns ze liegen geschiht|von der âventiure rât, wan si bezeichnunge hât|der zuht unde der wârheit;|daz wâr man mit lüge kleit. [… S]int die âventiur niht wâr,|si bezeichent doch vil gar,|waz ein ieglîch man tuon sol,|der nâch vrümkeit wil leben wol.|dâ von ich den danken wil,|die uns der âventiure vil|in tiusche zungen hânt verkêrt.|guot âventiure zuht mêrt.|doch wold ich in danken baz,|und heten si noch groezer êre." Thomasin von Zirclaere, *Der Welsche Gast*, ed. Eva Willms (Berlin: de Gruyter, 2004), 45–46. Cf. C. Stephen Jaeger, *The Origins of Courtliness: Civilizing Trends and the Formation of Courtly Ideals, 939–1210* (Philadelphia: University of Pennsylvania Press, 1985), 266.
21 Jaeger, *The Origins of Courtliness*, 232–33.
22 Jesús Montoya Martínez, "Juan Manuel (1282–1348)," in *Key Figures in Medieval Europe: An Encyclopedia*, ed. Richard K. Emmerson (London: Routledge, 2006), 385.

wellbeing and his estate. [... I]f he cannot sleep, he should bid someone to read him some good (hi)stories, from which he can take good example. [...] It is good to have them read those (hi)stories to him, because he will then leave those cares behind, which are unprofitable, and turn towards sleep; and if he cannot sleep, he will learn some things that will be beneficial.[23]

This passage echoes closely a section in the *Segunda Partida* of the legal code of Alfonso X, the *Siete Partidas*, dealing with chivalry and the knighthood, where it is suggested that while the knights eat, or if they cannot sleep, one should read histories to them or otherwise *cantares de gesta* (*chansons de geste*), i.e., epic songs.[24] To a modern reader, this might primarily signal two different genres of text, historical (*estoria*) or fictional (*cantar*), but the important function of these texts here is shared: that of providing examples in the form of good deeds done by outstanding men of the past.[25]

---

23 "Y si acaeciere que alguna noche non puede dormir luego cuando se echa en la cama, o después que á dormido una pieça y despierta y non puede dormir, deve cuidar en las cosas que deve fazer para [a] provechamiento y salvamiento de su alma, y acrecentamiento de su onra y de su pro y de su estado. [... S]i non pudiere dormir deve mandar que leyan ante él algunas buenas estorias, de que tome buenos exemplos. [...] Y por ende es bien que lean ant'él las dichas estorias, porque salga d'él aquel cuidado, que es sin provecho, y torne a dormir; y en cuanto non pudiere dormir, que aprenda algunas cosas que sean aprovechosas." Juan Manuel, *Obras completas*, 404 (*Libro de los estados*). The word *estoria* was likely meant to signify "history" (*res gesta*) in this context, but increasingly came to represent "story" (*res ficta*) as well: Carmen Benito-Vessels, *Juan Manuel: Escritura y recreación de la historia* (Madison: Hispanic Seminary of Medieval Studies, 1994), 93.
24 *Las Siete Partidas del rey Don Alfonso el Sabio*, 3 vols. (Madrid: Real Academia de la Historia, 1807), Part. 2, Tit. 21, Law 20.
25 Emily S. Beck, "'Porque oyéndolas les crescian los corazones': Chivalry and the Power of Stories in Alfonso X and Ramon Llull," *Bulletin of Spanish Studies* 88, no. 2 (2011): 171–72. On Juan Manuel's preference for history over trivialities (*fabliellas*), see Barry Taylor, "La fabliella de Don Juan Manuel," *Revista de poética medieval* 4 (2000): 197–98.

Medieval Autofiction and the Case against Self-Referentiality

Geoffrey Gust, in his 2009 monograph *Constructing Chaucer,* defines autofiction as "a story of the self" which is creative, unreliable, and essentially unreal, the main point being that the authorial persona created in medieval fictional works is not a representation of the "true" author.[26] In his *Libro de los estados* (*Book of the Estates;* 1330), Juan Manuel introduces a figure bearing his own name: Don Johán. This character is used only sparingly, mentioned by one of the two main characters, Julio, as a friend of his. This figure appears to act in support of the truth-value of the stories presented in the work.[27] References to an authorial "I," Don Juan ("yo, don Johán"), appear in the prologue to several of Juan Manuel's works and can be read as authorial assertions in line with those of his royal uncle ("Nos, don Alfonso"), as Manuel Hijano has shown.[28] They are thus analyzed as a discursive strategy used to legitimate the act of writing. Hijano argues that mentioning the life and work of this "don Johán" acts to indicate the authority of the enunciative "I," projecting an ideal image of its referent and establishing the *auctoritas* of the author function (in the Foucauldian sense).[29] However, when these self-references appear in relation to clearly fictional characters in the *Libro de los estados* and as judge of the value of the *exempla* in the *Conde Lucanor,* they serve further functions. Here, they become autofictional and metafictional

---

26 Geoffrey W. Gust, *Constructing Chaucer: Author and Autofiction in the Critical Tradition* (New York: Palgrave Macmillan, 2009), 2.

27 Dunn, "The Structure of Didacticism," 66.

28 Manuel Hijano Villegas, "Historia y poder simbólico en la obra de don Juan Manuel," *Voz y letra: Revista de literatura* 25, nos. 1–2 (2014): 71–110.

29 Ibid., 87–89. Michel Foucault developed the idea of the author as a function of the discourse in a 1969 lecture, printed in English as "What Is an Author?," trans. Donald F. Bouchard and Sherry Simon, in *Language, Counter-Memory, Practice: Selected Essays and Interviews,* ed. Donald F. Bouchard (Oxford: Blackwell, 1977), 113–38. Cf. Leonardo Funes, "Don Juan Manuel y la herencia alfonsí," in *Actas del VIII Congreso Internacional de la Asociación Hispánica de Literatura Medieval,* ed. Silvia Iriso and Margarita Freixas (Barcelona: AHLM, 2000), 788.

because of the complexity of the fictions and fictional structures in which they appear. Most of Juan Manuel's works do contain some autobiographical references, representing him as an expert in matters of knighthood and war against the Muslims,[30] but in line with Gust's reading, we can determine they are not a simple reference to the "real" Don Juan Manuel. On the other hand, reading them solely as an exponent of an author function risks separating the fictional discourse, as an autonomous entity, from its historical context.

One might wonder, in this case, if the introduction of referential or historical figures signifies an attempt to avoid the implied self-referentiality of fiction.[31] For if fictional narratives are characterized by their autonomy, by only referring to things contained within the fictional world created by the narrative, then the possibility of using fiction to comment on social reality would be questionable. On this theory, the separation of (implied) author and narrator — e.g., the works of Chrétien de Troyes or Wolfram von Eschenbach — is crucial;[32] it means that a narrator who is in himself fictional and separate from the author who composed the work has been created.[33] The Don Juan

---

30 Germán Orduna, "La autobiografía literaria de don Juan Manuel," in *Don Juan Manuel: VII centenario* (Murcia: Universidad de Murcia/Academia Alfonso X el Sabio, 1982), 245–58.
31 This was identified as a characteristic and defining feature of fiction by Green in *The Beginnings of Medieval Romance*, and has been explored also by Verbaal in a couple of articles. Green's argument takes the romances of Chrétien de Troyes as the ultimate exponent of fiction in the Middle Ages.
32 Roberta L. Krueger, "The Author's Voice: Narrators, Audiences, and the Problem of Interpretation," in *The Legacy of Chrétien de Troyes*, 2 vols., ed. Norris J. Lacy, Douglas Kelly, and Keith Busby (Amsterdam: Rodopi, 1987), 1: 115–40; Linda B. Parshall, *The Art of Narration in Wolfram's "Parzival" and Albrecht's "Jüngerer Titurel"* (Cambridge: Cambridge University Press, 1981), 164.
33 Fleischmann, "On the Representation of History and Fiction in the Middle Ages," 295–96. Cf. Laurence de Looze, *Manuscript Diversity, Meaning, and Variance in Juan Manuel's "El Conde Lucanor"* (Toronto: University of Toronto Press, 2006), 262, on the implied author Juan Manuel as recipient of the fifty stories of Part I of *El Conde Lucanor*, which the real Juan Manuel wrote.

character in Juan Manuel's works is a fictional character who by implication of its referent ties the fiction to its socio-historical context of composition. Correspondingly, the selection of historical figures included in the fictional discourse of *El Conde Lucanor* follows political criteria, according to Carmen Benito-Vessels, and thus demonstrates the close ties between literary discourse and socio-political context.[34]

According to some scholars, the introduction of historical figures into fictional narratives does not transform the narratives themselves, but rather transforms these historical personages into devices within the fictional world. In other words, they become part of the fiction.[35] For example, Charlemagne in the *Chanson de Roland* (*Song of Roland*; eleventh century) is not the historical figure we meet in a biography of him; he is a literary character. This description of the function of referentiality has some merit; yet we could distinguish between at least two different models for interpreting these aspects of fictional literature: the *supposed* intention of the text and the *assumed* reception by the audience(s). Surely, while some fictional narratives could be "received as history" in certain contexts, historical figures were most likely received as fiction in other literary contexts. Ramón Menéndez Pidal consequently argued that historical elements present in an epic poem are not incorporated because of their historicity, but because they serve a fictional poetics.[36] The difficulty here lies in distinguishing textual strategy from the potential reception of the work and its different aspects. Historical elements in a fictional discourse could serve different ends, depending upon the context of reception. The inclusion of a historical figure could serve mainly literary ends for the author while being received as a true story of a real person by certain

---

34 Cf. Benito-Vessels, *Juan Manuel*, 87–88.
35 See, for example, Alberto Voltolini, "Probably the Charterhouse of Parma Does Not Exist, Possibly Not Even That Parma," HUMANA.MENTE: *Journal of Philosophical Studies* 6, no. 25 (2013): 235–61, and Ioan-Radu Motoarca, "Fictional Surrogates," *Philosophia* 42, no. 4 (2014): 1033–53.
36 Ramón Menéndez Pidal, "Poesía e historia en el Mio Cid: El problema de la poesía épica," *Nueva Revista de Filología Española* 3, no. 2 (1949): 113–29.

audiences, or vice versa. For while Johán in the *Libro de los estados* may have been read as a character analogous to either of the fictional characters in the same work by a contemporaneous or latter-day reader, we should still be sensitive to its intended function within the text, in terms of literary strategy. The intention of the work on the whole — in this case a question of didactics rather than diversion or entertainment — then becomes crucial to the interpretation.

The autonomy of fiction has previously been questioned by Laura Ashe,[37] Robert Stein,[38] and others.[39] Ashe argued the case that insular romances of the late eleventh century shared an ethos with histories and embodied both the events of history and the pattern of romance. As well, they exercised (or enjoyed) "both the freedoms of fiction and the referentiality of history," occupying a space between the two.[40] We may compare these romances to the medieval *Íslendingasögur*, or Icelandic family sagas, which were also referential in terms of many historical events and characters, but followed a fictional pattern of discourse or mode of storytelling.[41]

Several scholars have argued that certain fictions were accepted as true in specific contexts.[42] So whereas a modern conception of fiction entails the ontological separation between the domains of fact and fiction[43] — where the latter is completely self-referential and even in reporting true facts does not bear any relation to actual persons or events — I would argue this dis-

---

[37] Laura Ashe, *Fiction and History in England, 1066–1200* (Cambridge: Cambridge University Press, 2007), 24–26.

[38] Robert Stein, *Reality Fictions: Romance, History, and Governmental Authority, 1025–1180* (South Bend: University of Notre Dame Press, 2006).

[39] But cf. Green, *The Beginnings of Medieval Romance*, 142.

[40] Ashe, *Fiction and History in England*, 26.

[41] Cf. Mundal, "The Growth of Consciousness of Fiction in Old Norse Culture"; Theodore M. Anderson, *The Growth of the Medieval Icelandic Sagas (1180–1280)* (Ithaca: Cornell University Press, 2006), 207–10.

[42] Cf. Paul Strohm, *Hochon's Arrow: The Social Imagination of Fourteenth-Century Texts* (Princeton: Princeton University Press, 1992).

[43] Tzvetan Todorov, *Genres in Discourse*, trans. Catherine Porter (Cambridge: Cambridge University Press, 1990), 25.

tinction was not generally in place in the Middle Ages. Stating that a historical novel about "Charlemagne" containing information drawn from history still only makes claims about this fictional character that bears a resemblance to the historical Frankish Emperor may be correct for modern fiction and the modern awareness of fictional discourses, but it seems a weak proposition in terms of explaining the functions and modalities of medieval literature.

Historical and Fictional Truths in the Works of Don Juan Manuel

In Juan Manuel's best-known work, *El Conde Lucanor,* it is possible to discern a difference in the treatment of fables on the one hand and historical *exempla* on the other. While the former are presented as useful or good *examples* (*enxiemplo bueno*), and both can be deemed *buen seso* (good reason), some of the latter are also judged as true or as reporting the truth (*verdat*). For whilst fables can contain *allegorical* or *figurative truths,* this aspect is distinguished from *historical* truth in the frametale narrative encapsulating these *exempla*. This is somewhat in contrast to the idea that the facts of history are subordinate to a higher truth which must be interpreted by the recipient of the text, in the sense of the *sensus moralis* of medieval romance.[44] Suzanne Fleischmann contends, based on the attitudes of Jean Bodel and Alfonso X of Castile-León, that there existed a distinction between historical and fictional discourse in the minds of originators and recipients of medieval texts, but that "this distinction cuts across different lines from our own."[45] However, Fleischmann goes so far as to state that "the distinction between the historical deeds of kings and heroes on the one hand, and the legendary embroidery on those deeds, or their invention out of fertile poetic imagination, on the other, was at best blurred

---

44 Fleischmann, "On the Representation of History and Fiction in the Middle Ages," 289–90.
45 Ibid., 299–300.

and probably nonexistent in the minds of intended audiences," and that "historical truth was anything that belonged to a widely accepted tradition."[46]

It appears Juan Manuel did distinguish between good stories and true stories, and that the latter were often deemed true due to some idea of historical referentiality. These judgments come into play in the final comments of each *exemplum* in *El Conde Lucanor*, where the diegetic levels of the narrative are transcended, insofar as they report that the count was pleased with the advice given him by Patronio, and acted upon it, and then that "don Johán" deemed it a good example, had it written in "this book", and composed a verse to summarize the lesson.[47] The few tales in *El Conde Lucanor* that are given the epithet of true are almost exclusively based on actual historical people.[48] This is not likely an attempt to wrest these narratives out of their wider (fictional) context, but rather a means of demonstrating how historically true accounts and fables can be both profitable stories, if understood and acted upon correctly by the intended audience, and, as principally, a mode of overstepping the boundaries of genre and modality.

---

46 Ibid., 303, 305.
47 Cf. James Mandrell, "Literary Theory and Medieval Texts: Authority and the Worldly Power of Language in *El Conde Lucanor*," *South Central Review* 8, no. 2 (1991): 10: "what was initially to seem real becomes part of the fiction proper. The inclusion of Don Juan Manuel at this point not only brings into the body of the fiction the putative author, it also details the authorial process by which El Conde Lucanor was composed. [...] El Conde Lucanor shows Don Juan Manuel not as an author or a compiler or even merely a scribe, but, rather, as a kind of 'commentator' [...]."
48 Ex. 18, Don Pero Meléndez de Valdés (doubtful) ("El conde tovo que Patronio le dezía la verdat," 584); Ex. 25, Saladin ("El conde plogo mucho d'estas razones que Patronio le dixo, y tovo que era verdat todo assí como él le dizía." 605); Ex. 27, Alvar Fáñez ("El conde plogo mucho d'estas cosas que Patronio le dixo, y tovo que dezía verdat y muy buen seso." 616); Ex. 40, a Seneschal of Carcassone ("El conde tovo que era verdat lo que Patronio le dizía," 640); Ex. 42, a false Beguine ("el conde tovo que era verdad esto que Patronio le dixo y puso en su coraçón de lo fazer assí." 645); Ex. 44, Pedro Núñez et al. ("El conde tovo este por buen consejo y por verdadero." 652).

The story of the three knights in example 15 — Lorenzo Suárez Gallinato, Garci Pérez de Vargas, and a third whose name the author cannot recall (*non me acuerdo del nombre,* 578), though they were the best in the world — uses an historical episode and a setting that was recognizable to its intended audience. It is set during the siege of Seville by King Fernando III (Juan Manuel's grandfather) in 1247–1248. The brave and saintly king in the example is implicitly contrasted with the powerful but hostile king who seeks an excuse to attack the count Lucanor, his erstwhile enemy, which in the frame of the narrative is recounted to Patronio. This hostile relationship, which causes the count to seek his councilors' advice, echoes Juan Manuel's own contentious experiences with Alfonso XI (r. 1312–1350), and thus becomes a commentary on his own life as well as a profitable example for others in a similar situation. The story Patronio uses to illustrate why Lucanor should be patient and suffer the fear and anxiety of the situation without acting rashly, recounts how the knights in a test of courage went up to strike the gate of the city with their lances, provoking the attack of ten thousand defending Muslim soldiers. When the defenders attack, the knight who waits longest to clash with the multitude, Lorenzo Suárez, is deemed the bravest, since he quietly withstood the fear and did not panic. The narrative marries an anecdote about historical figures to literary structural principles in order to present the didactic message of the fiction in an appealing way.[49] The historical account is not represented mimetically, in full detail, but rather a single aspect of that narrative is used to symbolically illustrate a moral, determined by Juan Manuel.[50]

In another example (28) using the knight Lorenzo Suárez as protagonist, Juan Manuel seems to exculpate him for his disloyalty, for which he was exiled by Fernando III, perhaps in an attempt to excuse his own recurring conflicts with Alfonso XI. This rebellious trait is a recurring characteristic in several of the

---

49 Reinaldo Ayerbe-Chaux, *El Conde Lucanor: Materia tradicional y originalidad creadora* (Madrid: J. Porrúa, 1975), 91–95.
50 Benito-Vessels, *Juan Manuel,* 97.

historical figures represented in *El Conde Lucanor* (among them Fernán González).[51] In all this, Juan Manuel uses a historical mode — in contrast to other instances, for example, those based on fables — wherein an aspect of a reality element is adapted to the moral-didactic intention of the text. Unlike Reinaldo Ayerbe-Chaux, who points out the entirely imaginative character of this example, history subsumed into fiction, Carmen Benito-Vessels does not defend the autonomy of the fictional narrative, but rather signals its pseudo-referentiality. Referentiality here is not representational (mimetic) but illustrative (symbolic): Juan Manuel chose to represent those aspects of the history or legend of a historical figure that he considered exemplary.[52] Reality elements serve to upset the autonomy of the fictional and reinforce its (pseudo-)referentiality, serving the didactic aims of the text but resulting in a form of modal instability. The text reimagines an episode from the *Estoria de Espanna*, retaining the historical setting but recreating its significance in a new discursive context. In so doing, Juan Manuel is able to appropriate the truth claims of the historical genre (having presented his biased selection of history in the abbreviated version of the *Estoria de Espanna*, the *Crónica abreviada*), the modalities of which he incorporates into his story, while using the exemplarity inherent in the structure of the *exempla* genre, thus making possible the elevation of rebellion and political ambition to the status of praiseworthy example.[53]

---

51 Ayerbe-Chaux, *El Conde Lucanor*, 87–88; María Cecilia Ruiz, *Literatura y política: el "Libro de los estados" y el "Libro de las armas" de don Juan Manuel* (Potomac: Scripta Humanistica, 1989), 110, 118–19. Cf. Olivier Biaggini, "Histoire et fiction dans l'œuvre de Don Juan Manuel: de la *Crónica abreviada* à *El Conde Lucanor*," *e-Spania* 23 (2016), https://journals.openedition.org/e-spania/25253

52 Ayerbe-Chaux, *El Conde Lucanor*, 91; Benito-Vessels, *Juan Manuel*, 97–101, 108. Cf. Robert Scholes, James Phelan, and Robert L. Kellogg, *The Nature of Narrative* (Oxford: Oxford University Press, 2006), 84.

53 Benito-Vessels, *Juan Manuel*, 108–9.

When the fiftieth and final *exemplum* of *El Conde Lucanor*—which uses Saladin as its protagonist[54]—is presented as a means of knowing the truth of what is the most important virtue for a man to possess, Patronio is not referring to historical truth.[55] Neither was Juan Manuel interested in this story for its historical accuracy but rather because of its ability to demonstrate in a pleasing and entertaining manner a perpetual truth. The memory of things that have happened (i.e., the events of history), are essential to what Juan Manuel considered knowledge (*saber*) and that the ancients recorded in books, but they are valuable because of their utility and exemplarity.[56] Similarly, John of Salisbury defended "the notion that the truth of a thing lies more in its moral utility than in its actual relation to 'reality.'"[57] Thus, historical truth need not be a matter of fact.

Nevertheless, apart from the fact of a consciousness of fiction, or a boundary—however porous—between history and fiction, there exists the question of the presence of a playfulness in overstepping that boundary. The *Libro de las tres ra-*

---

54 Ayerbe-Chaux, *El Conde Lucanor*, 124–37; María Cecilia Ruiz, "Theft in Juan Manuel's *El Conde Lucanor*," in *Crime and Punishment in the Middle Ages: Mental-Historical Investigations of Basic Human Problems and Social Responses*, ed. Albrecht Classen and Connie Scarborough (Berlin: de Gruyter, 2012), 263–70.

55 Juan Manuel, *Obras completas*, 666–73.

56 "Comoquier que entre Dios y los omnes á muy pequeña comparación, como puede seer entre criador y criatura, pero porque tovo nuestro señor Dios por bien qu'el omne fuese fecho a su semejança, y esta semejanza es la razón y el saber y el libre albedrío que Dios puso en el ombre, y porque los omnes son cosa fallecedera muy aína, tan bien en la vida como en el saber, que fue una de las señaladas cosas para que Dios nuestro señor lo crio, tovieron por bien los sabios antiguos de fazer libros en que posieron los saberes y las remembranças de las cosas que pasaron, tan bien de las leyes que an los omnes para salvar las ánimas (a que llaman Testamento Viejo y Testamento Nuevo), como de los ordenamientos y posturas que fizieron los papas, y los emperadores y reyes (a que llaman decreto y decretales y leyes y fueros), como de los saberes (a que llaman 'ciencias' y 'artes'), como de los grandes fechos y cosas que pasaron (a que llaman 'crónicas')." Juan Manuel, *Obras completas*, 46 (*Crónica abreviada*).

57 Siân Echard, *Arthurian Narrative in the Latin Tradition* (Cambridge: Cambridge University Press, 1998), 32.

zones (*Book of the Three Reasons*; 1345),⁵⁸ often interpreted as the political testament of Don Juan Manuel, is a singular work of fictional history writing. This late work is also highly characterized by his own personal experiences, both in terms of his interactions with kings and experiences in his daily life.⁵⁹ In the text, Juan Manuel sets out to present to the reader his rights to the Castilian throne, representing himself as the culmination of a lineage characterized by the fulfilment of Christian, aristocratic, and warrior virtues. In so doing, he creates a narrative that is intended to be historically accurate, based on eyewitness accounts, and which explicitly aims to convey historical truths; yet to modern scholarship his text appears highly fictionalized, influenced by folklore and marked by a conscious distortion of facts.⁶⁰ Why? It can be related to the idea of plausibility.

David Wacks has analyzed Juan Manuel's complex relationship to Andalusī culture as a colonizer's experience.⁶¹ His works were influenced, to some degree, by Arabic storytelling, not least the frametale structure of the *Sendebar* and *Calila e Dimna*, and "[i]n the *maqāmāt* of the Andalusī author al-Saraqusti, the anecdotal frame of performance suggests a continuity between the world of the tale and that of the audience, with the narrator linking the two through first person perspective (i.e., 'I saw x happen and now I relate it to you'). It heralds the introduction of plausible fictionality to medieval narrative."⁶² This speaks to the discursive common ground shared with historiography.

---

58 Previously known as the *Libro de las armas*.
59 Alan Deyermond, "Cuentos orales y estructure formal en el Libro de las tres razones (Libro de las armas)," in *Don Juan Manuel: VII centenario* (Murcia: Universidad de Murcia/Academia Alfonso X el Sabio, 1982), 75–87.
60 Ruiz, *Literatura y política*, 108–11; Leonardo Funes, "Entre política y literatura: estrategias discursivas en don Juan Manuel," *Medievalia* 18, no. 1 (2015): 9–25.
61 David A. Wacks, "Reconquest Colonialism and Andalusī Narrative Practice in the 'Conde Lucanor,'" *Diacritics* 36, nos. 3–4 (2006): 87–103.
62 David A. Wacks, *Framing Iberia: "Maqāmāt" and Frametale Narratives in Medieval Spain* (Boston and Leiden: Brill, 2007), 49. See also Rina Drory, *Models and Contacts: Arabic Literature and Its Impact on Medieval Jewish Culture* (Boston and Leiden: Brill, 2000).

But Juan Manuel's debt to Arabic storytelling in the form of the frametale genre also affects the message, since, as Wacks highlights, it "juxtaposes the explicit didactic program of the author with the more ambiguous lessons expressed by the tales themselves and decoded by the reader. This juxtaposition opens a space between our author and his narrative."[63] Again, Juan Manuel's strategic use of reality elements need not correspond to his audience's reading of the *exempla*, since these polyphonously are open to multiple interpretations. The type of discourse suggests that the truth present in the narratives is exterior and prior to the composition of the work, and that this truth is thus not created by its author, but merely revealed to its audience.[64]

Nonetheless, plausible fictionality can be achieved without the need to introduce "reality elements" or autobiographical details. The use of personal details and the creation of autofiction in this period must be explained by reference to other aspects of the discourse. One suggestion is that personal details and self-naming would have worked to establish precisely a means of contact and a specific relationship to the intended audience.[65] It might also be a play on the discursive common ground between history and fiction, sharing their pursuit of plausibility, a way of grounding the fictional world in the lived experience of the audience. Correspondingly, Boccacio's Decameron — another frametale narrative akin to *El Conde Lucanor* — is set in a context that would have a very direct relevance to its audience

---

[63] Wacks, *Framing Iberia*, 133. Mario Cossío Olavide, "*Algunos moros muy sabidores*: Virtuous Muslim Kings in Examples 30 and 41 of *El conde Lucanor*," *Bulletin of Spanish Studies* 97, no. 2 (2020): 127–38, analyzes a couple of narratives from the *Conde Lucanor* to demonstrate how Juan Manuel, using the example of two Muslim kings — al-Mu'tamid of Seville and al-Ḥakam al-Mustanṣir, the Umayyad caliph — offers positive models of virtuous kingship by adapting Andalusī historical and folkloric traditions.

[64] Marta Lacomba, "Escritura, ética y política en la segunda parte de El libro del Conde Lucanor," *e-Spania* 21 (2015), https://journals.openedition.org/e-spania/24747.

[65] Haug, *Vernacular Literary Theory in the Middle Ages*, 135.

in their social and historical situation. This would speak against the autonomy of the fictional world.[66]

Did these reality elements then raise or deconstruct the status of the discourse as fiction — turning it into something akin to history or historically based didactic fiction? Did they unsettle the reader's sense of what was real and what was make-believe? If we look to similar literary elements in modern literature, they signal an acute awareness of generic boundaries. The play on these boundaries destabilizes them and gives rise to questions about the nature of reality and the stories we tell. For Juan Manuel, the primary motivation was to create plausible and convincing exemplary stories. He was determined to write effective didactic tales. The reality elements that he sometimes used, some of them based on the introduction of an authorial alter ego, others on episodes or figures from historiography, must be read in line with his overall didactic aims. This upsetting of the narrative voice can be compared to Mundal's discussion of how saga authors played with the boundaries between the real and the fantastic. The play on the borderline between realism and fantasy marks an awareness of that line rather than a lack of consciousness and so complicates our understanding of history and fiction in the Old Norse context.[67] Likewise, the conscious playfulness with the boundary between the fictional world of the *exempla* and the lived experience of the author and audience in fourteenth-century Castile is a literary device that demonstrates the complexity and multivalence of medieval fiction.

---

66 According to Mandrell, "Literary Theory and Medieval Texts," 9: "at the level of narrative organization, the diegetic and situational repetitions tend towards the commonality of everyday existence. It is the nature of *El Conde Lucanor* to extend outwards in an increasingly generalized way and not to close in upon itself, either as a function of its being read or of its being the embodiment of the author who created the fiction and the role that he plays."

67 Mundal, "The Growth of Consciousness of Fiction in Old Norse Culture," 192–93.

Conclusion: Reality Elements in Medieval Fiction

Factual and fictional discourses were distinct, but there was significant discursive common ground, and authors quite consciously played with this aspect of literary discourse. In effect, Juan Manuel and other medieval authors had a sophisticated grasp of what they and their audiences would expect from a historical or a fictional work of literature. This does not imply that these discourses were entirely distinct or wholly stable. On the contrary, there is research on several medieval European literary contexts that strongly suggests that the discursive common ground shared between historical and fictional modes of storytelling was continuously in effect during several centuries after the "invention" of medieval fiction — a process that in itself was not a sudden revolution but rather a gradual and processual development.[68] There is good reason to believe that authors wrote fictions that used reality elements not principally to *verify* the authenticity or historicity of their tales, but to embrace the discursive common ground between the two modes — foregrounding plausibility, embracing pseudo-referentiality, destabilizing the vague distinctions between history and fiction — ultimately to enhance the fictional mode as an interpretation of lived reality. It was a model for commenting on society in the guise of literary play. The aim was to achieve the balance between *entertainment, example,* and *history* that Lars Boje Mortensen argues for in relation to twelfth-century historical culture.[69] To be sure, the further investigation of these traits in medieval fiction might augment our knowledge of another kind of *historicity* in medieval fiction: not its potential connection to actual events in the past, but rather the condition of fictional narratives as historically and socially situated cultural objects that vary and

---

[68] See Kim Bergqvist, "Truth and Invention in Medieval Texts," *Roda da Fortuna: Revista Eletrônica sobre Antiguidade e Medievo* 2, no. 2 (2013): 229–30.

[69] Lars Boje Mortensen, "The Glorious Past: Entertainment, Example or History? Levels of Twelfth-Century Historical Culture," *Culture and History* 13 (1994): 68–69.

transform in their movement between spatial and temporal contexts.[70]

---

[70] Cf. Francisco Bautista, "Pseudo-historia y leyenda en la historiografía medieval: la Condesa Traidora," in *El relato historiográfico: textos y tradiciones en la España medieval*, ed. Francisco Bautista (London: Department of Hispanic Studies, Queen Mary, University of London, 2006), 96.

Bibliography

Primary

Las Siete Partidas del rey Don Alfonso el Sabio. 3 volumes. Madrid: Real Academia de la Historia, 1807.

Manuel, Juan. *Obras completas.* Edited by Carlos Alvar and Sarah Finci. Valencia: Proyecto Parnaseo de la Universitat de València, 2014. http://parnaseo.uv.es/@Medieval.html.

von Zirclaere, Thomasin. *Der Welsche Gast.* Edited by Eva Willms. Berlin: de Gruyter, 2004; *Der Welsche Gast* (The Italian Guest). Translated by Marion Gibbs and Winder McConnell. Kalamazoo: Medieval Institute Publications, 2009.

Secondary

Anderson, Theodore M. *The Growth of the Medieval Icelandic Sagas (1180–1280).* Ithaca: Cornell University Press, 2006.

Ashe, Laura. *Fiction and History in England, 1066–1200.* Cambridge: Cambridge University Press, 2007.

Ayerbe-Chaux, Reinaldo. *El Conde Lucanor: Materia tradicional y originalidad creadora.* Madrid: Ediciones J. Porrúa, 1975.

Bautista, Francisco. "Pseudo-historia y leyenda en la historiografía medieval: la Condesa Traidora." In *El relato historiográfico: textos y tradiciones en la España medieval,* edited by Francisco Bautista, 59–101. London: Department of Hispanic Studies, Queen Mary, University of London, 2006.

Beck, Emily S. "'Porque oyéndolas les crescian los corazones': Chivalry and the Power of Stories in Alfonso X and Ramon Llull." *Bulletin of Spanish Studies* 88, no. 2 (2011): 159–76. DOI: 10.1080/14753820.2011.555359.

Benito-Vessels, Carmen. *Juan Manuel: Escritura y recreación de la historia.* Madison: Hispanic Seminary of Medieval Studies, 1994.

Bergqvist, Kim. "Truth and Invention in Medieval Texts." *Roda da Fortuna: Revista Eletrônica sobre Antiguidade e Medievo* 2, no. 2 (2013): 221–42. https://www.revistarodadafortuna.com/_files/ugd/3fdd18_c103488cd2704519a2371d-2e5d880468.pdf.

Biaggini, Olivier. "Histoire et fiction dans l'œuvre de Don Juan Manuel: de la *Crónica abreviada* à *El conde Lucanor*." *e-Spania* 23 (2016). https://journals.openedition.org/e-spania/25253. DOI: 10.4000/e-spania.25253.

———. "Stratégies du paratexte dans les œuvres de don Juan Manuel." *Cahiers d'études hispaniques médiévales* 35 (2012): 195–232. DOI: 10.3406/cehm.2012.2281.

Bizzarri, Hugo O. *La otra mirada: el "exemplum" histórico*. Vienna: Lit, 2019.

Boggs, Ralph Steele. *Index of Spanish Folktales*. Helsinki: Suomalainen Tiedeakatemia, Academia Scientiarum Fennica, 1930.

Catalán, Diego. "Don Juan Manuel ante el modelo alfonsí: El testimonio de la *Cronica abreviada*." In *Juan Manuel Studies*, edited by Ian Macpherson, 17–51. London: Tamesis, 1977.

Chinca, Mark. *History, Fiction, Verisimilitude: Studies in the Poetics of Gottfried's "Tristan."* London: The Modern Humanities Research Association for The Institute of Germanic Studies, University of London, 1993.

Cossío Olavide, Mario. "*Algunos moros muy sabidores*: Virtuous Muslim Kings in Examples 30 and 41 of *El conde Lucanor*." *Bulletin of Spanish Studies* 97, no. 2 (2020): 127–38. DOI: 10.1080/14753820.2020.1729619.

De Looze, Laurence. *Manuscript Diversity, Meaning, and Variance in Juan Manuel's "El conde Lucanor."* Toronto: University of Toronto Press, 2006. DOI: 10.3138/9781442676985.

Deyermond, Alan. "Cuentos orales y estructura formal en el *Libro de las tres razones* (*Libro de las armas*)." In *Don Juan Manuel: VII centenario*, 75–87. Murcia: Universidad de Murcia/Academia Alfonso X el Sabio, 1982.

Drory, Rina. *Models and Contacts: Arabic Literature and Its Impact on Medieval Jewish Culture*. Boston and Leiden: Brill, 2000.

Dunn, Peter N. "The Structure of Didacticism: Private Myths and Public Fictions." In *Juan Manuel Studies*, edited by Ian McPherson, 53–67. London: Tamesis, 1977.

Echard, Siân. *Arthurian Narrative in the Latin Tradition.* Cambridge: Cambridge University Press, 1998. DOI: 10.1017/CBO9780511518713.

Fleischmann, Suzanne. "On the Representation of History and Fiction in the Middle Ages." *History and Theory* 22, no. 3 (1983): 278–310. DOI: 10.2307/2504985.

Foucault, Michel. "What Is an Author?" Translated by Donald F. Bouchard and Sherry Simon. In *Language, Counter-Memory, Practice: Selected Essays and Interviews,* edited by Donald F. Bouchard, 113–38. Oxford: Blackwell, 1977.

Funes, Leonardo. "Don Juan Manuel y la herencia alfonsí." In *Actas del VIII Congreso Internacional de la Asociación Hispánica de Literatura Medieval,* edited by Silvia Iriso and Margarita Freixas, 782–88. Barcelona: AHLM, 2000.

———. *El modelo historiográfico alfonsí: Una caracterización.* London: Department of Hispanic Studies, Queen Mary, University of London, 1997.

———. "Entre política y literatura: Estrategias discursivas en don Juan Manuel." *Medievalia* 18, no. 1 (2015): 9–25. DOI: 10.5565/rev/medievalia.305.

———. *Investigación literaria de textos medievales: objeto y práctica.* Buenos Aires: Miño y Dávila, 2009.

Given-Wilson, Chris. *Chronicles: The Writing of History in Medieval England.* London: Hambledon and London, 2004.

Gómez Redondo, Fernando. "Géneros literarios en don Juan Manuel." *Cahiers de linguistique hispanique médiévale* 17 (1992): 87–125. DOI: 10.3406/cehm.1992.1078.

———. *Historia de la prosa medieval castellana II: El desarrollo de los géneros. La ficción caballeresca y el orden religioso.* Madrid: Cátedra, 1999.

Green, Dennis H. *The Beginnings of Medieval Romance: Fact and Fiction, 1150–1220.* Cambridge: Cambridge University Press, 2002. DOI: 10.1017/CBO9780511485787.

Gust, Geoffrey W. *Constructing Chaucer: Author and Autofiction in the Critical Tradition.* New York: Palgrave Macmillan, 2009. DOI: 10.1057/9780230621619.

Haug, Walter. *Vernacular Literary Theory in the Middle Ages: The German Tradition, 800–1300, in Its European Context.* Translated by Joanna M. Catling. Cambridge: Cambridge University Press, 1997.

Hijano Villegas, Manuel. "Historia y poder simbólico en la obra de don Juan Manuel." *Voz y letra: Revista de literatura* 25, nos. 1–2 (2014): 71–110.

Irvine, Martin. *The Making of Textual Culture: "Grammatica" and Literary Theory, 350–1100.* Cambridge: Cambridge University Press, 1994.

Jaeger, C. Stephen. *The Origins of Courtliness: Civilizing Trends and the Formation of Courtly Ideals, 939–1210.* Philadelphia: University of Pennsylvania Press, 1985. DOI: 10.9783/9780812200898.

Jeauneau, Édouard. "Note sur l'École de Chartres." *Mémoires de la Société archéologique d'Eure-et-Loir* 23 (1964–68): 1–45.

Knapp, Fritz Peter. "Historicity and Fictionality in Medieval Narrative." In *True Lies Worldwide: Fictionality in Global Contexts,* edited by Anders Cullhed and Lena Rydholm, 179–87. Berlin: de Gruyter, 2014.

Krueger, Roberta L. "The Author's Voice: Narrators, Audiences, and the Problem of Interpretation." In T*he Legacy of Chrétien de Troyes,* edited by Norris J. Lacy, Douglas Kelly, and Keith Busby, Volume 1, 115–40. Amsterdam: Rodopi, 1987.

Lacomba, Marta. "Escritura, ética y política en la segunda parte de El libro del Conde Lucanor." *e-Spania* 21 (2015). https://journals.openedition.org/e-spania/24747. DOI: 10.4000/e-spania.24747.

Mandrell, James. "Literary Theory and Medieval Texts: Authority and the Worldly Power of Language in *El Conde Lucanor.*" *South Central Review* 8, no. 2 (1991): 1–18. DOI: 10.2307/3189180.

Márquez Villanueva, Francisco. *El concepto cultural alfonsí.* Revised and expanded edition. Barcelona: Edicions Bellaterra, 2004.

Menéndez Pidal, Ramón. "Poesía e historia en el Mio Cid: El problema de la poesía épica." *Nueva Revista de Filología Española* 3, no. 2 (1949): 113–29. DOI: 10.24201/nrfh.v3i2.134/.

Montoya Martínez, Jesús. "Juan Manuel (1282–1348)." In *Key Figures in Medieval Europe: An Encyclopedia*, edited by Richard K. Emmerson, 383–85. London: Routledge, 2006.

Morse, Ruth. *Truth and Convention in the Middle Ages: Rhetoric, Representation, and Reality*. Cambridge: Cambridge University Press, 1991.

Mortensen, Lars Boje. "The Glorious Past: Entertainment, Example or History? Levels of Twelfth-century Historical Culture." *Culture and History* 13 (1994): 57–71.

Motoarca, Ioan-Radu. "Fictional Surrogates." *Philosophia* 42, no. 4 (2014): 1033–53. DOI: 10.1007/s11406-014-9522-1.

Mundal, Else. "The Growth of Consciousness of Fiction in Old Norse Culture." In *Medieval Narratives between History and Fiction: From the Centre to the Periphery of Europe, c. 1100–1400*, edited by Panagiotis A. Agapitos and Lars B. Mortensen, 167–98. Copenhagen: Museum Tusculanum Press, University of Copenhagen, 2012.

Orduna, Germán. "La autobiografía literaria de don Juan Manuel." In *Don Juan Manuel: VII centenario*, 245–58. Murcia: Universidad de Murcia/Academia Alfonso X el Sabio, 1982.

Parshall, Linda B. *The Art of Narration in Wolfram's "Parzival" and Albrecht's "Jüngerer Titurel."* Cambridge: Cambridge University Press, 1981.

Ruiz, María Cecilia. *Literatura y política: El "Libro de los estados" y el "Libro de las armas" de don Juan Manuel*. Potomac: Scripta Humanistica, 1989.

———. "Theft in Juan Manuel's *El Conde Lucanor*." In *Crime and Punishment in the Middle Ages: Mental-Historical Investigations of Basic Human Problems and Social Responses*, edited by Albrecht Classen and Connie Scarborough, 247–80. Berlin: de Gruyter, 2012.

Scholes, Robert, James Phelan, and Robert L. Kellogg. *The Nature of Narrative*. 1966; rpt. Oxford: Oxford University Press, 2006.

Stein, Robert. *Reality Fictions: Romance, History, and Governmental Authority, 1025–1180.* South Bend: University of Notre Dame Press, 2006.

Strohm, Paul. *Hochon's Arrow: The Social Imagination of Fourteenth-Century Texts.* Princeton: Princeton University Press, 1992.

Taylor, Barry. "La fabliella de Don Juan Manuel." *Revista de poética medieval* 4 (2000): 187–200.

Todorov, Tzvetan. *Genres in Discourse.* Translated by Catherine Porter. Cambridge: Cambridge University Press, 1990.

Verbaal, Wim. "Getting Lost in Worlds: The Fiction of Literature (Eleventh and Twelfth Century)." In *Fiction and Figuration in High and Late Medieval Literature,* edited by Marianne Pade, Anders Cullhed, Anders Hallengren, and Brian Møller Jensen, 55–62. Rome: Edizioni Quasar, 2016.

———. "How the West Was Won by Fiction: The Appearance of Fictional Narrative and Leisurely Reading in Western Literature (11th and 12th century)." In *True Lies Worldwide: Fictionality in Global Contexts,* edited by Anders Cullhed and Lena Rydholm, 189–200. Berlin: de Gruyter, 2014.

Voltolini, Alberto. "Probably the Charterhouse of Parma Does Not Exist, Possibly Not Even That Parma." HUMANA.MENTE: *Journal of Philosophical Studies* 6, no. 25 (2013),:235–61.

Wacks, David A. *Framing Iberia: "Maqāmāt" and Frametale Narratives in Medieval Spain.* Boston and Leiden: Brill, 2007. DOI: 10.1163/ej.9789004158283.i-279.

———. "Reconquest Colonialism and Andalusī Narrative Practice in the 'Conde Lucanor.'" *Diacritics* 36, nos. 3–4 (2006): 87–103. DOI: 10.1353/dia.0.0007.

2

How the Barking Nuns Forgot Their Abbesses

Cynthia Turner Camp

Forgetting the past is normally seen as a problem historians are tasked to overcome.[1] They strive to recover a past silenced by earlier generations or deliberately suppressed by authoritarian regimes,[2] or else to open up the repressed social trauma of an event like the Holocaust or the Norman Conquest.[3] Scholars of medieval English women's history grapple regularly with the parallel problem of missing, suppressed, or never produced records: female voices obscured within men's accounts of their

---

[1] I am grateful to the audience at the University of Missouri's 2018 Medieval and Renaissance Studies lecture for their input on an earlier version of this argument, and for Tynan Stewart, Bridget Whearty, and the anonymous reviewers' productive suggestions on this essay.

[2] George R. Lucas, Jr., "Recollection, Forgetting, and the Hermeneutics of History: Meditations on a Theme from Hegel," in *Hegel, History, and Interpretation*, ed. Shaun Gallagher (Albany: SUNY Press, 1997), 97–115, at 98–103.

[3] F.R. Ankersmit, "The Sublime Dissociation of the Past: Or How to Be(come) What One Is No Longer," *History and Theory* 40, no. 3 (2001): 295–323, and Elaine Treharne, *Living through Conquest: The Politics of Early English, 1020–1220* (Oxford: Oxford University Press, 2012), esp. 54–61, 69–90.

lives,[4] women's writings "overwritten by monastic historians,"[5] or anonymous texts whose authors' identities are lost to time. This is a particular issue for English nuns who, unlike monks and canons, did not write chronicles.[6] While David Knowles's claim that "intimate or detailed records of the nunneries are almost entirely wanting" is an overstatement, as witnessed by the foundation narratives the nuns created and the cartularies they compiled,[7] scholars face a dearth of materials for understanding nunnery history and nuns' own perception of their pasts.

Yet forgetting is not always an act of historical desecration or a symptom of traumatic repression; rather, history is "as much

---

4 Diane Watt, *Medieval Women's Writing: Works by and for Women in England, 1100–1500* (Cambridge: Polity Press, 2007), 31–37.

5 Diane Watt, "Literature in Pieces: Female Sanctity and the Relics of Early Women's Writing," in *The Cambridge History of Early Medieval English Literature*, ed. Clare A. Lees (Cambridge: University Press, 2013), 357–80, at 364.

6 Sally Thompson, "Why English Nunneries Had No History: A Study of the Problems of the English Nunneries Founded after the Conquest," in *Medieval Religious Women 1: Distant Echoes,* ed. John A. Nichols and Lillian Thomas Shank (Kalamazoo: Cistercian Publications, 1984), 131–49; Sally Thompson, *Women Religious, The Founding of English Nunneries after the Norman Conquest* (Oxford: Clarendon Press, 1991), 7–15; Sarah Foot, *Veiled Women,* 2 vols. (Burlington: Ashgate, 2000), vol. 1, 5–34; Jocelyn Wogan-Browne, *Saints' Lives and Womens' Literary Culture, 1150–1300: Virginity and Its Authorizations* (Oxford: Oxford University Press, 2001), 50–56.

7 David Knowles, *The Religious Orders in England,* vol. 2: *The End of the Middle Ages* (Cambridge: Cambridge University Press, 1955), viii. On foundation narratives, see Cynthia Turner Camp, *Anglo-Saxon Saints' Lives as History Writing in Late Medieval England* (Cambridge: D.S. Brewer, 2015), 33–35; Rebecca June, "The Languages of Memory: The Crabhouse Nunnery Manuscript," in *Language and Culture in Medieval Britain: The French of England, c. 1100–c.1500,* ed. Jocelyn Wogan-Browne et al. (York: York Medieval Press, 2009), 347–58; Emilie Amt, "The Foundation Legend of Godstow Abbey: A Holy Woman's Life in Anglo-Norman Verse," in *Writing Medieval Women's Lives,* ed. Charlotte Newman Goldy and Amy Livingstone (Gordonsville: Palgrave Macmillan, 2012), 13–31. On historical manuscripts, see Camp, *Anglo-Saxon Saints' Lives,* 42. On both, see Wogan-Browne, *Saints' Lives,* 197–204.

about forgetting as it is about remembering."[8] Forgetting — or more properly, the judicious privileging of some events over others — is a necessary historiographic operation, for it is impossible to emplot *everything* into a coherent presentation of a meaningful past. In the ever-shifting historiographic negotiations of sifting the meaningful from the incidental, forgetting indicates active choice. As Michel de Certeau explains, decisions of omission and inclusion "are signs of a selection between what is excluded as obsolete, and what is considered as homogeneous to the present time, or 'fundamental.'"[9] In extracting the recognizable aspects of the past to construct a useful identity for the present, the present exposes its unspoken values in what it relegates to obsolescence.[10]

In the field of women's history, the forgetting of female textual and social agency has recently become a methodological opportunity. Maximizing their approaches to extant documents, scholars have inferred writings that once existed, identifying now-lost saints' lives and historical narratives.[11] These lacunae in the written record have also engendered theoretically supple approaches that decenter linear narrative and genealogical models of history-production — exactly those structures that encourage selective forgetting — to consider instead webs of affinity and supratemporal connections.[12] Diane Watt in particular issues a

---

[8] Hayden White, "Guilty of History? The Longue Durée of Paul Ricoeur," *History and Theory* 46, no. 2 (2007): 233–51, at 237; see further Anders Schinkel, "History and Historiography in Process," *History and Theory* 43, no. 1 (2004): 39–56, at 46 et passim.

[9] Michel de Certeau, *The Writing of History*, trans. Tom Conley (New York: Columbia University Press, 1988), 137.

[10] See Jay Paul Gates, "The 'Worcester' Historians and Eadric Streona's Execution," in *Capital and Corporal Punishment in Anglo-Saxon England*, ed. Jay Paul Gates and Nicole Marafioti (Woodbridge: Boydell, 2014).

[11] Watt, "Literature in Pieces." For examples of such recovery, see Amt, "Foundation Legend"; Katie Ann-Marie Bugyis, "Recovering the Histories of Women Religious in England in the Central Middle Ages: Wilton Abbey and Goscelin of Saint-Bertin," *Journal of Medieval History* 42, no. 3 (2016): 285–303.

[12] Gabrielle M. Spiegel, "Genealogy: Form and Function in Medieval Historical Narrative," *History and Theory* 22, no. 1 (1983): 43–53. On webs of affinity,

call to "embrace the disrupted, discontinuous, fragmentary nature of the [women's] history that has come down to us":[13] that is, to use fractures in women's history both to interrogate the processes through which history gets made and to consider the possibilities of thinking beyond the normative linearity of history writing.

Both approaches to historiographic forgetting — the (medieval) discriminating preservation of past events and the (current) creative investigation of alternate memorial modes — inform my examination of Barking Abbey's memorial processes. I look beyond narrative evidence by turning to an oft-neglected body of material: the liturgy. In particular, I examine how the later medieval Barking nuns commemorated their early abbesses through yearly anniversary masses, both emphasizing their individual achievements and aggregating them into a collective whole. By doing so, they construct a conventual identity through this ritual form. Like most nunneries, Barking left no chronicle or cartulary, even though the nunnery enjoyed a robust literary culture.[14] However, the Barking *Ordinal* — the liturgical manuscript that contains the directions for how the Divine Office, Mass, and other rites were to be performed — includes entries that allow us to reconstruct the way the nuns remembered their community members. Of course, this remembrance was itself selective, and the *Ordinal* also forgets male figures key to the abbey's development, thus privileging female agency in Barking's history. By exercising careful control over the precise

---

see Camp, *Anglo-Saxon Saints' Lives*, 91–99; Cynthia Turner Camp, "Looking for Holy Grandmothers in Late Medieval Nunneries," in *Remembering the Present: Generative Uses of the Pre-Conquest Past*, ed. Jay Paul Gates and Brian O'Camb (Boston and Leiden: Brill, 2019).

13 Watt, "Literature in Pieces," 364. See further Wogan-Browne, *Saints' Lives*, 56; Liz Herbert McAvoy, "Introduction: *In Principio*: The Queer Matrix of Gender, Time and Memory in the Middle Ages," in *Reconsidering Gender, Time, and Memory in Medieval Culture*, ed. Elizabeth Cox, Liz Herbert McAvoy, and Roberta Magnani (Cambridge: D.S. Brewer, 2015), 1–12.

14 Jennifer N. Brown and Donna Alfano Bussell, eds., *Barking Abbey and Medieval Literary Culture: Authorship and Authority in a Female Community* (York: York Medieval Press, 2012).

rites through which they prayed for their early abbesses' souls, the nuns of Barking engaged in the historiographic dialectic of remembering and forgetting to craft a decidedly, almost exclusively, female heritage that negotiates the achievements of individual abbesses with a singular nunnery identity.

This recuperation of Barking's ritual commemorative processes is also, therefore, a recuperation of the liturgy not just as a religious performance but also as a key recollective — even historiographic — mode. These are the practices that most shaped monks' and nuns' daily lives, informing the way institutions remembered. As Margot Fassler has argued, "liturgy is indeed the foundation for understanding and representing the past during several centuries in the Middle Ages," and her own work with Chartres has demonstrated the centrality of liturgical forms for both secular and ecclesiastical understandings of the past.[15] Because the Mass, Divine Office, and ad hoc ceremonies are enacted practices rather than static texts, liturgical rites transmit historical information differently than narrative writing. The intensely somatic nature of liturgical performance — standing and kneeling, singing and listening — would have enabled invisible theological concepts and past events to become experientially present in the minds and bodies of those who enacted it.[16] More-

---

15 Margot E. Fassler, "The Liturgical Framework of Time and the Representation of History," in *Representing History, 900–1300: Art, Music, History*, ed. Robert A. Maxwell (University Park: Pennsylvania State University Press, 2010), 149–71, at 155, and Fassler, *The Virgin of Chartres: Making History through Liturgy and the Arts* (New Haven: Yale University Press, 2010). See further Susan Boynton, "Writing History with Liturgy," *Representing History, 900–1300: Art, Music, History*, ed. Robert A. Maxwell (University Park: Pennsylvania State University Press, 2010), 187–200. For a contrasting view, see Gabrielle Spiegel, "Memory and History: Liturgical Time and Historical Time," *History and Theory* 41, no. 2 (2002): 1–13.

16 Carol Symes, "Liturgical Texts and Performative Practices," in *Understanding Medieval Liturgy: Essays in Interpretation*, ed. Helen Gittos and Sarah Hamilton (Burlington: Ashgate, 2016), 239–67, and Eric Palazzo, "Art, Liturgy, and the Five Senses in the Early Middle Ages," *Viator* 41, no. 1 (2010): 25–56. Jill Stevenson makes compatible arguments from the perspective of cognitive theory in "Rhythmic Liturgy, Embodiment and Female Authority in Barking's Easter Plays," in *Barking Abbey*, ed. Brown and Bussell, 245–66.

over, its multitemporal interweaving of Biblical and historical events, which were experienced repeatedly within the rhythms of individual services and across the liturgical year, reinforced the typological and cyclical temporal patterns of medieval historiography.[17] As communally performed prayer, the liturgy's constant repetition by the convent would have cultivated a collective experience of this embodied mode of encountering the past; the convent "will be realized as a communal entity through shared supplication" to God on behalf of the community's members, living and dead.[18]

As one of England's most ancient nunneries, Barking had a long history to manage. Founded in the seventh century by Erkenwald, bishop of London, for his sister Ethelburg, it features prominently in Bede's *Ecclesiastical History*.[19] After being devastated by the Viking invasions of the ninth century, Barking was re-established in the tenth,[20] and it grew to be the third wealthiest nunnery in England at Domesday even though it was not patronized by the House of Wessex like the other ma-

---

17 Owain Tudor Edwards, "Dynamic Qualities in the Medieval Office," in *Liturgy and the Arts in the Middle Ages: Studies in Honour of C. Clifford Flanigan*, ed. Eva Louise Lillie and Nils Holger Petersen (Copenhagen: Museum Tusculanum Press, 1996), 36–63; Cynthia Hahn, "Picturing the Text: Narrative in the Life of Saints," *Art History* 13, no. 1 (1990): 1–33; Fassler, "Liturgical Framework"; Gabrielle M. Spiegel, "Structures of Time in Medieval Historiography," *Medieval History Journal* 19, no. 1 (2016): 1–13.

18 Sara Gorman, "Anglo-Norman Hagiography as Institutional Historiography: Saints' Lives in Late Medieval Campsey Ash Priory," *The Journal of Medieval Religious Cultures* 37, no. 2 (2011): 110–28, at 123, speaking of calls to corporate prayer in saints' lives. For a sociological perspective on this phenomenon, see Todd Nicholas Fuist, "Talking to God Among a Cloud of Witnesses: Collective Prayer as a Meaningful Performance," *Journal for the Scientific Study of Religion* 54, no. 3 (2015): 523–39.

19 *Bede's Ecclesiastical History of the English People*, ed. Bertram Colgrave and R.A.B. Mynors (Oxford: Clarendon Press, 1969), 4.6–11, pp. 354–66.

20 Foot, *Veiled Women*, 2.27–33; Donna Bussell and Jennifer N. Brown, "Barking's Lives, the Abbey and Its Abbesses," in *Barking Abbey*, ed. Brown and Bussell, 1–30, at 9, 31; Barbara Yorke, *Nunneries and the Anglo-Saxon Royal Houses* (London: Continuum, 2003), 84, 87–88, 156–57, 167–70.

jor pre-Conquest nunneries.²¹ Its post-Conquest fortunes were cemented when William the Conqueror, residing there temporarily while waiting for the Tower of London to be constructed, confirmed the convent's landholdings and privileges.²² This occurred during the tenure of Abbess Ælfgifu, an intrepid leader who directed the rebuilding of the abbey precinct, translated the relics of Barking's three saints into the new abbey church in the face of episcopal resistance, and commissioned the itinerant hagiographer Goscelin of Saint-Bertin to write formal *vitae* for the abbey's saints.²³ Throughout the later Middle Ages, Barking had a thriving literary community, where the nuns wrote, read, and commissioned devotional texts in many genres.

Those devotional texts included liturgical productions, and we can partly recover Barking's ritual life from three extant manuscripts.²⁴ Cardiff Public Library MS 1.381 contains Goscelin's late eleventh-century *vitae* and *lectiones* for the three Barking

---

21 Julia Crick, "The Wealth, Patronage, and Connections of Women's Houses in Anglo-Saxon England," *Revue Bénédictine* 109 (1999): 154–85, at 165, 161–2.

22 William of Poitiers, *Gesta Gvillelmi: The Deeds of William*, ed. and trans. R.H.C. Davis and Marjorie Chibnall (Oxford: Clarendon Press, 1998), 160–62; *Calendar of the Charter Rolls Preserved in the Public Record Office*, vol. 5 (London: Stationery Office, 1916), 284 (Barking 9).

23 On the reconstruction and translation efforts, see Kay Slocum, "Goscelin of Saint-Bertin and the Translation Ceremony for Saints Ethelburg, Hildelith and Wulfhild," in *Barking Abbey*, ed. Brown and Bussell, 78, 82–85, and Paul Antony Hayward, "Translation Narratives in Post-Conquest Hagiography and English Resistance to the Norman Conquest," *Anglo-Norman Studies* 21 (1998): 67–93, at 81–83. For Goscelin's *vitae* and *lectiones*, see below, n. 25.

24 Bussell and Brown, "Barking's Lives," 14–16. Studies of Barking's liturgical efforts include Slocum, "Goscelin"; Slocum, "Ritual and Ceremony at Barking Abbey," *Magistra* 16, no. 2 (2010): 94–110; Stevenson, "Rhythmic Liturgy"; Anne Bagnall Yardley, "Liturgy as the Site of Creative Engagement: Contributions of the Nuns of Barking," in *Barking Abbey*, ed. Brown and Bussell, 267–82; Anne Bagnall Yardley, *Performing Piety: Musical Culture in Medieval English Nunneries* (New York: Palgrave Macmillan, 2006), esp. 179–202. For Barking's manuscripts, see David N. Bell, *What Nuns Read: Books and Libraries in Medieval English Nunneries* (Kalamazoo: Cistercian Publications, 1995), 107–20.

saints, Ethelburg, Hildelith, and Wulfhild.[25] Barking's fifteenth-century hymnal, Cambridge, Trinity College, MS 1226 (O.3.54), includes standard hymns and hymns specifically composed (possibly by the Barking nuns) for the convent's feasts.[26] Finally, the early fifteenth-century *Ordinal,* Oxford, University College MS 169, outlines the way that the Office and Mass were to be performed at Barking.[27] It also includes a detailed calendar, directions for special rites (such as the Easter liturgical drama), and orders for auxiliary rituals like a royal entry or the profession of a nun. Importantly, the *Ordinal* positions itself not simply as a prompt for liturgical performance, but as a memorial document; an opening memorandum, immediately following the calendar, explains that the manuscript was compiled under the direction of Abbess Sybil de Felton (1393–1419) to be a "perpetual remembrance" for use by "future abbesses."[28] At various points it also names nuns who oversaw ritual changes and articulates the reasons for these changes, commemorating the nunnery's past on multiple levels.[29] This rich, detailed document — so distinctive in its customs that Richard Pfaff warns against extrapolating other nunneries' observances from it[30] — codifies the rituals specific to Barking as a carefully orchestrated configuration of nunnery identity, a "*prescriptive* template for what should occur

---

25 Edited in Marvin L. Colker, "Texts of Jocelyn of Canterbury Which Relate to the History of Barking Abbey," *Studia Monastica* 7 (1965): 383–460. I cite from this edition of Goscelin's *vitae* and *lectiones*.

26 Available online as a digital facsimile from the Trinity College Cambridge website at https://mss-cat.trin.cam.ac.uk/Manuscript/O.3.54. See Yardley, *Performing Piety*, 192–98.

27 The ordinal has been edited in full by J.B.L. Tolhurst as *The Ordinale and Customary of the Benedictine Nuns of Barking Abbey*, 2 vols., HBS 65–66 (London: Henry Bradshaw Society, 1927–28), hereafter cited as *Ordinal*.

28 *Ordinal*, 1.13: "perpetuum commemoraturum"; "ad usum Abbitssarum [...] in futurum"; see Yardley, "Liturgy as the Site," 270–71.

29 Yardley, "Liturgy as the Site"; Stevenson, "Rhythmic Liturgy," 245–46.

30 Richard W. Pfaff, *The Liturgy in Medieval England. A History* (Cambridge: Cambridge University Press, 2009), 347–49.

in performance," that reveals the nuns' spiritual and memorial priorities.³¹

The *Ordinal* consistently emphasizes Barking's female agency and lineage. Beyond highlighting the nuns' roles in its textual production and liturgical innovation, the *Ordinal* highlights holy women as the abbey's spiritual grandmothers, especially in the calendar's emphasis on female saints. It records twelve non-Barking English female saints to be honored in the Daily Office and/or at Mass, some rarely commemorated outside their home institutions.³² The three Barking saints, Ethelburg, Hildelith, and Wulfhild, were celebrated eleven times during the year, counting octaves, and select pre-Conquest nuns were commemorated as well. The March 7th feast for the eleventh-century relic translation foregrounds Edith and Tortgyth, the two Barking nuns discussed in Bede's *Ecclesiastical History,* in the Vespers and Matins antiphons, versicles, and prayers. The same day's readings also honor Abbess Ælfgifu, and the Matins lessons come from Goscelin's *lectiones* for the translation, in which Ælfgifu is the major player. Goscelin emphasizes her initiative in rebuilding the abbey, getting episcopal authorization for the translations, and overseeing the translations themselves.³³ The March 7 feast thereby confirms the central role of famed pre-Conquest nuns while also establishing Abbess Ælfgifu's reconstruction of the abbey precinct as the modern nunnery's starting point. Bringing together these holy women within the liturgical year, the *Ordinal* enables a supratemporal recognition of female accomplishment, associating significant women across the centuries and bringing them into focus in the modern nuns' devotions.

This emphasis on female affinities is more pronounced in its arrangements for abbesses' and prioresses' obits. Praying for the dead was a core function of every religious house, and obits, recorded in calendars or in separate lists, preserve the names and

---

31 Symes, "Liturgical Texts," 244, italics in original. See also Boynton, "Writing History with Liturgy," 188.
32 Camp, "Looking for Grandmothers," 156–57.
33 "Two Accounts of the Translation" in Colker, "Texts of Jocelyn," 435–52; Slocum, "Goscelin," 74, 81–85.

death-dates (rarely death-years) of those individuals, including lay patrons, for whose souls the institution was bound to pray.[34] On the individual's death-day, the community typically said a memorial mass, sometimes with special prayers and antiphons. There may have been a procession, alms were distributed to the poor or assigned to the convent, and the convent also received pittances (extra dishes at mealtime).[35] Because anniversary masses were arranged by the individual before death, historians typically study them as evidence for relationships between institutions and patrons, and for lay individuals' devotional inclinations, not as evidence of institutional identity construction. However, the recording of obits in calendars could be a historical activity (preserving for later generations the names of abbesses and patrons) as well as a historiographic one (the creation of an institutional past through the selective action of recording).[36] As

---

[34] For a useful distinction between necrologies (lists of names to be read on the death-day) and obituaries (lists for the performance of anniversary masses), see Jean-Loup LeMaitre, "Nécrologes et obituaires: une source privilégiée pour l'histoire des institutions ecclésiastiques et de la société au Moyen Âge?" in *Le médiéviste devant ses sources: Questions et Méthodes*, ed. Claude Carozzi and Huguette Taviani-Carozzi (Aix-en-Provence: Publications de l'Université de Provence, 2004), 25–39; K.S.B. Keats-Rohan, "Testimonies of the Living Dead: The Martyrology-Necrology and the Necrology in the Chapter-Book of Mont-Saint-Michel (Avranches, Bibliothèque municipale, MS 214)," in *The Durham "Liber Vitae" and Its Context*, ed. David Rollason et al. (Woodbridge: Boydell Press, 2004), 165–89, at 169.

[35] Practices varied widely. For examples, see Emilie Amt, "Ela Longespee's Roll of Benefits: Piety and Reciprocity in the Thirteenth Century," *Traditio* 64 (2009): 1–56; Janet Burton, "Commemoration and Memorialization in a Yorkshire Context," in *The Durham "Liber Vitae" and Its Context*, ed. Rollason et al., 221–31, at 225–27, 228–29; William of Malmesbury, *The Early History of Glastonbury: De antiquitate Glastonie ecclesie*, ed. and trans. John Scott (Woodbridge: Boydell Press, 1981), 162–63. Compare the anniversaries Catherine de' Medici established for herself at the Italian convent of Santa Maria Annunziata in Florence: K.J.P. Lowe, *Nuns' Chronicles and Convent Culture in Renaissance and Counter-Reformation Italy* (Cambridge: Cambridge University Press, 2003), 276–77.

[36] Robin Fleming, "History and Liturgy at pre-Conquest Christ Church," *Haskins Society Journal* 6 (1994): 67–82; Keats-Rohan, "Testimonies," 174; Lynda Rollason, "The Late Medieval Non-Monastic Entries in the Durham Liber Vitae," in *The Durham "Liber Vitae" and Its Context*, ed. Rollason et al.,

Robin Fleming has shown for Christ Church Canterbury, such lists "are skillfully crafted portrayals of the past,"[37] modified by the institution to shape who they remembered — and who they forgot.

The *Ordinal* engages in this kind of institutional memory-making through three items: the calendar, a list of abbess burial places, and a memorandum on how abbess anniversaries were to be celebrated.[38] Nearly every Barking abbess from Ælfgifu (1066–87) through Sybil de Felton (d. 1419), the *Ordinal*'s commissioner, is listed on her death-date in the calendar.[39] The abbesses who died between the Conquest and 1215 are marked with "missa," while those who died 1215–1258 are marked "processio" but, other than the data provided in the anniversary memorandum, we have no more detailed information on precisely how the abbesses' anniversaries were recognized. The later medieval nuns also provided masses for themselves and sometimes their

---

127-37, at 132–37, and Simon Keynes, "The *Liber Vitae* of the New Minster, Westminster," 149–63, at 152–53, 158–60, both in *The Durham "Liber Vitae" and Its Context*, ed. Rollason et al. Biographical obits played this role in early modern English convents on the Continent, on which see Caroline Bowden, "Collecting the Lives of Early Modern Women Religious: Obituary Writing and the Development of Collective Memory and Corporate Identity," *Women's History Review* 19, no. 1 (2010): 7–20.

37 Fleming, "History and Liturgy," 82.

38 The death dates of prioresses are also listed in the calendar, and the process for celebrating their obits is also noted in the anniversary memorandum.

39 The calendar is missing one folio, for November and December; I postulate that the four missing abbesses between Ælfgifu and Sybil had death-dates in these months. Neither the calendar nor the burial-place list include the queens, Edith-Matilda, wife of Henry I, or Matilda, wife of Stephen, whom modern scholarship occasionally includes in lists of Barking's abbesses: see *History of the Count of Essex*, vol. 2: *Religious Houses*, Victoria History of the Counties of England (London: Victoria County History, 1907), 120–21, and Bussel and Brown, "Barking's Lives," 7. Whatever their administrative relationship to Barking, the fourteenth-century nuns did not recognize them as abbesses. *The Heads of Religious Houses of England and Wales*, vol. 1: *940–1216*, 2nd edn., ed. David Knowles, C.N.L Brooke, and Vera C.M. London (Cambridge: Cambridge University Press, 2001), 208, also excludes them.

families; Sybil de Felton established a chantry for her soul and those of family members,[40] and others likely followed suit.

The list of abbess resting-places is also nearly complete from Ælfgifu through Sybil de Felton. This French document, located toward the end of the *Ordinal* immediately after the anniversary memorandum (discussed below), was compiled specifically for use by the convent when celebrating the abbesses' anniversaries.[41] It demonstrates the way that abbesses' tombs functioned as a "commemorative medium," visibly honoring the dead within the abbey precinct.[42] The list identifies the abbesses' burial locations by reference to the abbey's architectural features.[43] While some tombs were set into the abbey church floor,[44] others were probably prominent, especially those set in arches in the church walls.[45] Together, the abbey's mortuary architecture and burial list actively inscribed a topography of remembrance, ensuring

---

40 Richard Newcourt, *Repertorium Ecclesiasticum Parochiale Londinense*, vol. 2 (London, 1710), 32–33.

41 The heading reads "This entry is made to record the tombs of the abbesses who have their anniversary services within the convent yearly" (*Ordinal*, 2.361: "Ceste escripture fait a remembrer de les sepultures de Abbesses qe ount lour seruices entre conuent a les anniuersaries par lan").

42 Roberta Gilchrist and Barney Sloane, *Requiem: The Medieval Monastic Cemetery in Britain* (London: Museum of London Archaeological Service, 2005), 30.

43 Although the abbey precinct was razed during the Dissolution of the Monasteries, early twentieth-century excavations reconstructed the floorplan of abbey grounds: Alfred W. Clapham, "The Benedictine Abbey of Barking: A Sketch of its Architectural History and an Account of Recent Excavations on its Site," *Transactions of the Essex Archaeological Society* 12 (1911): 69–87.

44 Christiania de Valoniis was buried "in the middle of the chapter-house under a marble stone" (*Ordinal*, 2.362: "en mylieu del chapitre ou la pere du margre"). A nineteenth-century excavation of the Lady Chapel revealed three interments in the east, probably the tombs of Matilda Plantagenet, Maud daughter of John, Maud de Leveland, and/or Yolande de Sutton, all buried in the Lady Chapel according to the burial list: Clapham, "Benedictine Abbey," 79; *Ordinal*, 2.361.

45 These include Ælfgifu (near the high altar), Mary Becket (near the altar of Our Lady and Paul, in an aisle), Mabel de Boseham (in an unspecified arch), Alice de Merton (near the nuns' cemetery), Katherine de Sutton (in the Lady Chapel), and Maud Montagu (near the high altar): *Ordinal*, 2.361–62.

that the abbesses' physical remains persisted meaningfully within the nuns' daily experience of the conventual grounds.

The calendar and burial list witness a concerted effort to remember the abbey's institutional dead. They also reveal how forgetting is always implicated in commemorating. In constructing its dominantly female past, institutionally and nationally, the *Ordinal* forgets most of its male supporters. Although Erkenwald, as Ethelburga's brother and the nunnery's first founder, is recognized on his feast day of April 30 and with a unique hymn in the hymnal,[46] the *Ordinal* is otherwise stingy in its recognition of male aid. Nowhere does it honor its royal patrons, either the early English *thegns* who endowed the nunnery with land or later kings like Edgar or William I.[47] While the calendar does preserve the death dates for some priests and two bishops,[48] as well as several lay persons, mostly relatives of Barking's abbesses,[49] abbesses and prioresses are unusually prevalent for a later medieval nunnery. By contrast, the late fifteenth-century "Leiger Book" from Wroxall Abbey provides an extensive list of royal and noble patrons for whose souls the nuns would pray.[50] A similar, Middle English obit list for Kingston St. Michael's Priory, arranged in calendrical order, intertwines prioresses, nuns, male and female patrons, and ecclesiastical benefactors.[51] The paucity of highly placed lay and ecclesiastical obits in the Barking *Ordinal*'s calendar is therefore a deliberate act

---

46 *Ordinal*, 2.221–23; Slocum, "Goscelin," 85–86. The hymn, *Festiva dies annua*, is no. 204 in *Analecta Hymnica Medii Aevii*, ed. Guido Maria Dreves, vol. 11 (Leipzig: O.R. Reisland, 1891), 119.

47 Crick, "The Wealth," 169–70.

48 These obits are for two early thirteenth-century bishops of London, William of Ste-Mère-Eglise (r. 1198–1221, March 27) and Roger Niger (d. 1241, October 1).

49 I count eight men marked "presbiter" or "magister," probably priests who served the nuns; fourteen lay persons, half identifiable by last name as relatives of fourteenth-century abbesses and prioresses, the other half possibly also family members of nuns, and the two bishops (n. 48).

50 Printed in John William Ryland, *Records of Wroxall Abbey and Manor, Warwickshire* (London: Spottiswoode, 1903), 217–18.

51 Printed in J.E. Jackson, "Kington St. Michael," *Wiltshire Archaeological and Natural History Society Magazine* 4 (1858): 36–124, at 60–67.

of institutional identity construction: the calendar communicates that Barking is primarily the sum of its family members and female religious forebearers. By downplaying male aid in favor of female antecedents, the *Ordinal* aligns with other nunneries' historiographic priorities. Crabhouse and Godstow, for instance, "place women front and centre in their community's formation," privileging in their foundation narratives female agency over male aid recorded in early charters.[52] The Barking *Ordinal* undertakes a similar venture in the performed realm of anniversary and liturgical services. Masses for the souls of former abbesses and other supporters unite the dead with the praying community in the hope of a shared afterlife, constructing for Barking a (primarily) female corporate identity across time.

The *Ordinal*'s historiographic process of forgetting in the act of remembering is, however, more complex than simply prioritizing women, as a close examination of the anniversary memorandum reveals. The memorandum states that, in the time of Abbess Anne de Veer (d. 1318), the convent reduced the anniversaries of the abbesses and prioresses who had died 200 years earlier to a simple, customary mass in common, as a way to simplify the convent's liturgical commitments. The memorandum names the six abbesses whose anniversaries were to be simplified — Ælfgifu, Agnes, Adeliza, Mary sister of Thomas Becket, Matilda daughter of Henry II, and Sybil — before suggesting that later generations of nuns also simplify the anniversaries of later abbesses "as was said above," that is, once the 200-year mark had passed.[53] Returning to the calendar, we see that the six abbesses marked "missa" are those listed in the memorandum, and that the next three abbesses, marked "processio," would have passed the 200-year mark about fifty years before Sybil de Felton compiled the *Ordinal*. The calendar therefore indicates

---

52 June, "Languages of Memory," 351 (on Crabhouse). For Godstow, see Amt, "Foundation Legend." For continental examples, see Lowe, *Nuns' Chronicles*, 97–115, and Anne Winston-Allen, *Convent Chronicles: Women Writing About Women and Reform in the Late Middle Ages* (University Park: Penn State University Press, 2004), esp. 67–76.

53 *Ordinal*, 2.359: "sicut supradictum est."

that later nuns implemented or adapted the memorial simplifications that Anne de Veer's convent had initiated.

While these changes have been interpreted as the Barking nuns' liturgical laziness,[54] that interpretation does not accord with the *Ordinal* itself, which reveals the nuns' distinctive, even expansive liturgical expression.[55] Rather, these are alterations to institutional memory that efface some elements of the earlier abbesses' memorial preferences. Anniversary masses were a way for individuals to assert their devotional priorities beyond the grave, impressing their spiritual personalities upon later generations tasked with fulfilling these requests. Although we do not know what form the Barking abbesses' original anniversaries took, they may have been quite elaborate, as parallel examples from Godstow and Westminster Abbey suggest. Ela Longespee (c. 1209–1298), a patron of Godstow Abbey, left a roll detailing the anniversary services she contracted the nuns of Godstow (and other religious institutions) to perform for her. Godstow would say mass twice daily, two additional masses per month, St. Gregory's Trental on the anniversary of her death, and weekly Our Fathers and Hail Marys by the nuns; Ela specifies exactly which collects and postcommunion texts were to be used, and which altars would serve for which masses.[56] Ela's documents are unusually precise, but John Flete's mid-fifteenth-century history of Westminster Abbey demonstrates that abbots might arrange for equally complex, or much simpler, anniversary masses. Abbot Richard Crokesley (d. 1258) lists how many masses he wanted said at which altars with how many candles, while abbot Richard Ware (1258–1283) simply requested a single anniversary mass as said for other abbots.[57] These examples demonstrate the wide variety of forms that anniversaries could take, and this variation would have been viscerally experienced by the nuns

---

54 George Henry Cook, *Medieval Chantries and Chantry Chapels* (London: Phoenix House, 1947), 12.
55 Yardley, "Liturgy as the Site," 268, 271–74; Pfaff, *The Liturgy,* 347.
56 Amt, "Ela Longespee's Roll," 10–11, 37–41, et passim.
57 John Flete, *The History of Westminster Abbey,* ed. J. Armitage Robinson (Cambridge: Cambridge University Press, 1909), 111–12, 116.

and monks performing these services. At Barking, remnants of Ælfgifu's original arrangements may be preserved in the *Ordinal*. Although her anniversary was reduced to a communal mass, the burial-place list records that the nuns additionally said the seven penitential psalms for her soul while kneeling before her tomb, specifying the specific trope for the Kyrie at mass.[58] It is also likely that Matilda Plantagenet originally established distinctive anniversary celebrations for herself; she had contracted Ilford Hospital, established by Barking Abbey under Adeliza's tenure as abbess, to observe an anniversary for her and her parents, and likely did the same at Barking.[59] Undoubtedly, other abbesses took equal care for their souls.

In simplifying these anniversary masses, Anne de Veer's convent not only updates their liturgy; they also alter the convent's history. As the memorandum's verbs reveal, this change actively forgets the earliest abbesses's spiritual preferences. The anniversaries "should be thoroughly disbanded," and the six named abbesses "were removed."[60] Both verbs, *dimittere* and *auferre*, suggest dispersal, abandoning, and even destruction. Although the abbesses themselves continue to be remembered, their spiritual personalities, formerly impressed upon nuns praying yearly (or more frequently) for their souls, are effaced. Forgotten in prayer are the powerful personalities and highly placed women who materially benefited the Norman convent: Matilda Plantagenet, the daughter of a king; Mary Becket, the sister of a saint; Adeliza, sister of the Norman barons Eustace and Payn FitzJohn and founder of a hospital.[61] The one exception is Ælfgifu. Al-

---

58 *Ordinal*, 2.362: "Dame Aluine gist en larche deuers le haut auter qe ad vij. psaumes en genulant. E messe capital oue Kyrie par vers .s. Hominum plasmator. et Offertorium."

59 Emily Mitchell, "Patrons and Politics at Twelfth-Century Barking Abbey," *Revue Bénédictine* 113 (2003): 347–64, at 354.

60 *Ordinal*, 2.359: "anniversaria Abbatissarum antiquarum [...] penitus dimittantur"; "Ista sunt nomina auferendarum."

61 Matilda (c. 1175–after 1198), natural daughter of Henry II, does not appear in the literature on her father; Mary Becket (1173–c. 1175) is named in Guernes de Pont-Sainte-Maxence's *Vie de saint Thomas*; Adeliza (1137?–c. 1166) founded Ilford Hospital, one of Barking's major holdings, and correspond-

though she too is put on the same commemorative footing as the other early abbesses, she is allowed a distinctive liturgical profile, befitting her status as a founding figure, in the March 7 *lectiones* and the penitential psalms the nuns intoned at her tomb on May 10.

As it forgets its earliest abbesses' personalized anniversary rites while remembering the innovations of other abbesses, the *Ordinal* negotiates the historiographic implications of two rhetorical features common in nunnery writing. The first is the tendency to locate a convent's past in the initiative of exceptional women. This medieval historiographic decision is familiar to modern scholars of women's history, who are trained to recover the actions of notable women. Examples include the Wherwell Abbey cartulary, which praises the building efforts of its twelfth-century abbesses;[62] the Wroxall "Leiger Book," which lauds abbess Alice Croft for constructing the nunnery's Lady Chapel;[63] and the many foundation narratives that place conventual origins in laywomen's spiritual and economic drive.[64] The *Ordinal*, in identifying Sybil as the *Ordinal*'s mastermind, naming Katherine de Sutton as the agent behind the nunnery's Easter drama,[65] and preserving the extra features for Ælfgifu's anniversary celebrations, similarly positions Barking's architectural and liturgical achievements as the actions of specific nuns. Yet the "notable women" historiographic model has its limits. It invites, but is too fragmentary to fulfill, a linear conventual history in the "lives of the abbots" model, where the successes of each generation can be listed in chronological order.[66] Instead, the

---

ed with Osbert of Clare, Prior of Westminster. On all three, see Mitchell, "Patrons and Politics"; on Mary and Adeliza, see Thomas O'Donnell, "'The Ladies Have Made Me Quite Fat': Authors and Patrons at Barking Abbey," in *Barking Abbey*, ed. Brown and Bussell, 94–114.

62 Wogan-Browne, *Saints' Lives*, 201–3; Rhoda P. Bucknill, "Wherwell Abbey and Its Cartulary" (PhD diss., King's College London, 2003), 173–88.

63 Ryland, *Records of Wroxall*, 216.

64 See above, n. 52.

65 *Ordinal*, 2.273; Yardley, "Liturgy as the Site," 272–74.

66 E.g., Flete, *History of Westminster*. On the inability of nunnery writings to meet this expectation, see Wogan-Browne, *Saints' Lives*, 202.

achievements of some women point up the silence elsewhere in the historical record.

The second rhetorical feature is the trope of the "timeless nun," a figure common in hortatory writings for nuns. Entering a convent and becoming a Bride of Christ, the nun notionally steps outside the flow of secular time, subordinating personal aspirations to a homogenized professional identity.[67] Such privileging of the collective over the individual in nunnery writings at times takes on historiographic weight. For example, Rebecca June argues that the Crabhouse foundation narrative deliberately leaves its earliest nuns nameless in order to "describ[e] the Crabhouse nunnery's identity as an anonymous and collective body of women."[68] The Barking anniversary memorandum too prefers collectivity; in honoring its early abbesses through the same mass, it privileges a collective identity unified in nunhood. Additionally, although its opening lines name both Anne and her prioress, Lady Wymark, the changes themselves were "ordered by the common assent of the convent," the community rather than the abbess or prioress taking responsibility.[69] This structure for organizing the conventual past locates successes not in the deeds of singular women but in the collective action of the whole. It is less easily assimilated to linear history-writing, as June's analysis reveals, but it aligns neatly with liturgical memorial modes, which can also incorporate elements of the "notable women" structure. Within the yearly round of anniversaries and saints' feasts, the convent's holy dead are remembered both as singular actors within mundane time and valued members of the convent's community across time. These liturgi-

---

67 Nancy Bradley Warren, *Spiritual Economies: Female Monasticism in Later Medieval England* (Philadelphia: University of Pennsylvania Press, 2001), 3–29. Examples include, from the early thirteenth century, the Anglo-Norman hortatory poem for nuns edited in Tony Hunt, "An Anglo-Norman Treatise on Female Religious," *Medium Ævum* 64, no. 2 (1995): 205–31;,and, from the late fifteenth century, John Alcock, *Desponsacio virginis xpristo. Spousage of a virgyn to chryste* (London: Wyndyn de Worde, 1497).
68 June, "Languages of Memory," 331–55, at 354.
69 *Ordinal*, 2.359: "ordinatum est per comunem assensum conuentus."

cal structures can accommodate, and to a point reconcile, both rhetorical nunnery modes.

Liturgical commemoration cements the past more firmly in institutional memory than could have a written chronicle, which would rarely have been experienced corporately. Significant changes to rites for the dead therefore impact the community's memory. The collective performance of anniversary masses not only speeds the nuns' souls through purgatory, but it also incorporates the conventual dead into the living's experience of their institutional past. By limiting the anniversary celebrations for their earliest abbesses, the Barking nuns actively change the convent's relationship with its past, as enacted communally within its yearly ritual life. Between feast days and abbess anniversaries, Sybil's nuns would have been commemorating Barking's most honored dead at least thirty-three days, or one tenth, of the year.[70] Celebrating their predecessors multiple times a month — standing and kneeling during Mass and Office, singing antiphons and responsories, processing through the abbey church on some saints' feasts and abbess anniversaries, listening to the March 7 *lectiones* within sight of Ælfgifu's tomb — the Barking nuns engrained the community's past in their bodies' somatic memories. It is this haptic repetition that makes the anniversary simplifications crucial, for the nuns perform exactly the same movements, chants, and words for Agnes as for Matilda Plantagenet as for Mary Becket. It also makes the additions to Ælfgifu's anniversary critical. In kneeling before her tomb, moving lips and tongue to say the seven penitential psalms on her behalf, singing and hearing the Kyrie performed by female voices within the sonic space of the Barking church choir, the nuns enact Ælfgifu's exceptional role in Barking's history.

The seeming absence of English nuns from the historical record results from both their active exclusion from male-produced, chronicle history and their own disinclination to keep

---

70 This count includes the anniversaries I anticipate were present on the missing calendar leaf for November–December and does not include the obits for the prioresses and family members.

the same kinds of records male houses did. Nevertheless, the lack that scholars of women's history feel acutely may not have been apparent to the nuns themselves. They already had structures in place to ensure the memory of their predecessors stayed vivid and relevant. Those structures were not written narrative, but rather the internalized *habitus* of individual nuns trained in the *opus Dei* and reproduced through the continual performance of these anniversaries. Where scholarship laments the forgetting of English nuns, perhaps the problem is not with the nuns but with our own historiographic expectations. And if we can align our ways of engaging with history more closely with theirs, we can come to a better understanding of how all medieval people remembered, and forgot, their pasts.

Bibliography

Primary

Alcock, John. *Desponsacio virginis xpristo. Spousage of a virgyn to chryste.* London: Wyndyn de Worde, 1497.

Analecta Hymnica Medii Aevii. Volume 11. Edited by Guido Maria Dreves. Leipzig: O.R. Reisland, 1891.

Bede. *Historiam Ecclesiasticum Gentis Anglorum.* In *Bede's Ecclesiastical History of the English People,* edited and translated by Bertram Colgrave and R.A.B. Mynors. Oxford: Clarendon Press, 1969.

Calendar of the Charter Rolls Preserved in the Public Record Office. Volume 5. London: Stationery Office, 1916.

Colker, Marvin L. "Texts of Jocelyn of Canterbury Which Relate to the History of Barking Abbey." *Studia Monastica* 7 (1965): 383–460.

Flete, John. *The History of Westminster Abbey.* Edited by J. Armitage Robinson. Cambridge: Cambridge University Press, 1909.

Ryland, John William. *Records of Wroxall Abbey and Manor, Warwickshire.* London: Spottiswoode, 1903.

The Ordinale and Customary of the Benedictine Nuns of Barking Abbey. 2 volumes. Henry Bradshaw Society 65–66. Edited by J.B.L. Tolhurst. London: Henry Bradshaw Society, 1927–1928.

William of Malmesbury. *The Early History of Glastonbury: De antiquitate Glastonie ecclesie.* Edited and translated by John Scott. Woodbridge: Boydell Press, 1981.

William of Poitiers. *Gesta Gvillelmi: The Deeds of William.* Edited and translated by R.H.C. Davis and Marjorie Chibnall. Oxford: Clarendon Press, 1998.

Secondary

Amt, Emilie. "Ela Longespee's Roll of Benefits: Piety and Reciprocity in the Thirteenth Century." *Traditio* 64 (2009): 1–56. DOI: 10.1017/S0362152900002245.

———. "The Foundation Legend of Godstow Abbey: A Holy Woman's Life in Anglo-Norman Verse." In *Writing Medieval Women's Lives*, edited by Charlotte Newman Goldy and Amy Livingstone, 13–31. Gordonsville: Palgrave MacMillan, 2012. DOI: 10.1057/9781137074706_2.

Ankersmit, F.R. "The Sublime Dissociation of the Past: Or How to Be(come) What One Is No Longer." *History and Theory* 40, no. 3 (2001): 295–323. DOI: 10.1111/0018-2656.00170.

Bell, David N. *What Nuns Read: Books and Libraries in Medieval English Nunneries*. Kalamazoo: Cistercian Publications, 1995.

Bowden, Caroline. "Collecting the Lives of Early Modern Women Religious: Obituary Writing and the Development of Collective Memory and Corporate Identity." *Women's History Review* 19, no. 1 (2010): 7–20. DOI: 10.1080/09612020903444619.

Boynton, Susan. "Writing History with Liturgy." In *Representing History, 900–1300: Art, Music, History*, edited by Robert A. Maxwell, 187–200. University Park: Pennsylvania State University Press, 2010.

Brown, Jennifer N., and Donna Alfano Bussell, eds. *Barking Abbey and Medieval Literary Culture: Authorship and Authority in a Female Community*. York: York Medieval Press, 2012.

Bucknill, Rhoda P. "Wherwell Abbey and Its Cartulary." PhD diss., King's College London, 2003.

Bugyis, Katie Ann-Marie. "Recovering the Histories of Women Religious in England in the Central Middle Ages: Wilton Abbey and Goscelin of Saint-Bertin." *Journal of Medieval History* 42, no. 3 (2016): 285–303. DOI: 10.1080/03044181.2016.1163505.

Burton, Janet. "Commemoration and Memorialization in a Yorkshire Context." In *The Durham "Liber Vitae" and Its Context*, edited by David Rollason, A.J. Piper, Margaret Harvey, and Lynda Rollason, 221–31. Woodbridge: Boydell, 2004.

Bussell, Donna Alfano, and Jennifer N. Brown. "Barking's Lives, the Abbey and Its Abbesses." In *Barking Abbey and Medieval Literary Culture: Authorship and Authority in a Female Community*, edited by Jennifer N. Brown and Donna Alfano Bussell, 1–30. York: York Medieval Press, 2012.

Camp, Cynthia Turner. *Anglo-Saxon Saints' Lives as History Writing in Late Medieval England.* Cambridge: D.S. Brewer, 2015.

———. "Looking for Holy Grandmothers in Late Medieval Nunneries." In *Remembering the Present: Generative Uses of the Pre-Conquest Past,* edited by Jay Paul Gates and Brian T. O'Camb, 144–67. Boston and Leiden: Brill, 2019. DOI: 10.1163/9789004408333_007.

Clapham, Alfred W. "The Benedictine Abbey of Barking: A Sketch of its Architectural History and an Account of Recent Excavations on its Site." *Transactions of the Essex Archaeological Society* 12 (1911): 69–87.

Cook, George Henry. *Medieval Chantries and Chantry Chapels.* London: Phoenix House, 1947.

Crick, Julia. "The Wealth, Patronage, and Connections of Women's Houses in Anglo-Saxon England." *Revue Bénédictine* 109 (1999): 154–85. DOI: 10.1484/J.RB.5.105443.

De Certeau, Michel. *The Writing of History.* Translated by Tom Conley. New York: Columbia University Press, 1988.

Edwards, Owain Tudor. "Dynamic Qualities in the Medieval Office." In *Liturgy and the Arts in the Middle Ages: Studies in Honour of C. Clifford Flanigan,* edited by Eva Louise Lillie and Nils Holger Petersen, 36–63. Copenhagen: Museum Tusculanum Press, 1996.

Fassler, Margot E. "The Liturgical Framework of Time and the Representation of History." In *Representing History, 900–1300: Art, Music, History,* edited by Robert A. Maxwell, 149–71. University Park: Pennsylvania State University Press, 2010.

———. *The Virgin of Chartres: Making History through Liturgy and the Arts.* New Haven: Yale University Press, 2010.

Fleming, Robin. "History and Liturgy at Pre-Conquest Christ Church." *Haskins Society Journal* 6 (1994): 67–82.

Foot, Sarah. *Veiled Women.* 2 volumes. Burlington: Ashgate, 2000.

Fuist, Todd Nicholas. "Talking to God Among a Cloud of Witnesses: Collective Prayer as a Meaningful Performance." *Journal for the Scientific Study of Religion* 54 (2015): 523–39. DOI: 10.1111/jssr.12209.

Gates, Jay Paul. "The 'Worcester' Historians and Eadric Streona's Execution." In *Capital and Corporal Punishment in Anglo-Saxon England*, edited by Jay Paul Gates and Nicole Marafioti, 165–80. Woodbridge: Boydell and Brewer, 2014.

Gilchrist, Roberta, and Barney Sloane. *Requiem: The Medieval Monastic Cemetery in Britain*. London: Museum of London Archaeological Service, 2005.

Gorman, Sara. "Anglo-Norman Hagiography as Institutional Historiography: Saints' Lives in Late Medieval Campsey Ash Priory." *The Journal of Medieval Religious Cultures* 37, no. 2 (2011): 110–28. DOI: 10.5325/jmedirelicult.37.2.0110.

Hahn, Cynthia. "Picturing the Text: Narrative in the Life of the Saints." *Art History* 13, no. 1 (1990): 1–33. DOI: 10.1111/j.1467-8365.1990.tb00377.x.

Hayward, Paul Antony. "Translation Narratives in Post-Conquest Hagiography and English Resistance to the Norman Conquest." *Anglo-Norman Studies* 21 (1998): 67–93.

History of the County of Essex, Volume 2: *Religious Houses*. Victoria History of the Counties of England. London: Victoria County History, 1907.

Hunt, Tony. "An Anglo-Norman Treatise on Female Religious." *Medium Ævum* 64, no. 2 (1995): 205–31. DOI: 10.2307/43633092.

Jackson, J.E. "Kingston St. Michael." *Wiltshire Archaeological and Natural History Society Magazine* 4 (1858): 36–124.

June, Rebecca. "The Languages of Memory: The Crabhouse Nunnery Manuscript." In *Language and Culture in Medieval Britain: The French of England, c. 1100-c. 1500*, edited by Jocelyn Wogan-Browne, Carolyn Collette, Maryanne Kowaleski, Linne Mooney, Ad Putter, and David Trotter, 347–58. York: York Medieval Press, 2009.

Keats-Rohan, K.S.B. "Testimonies of the Living Dead: The Martyrology-Necrology and the Necrology in the Chapter-Book of Mont-Saint-Michel (Avranches, Bibliothèque municipale, MS 214)." In *The Durham "Liber Vitae" and Its Context*, edited by David Rollason, A.J. Piper, Margaret Harvey, and Lynda Rollason, 165–89. Woodbridge: Boydell, 2004.

Keynes, Simon. "The *Liber Vitae* of the New Minster, Westminster." In *The Durham "Liber Vitae" and Its Context*, edited by David Rollason, A.J. Piper, Margaret Harvey, and Lynda Rollason, 149–63. Woodbridge: Boydell, 2004.

Knowles, David. *The Religious Orders in England*, Volume 2: *The End of the Middle Ages*. Cambridge: Cambridge University Press, 1955.

Knowles, David., C.N.L Brooke, and Vera C.M. London, eds. *The Heads of Religious Houses of England and Wales*, Volume 1: *940–1216*. 2nd edition. Edited by Vera C.M. London. Cambridge: Cambridge University Press, 2001. DOI: 10.1017/CBO9780511496226.

LeMaitre, Jean-Loup. "Nécrologes et obituaires: une source privilégiée pour l'histoire des institutions ecclésiastiques et de la société au Moyen Âge?" In *Le médiéviste devant ses sources: Questions et Méthodes*, edited by Claude Carozzi and Huguette Taviani-Carozzi, 25–39. Aix-en-Provence: Publications de l'Université de Provence, 2004. DOI: 10.4000/books.pup.6524.

Lowe, K.J.P. *Nuns' Chronicles and Convent Culture in Renaissance and Counter-Reformation Italy*. Cambridge: Cambridge University Press, 2003.

Lucas, George R., Jr. "Recollection, Forgetting, and the Hermeneutics of History: Meditations on a Theme from Hegel." In *Hegel, History, and Interpretation*, edited by Shaun Gallagher, 97–115. Albany: SUNY Press, 1997.

McAvoy, Liz Herbert. "Introduction: *In Principio*: The Queer Matrix of Gender, Time and Memory in the Middle Ages." In *Reconsidering Gender, Time, and Memory in Medieval Culture*, edited by Elizabeth Cox, Liz Herbert McAvoy, and Roberta Magnani, 1–12. Cambridge: D.S. Brewer, 2015.

Mitchell, Emily. "Patrons and Politics at Twelfth-Century Barking Abbey." *Revue Bénédictine* 113, no. 2 (2003): 347–64. DOI: 10.1484/J.RB.5.100636.

Newcourt, Richard. *Repertorium Ecclesiasticum Parochiale Londinense.* Volume 2. London, 1710.

O'Donnell, Thomas. "'The Ladies Have Made Me Quite Fat': Authors and Patrons at Barking Abbey." In *Barking Abbey and Medieval Literary Culture: Authorship and Authority in a Female Community,* edited by Jennifer N. Brown and Donna Alfano Bussell, 94–114. York: York Medieval Press, 2012.

Palazzo, Eric. "Art, Liturgy, and the Five Senses in the Early Middle Ages." *Viator* 41, no. 1 (2010): 25–56. DOI: 10.1484/J.VIATOR.1.100566.

Pfaff, Richard W. *The Liturgy in Medieval England: A History.* Cambridge: Cambridge University Press, 2009. DOI: 10.1017/CBO9780511642340.

Rollason, Lynda. "The Late Medieval Non-Monastic Entries in the Durham *Liber Vitae.*" In *The Durham "Liber Vitae" and Its Context,* edited by David Rollason, A.J. Piper, Margaret Harvey, and Lynda Rollason, 127–37. Woodbridge: Boydell, 2004.

Schinkel, Anders. "History and Historiography in Process." *History and Theory* 43, no. 1 (2004): 39–56. DOI: 10.1111/j.1468-2303.2004.00264.x.

Slocum, Kay. "Goscelin of Saint-Bertin and the Translation Ceremony for Saints Ethelburg, Hildelith and Wulfhild." In *Barking Abbey and Medieval Literary Culture: Authorship and Authority in a Female Community,* edited by Jennifer N. Brown and Donna Alfano Bussell, 73–93. York: York Medieval Press, 2012.

———. "Ritual and Ceremony at Barking Abbey." *Magistra* 16, no. 2 (2010): 94–110.

Spiegel, Gabrielle M. "Genealogy: Form and Function in Medieval Historical Narrative." *History and Theory* 22, no. 1 (1983): 43–55. DOI: 10.2307/2505235.

———. "Memory and History: Liturgical Time and Historical Time." *History and Theory* 41, no. 2 (2002): 149–62. DOI: 10.1111/0018-2656.00196.

———. "Structures of Time in Medieval Historiography." *Medieval History Journal* 19, no. 1 (2016): 1–13. DOI: 10.1177/0971945816638616.
Stevenson, Jill. "Rhythmic Liturgy, Embodiment and Female Authority in Barking's Easter Plays." In *Barking Abbey and Medieval Literary Culture: Authorship and Authority in a Female Community*, edited by Jennifer N. Brown and Donna Alfano Bussell, 245–66. York: York Medieval Press, 2012.
Symes, Carol. "Liturgical Texts and Performative Practices." In *Understanding Medieval Liturgy: Essays in Interpretation*, edited by Helen Gittos and Sarah Hamilton, 239–67. Burlington: Ashgate, 2016. DOI: 10.4324/9781315562988-11.
Thompson, Sally. "Why English Nunneries Had No History: A Study of the Problems of the English Nunneries Founded after the Conquest." In *Medieval Religious Women 1: Distant Echoes*, edited by John A. Nichols and Lillian Thomas Shank, 131–49. Kalamazoo: Cistercian Publications, 1984.
———. *Women Religious: The Founding of English Nunneries After the Norman Conquest*. Oxford: Clarendon Press, 1991.
Treharne, Elaine. *Living Through Conquest: The Politics of Early English, 1020–1220*. Oxford: Oxford University Press, 2012.
Warren, Nancy Bradley. *Spiritual Economies: Female Monasticism in Later Medieval England*. Philadelphia: University of Pennsylvania Press, 2001. DOI: 10.9783/9780812204551.
Watt, Diane. "Literature in Pieces: Female Sanctity and the Relics of Early Women's Writing." In *The Cambridge History of Early Medieval English Literature*, edited by Clare A. Lees, 357–80. Cambridge: University Press, 2013. DOI: 10.1017/CHO9781139035637.017.
———. *Medieval Women's Writing: Works by and for Women in England, 1100–1500*. Cambridge: Polity Press, 2007.
White, Hayden. "Guilty of History? The Longue Durée of Paul Ricoeur." *History and Theory* 46, no. 2 (2007): 233–51. DOI: 10.1111/j.1468-2303.2007.00404.x.
Winston-Allen, Anne. *Convent Chronicles: Women Writing About Women and Reform in the Late Middle Ages*. University Park: Penn State University Press, 2004.

Wogan-Browne, Jocelyn. *Saints' Lives and Womens' Literary Culture, c. 1150–1300: Virginity and Its Authorizations.* Oxford: Oxford University Press, 2001. DOI: 10.1093/acprof:oso/9780198112792.001.0001.

Yardley, Anne Bagnall. "Liturgy as the Site of Creative Engagement: Contributions of the Nuns of Barking." In *Barking Abbey and Medieval Literary Culture: Authorship and Authority in a Female Community,* edited by Jennifer N. Brown and Donna Alfano Bussell, 267–82. York: York Medieval Press, 2012.

———. *Performing Piety: Musical Culture in Medieval English Nunneries.* New York: Palgrave Macmillan, 2006.

Yorke, Barbara. *Nunneries and the Anglo-Saxon Royal Houses.* New York: Continuum, 2003.

3

Alternative Histories: Phantom Truths in Stone

Catherine E. Karkov

Introduction

Stone has been described by Michel Serres as both preceding and buried by language; as such, it is the foundation of human stories.[1] For Jeffrey Jerome Cohen, stone is foundation, the ultimate archive,[2] and for Jan Zalasiewicz, stone is the ultimate history because in stone is preserved the record of both human endeavor and the deep history of the planet.[3] Stone records all; stone cannot lie, although it can be used to convey stories not its own. Isidore of Seville (c. 560–636), who was both closer in time to early medieval England, and whose writings were well known to its learned elite, wrote about the link between stone and memory or history, describing stone monuments as speaking to the mind, instructing it to remember that which had been

---

1 Michel Serres, *Statues: The Second Book of Foundations*, trans. Randolph Burks (London: Bloomsbury, 2015), 23.
2 Jeffrey Jerome Cohen, *Stone: An Ecology of the Inhuman* (Minneapolis: University of Minnesota Press, 2015).
3 Jan Zalasiewicz, *The Planet in a Pebble: A Journey into Earth's Deep History* (Oxford: Oxford University Press, 2012).

memorialized in stone.⁴ Stone, then, both had agency and was the agent through which certain histories could be constructed — it spoke and instructed and it was or was a sign of, what was to be remembered through that instruction. The use of stone for architectural purposes in seventh- and eighth-century England has a troubled history amongst modern scholars who study the period. We have tended to listen to the written histories rather than to interrogate the stone itself, and we thus have failed to hear its instruction, preferring to understand only through the secondary written record — the human endeavor and not the deeper history. According to Bede (c. 673–735), for example, the Northumbrians did not know how to build in stone, and so they sent for stonemasons from the Continent,⁵ and so their architecture spoke of imported ideas and ideals. But the stone itself was not imported, and that stone could thus record a very different history from that which it was asked to convey. Of course, it is impossible not to rely in some measure on the written sources as they provide information on dates, patrons, the historical contexts in which stone buildings were constructed, and sometimes even the sources of the stone. This chapter is an attempt to begin to put those sources in dialogue with the stone itself.

The ability of stone to relate stories and to create or remember histories has been exploited by conquerors and colonizers across the globe for centuries, and studies of the use of stone in both the Inkan Andes and in medieval India provide useful examples of ways that we might think differently about the use and reuse of stone in early medieval England, and about its peoples' relationship with both land and history. In looking to these other times and cultures I do not intend to draw comparisons amongst three very different postcolonial situations; rather, this

---

4 Isidore of Seville, *The Etymologies of Isidore of Seville* 15.11.1, trans. Stephen A. Barney, W.J. Lewis, J.A. Beach, and Oliver Berghof (Cambridge: Cambridge University Press, 2006), 313.

5 Bede, *History of the Abbots of Wearmouth and Jarrow*, ch. 5, in *Abbots of Wearmouth and Jarrow*, ed. Christopher Grocock and Ian N. Wood (Oxford: Clarendon Press, 2013), 33.

chapter will focus specifically on what the use of stone in these cultures might have to contribute to our understanding of the use and reuse of stone along the Hadrian's Wall frontier and of what stone had to say to the inhabitants of early medieval England as well as what it has to say to us today. But I also want to think more deeply about the gap, distance, or echo that exists between stone and the working or reworking of that stone, and about the sorts of buried truths or alternative histories that might lie within that gap or echo. Isidore described common stone as an icon because it had the ability to capture "the sound of the human voice":

> An *icon* is a rock that, by capturing the sound of the human voice, imitates the words of someone speaking. It is an icon in Greek and "image" (*imago*) in Latin, because an image of someone else's speech is produced in response to one's voice.[6]

However, Pliny, his source, described such stone as *echo* rather than *icon*,[7] consequently Isidore's translation opens a gap in meaning between that which is heard and that which is seen, a gap in translation that might be said to echo the one that exists between what is written about stone and what is seen in the materiality of the stone before us. Moreover, the semantic range of both icon and *imago* extended to include the unseen or intangible, to such things as shadows, ghosts or phantoms, and this will be taken up further below.[8]

But let's begin with two different attitudes to stone and its reuse that are temporally and geographically distant from early

---

6 Isidore of Seville, *The Etymologies of Isidore of Seville*, 16.3.4 (Barney et al., trans., 319). "Icon saxum est, qui humanae vocis sonum captans, etiam verba loquentium imitatur: icon autem Graece, Latine imago vocatur, eo quod ad vocem respondens alieni efficitur imago sermonis." The Latin Library: http://www.thelatinlibrary.com/isidore/16.shtml.

7 Barney et al, trans., *The Etymologies of Isidore of Seville*, 319, n. 5. In Greek, *icon* (*eikōn*) meant image or likeness, while *echo* was a noise or sound.

8 On the origin and changing meanings of "icon" from the classical to the early Christian world see Patrick R. Crowley, *The Phantom Image: Seeing the Dead in Ancient Rome* (Chicago: Chicago University Press, 2019).

medieval England, but that also provide documented evidence for some of the multiple ways in which stone speaks from and about both the past and the present. For the Inka, stone was simultaneously a part of nature and a part of culture, a place and medium in which the two met, and a means by which the natural world could be ordered and domesticated.[9] The Inka also considered themselves to be "the agents of order, the civilizers of the Andes,"[10] and stone, both in the form of the built environment and the natural mountain and rock formations in which their architecture was located, was very much a part of the territorial expansion of the state and the bringing of civilization to the "untamed" people of the Andes.[11] The Spanish, in their turn, would dismantle Inka monuments in order to construct towns and churches in their own style, as statements of *their* conquest and the bringing of a new *Christian* order to the polytheistic peoples of the Andes. They described Cuzco as an empty city,[12] unowned and available for the taking, and they turned the Inka's limestone fortress of Saqsaywaman (begun 900–1100 CE) into a quarry for already worked stone for the cathedral and other buildings of Cuzco, in part because of its convenience, but also because they were both impressed by and envious of its megalithic grandeur.[13] As important to the Spanish as their new architecture was the creation of a ruined Inka monument. The life and histories of the Inka stone were replaced by death and the written word. According to stories still told today, the earth and its stone were integral to the identities of both cultures, though their agency was somewhat different. The ancient Inka married Mother Earth (Pachamama), a union which produced human offspring and which also remained apparent in

---

9   Carolyn Dean, *A Culture of Stone: Inka Perspectives on Rock* (Durham: Duke University Press, 2010), 14, 21, 70.
10 Ibid., 70.
11 Ibid., 70, 103.
12 Michael J. Schreffler, "Inca Architecture from the Andes to the Adriatic: Pedro Sancho's Description of Cuzco," *Renaissance Quarterly* 67, no. 4 (2014): 1191–223, at 1205.
13 Dean, *A Culture of Stone*, 145–48.

the rocky outcrops of the land, many of which were worked into Inka structures in ways that fully integrated the natural and built environments.[14] Jesus Christ and the Inka were both the sons of God, but Jesus Christ became jealous of the Inka and sent him a page of writing; and because Inka could not understand writing, he fled. "With the Inka gone and unable to do anything, Jesus Christ attacked Mother Earth, cut off her head, then built churches on her."[15] This stone speaks of two separate conquests, that of the Inka and that of the Spanish, and both these stone structures and the larger landscapes of stone and mountain into which they were set remained a constant record and reminder of that fact.

The story of the Inka and their stone, as well as the Spanish and theirs, does have some parallels with that of the early medieval Britons, Romans, and English and their stone, though they are by no means exact. For each of these peoples, stone architecture brought order, tamed that which was untamed, and was a means of publicly marking and memorializing the expansion of kingdoms. British and Celtic monuments or sites such as the fortress of Dunadd in Scotland, or Tintagel off the north coast of Cornwall incorporated stone and other geographical features in a way that most Roman and English medieval structures did not—although the Angles, Saxons, and Jutes who settled in the country certainly made significant use of islands.[16] Stone buildings wrote history and memory into the landscape. And, as the Spanish quarried Saqsaywaman for stone for Cuzco, so the Angles and Saxons quarried earlier sites like Corbridge and other Roman towns and monuments for stone for their towns and churches. The story of the Inka also asks us to think about

---

14 Carolyn Dean, "The Inka Married the Earth: Integrated Outcrops and the Making of Place," *The Art Bulletin* 89, no. 3 (2007): 502–18.

15 Ibid., 66, quoting a story recorded in Quechua in 1971. For the full story, see Alejandro Ortiz Rescaniere, "Mito de la Escuela," in *Ideología Mesiánica del Mundo Andino*, ed. Juan M. Ossio Acuña (Lima: Ignacio Prado Pastor, 1973), 237–50.

16 See especially Catherine A.M. Clarke, *Literary Landscapes and the Idea of England 700–1400* (Cambridge: D.S. Brewer, 2006).

the role of stone as a porous frontier between the human and the land on and into which humans built, as well as about larger landscapes, about the deeper histories of stone and the monuments built with it, about the death and destruction of monuments, and about the ghosts that continue to haunt these landscapes of stone.

In his study of the Hindu/Muslim encounter in South Asia, Finbarr Flood complicates our understanding of the reuse of stone, cautioning us about interpreting such postcolonial situations in exclusively binary terms. It is not simply a matter of Inka vs. the other peoples of the Andes, or Spanish vs. Inka, or the Angles and Saxons vs. the Britons or the Romans, the present vs. the past, and so on. In viewing the postcolonial in binary terms, or as a state of hybridity or synchronism, there is a danger that we "presuppose (if not produce) 'pure' original or parent cultures" that simply did not exist.[17] He prefers to understand the postcolonial as a network of processes and relationships, a "complex interplay between past and present, tradition and innovation," religions and peoples,[18] proposing a Benjaminian dialogic model of translation as methodology through which translation continues the creative process of the work being translated. He focuses on things rather than texts, and the ability of things to subvert the very texts they accompany or that are used to describe them. The idea of "translation" I find particularly useful as it captures the sense of both physical movement (as in the translation of a saint), and the presence of words and voices (as in translation from one language to another), and hence helps to reveal stone's nature as both translated and translator. In Flood's model of translation there is no original or copy, but rather that which is translated lives on in the translation, even in its absence or in the act of discarding it,[19] creating gaps and echoes akin to those we find in the act of re-

---

17 Finbarr B. Flood, *Objects of Translation: Material Culture and Medieval "Hindu–Muslim" Encounter* (Princeton: Princeton University Press, 2009), 5.
18 Ibid., 158.
19 Ibid., 182–83.

use more generally. In terms of stone architecture and sculpture then, Roman monuments live on in the early medieval English structures into which they have been translated. To take one of the best known and perhaps most large-scale instances of reuse, one which will be considered further below, parts of Roman Corbridge live on in Anglian Hexham, and Anglian Hexham in parts of Roman Corbridge, their respective identities being an ongoing intra-action of the spaces,[20] materials, and materialities of the two, and indeed of the British landscape into which both were intruders, and onto which both built in stone. This may, indeed have been one of the purposes of the mining of Corbridge to build Hexham.[21]

Equally important, however, is the ability of things, in this case of stone as object and material, to subvert the linear histories or narratives they are asked to construct. In his study of the Delhi Mosque, Flood identifies the building's evolving status as a sort of heterotopia:

---

20 I borrow the term "intra-action" from Donna Haraway, Karen Barad, and entanglement theory. Unlike "interaction," in which two discreet entities exert some kind of influence on each other, "intra-action" breaks down the idea that there are such things as discreet entities, times, or places, or actions such as cause and effect. Things and times are continuously and inextricably entangled and demand being read through each other, they are continually intra-acting with each other. See further Donna Haraway, "The Promises of Monsters: A Regenerative Politics for Inappropriate/d Others," in *The Haraway Reader* (New York: Routledge, 2014), 23–124; Karen Barad, *Meeting the Universe Halfway: Quantum Physics and the Entanglement of Matter and Meaning* (Durham: Duke University Press, 2006); Birgit Mara Kaiser and Kathrin Thiele, eds., *Diffracted Worlds — Diffracted Readings: Onto-epistemologies and the Critical Humanities* (London: Routledge, 2018).
21 See further Paul Bidwell, "A Survey of the Anglo-Saxon Crypt at Hexham and Its Reused Roman Stonework," *Archaeologia Aeliana* 5th ser. 39 (2010): 53–145, and Paul Bidwell, "Wilfrid and Hexham: The Anglo-Saxon Crypt," in *Wilfrid Abbot, Bishop, Saint: Papers from the 1300th Anniversary Conference*, ed. Nicholas J. Higham (Donington: Shaun Tyas, 2013), 152–62. See also the description of the size and grandeur of the church in Eddius Stephanus, *The Life of Bishop Wilfrid by Eddius Stephanus*, ed. and trans. Bertram Colgrave (Cambridge: Cambridge University Press, 1927), 44–47.

In its role as an agglomeration of signs that both addressed and sought to mold the nature of Muslim identity in the newly emerging capital of a triumphant Indian sultanate, the Delhi mosque provides a precocious example of what Michel Foucault termed a heterotopia. Heterotopias are spaces in which a variety of sites including those that are incompatible or incommensurate, "are simultaneously represented, contested, and inverted." They are often likened "to the accumulation of time," or what Foucault terms heterochrony, a term that denotes the synchronous representation of different (and possibly incommensurate) eras or times with the same space. The best example is the modern museum. As the case of the museum demonstrates, space itself is hardly devoid of narrative context, despite the temptation for art historians to approach it as a series of forms and dates.[22]

Flood's primary interest here is in the narrative continuity and transculturation such monuments are capable of expressing. My interest, however, is in the ability of stone as both worked material and as material that has its source in land and place to subvert such narratives. Along the Hadrian's Wall frontier, the echo of the Britons through the landscape was something that both the Romans and the English in their different ways sought to silence. Nevertheless, we can hear that echo on and in the stone of that land. Gildas (d. 570), Bede, and others repeatedly associated the Britons with spaces beneath the earth, describing the Picts, Scots, and Britons as emerging from, fleeing into, or simply lurking in rocks, fens and mountains. For example, Gildas describes the arrival of "the foul hordes of Scots and Picts, like dark throngs of worms who wriggle out of narrow fissures in the rock when the sun is high and the weather grows warm."[23] A similar attitude is enshrined in the fen dwelling Welsh de-

---

[22] Flood, *Objects of Translation*, 252.
[23] Gildas, *The Ruin of Britain and Other Documents*, trans. Michael Winterbottom (London: Phillimore, 1978), 23. Original Latin in ibid., 92–93: "quasi in alto Titane incalescenteque caumate de artissimis foraminum caveerniculis fusci vermiculorum cunei, tetri Scottorum Pictorumque greges."

mons of Felix's *Life of Guthlac,* or the Mere-dwelling Grendel and his mother in *Beowulf.*[24] In these texts, it is the demons and the Grendel-kin who are in and of the land, and the English and Danes who are the intruders. It is only when Guthlac enters into the land by building his hut over a cistern within a burial mound (*tumulus*) that the demons begin to plague him, and Beowulf must dive down through the fen into the Grendel-kin's cave in order to finally defeat Grendel's mother. Both episodes resonate with Isidore's claim that stone as icon and *imago* can capture and project, as well as with the extended meanings of the terms. Stone holds shadows and phantoms and Grendel is a death-shadow (*deaþscua,* line 160a), while the fen dwellers that Guthlac encounters are phantoms of demons (*fantasias demonum,* chapter XXV) who are contained within but also emerge from earth and stone.

Early Medieval England

That people in early medieval England did understand stone as something that both held and memorialized life and had a life in the world is evident in both their texts and their approach to the landscape of the past. I turn first to textual descriptions and artistic representations of land and stone to provide a basis for the ways in which the agency and voice of stone as a material could have been manifested. The Britons or the phantoms of

---

24 *Felix's Life of Guthlac,* ed. Bertram Colgrave (Cambridge: Cambridge University Press, 1956), ch. 34 (110–11) explicitly identifies a host of phantoms that attack Guthlac's cell in the night as British, i.e., Welsh, that he recognizes through their sibilant speech, with which he had become familiar while previously in exile amongst the Britons: "Verba loquentis vulgi Brittannicaque agmina tectis succedere agnoscit; nam ille aliorum temporum praeteritis voluminibus inter illos exulabat quoadusque eorum strimulentas loquelas intelligere valuit." See also Alfred K. Siewers, "Landscapes of Conversion: Guthlac's Mound and Grendel's Mere as Expressions of Anglo-Saxon Nation-Building," *Viator* 34 (2003): 1–39, and Fabienne Michelet, *Creation, Migration, and Conquest: Imaginary Geography and Sense of Space in Old English Literature* (Oxford: Oxford University Press, 2006), esp. chs. 3 and 5.

them, as we have seen, could emerge like worms from the rocks and ancient burial mounds that still stood in the landscape. Such openings into the earth were represented as both gateways to hell and the haunts of demons in manuscript illumination, while the right-side panel of the eighth-century Franks Casket depicts what appears to be one of the living dead enclosed within in a mound at its center.[25] Individual types of stone were said to have certain powers. If burned, jet could drive away serpents and if rubbed had magnetic qualities,[26] and stone buildings were witnesses to the passing of time and human existence. The dead warriors and their glorious hall live on, watched over by, written into, and memorialized in the decaying stone of their architecture in *The Ruin*.

Often this wall, covered with moss and red-stained, endured one kingdom after another, withstood the storms, the steep arch has now fallen. The place where the wall stands still crumbles hewn by weapons; it fell on the earth, the creation broken, grimly ground down, the ground swallowed all [...] shone [...] the ancient work of skill [...] bowed with coats of mud; an intent mind was urged swiftly to a crafty plan, strongly in circles the strong-minded one bound the foundation wondrously together with wires. The city buildings were bright, many bath-houses, an abundance of high roofs, great army-sounds, many mead-halls full of human-joys, until mighty fate changed all that. The slain died widely, pestilence came and death took away all the brave warriors. Their bulwarks (or altars) became wastelands, the city crumbled. Its

---

25 For manuscript illumination see Sarah J. Semple, "Illustrations of Damnation in Late Anglo-Saxon Manuscripts," *Anglo-Saxon England* 32 (2003): 31–45. The panel in the British Museum is a replica and the original is in the Museo Nazionale del Bargello, Florence. On the back panel the eye of the man within the mound is open as if he were alive, while on the front panel no eyes are represented on the severed head of a dead prince that Weland the Smith holds in his tongs. For images of both panels see: https://www.britishmuseum.org/collection/object/H_1867-0120-1.
26 Bede, *Ecclesiastical History of the English People*, ed. Bertram Colgrave and R.A.B. Mynors (Oxford: Oxford University Press, 1969), 17.

rebuilders perished, armies in the earth. For that these buildings decay, and the red vaults shed their tiles, the curved wooden roofs. The ruin fell to the earth broken into stone mounds, where once many men glad-minded and gold-bright, ornamented with splendor, proud and flushed with wine shone in battle-gear; looked on treasure, on silver, on crafted gems, on wealth, on possessions, on precious stones, on the bright city, the broad kingdom.[27]

The literary fascination with ruins in early medieval England is well documented. Heide Estes suggests that it may reflect the culture's own "anxieties about loss and displacement." She suggests further that the presence of ruins in both literature and the landscape "challenges" the way the English thought "about themselves and their relationship to dwellings and to the features of their lived environments."[28] In *The Ruin* everything — men, buildings, cultures — crumbles back into the earth from which it arose. The crumbling ruin and *ubi sunt* topos of the poem may be poetic conventions but, as Estes notes, crumbling ruins built by dead armies were common fixtures of the landscape of early

---

27 *The Ruin*, ll. 9–37: "Oft þæs wag gebad, ræg-har ond read-fah rice æfter oþrum, oftstonden under stormum; steap geap gedreas. Worað giet se weall-steall wæpnum geheapen; fel on foldan forð-gesceaft bærst grimme gegrunden, grund eall forswealg [...] scan heo [...]g or-þonc ærsceaft [...] g lam-rindum gebeag; mod monade myne swiftne gebrægd hwæt-red in hringas, hyge-rof gebond weall-walan wirum wundrum togædre. Beorht wæron burg-ræced, burn-sele monige, heah horn-gestreon, here-sweg micel, meodo-heall monig monn-dreama full, oþþæt þæt onwende wyrd seo swiþe. Crungon walo wide, cwoman wol-dagas, swylt eall fornom secg-rofa wera; wurdon hyra wig-steal westen staþolas, brosnade burg-steall. Betend crungon hergas to hrusan. Forþon þas hofu dreorgiað, ond þæs teafor-geapa tigelum sceadeð hrost-beages hrof. Hryre wong gecrong gebrocen to beorgum, þær iu beorn monig glæd-mod ond gold-beorht gleoma gefrætwed, wlong ond win-gal wig-hyrstum scan; seah on sinc, on sylfor, on searo-gimmas, on ead, on æht, on eorcan stan, on þas beorhtan burg braden rices." In *Old English Shorter Poems*, Vol. 2: *Wisdom and Lyric*, ed. and trans. Robert E. Bjork (Cambridge: Harvard University Press, 2014), 118, 120. All Old English translations are my own unless otherwise stated.
28 Heide Estes, *Anglo-Saxon Literary Landscapes: Ecotheory and the Environmental Imagination* (Amsterdam: Amsterdam University Press, 2017), 63.

medieval England, most especially along the Hadrian's Wall corridor where evidence for the occupation and reuse of Roman (and earlier) sites is strong.[29]

The Ruin's treatment of the stone building as a living thing that rises from and returns to the earth with its builders suggests an intra-action of stone and the human. The buildings were bright and their inhabitants bright with gold, and just as builders and armies fall dead to the ground the ruin falls to the earth. But the ruin does more than just fall, it falls broken into stone mounds (*gebrocen to beorgum*). Beorg can mean both hill and burial mound, and the connection or play between the two occurs elsewhere in Old English poetry. The inscription on the front panel of the eighth-century Franks Casket, for example, begins by telling us that the whale from whose bones the casket is made was cast up onto a high hill or mound (*fergenberig*) where it died, the hill becoming its burial mound. But while the hill in the casket's inscription is a passive recipient of the whale's body, the building in *The Ruin* has agency, forming itself into mounds as it falls, creating a tomb for the builders that had created it. Building and inhabitants demand to be read through each other, as do the times of the buildings' creation and the much later time of their decay and fall.

Bewcastle

Turning from text to stone, a story similar to that told in words in *The Ruin* is told in stone and earth at Bewcastle, Cumbria, where the Roman fort of Fanum Cocidii was abandoned in the fourth century and left to decay and fall into ruin. The warriors who had manned it had departed either through death or the Roman withdrawal of their troops. Its falling stones marked the graves of some and lay as memorials to others. It is not clear how

---

[29] For a useful overview of the Wall corridor see Richard Hingley, *Hadrian's Wall: A Life* (Oxford: Oxford University Press, 2012). For the reuse of earlier sites across England, see Sarah J. Semple, *Perceptions of the Prehistoric in Anglo-Saxon England: Religion, Ritual, and Rulership in the Landscape* (Oxford: Oxford University Press, 2013).

far back in time the cemetery at Bewcastle goes, but it is still possible to see some of the larger stones from the fort's ramparts at the base of the hill on which the present church and cemetery sit, and down which they have slid over the centuries, giving the entire hill the appearance of a monumental barrow.

The area around Bewcastle hill was the site of prehistoric activity, traces of which can still be seen in the surviving Bronze Age stone cairns that dot the landscape. The stone of the cairns is, presumably, local although to the best of my knowledge it has not undergone geological analysis. It is therefore with the arrival of the Romans that the story of stone at Bewcastle can begin to be read. Fanum Cocidii was an outpost fort located approximately ten miles north of Hadrian's Wall and its main line of forts. It was begun in Hadrianic times (ca. 120 CE) and abandoned at some point in the fourth century. The ruins of its buildings must have stood for some time after the fort was abandoned as stones from the bathhouse were incorporated into the Norman Castle built in 1092 and rebuilt in the fourteenth century, and into the thirteenth-century church (now gone), as well as numerous other buildings in the vicinity.[30]

The bathhouse was particularly well-built and remained standing the longest of all the fort's buildings. Thirteenth- and fourteenth-century pottery fragments discovered in the disturbed soil of the bathhouse indicate that it was still accessible to those in search of stone at that point.[31] Excavations in 1949 uncovered portions of the bathhouse with walls still standing up to ten courses high, and further excavations were carried out in the mid-1950s. It was built almost entirely of local stone, primarily sandstone with some limestone and tufa, and tiles made from clay obtained eight miles to the south at Bampton.[32]

---

30 J.P. Gillam et al., *The Roman Bath-House at Bewcastle, Cumbria* (Kendal: Cumberland and Westmorland Antiquarian and Archaeological Society, 1993), 24; J.B.W. Day et al., *Geology of the Country around Bewcastle* (London: Her Majesty's Stationary Office, 1970), 267.

31 Gillam et al., *The Roman Bath-House at Bewcastle, Cumbria*, 18.

32 Ibid., 5, 10, 14; see also Paul S. Austin, *Bewcastle and Old Penrith: A Roman Outpost Fort and a Frontier Vicus* (Kendal: Cumberland and Westmorland

Figure 1. The Bewcastle Cross. Photo by the author.

The primary stone was the same as that used for the eighth-century Anglian cross that still stands on the site, a Carboniferous medium-grained yellow sandstone with grains of feldspar, quartz, and muscovite mica held in a matrix of clay minerals.[33] The sandstone was formed through a long process of sand and marine sedimentation during which marine organisms were entombed as the layers of sedimentation built up.[34] It was most likely sourced from the "ancient quarries" in the Earthwork and Parkhead sandstones near Crossgreens, with some of the larger stones possibly brought from the great crags of the Long Bar on Whitlyne Common.[35]

Like the buildings of *The Ruin*, "at some time the whole bathhouse collapsed; the vaults had fallen in and the walls had fallen over."[36] That this was prior to the thirteenth/fourteenth century was indicated to the excavators by the lack of debris in places that provided evidence of stone robbing,[37] but that stone was still accessible in some form is indicated by its reuse in the church and castle, as note above. That stone is no longer accessible to visitors to the site, but the Anglian cross carved from the same sandstone is (fig. 1).[38] Plans of the fort indicate that the cross was erected on what would have been a terrace in front of the ruined bathhouse.[39] There is some debate about whether this

---

Antiquarian and Archaeological Society, 1991), 17, 46

33 Richard N. Bailey and Rosemary Cramp, *Cumberland, Westmorland and Lancashire North-of-the Sands*, vol. 2, Corpus of Anglo-Saxon Stone Sculpture (Oxford: Oxford University Press, 1988), 7.

34 On the long geological history of the area see Day et al., *Geology of the Country around Bewcastle*, 5–6; J. Ward, "Early Dinantian Evaporates of the Easton-I Well, Solway Basin, Onshore Cumbria, England," in *The Petroleum Geology of the Irish Sea and Adjacent Areas*, ed. Neil S. Meadows, S.P. Trueblood, M. Hardman, and G. Cowan, Geological Society Special Publication 124 (Bath: The Geological Society, 1997), 277–96, at 281.

35 Day et al., *Geology of the Country around Bewcastle*, 266–77.

36 Gillam et al., *The Roman Bath-House at Bewcastle, Cumbria*, 22.

37 Ibid.

38 For detailed images of the cross, see: http://www.ascorpus.ac.uk/catvol2.php?pageNum_urls=30.

39 See Fred Orton and Ian Wood with Clare A. Lees, *Fragments of History: Rethinking the Ruthwell and Bewcastle Monuments* (Manchester: Man-

monument was originally intended to be a cross or an obelisk or a column,[40] but that is less crucial to the story told by its stone than it is to the form into which that stone was worked. I will refer to it as a cross because the play on hidden crosses within its individual carved panels suggests to me that that is what it was intended to be, but the important point is that when it was carved and erected it would have been part of a much larger landscape of stone cairns, ruined buildings, and sculptures. Its stone has endured and been witness to the rise and fall of armies and empires. It holds, as does all stone, the deep history of geologic time, but also the far shorter history of human activity and conquest in the area. J.B.W. Day speculated that, rather than being newly quarried, the stone from which the cross is carved came from the ruined fort,[41] while Martin Henig has suggested that the cross might have been intended as a replacement for a Roman votive column, a powerful statement of a new claim to the land by the Northumbrian church and kingdom.[42] This is part of the history and meaning of worked and reworked stone rather than that of the material itself, but as was the case with the stone of Inkan and Hindu/Muslim monuments, the two are not always so easily separated. Moreover, as Flood demonstrated, through the process of its translation, stone and things made from it have the power to subvert the texts that are used to describe them. Times, materials, and processes intra-act and

---

chester University Press, 2007), fig 4. Image available at: https://www.researchgate.net/figure/Plan-of-fort-showing-location-of-excavated-areas_fig4_294261287.

40 See especially Orton and Wood with Lees, *Fragments of History*.
41 Day et al., *Geology of the Country around Bewcastle*, 267.
42 Martin Henig, "*Murem civitatis et fontem in ea a Romanis mire olim constructum*: The Arts of Rome in Carlisle and the civitatis of the Carvetii and Their Influence," in *Carlisle and Cumbria: Roman and Medieval Architecture, Art and Archaeology*, ed. Mike McCarthy and David Weston, British Archaeology Association Conference Transactions 27 (Leeds: Maney Publishing, 2004), 11–28, at 22–23. Henig speculates that what the excavators of the fort interpreted as the base of a life-sized statue was more likely to have been the base for a votive column.

demand to be read through each other. I'll begin with material and process.

The surfaces of the cross are now badly weathered, many panels are covered with lichen or mosses, and the north side has been damaged by fire so it is impossible to know whether the fossils or traces of them that would have become part of the stone during the process of sedimentation could once be seen — none have been observed in modern times — but they might well have been encountered by the sculptor(s). Fossils can still be seen on many surviving sculptures from pre-1066 England.[43] Fossils were evidence of the deep time preserved in stone. While early medieval persons may not have known how stone was created, they did recognize its iconic nature, its agency in preserving the shadows of life. For Isidore, whose writings were popular in early medieval England, stones that contained fossils provided proof that the biblical deluge had covered the earth.[44] Biblical time was made real and brought into the present by their presence, and they were visual reminders of the destruction that could so easily overturn worlds. The sundial carved into the south side of the Bewcastle Cross (fig. 2), brings this deep time to the stone's surface, setting this particular monument and this particular place within the schemes of biblical and cosmic time. Whether the sundial was intended to signal the hours of the monastic day or whether it was primarily symbolic, it establishes a direct connection between the cross and the sun and the course of the sun as it moves through days, years, decades, and centuries, a movement that was also important to the liturgical meaning of the cross.[45] Time might bring salvation, that is certainly

---

43 See, for example, the descriptions of the following monuments in the Corpus of Anglo-Saxon Stone Sculpture (hereafter CASSS), http://www.ascorpus.ac.uk. CASSS 3: York Minster 12, York Minster 44, Amotherby 1 and 2, Ellburn several, Levisham 5, Middleton 2, Old Malton 2; CASSS 4, Langford 3, Oxford St. Aldates 1; CASSS 5, Lincoln St. Mark 15; CASSS 10, Deerhurst St. Mary 1. I am grateful to Derek Craig for his help with this information.

44 Isidore of Seville, *Etymologies*, 13.22 (Barney et al., trans., 282).

45 Éamonn Ó Carragáin, *Ritual and the Rood: Liturgical Images and the Old English Poems of the Dream of the Rood Tradition* (London and Toronto: The British Library and University of Toronto Press, 2005), 46, 106–7.

Figure 2. The Bewcastle Cross, detail of the sundial on the south side. Photo by the author.

Figure 3. Bewcastle Cross, north side showing the female name Kynibur*g inscribed in runes and fire damage. Photo by the author.

the hope of the cross as a memorial monument to the men and women whose names are inscribed into it (fig. 3), but time also brings death and decay. The past, death, and decay continue to haunt the present, and what we think of as past events, or as things that have been abandoned, ruined, or forgotten, persist and refuse to go away. For ruins, this can be a complicated past.

If the worked stone of the monument that is the cross was meant to lay claim to a territory previously inhabited by Romans and Britons or to overturn their polytheistic religions, the extended landscape from which the stone was quarried and in which it stood also had the power to keep these pasts alive and cultures present. The cross may have been a sign of Northumbrian expansion into the British kingdom of Rheged,[46] but stone stood as testament to a longer history. The Bronze Age stone cairns held the ghosts of the Britons and the ever-present threat of their return. The Welsh demons released from the barrow in the *Life of Guthlac* were defeated and driven out, but Guthlac was a saint, and ordinary men and women did not have his pow-

---

46 Orton and Wood, with Lees, *Fragments of History*, 110–17.

ers. The Romans may have conquered the area for a time, but they left and the land and the stone they had worked returned to the Britons — in fact Bewcastle alternated between being part of England or part of Scotland down into modern times. The Romans had an empire but eventually that too vanished. The ruined fort spoke as loudly about the death and decay of empire as it did about Roman presence in the area — the two moments intra-acting in this place. And if the cross was intended as a sign of the triumph of Christianity and the Northumbrian church, polytheistic culture, that which was translated into the stone of the cross, lived on in the act of translation from column or obelisk to cross, or a different form of obelisk. It was ultimately stone that held these multiple pasts, peoples, and their ghosts together.

The sundial on the south side of the Bewcastle Cross is a reminder that the monument was always about time, and time by its very nature and the way we experience is about loss and the past. Like the fossils preserved in stone, the sundial carved into this stone and the movement of the sun around it make present the cycles of cosmic and biblical time, the intra-action of time past, present, and future. Time brings death and decay, the death of the men and women commemorated by the cross, of the Romans, the decay of the stone buildings from which the cross may have been quarried. In time stone too dies, returning to dust and earth, and we see this now at Bewcastle as the weathered and burnt cross-shaft crumbles, sheds its grains, and tilts evermore noticeably towards the earth that gave birth to it.

Hexham

Hadrian's Wall with its Roman ruins has always been a locus of contention and multiple narratives. From the time of its building, it has been a symbol of cultural, ethnic, or political difference. To the north were the Scots and the Picts, peoples who, like Guthlac's Welsh demons, were cast as uncivilized barbarians by authors such as Gildas and Bede. To those people north of the Wall it was to a certain extent a line of resistance. Indeed, one of the historical scenarios for the destruction of Fanum Cocidii has it having been overrun by the Picts and Scots, and the border area was certainly at the center of the recurring rebellions led by the Scots and Danes against William the Conqueror in the late eleventh and twelfth centuries. For those living south of the Wall, for Bede or William, or the centuries of English expansion that followed them, it was a symbol of conquest, empire, and a fantasy of English superiority. As Richard Hingley has written, "This myth of the origins of English civilization links the people south of the Wall directly to the imperial Romans [...] [and] the English myth of a direct inheritance from the Romans has informed many popular images of the Wall and the work of scholars [...] right down to the present day."[47] But stone can allow us to read the narratives on which this myth is based differently. The deeper history of stone can expose the frailties and failures of those written narratives of conquest and conversion that it is asked to support.

In the seventh and eighth centuries, Hadrian's Wall was the locus of ongoing intra-action and translation amongst times, lands, cultures, and peoples. The complexity of that encounter is demonstrated by recent work on sites such as Hexham (by Paul Bidwell),[48] and Wearmouth, Jarrow, and Escomb (by Sarah Semple and María de Los Ángeles Utrero).[49] These differing projects demonstrate: (A) we cannot rely on any one explanation for the translation or transformation of stone, site, and architecture over time; each site must be approached individually and understood as the work of individuals with differing

---

47 Hingley, *Hadrian's Wall: A Life*, 107. See also Nicholas Howe, "Rome: Capital of Anglo-Saxon England," *Journal of Medieval and Early Modern Studies* 34, no. 1 (2004): 147–72.
48 Bidwell, "A Survey of the Anglo-Saxon Crypt at Hexham and Its Reused Roman Stonework"; Bidwell, "Wilfrid and Hexham: The Anglo-Saxon Crypt."
49 Sarah Semple, in a personal communication. This work currently remains unpublished.

agendas;[50] (B) In some cases there are centuries of continuity and reuse or transformation of site that, as at Bewcastle, stretch back well beyond the Roman.[51] At St. Andrew's Hexham (Northumberland), built by Bishop Wilfrid between 672 and 678, two conflicting explanations for the massive reuse of stone from Corbridge and, to a lesser extent, Chesters and other sites, have been proposed. Some scholars have described it as entirely opportunistic as the Northumbrians in the seventh century did not have a history of building in stone and Corbridge and Chesters provided convenient sources for pre-cut and carved material for the taking.[52] Others have interpreted it as a calculated appropriation of *romanitas* — both imperial and Christian — on Wilfrid's part, a deliberate attempt to imitate something of the grandeur of the churches he had seen in Rome.[53]

All of the stone used at Hexham is sandstone and was quarried locally. In 1888 Charles C. Hodges determined that most of the stone used for St. Andrew's was redressed stone quarried by the Romans from the nearby stone quarries at Birkey Burn and Fallowfield Fell. Some stone of a slightly different color and softer and coarser than the reused Roman stone seems to have

---

50 Semple, *Perceptions of the Prehistoric*, 135–36. See also Tim Eaton, *Plundering the Past: Roman Stonework in Medieval Britain* (Stroud: Tempus, 2000), and Nicholas Howe, *Writing the Map of Anglo-Saxon England: Essays in Cultural Geography* (New Haven: Yale University Press, 2008).

51 Semple, *Perceptions of the Prehistoric*.

52 For a summary of the major arguments, see Eric Cambridge, "The Sources and Function of Wilfrid's Architecture at Ripon and Hexham," in *Wilfrid Abbot, Bishop, Saint*, ed. Higham, 136–51.

53 See, for example, Rosemary Cramp, "The Anglo-Saxons and Rome," *The Architectural and Archaeological Society of Durham and Northumberland* 3, no. 27 (1974): 27–37; Cambridge, "The Sources and Function of Wilfrid's Architecture at Ripon and Hexham"; and the essays in David P. Kirby, ed., *Saint Wilfrid at Hexham* (Newcastle upon Tyne: Oriel Press, 1974). Bidwell believes that the overall inspiration for Hexham was Mediterranean, but that "another was surely its setting amongst monuments to Roman power and its architectural achievements" ("Wilfrid and Hexham: The Anglo-Saxon Crypt," 162). Eaton understands Hexham as referring specifically to the new authority of the Roman church built on the old authority of imperial Rome (*Plundering the Past*, 125–27).

been newly quarried, but it too is local.⁵⁴ Paul Bidwell's work on Hexham has revealed that as far as the sort of stone that Wilfrid chose for reuse shows the picture is far from simple. Some reuse was opportunistic, but some was strategic, and all was selective. Specific structures that were quarried include a bridge, granary, mausoleum, and altars at Corbridge and a bridge and temple at Chesters. The bridges and mausoleum were methodically dismantled down to their foundations, which was far easier and cheaper than quarrying, cutting, and carving new stone, and the foundations, which would have been far more difficult to quarry, were left intact.⁵⁵ It is possible, however, that the mausoleum might have been believed to have specific imperial and/or Christian significance, like the Igel monument at Trier, which was erroneously associated with Constantine and Helena. If Wilfrid's biographer is to be believed, St. Andrew's, Hexham was a truly impressive structure:

> My feeble tongue will not permit me to enlarge here upon the depth of the foundations in the earth, and its crypt of wondrously dressed stone, and the manifold building above ground. Supported by various columns and many side aisles, and adorned with walls of notable length and height, surrounded by various winding passages with spiral stairs leading up and down; for our holy bishop, being taught by the Spirit of God thought on how to construct these buildings; nor have we heard of any other house on this side of the Alps built on such a scale.⁵⁶

---

54 Bidwell, "A Survey of the Anglo-Saxon Crypt at Hexham and Its Reused Roman Stonework," 80–81; Charles C. Hodges, *The Abbey of St Andrew Hexham* (London: the author, 1888).
55 Bidwell, "A Survey of the Anglo-Saxon Crypt at Hexham," 78, 81.
56 "Cuius profunditatem in terra cum domibus mire politis lapidibus fundatam et superterram multiplicem domum columnis variis et porticibus multis suffultam mirabilique longitudine et altitudine murorum ornatam et liniarum variis anfractibus viarum, aliquando sursum aliquando deorsum per cocleas circumductam, non est meae parvitatis hoc sermone explicare, quod sanctus pontifex noster, a spiritu Dei doctus opera facere excogitavit,

Figure 4. Fragments of a Roman frieze decorated with leaf and berry ornament, Hexham crypt, south passage. Photo by the author.

Figure 5. Fragments of a Roman frieze decorated with dentils, cable molding, and leaf and berry ornament, Hexham crypt, north passage. Photo by the author.

As this passage makes clear, however, it was the scale of the building and the quality of the dressed stone that was most impressive, not the source of the stone or its history.

Wilfrid's crypt is the only part of the original structure to survive largely intact, and it is as striking for its discordant appearance as it is for the neatly cut and dressed nature of much of its stonework. Flood described the Delhi Mosque as a heterotopia, a building in which a variety of elements "including those that are incompatible or incommensurate," are juxtaposed in a manner that creates a space that is simultaneously ordered yet filled with conflict,[57] and the same is true of the crypt at Hexham. While some of the original stonework has been moved or removed, the earliest descriptions of the crypt made shortly after its rediscovery in the eighteenth century indicate that its appearance was very close to what can be seen at Hexham today.[58] The walls include decorative blocks from four different Roman architectural friezes (figs. 4, 5) and a slab carved with a dedication to Apollo Maponus cut to form the lintel of a doorway in the north-side chamber (fig. 6).[59] The sections of frieze are at eye-level and grouped together and were clearly intended to compose a decorative display despite the fact that there is no unified pattern to them or the manner in which they have been inserted into the wall. Cut to pieces, grouped together in no apparent pattern, sometimes turned upside down or on their sides, these reused stones make no clear statement one way or the other about a link with or appropriation of empire, or the overturning of an older political or religious order. On the other hand, their reuse cannot be described simply as a mere matter of convenience as the frieze fragments are clearly arranged to be seen for some reason and other stones were certainly available

---

necque enim ullam domum aliam citra Alpes montes talem aedificatam audivimus." Eddius Stephanus, *The Life of Bishop Wilfrid*, 44–46.
57 Ibid., 7–8.
58 Bidwell, "A Survey of the Anglo-Saxon Crypt at Hexham," 55–60.
59 Ibid., 117, 120. Bidwell notes that it is possible that the crypt was originally covered with a fine layer of plaster but that the large, deeply cut, and "eye-catching" letters of the inscription had most likely shown through it.

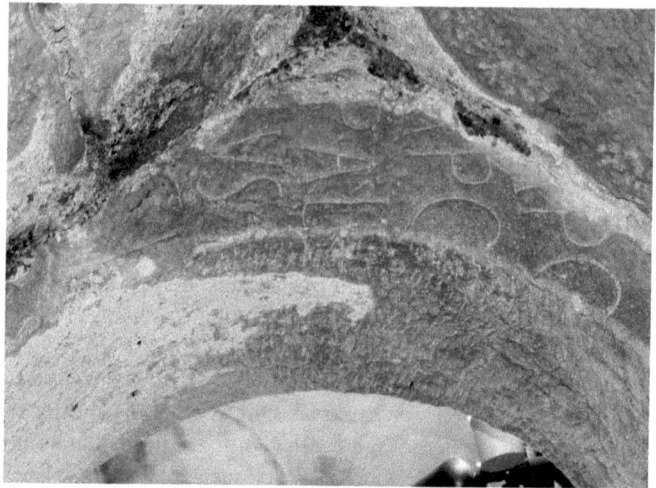

Figure 6. Roman dedicatory inscription used as a lintel, Hexham crypt, north side chamber. Photo by the author.

for use as the lintel of the doorway. If they make any statement, it is one of ambivalence, with representations of past cultures set alongside each other in a manner in which one can find both harmony (the repeated motifs of the friezes) and discord or incompatibility. As a heterotopian space, the crypt has connections with the Franks Casket discussed above, which some have suggested might have associations with Wilfrid and his other ecclesiastical center at Ripon.[60] On the casket, narrative fragments of different histories, places, and religions are juxtaposed in no narrative order and with no clear overall statement.[61]

A similar sort of heterotopian ambivalence emerges if we think about the fact that this is a crypt dug into the earth, a space for the display of an assemblage of relics, fragments of the

---

60 Ian Wood, "Ripon, Francia, and the Franks Casket in the Early Middle Ages," *Northern History* 26, no. 1 (1990): 1–19.
61 Catherine E. Karkov, *Imagining Anglo-Saxon England: Utopia, Heterotopia, Dystopia* (Woodbridge: Boydell & Brewer, 2020), 77–124.

dead, but fragments that have the living power of the saints. The stones that form the crypt were dug from the ground and in it they return to that ground, living reminders of the Roman and British pasts and land from which they have come. That double past is also both memorialized and kept present by the dedicatory inscription reconstructed as "To the god Maponus Apollos, Publius Ælius centurion of the Sixth Legion Victrix, willingly and deservedly fulfilled his vow.[62] Maponus was a god of youth in northern Britain and Gaul, a god with whom the Romans equated Apollo, the god of victory and death. Rather than making a clear statement of Christianity or romanitas, fragments of different gods, religions, and devotees brush up against each other in the crypt — gone, but still present. It is also a space in which the different meanings of translation intra-act. The translation of stone from earth to Roman building, to crypt, the translation of the relics of the saints, and the act of translation involved in reading the Latin inscription and its Romano-British references. Heterotopias place things together but they do not resolve them into a single unity, and the crypt is a particularly appropriate space for this type of encounter. The crypt is a physical place of the dead, of phantoms and ghosts, but it is also a psychic space of unresolved traumas and histories. It is a space that "buries a lost person or object or even a disavowed part of one's self or one's history, while keeping it psychically alive."[63] The violence inherent in the creation of nations and empires, the death and displacement of the peoples of the Andes, of the Inka, of the Britons are examples of disavowed or unresolved

---

62 "Deo Mapono Apollini Aelus centurio legionis VI Victricis uotum soluit libens merito". *Roman Inscriptions of Britain*, 1122: https://romaninscriptionsofbritain.org/inscriptions/1122.

63 Gabriele Schwab, *Haunting Legacies: Violent Histories and Transgenerational Trauma* (New York: Columbia University Press, 2010), 2. See also Nicholas Abraham and Maria Torok, *The Wolfman's Magic Word: A Cryptonymy*, trans. Nicholas T. Rand with a foreword by Jacques Derrida (Minneapolis: University of Minnesota Press, 1986) and *The Shell and the Kernel: Renewals of Psychoanalysis*, vol. 1, ed and trans. Nicholas T. Rand (Chicago: University of Chicago Press, 1994).

histories that encrypt trauma.[64] That violence was played out in the landscape around Hexham in the Battle of Heavenfield at which King Oswald, a Northumbrian Constantine, won victory over the Welsh "pagan tyrant" Cadwallon ap Cadfa, thereby uniting Northumbria. The Hexham community celebrated the vigil of Oswald's feast at the church of St. Oswald-in-Lee four miles from the abbey. At the very time that Wilfrid was building Hexham, however, there were multiple revolts of and battles against the Mercians, the Irish (Scotti), and most especially the Picts, the peoples to the north of Hadrian's Wall: the battle of Two Rivers took place in 670, and there were further battles against the Picts in 680 and 682, as well as against the Mercians in 679, and finally the Battle of Nechtansmere in 685, the battle that marked the beginning of Pictish independence and a decline in the power of Northumbria.[65] Stone at Hexham held ghosts, but it was also a reminder that the very real and tangible conflicts of the past refused to go away.

Conclusion, by way of Carlisle

Nechtansmere brings us to Carlisle and also back to Bewcastle and Hexham and Northumbrian ambitions. Carlisle under the Romans had a large military population, with two forts, Luguvalium, located in the area between the Eden and Carwent rivers, and Stanwix (now a suburb of the city) on the north bank of the Eden. It also housed a significant population of merchants and traders. Its coastal setting no doubt contributed to its size and diversity. An impressive collection of sculpture, most notably

---

64 Karkov, *Imagining Anglo-Saxon England*. See also Donna Beth Ellard, *Anglo-Saxon(ist) Pasts, postSaxon Futures* (Earth: punctum books, 2019).

65 Bede, *Historia ecclesiastica*, 4.26 (Colgrave and Mynors, ed. and trans., 428–29): "From this time the hopes and strength of the English kingdom began to 'ebb and fall away'. For the Picts recovered their own land which the English had formerly held, while the Irish who lived in Britain and some part of the British nation recovered their independence." On Wilfrid and the Britons, especially the Picts, see Thomas M Charles-Edwards, "Wilfrid and the Celts," in *Wilfrid Abbot, Bishop, Saint*, ed. Higham, 243–59.

the beautifully carved tombstones of the trading families as well as many other types of artefacts survive from the Roman period. The sculptures have been shown to have been highly influential on seventh- and eighth-century sculpture in the area, most notably on the figural panels of the Bewcastle Cross. In particular, scholars have noted echoes between the ways in which Roman and Northumbrian figures inhabit the stone niches and other spaces into which they are set.[66] Nothing now survives of the Roman architecture of Carlisle, but William of Malmesbury and other post-Conquest sources record that ruined Roman buildings were still standing in the eleventh and twelfth centuries.[67] By the seventh century, Carlisle was a center of ecclesiastical power, in which the remains of Rome were a wonder if not an object of admiration. Both the anonymous *Life of Saint Cuthbert* and Bede's *Prose Life* of the saint record that on May 20, 685, while Cuthbert and the Northumbrian queen Iurminburh awaited the outcome of the Battle of Nechtansmere in the city, they were shown the "the city wall and the well [or fountain] formerly built in a wonderful manner by the Romans."[68] It was at that moment that Cuthbert had his vision of Ecgfrith's death in the Battle of Nechtansmere. In the *Historia Ecclesiastica,* Bede describes how his death occurred: "The enemy feigned flight and lured the king into some narrow passes in the midst of inaccessible mountains; there he was killed with the greater part

---

66 Henig, "*Murem civitatis et fontem in ea a Romanis mire olim constructum*"; Jane Hawkes "*Iuxta Morem Romanorum*: Stone and Sculpture in the Style of Rome," in *Anglo-Saxon Styles,* ed. Catherine E. Karkov and George Hardin Brown (Albany: SUNY Press, 2003), 60–100. For the possible influence of Roman art from the area on the Ruthwell Cross see Karkov, *The Art of Anglo-Saxon England,* 80.

67 Mike McCarthy, "The Roman Town of Luguvalium and the Post-Roman Settlement," in *Carlisle and Cumbria,* ed. McCarthy and Weston, 1–10, at 9; Henig, "Murem civitatis et fontem in ea a Romanis mire olim constructum," 13.

68 *Vita Sancti Cuthberti Auctore Anonymo & Vita Sancti Cuthberti Auctore Beda,* in *Two Lives of Saint Cuthbert,* ed. and trans., Bertram Colgrave (Cambridge: Cambridge University Press, 1940), 122–23: "murum ciuitatis, et fontem in ea a Romanis mire olim constructum."

of the forces he had taken with him."⁶⁹ While the battle took place far to the north of Hadrian's Wall, the description of the landscape of Ecgfrith's death ironically recalls that of the Wall's craggy outcrops and narrow passes; indeed part of its purpose was to control traffic between north and south by funneling it through strategically placed narrow stone gateways. The irony is furthered by the multiple descriptions in the writings of Gildas, Bede, Felix, the *Beowulf* poet, and others of the Britons emerging from, fleeing into, or lurking in rocks, fens, and mountains. The Britons live comfortably in stone and earth, these texts tell us, and Ecgfrith dies when he is lured into this world.

The simultaneity of the queen admiring the remains of one colonizing culture while the king, representative of a second such culture, dies in battle demonstrates the intra-action of the two cultures, the rise and fall of ambitions of conquest, and the stones of Carlisle and of Necthansmere, along with those of Hexham and Bewcastle. The land that had given birth to the stones of the structures built in these places now reclaimed the aspirations of those who had constructed them, and the historical narratives they had hoped they would convey. In their turn, of course, the stones of Bewcastle, Hexham, and Carlisle would become mere waste to be quarried by later conquerors or conquering ideologies, and that process continued for centuries. Still, the ruined and crumbling settlements and buildings of the wall were also an enduring sign of the fall of empires and cultures, the ghosts of the past, of wasted lives, displaced peoples, and ruined buildings that would not leave. They were the foundation of human stories, a record of human endeavor, but a record too of deeper histories.

---

69 Bede, *Historia ecclesiastica,* 4.26 (Colgrave and Mynors, ed. and trans., 428–29): "introductus est simulantibus fugam hostibus in angustias inaccessorum montium, et cum maxima parte copiarum quas secum adduxerat, extinctus."

Bibliography

Primary

Bede. *History of the Abbots of Wearmouth and Jarrow*. In *Abbots of Wearmouth and Jarrow*, edited by Christopher Grocock and Ian N. Wood, 22–76. Oxford: Clarendon Press, 2013.

Eddius Stephanus. *The Life of Bishop Wilfrid by Eddius Stephanus*. Edited and translated by Bertram Colgrave. Cambridge: Cambridge University Press, 1927.

Gildas. *The Ruin of Britain and Other Documents*. Translated by Michael Winterbottom. London: Phillimore, 1978.

Isidore of Seville. *Etymologies*. In *The Etymologies of Isidore of Seville*, translated by Stephen A. Barney, W.J. Lewis, J.A. Beach, and Oliver Berghof, 34–405. Cambridge: Cambridge University Press, 2006. The Latin Library: http://www.thelatinlibrary.com/isidore/16.shtml.

Old English Shorter Poems, Volume 2: *Wisdom and Lyric*. Edited and translated by Robert E. Bjork. Cambridge: Harvard University Press, 2014.

Vita Sancti Cuthberti Auctore Anonymo & Vita Sancti Cuthberti Auctore Beda. In *Two Lives of Saint Cuthbert*, edited and translated by Bertram Colgrave, 59–306. Cambridge: Cambridge University Press, 1940.

Secondary

Abraham, Nicholas, and Maria Torok. *The Shell and the Kernel: Renewals of Psychoanalysis*. Volume 1. Edited and translated by Nicholas T. Rand. Chicago: University of Chicago Press, 1994.

———. *The Wolfman's Magic Word: A Cryptonymy*. Translated by Nicholas Rand with a forward by Jacques Derrida. Minneapolis: University of Minnesota Press, 1986.

Austin, Paul S. *Bewcastle and Old Penrith: A Roman Outpost Fort and a Frontier Vicus*. Kendal: Cumberland and Westmorland Antiquarian and Archaeological Society, 1991.

Bailey, Richard N., and Rosemary Cramp. *Corpus of Anglo-Saxon Stone Sculpture*, Volume 2: *Cumberland, Westmorland*

and *Lancashire North-of-the-Sands*. Oxford: Oxford University Press, 1988.

Barad, Karen. *Meeting the Universe Halfway: Quantum Physics and the Entanglement of Matter and Meaning*. Durham: Duke University Press, 2006. DOI: 10.1515/9780822388128.

Bidwell, Paul. "A Survey of the Anglo-Saxon Crypt at Hexham and Its Reused Roman Stonework." *Archaeologia Aeliana* 5th ser. 39 (2010): 53–145.

———. "Wilfrid and Hexham: the Anglo-Saxon Crypt." In *Wilfrid Abbot, Bishop, Saint: Papers from the 1300th Anniversary Conference,* edited by Nicholas J. Higham, 152–62. Donington: Shaun Tyas, 2013.

Cambridge, Eric. "The Sources and Function of Wilfrid's Architecture at Ripon and Hexham." *Wilfrid Abbot, Bishop, Saint: Papers from the 1300th Anniversary Conference,* edited by Nicholas J. Higham, 136–51. Donington: Shaun Tyas, 2013.

Charles-Edwards, Thomas M. "Wilfrid and the Celts." In *Wilfrid Abbot, Bishop, Saint: Papers from the 1300th Anniversary Conference,* edited by Nicholas J. Higham, 243–59. Donington: Shaun Tyas, 2013.

Clarke, Catherine A.M. *Literary Landscapes and the Idea of England 700–1400*. Cambridge: D.S. Brewer, 2006.

Cohen, Jeffrey Jerome. *Stone: An Ecology of the Inhuman*. Minneapolis: University of Minnesota Press, 2015. DOI: 10.5749/minnesota/9780816692576.001.0001.

Colgrave, Bertram, ed. *Felix's Life of Guthlac*. Cambridge: Cambridge University Press, 1956.

Cramp, Rosemary. *County Durham and Northumberland, Corpus of Anglo-Saxon Stone Sculpture*. Volume 1. Oxford: Oxford University Press, 1984.

———. "The Anglo-Saxons and Rome." *The Architectural and Archaeological Society of Durham and Northumberland* 3, no. 27 (1974): 27–37.

Crowley, Patrick R. *The Phantom Image: Seeing the Dead in Ancient Rome*. Chicago: Chicago University Press, 2019. DOI: 10.7208/chicago/9780226648323.001.0001.

Day, J.B.W., et al. *Geology of the Country around Bewcastle.* London: Her Majesty's Stationary Office, 1970.

Dean, Carolyn. *A Culture of Stone: Inka Perspectives on Rock.* Durham: Duke University Press, 2010. DOI: 10.1515/9780822393177.

———. "The Inka Married the Earth: Integrated Outcrops and the Making of Place." *The Art Bulletin* 89, no. 3 (2007): 502–18. DOI: 10.1080/00043079.2007.10786358.

Eaton, Tim. *Plundering the Past: Roman Stonework in Medieval Britain.* Stroud: Tempus, 2000.

Ellard, Donna Beth. *Anglo-Saxon(ist) Pasts, postSaxon Futures.* Earth: punctum books, 2019. DOI: 10.21983/P3.0262.1.00.

Estes, Heide. *Anglo-Saxon Literary Landscapes: Ecotheory and the Environmental Imagination.* Amsterdam: Amsterdam University Press, 2017. DOI: 10.5040/9789048551408.

Flood, Finbarr B. *Objects of Translation: Material Culture and Medieval "Hindu–Muslim" Encounter.* Princeton: Princeton University Press, 2009.

Gillam, J.P., et al. *The Roman Bath-House at Bewcastle, Cumbria.* Kendal: Cumberland and Westmorland Antiquarian and Archaeological Society, 1993.

Haraway, Donna. "The Promises of Monsters: A Regenerative Politics for Inappropriate/d Others." In *The Haraway Reader,* 23–124. New York: Routledge, 2014.

Hawkes, Jane. "*Iuxta Morem Romanorum*: Stone and Sculpture in the Style of Rome." In *Anglo-Saxon Styles,* edited by Catherine E. Karkov and George Hardin Brown, 60–100. Albany: SUNY Press, 2003.

Henig, Martin. "*Murem civitatis et fontem in ea a Romanis mire olim constructum*: The Arts of Rome in Carlisle and the civitatis of the Carvetii and Their Influence." In *Carlisle and Cumbria: Roman and Medieval Architecture, Art and Archaeology,* edited by Mike McCarthy and David Weston, British Archaeological Association Conference Transactions 27, 11–28. Leeds: Maney Publishing, 2004.

Higham, Nicholas J., ed. *Wilfrid Abbot, Bishop, Saint: Papers from the 1300th Anniversary Conference*. Donington: Shaun Tyas, 2013.

Hingley, Richard. *Hadrian's Wall: A Life*. Oxford: Oxford University Press, 2012. DOI: 10.1093/acprof:oso/9780199641413.001.0001.

Hodges, Charles C. *The Abbey of St Andrew Hexham*. London: the author, 1888.

Howe, Nicholas. "Rome: Capital of Anglo-Saxon England." *Journal of Medieval and Early Modern Studies* 34, no. 1 (2004): 147–72. DOI: 10.1215/10829636-34-1-147.

———. *Writing the Map of Anglo-Saxon England: Essays in Cultural Geography*. New Haven: Yale University Press, 2008.

Kaiser, Birgit Mara, and Kathrin Thiele, eds. *Diffracted Worlds — Diffracted Readings: Onto-epistemologies and the Critical Humanities*. London: Routledge, 2018.

Karkov, Catherine E. *Imagining Anglo-Saxon England: Utopia, Heterotopia, Dystopia*. Woodbridge: Boydell & Brewer, 2020. DOI: 10.1017/9781787448940.

Karkov, Catherine E., and George Hardin Brown, eds. *Anglo-Saxon Styles*. Albany: SUNY Press, 2003.

Kirby, David. P., ed. *Saint Wilfrid at Hexham*. Newcastle upon Tyne: Oriel Press, 1974.

McCarthy, Mike. "The Roman Town of Luguvalium and the Post-Roman Settlement." In *Carlisle and Cumbria: Roman and Medieval Architecture, Art and Archaeology*, edited by Mike McCarthy and David Weston, British Archaeological Association Conference Transactions 27, 1–10. Leeds: Maney Publishing, 2004.

McCarthy, Mike, and David Weston, eds. *Carlisle and Cumbria: Roman and Medieval Architecture, Art and Archaeology*. British Archaeological Association Conference Transactions 27. Leeds: Maney Publishing, 2004.

Michelet, Fabienne. *Creation, Migration, and Conquest: Imaginary Geography and Sense of Space in Old English Literature*. Oxford: Oxford University Press, 2006.

Ó Carragáin, Éamonn. *Ritual and the Rood: Liturgical Images and the Old English Poems of the Dream of the Rood Tradition.* London and Toronto: The British Library and University of Toronto Press, 2005.

Ortiz Rescaniere, Alejandro. "Mito de la Escuela." In *Ideología Mesiánica del Mundo Andino,* edited by Juan M. Ossio Acuña, 237–50. Lima: Ignacio Prado Pastor, 1973.

Orton, Fred, and Ian Wood, with Clare A. Lees. *Fragments of History: Rethinking the Ruthwell and Bewcastle Monuments.* Manchester: Manchester University Press, 2007.

Schreffler, Michael J. "Inca Architecture from the Andes to the Adriatic: Pedro Sancho's Description of Cuzco." *Renaissance Quarterly* 67, no. 4 (2014): 1191–223. DOI: 10.1086/679781.

Semple, Sarah J. "Illustrations of Damnation in Late Anglo-Saxon Manuscripts." *Anglo-Saxon England* 32 (2003): 31–45. DOI: 10.1017/S0263675103000115.

———. *Perceptions of the Prehistoric in Anglo-Saxon England: Religion, Ritual, and Rulership in the Landscape.* Oxford: Oxford University Press, 2013.

Serres, Michel. *Statues: The Second Book of Foundations.* Translated by Randolph Burks. London: Bloomsbury, 2015.

Schwab, Gabriele. *Haunting Legacies: Violent Histories and Transgenerational Trauma.* New York: Columbia University Press, 2010.

Siewers, Alfred K. "Landscapes of Conversion: Guthlac's Mound and Grendel's Mere as Expressions of Anglo-Saxon Nation-Building." *Viator* 34 (2003): 1–39. DOI: 10.1484/J.VIATOR.2.300380.

Ward, J. "Early Dinantian Evaporates of the Easton-I Well, Solway Basin, onshore Cumbria, England," in *The Petroleum Geology of the Irish Sea and Adjacent Areas,* eds. Neil S. Meadows, S.P. Trueblood, M. Hardman and G. Cowan, Geological Society Special Publication 124, 277–96. Bath: The Geological Society, 1997. DOI: 10.1144/GSL.SP.1997.124.01.17.

Wood, Ian. "Ripon, Francia, and the Franks Casket in the Early Middle Ages." *Northern History* 26, no. 1 (1990): 1–19. DOI: 10.1179/007817290790175872.

Zalasiewicz, Jan. *The Planet in a Pebble: A Journey into Earth's Deep History.* Oxford: Oxford University Press, 2012.

3

Narratio Probabilis in Early Medieval Historiography: A Reconsideration

Justin Lake

To what extent did early medieval historians give themselves license to invent plausible fictions based on their understanding of the precepts of *narratio probabilis* laid down by the rhetorical handbooks of antiquity? This question arises out of certain statements found in Cicero's *De inventione* (written c. 91 BCE) and the pseudo-Ciceronian *Rhetorica ad Herennium* (written 86–82 BCE), which, together with the commentary on the *De inventione* by the fourth-century Neoplatonist and later Christian polymath Marius Victorinus,[1] contained the most detailed, widely available, and influential treatments of rhetorical invention in the Early Middle Ages.[2] In all three of these texts history is defined as a type of *narratio*, specifically a "narrative of past

1 *C. Marius Victorinus: Commenta in Ciceronis Rhetorica*, ed. Thomas Riesenweber, Bibliotheca Teubneriana (Berlin: de Gruyter, 2013). See also the monumental commentary by Riesenweber: *C. Marius Victorinus, Commenta in Ciceronis Rhetorica: Prolegomena und kritischer Kommentar*, 2 vols., Untersuchungen zur antiken Literatur und Geschichte, Bd. 120.1–2 (Berlin: De Gruyter, 2015).

2 See in particular John O. Ward, "Cicero's *De inventione* and the *Rhetorica ad Herennium*: Commentaries and Contexts," in *The Rhetoric of Cicero in its Medieval and Renaissance Commentary Tradition*, ed. Virginia Cox and John O. Ward (Boston and Leiden: Brill, 2006), 3–69 and *Ciceronian Rheto-*

events" (*narratio rerum gestarum*), and, in contradistinction to *fabula* and *argumentum*, a narrative of events that actually happened.³ Each also places history into the third of three categories of narratives, namely, those which are "separate from civil cases" (*remotum a civilibus causis*).⁴ And each enumerates three virtues of narrative: brevity, clarity, and plausibility.⁵ Whether or not these three virtues were meant to apply to *historia* (a subdivision of the third type of *narratio*) is not entirely clear. Both Cicero and the author of the *Rhetorica ad Herennium* seem to be referring specifically to forensic or deliberative speeches when discussing the virtues, and thus not necessarily prescribing a standard of mere plausibility for historical narratives.⁶ Crucially, however, Marius Victorinus, whose commentary on the *De inventione* was often accorded equal or greater importance than the source text itself in the Middle Ages, believed that all three virtues of narrative applied to the third category of narrative, and hence to history:

---

    ric in Treatise, Scholion, and Commentary, Typologie des sources du moyen âge occidental 58 (Turnhout: Brepols, 1995).

3 Cicero, *De inventione*, 1.19.27, ed. and trans. H.M. Hubbell, *Cicero, "De inventione"* (Cambridge: Harvard University Press, 1949), 54: "Historia est gesta res, ab aetatis nostrae memoria remota." Pseudo-Cicero's *Rhetorica ad Herennium* has an identical definition at 1.8.13, ed. and trans. Harry Caplan (Cambridge: Harvard University Press, 1964), 22. Cf. Victorinus, *Commenta in Ciceronis Rhetorica*, 1.19.27, ed. Riesenweber, 69: "Deinde historia est, inquit, quae res veras continet, sed a nostra memoria remotas."

4 Cicero, *De inventione*, 1.19.27, ed. Hubbell, 54: "Tertium genus est remotum a civilibus causis"; *Rhetorica ad Herennium*, 1.8.12, ed. and trans. Caplan, 22: "Tertium genus est id quod a causa civili remotum est."

5 *Rhetorica ad Herennium*, 1.9.14, ed. and trans. Caplan, 24: "Tres res convenit habere narrationem: ut brevis, ut dilucida, ut veri similis sit."

6 Cicero seems to be making a break from his discussion of *historia*, *argumentum*, and *fabula* to discuss forensic oratory at *De inventione*, 1.20.28, ed. Hubbell, 56: "Nunc de narratione ea, quae causae continet expositionem, dicendum videtur. Oportet igitur eam tres habere res: ut brevis, ut aperta, ut probabilis sit." The same seems to be true of the author of the *Rhetorica ad Herennium* at 1.8.13, ed. and trans. Caplan, 24: "Verum haec in exercendo transigentur; illud quod ad veritatem pertinet quomodo tractari conveniat aperiamus."

These three virtues of oratorical narrative, therefore, can apply also to that type of narrative that is outside of civil cases. For history ought to be concise in exposition, and clear, and plausible, as Sallust attributed all of these to himself in *Catiline*.[7]

Victorinus's opinion is important because, in order to endow a narrative with the rhetorical virtue of plausibility, circumstantial details that were not true but seemed to be true could be invented; indeed, they virtually had to be.[8] Whether or not this represented Cicero's own view on how to write history — to say nothing of the views of the authors of classical and late-antique Latin histories — is difficult to say, but the belief that history was a type of narrative subject to rhetorical amplification through the "discovery" (*inventio*) of merely plausible details could easily be read into both the *De inventione* and the *Rhetorica ad Herennium*. Did early medieval historians, therefore, take the statements about *narratio probabilis* in these texts as a license to evade the constraining standard of truthfulness for the laxer requirement of mere plausibility?

Because medieval historians invariably claimed to be writing the truth rather than purveying plausible fictions,[9] this question can for the most part only be approached indirectly, by looking at the intellectual formation of authors, the traces of rhetorical

---

7 *Commenta in Ciceronis Rhetorica*, 1.20.28, 70: "Igitur tres istae virtutes narrationis oratoriae convenire possunt et illi narrationi, quae extra civiles causas est. Namque historia et brevis esse debet in expositione et aperta et probabilis, ut Sallustius sibi omnia in Catilina tribuit."

8 Cicero, *De inventione*, 1.7.9, ed. Hubbell, 18: "Inventio est excogitatio rerum verarum aut veri similium quae causam probabilem reddant"; *Rhetorica ad Herennium*, 1.2.3, ed. and trans. Caplan, 6: "Inventio est excogitatio rerum verarum aut veri similium quae causam probabilem reddant."

9 See Gertrud Simon, "Untersuchungen zur Topik der Widmungsbriefe mittelalterlicher Geschichtsschreiber bis zum Ende des 12. Jahrhunderts," *Archiv für Diplomatik* 4 (1958): 52–119 and 5/6 (1959/60): 73–153, and Marie Schulz, *Die Lehre von der historischen Methode bei den Geschichtsschreibern des Mittelalters (VI.-XIII. Jahrhundert)* (Berlin and Leipzig: W. Rothschild, 1909), 15–42.

amplification found in their works, and their own statements about history-writing. There is ample evidence that by the twelfth century many medieval Latin historians had acquired a sophisticated understanding of classical rhetoric, which provided theoretical justification for the introduction of all kinds of plausible or verisimilar material into historical accounts.[10] Roger Ray has argued that the Ciceronian conception of history as a rhetorical genre subject to amplification (*exaedificatio*) in terms of both content (*res*) and words (*verba*) was widely shared throughout the Early Middle Ages.[11] I am convinced, however, that while the invention of plausible fictions was always a latent potentiality of medieval history-writing, the conscious application of rhetorical invention to history only emerged in the late tenth century. It is highly likely, moreover, that this shift was brought about by a change in the nature of rhetorical instruction in the Latin West, specifically an increasing focus on invention as a branch of rhetoric worthy of attention on the same scale as style (*elocutio*).

The question of the role of plausible fictions in medieval history cannot be detached from the theory and practice of classical historiography, which inevitably shaped the contours of medieval history-writing. Unfortunately, there is no consensus on the degree to which classical historians allowed themselves

---

10 Matthew Kemphsall, *Rhetoric and the Writing of History, 400–1500* (Manchester: Manchester University Press, 2011); Nancy Partner, *Serious Entertainments: The Writing of History in Twelfth-Century England* (Chicago: University of Chicago Press, 1977); Jeanette Beer, *Narrative Conventions of Truth in the Middle Ages* (Geneva: Droz, 1981); Ruth Morse, *Truth and Convention in the Middle Ages: Rhetoric, Representation, and Reality* (Cambridge: Cambridge University Press, 1991); Monika Otter, *Inventiones: Fiction and Referentiality in Twelfth-Century English Historical Writing* (Chapel Hill: University of North Carolina Press, 1996). Apart from Kemphsall, all of these works focus on the twelfth century or later and give relatively little attention to early medieval historical writing.

11 Roger Ray, "The Triumph of Greco-Roman Rhetorical Assumptions in pre-Carolingian Historiography," in *The Inheritance of Historiography 350–900*, ed. Christopher Holdsworth and T.P. Wiseman (Exeter: University of Exeter Press, 1986), 67–84.

the license to invent. On the one hand, it was generally accepted in antiquity that speeches could be freely composed; this procedure had been licensed by the authority of no less a figure than Thucydides (c. 460–400 BCE), who, in the opening section of his history of the Peloponnesian War, explained that his practice was "to make the speakers say what was in my opinion demanded of them by the various occasions, of course adhering as closely as possible to the general sense of what they really said."[12] But the invention of merely plausible content outside of set-piece orations is nowhere explicitly endorsed by Roman historians, even if there are reasons to think that it happened.

Perhaps the best-known discussion of history-writing in classical Latin literature is found in Book 2 of Cicero's *De oratore*, where Marcus Antonius, who is usually taken to be a mouthpiece for Cicero's own views about how to write history, states that:

> Everybody knows that the first law of history is not daring to say anything false; that the second is daring to say everything that is true; that there should be no suggestion of partiality, none of animosity when you write. These foundations (*fundamenta*) are, of course, familiar to everyone. The actual superstructure (*exaedificatio*) is a matter of content (*rebus*) and words (*verbis*).[13]

This seems to introduce a new wrinkle: what did it mean for the *exaedificatio* to be constructed out of *res*? Were historians, like orators, entitled to build up their narratives through the inven-

---

[12] Translation in Richard Crawley, *The History of the Peloponnesian War by Thucydides* (London: Longmans, Green, and Co., 1874), 14.

[13] Cicero, *De oratore*, 2.62–3: "Nam quis nescit primam esse historiae legem, ne quid falsi dicere audeat, deinde ne quid veri non audeat? Ne quae suspicio gratiae sit in scribendo? Ne quae simultatis? Haec scilicet fundamenta nota sunt omnibus; ipsa autem exaedificatio posita est in rebus et verbis." Translation in James M. May and Jakob Wisse, *Cicero: On the Ideal Orator* (Oxford: Oxford University Press, 2001). For the Latin of *De oratore*, see A.S. Wilkins, ed., *M. Tulli Ciceronis Rhetorica*, vol. 1 (Oxford: Clarendon Press, 1902), 88.

tion of merely plausible details? The prevailing view of most of twentieth-century scholarship was that the theoretical underpinnings of classical historiography were not radically different from our own.[14] This understanding applied to Cicero's statements on the relationship between rhetoric and historiography as well. Peter Brunt, for example, was unfazed by Antonius's mention of *exaedificatio* through *res,* explaining it as a reference to chronological and geographical exposition, not the invention of plausible, but untrue, historical content.[15] Charles William Fornara argued that the process of amplification described by Cicero "subserves the laws of history and is tested by the standard of the truth."[16] A vigorous challenge to this comparatively sanguine view of the relationship of rhetoric and history was mounted by T.P. Wiseman in *Clio's Cosmetics* (1979), and Anthony Woodman in *Rhetoric and Classical Historiography* (1988). Wiseman argued that later Roman annalists (most importantly Gnaeus Gellius and Valerius Antias) had taken a core of true material about early Rome and elaborated upon it through the techniques of rhetorical invention.[17] For Wiseman, the boundary between oratory and history-writing was permeable, and it was only the most rigorous historians, such as Polybius, who did not allow space for free invention when necessary.[18] Woodman

---

14 See in particular Charles William Fornara, *The Nature of History in Ancient Greece and Rome* (Berkeley: University of California Press, 1988), 91–141; Peter A. Brunt, "Cicero and Historiography," in *Studies in Greek History and Thought* (Oxford: Clarendon Press, 1993), 181–209.
15 Brunt, "Cicero and Historiography," 187.
16 Fornara, *The Nature of History,* 136.
17 T.P. Wiseman, *Clio's Cosmetics: Three Studies in Greco-Roman Literature* (Leicester: Leicester University Press, 1979), esp. 9–40. On Gellius, see the introductory article by John Briscoe in *The Fragments of the Roman Historians,* vol. 1, ed. John Briscoe and Tim J. Cornell (Oxford: Oxford University Press, 2013), 252–55, where Briscoe concludes that "Gellius must be credited with expansion, and perhaps invention, on a huge scale" (254). For Valerius Antias, see John Rich in *Fragments,* ed. Cornell, vol. 1, 293–304: "Antias' history was replete with inventions and exaggerations, both his own and his predecessors.'"
18 T.P. Wiseman, "Lying Historians: Seven Types of Mendacity," in *Lies and Fiction in the Ancient World,* ed. Christopher Gill and T.P. Wiseman (Liver-

argued that classical historiography was in essence a branch of rhetoric, and that just as orators were allowed to invent plausible details to strengthen their case, historians practiced *inventio* on a large scale — not merely padding out events that were known to have happened, but inventing them wholesale. Moreover, in an adventurous reading of Antonius's disquisition on history-writing in the *De oratore,* he argued that *exaedificatio* as used by Antonius refers to content rather than style (thus making amplification a matter of creating historical events rather than cloaking them in pleasing language), and that truth in historical writing was largely understood as freedom from partiality and bias rather than strict factual accuracy.[19]

In the last three decades opinion has inclined towards the Wiseman and Woodman view of history as literature,[20] but there are reasons to be skeptical of the notion that Roman historians practiced outright invention on a large scale. Cynthia Damon has noted the many practical constraints against *inventio*: refutation by other authorities, the restricted scope of *inventio* when it was actually practiced (*inventio* did not create the event, but the description), and the strong evidence that ancient audiences were able to spot rhetorical invention easily and thus distinguish it from fact.[21] Simon J. Northwood has argued persuasively that the discussion at *De oratore* 2.51–64 is about style and not content, and that the *fundamenta* mentioned by Antonius are the laws of history — most importantly, the requirement to tell the truth — to which the process of *exaedificatio* was wholly sub-

---

pool: Liverpool University Press, 1993), 122–46, esp. 132–34.

19 Anthony Woodman, *Rhetoric and Classical Historiography: Four Studies* (London: Croom Helm, 1988), 70–95.

20 See, for example, the discussion of this issue in *Latin Historians,* ed. Christina Shuttleworth Kraus and Anthony J. Woodman (Oxford: Oxford University Press, 1997), 5–6. Rohert W. Cape, "Persuasive History: Roman Rhetoric and Historiography," in *Roman Eloquence: Rhetoric in Society and Literature,* ed. William J. Dominik (London: Routledge, 1997), 212–28, accepts many of the conclusions of Wiseman and Woodman.

21 Cynthia Damon, "Rhetoric and Historiography," in *A Companion to Roman Rhetoric,* ed. William Dominik and Jon Hall (Malden: Wiley-Blackwell, 2007), 439–50.

ordinate.²² And in a blistering attack on the assumptions of the Wiseman-Woodman school, J.E. Lendon makes the case that Latin historians were considerably more concerned with the truth than much modern scholarship gives them credit for.²³

Where does this leave us? The most reasonable conclusion is that while expansion or amplification, particularly in speeches and descriptive passages, was a licit and virtually inevitable, practice, invention of events themselves was less tolerated. This is the impression we get from the one case in which we can actually examine in detail the process by which a classical historian rewrote the work of his predecessor, namely Livy's use of Polybius in the *Ab urbe condita*.²⁴ The Roman historian, as Lendon puts it, "practiced his creativity within a tight box of acknowledged fact."²⁵

Outside of the composition of chronicles, history-writing in the Latin West ebbed and then virtually disappeared in the fifth and sixth centuries, and a thin thread connects the canonical works of classical Latin historiography to their early medieval descendants.²⁶ At the same time, the political disruptions of the fifth and sixth centuries brought the Roman school tradition to

---

22 Simon J. Northwood, "Cicero's *De Oratore* 2.51–64 and Rhetoric in Historiography," *Mnemosyne* 61, no. 2 (2008): 228–44. Northwood is also surely correct that the famous letter to L. Lucceius (*Ad familiares*, 5.12) confirms, rather than undermines, the paramount importance of the *leges historiae*. On this point, see also Fornara, *The Nature of History*, 101–2.

23 J.E. Lendon, "Historians without History: Against Roman Historiography," in *The Cambridge Companion to the Roman Historians*, ed. Andrew Feldherr (Cambridge: Cambridge University Press, 2009), 41–61.

24 P.G. Walsh, *Livy: His Historical Aims and Methods* (Cambridge: Cambridge University Press, 1961), 138–90 and passim; T.J. Luce, review of Woodman, *Rhetoric and Classical Historiography: Four Studies*, *Phoenix* 43, no. 2 (1989): 177: "the added touches are not extensive, and do not impair the essential integrity of the Polybian narrative;" Lendon, "Historians without History," 44: "innocent rhetorical gussying and cosmetic surgery."

25 Lendon, "Historians without History," 43.

26 Walter Goffart, *The Narrators of Barbarian History (A.D. 550–800): Jordanes, Gregory of Tours, Bede, and Paul the Deacon* (Princeton: Princeton University Press, 1988), 117–8: "The historiographic 'tradition' that Gregory [of Tours] looked back to was as far removed from him as if a fiction writer today were to undertake to be the first novelist since Jane Austen."

an end. Classical rhetoric survived in derivative handbooks such as Martianus Capella's *De nuptiis,* Fortunatinus's *Ars rhetorica,* Cassiodorus's *Institutiones,* and Isidore of Seville's *Etymologiae,* but the institutional and political framework that made rhetoric the pinnacle of literary studies in imperial Rome had vanished. To some extent, therefore, early medieval historians reinvented the genre of historiography as they went, picking and choosing between classical and late-antique models, while incorporating vernacular traditions as well, and in many cases puzzling modern readers with finished products that depart from more familiar classical genre distinctions (hence the debate about whether or not there is such a thing as "national" history among the barbarian successor states). We cannot, therefore, assume that the beliefs about the interrelationship of history and rhetoric expounded by Cicero in the first century BCE and appreciated anew by the *litterati* of the twelfth century—the great age of Latin historiography—were widely shared during the intervening centuries.

For most of the Early Middle Ages, it is difficult to find evidence for the conscious application of rhetorical invention based on an understanding of the doctrine of *narratio probabilis.* Invented speech, for example, can be found in both histories and saints' lives, but it tends to take the form either of direct dialogue or sermons and expositions of religious doctrine, neither of which necessarily entails the application of the techniques of classical rhetoric. In his classic study of the dramatic scene in early medieval narrative, Joaquín Martínez Pizarro demonstrated that direct dialogue (along with other features like the use of dramatic gestures and objects) is one of the hallmarks of oral-traditional narrative.[27] Conversations in an author like Gregory of Tours (538–594), for example, are more likely to be the literary deposit of orally circulating traditions than free inventions by the author. In any case, there is no reason to suspect the influence of classical rhetoric in Gregory's histories.

---

27 Jaoquín Martínez Pizarro, *A Rhetoric of the Scene: Dramatic Narrative in the Early Middle Ages* (Toronto: University of Toronto Press, 1989).

The same holds true for other well-known historians of the pre-Carolingian and Carolingian periods. There is no evidence, for example, that Bede — or any insular author of the seventh or eighth centuries — was familiar with the *De inventione* or the Victorinus commentary.[28] Gabriele Knappe has argued that classical rhetoric as such was not studied in Anglo-Saxon England, pointing out that "Alcuin was the only Anglo-Saxon who was well acquainted with the rhetorical tradition of antiquity."[29] The *De inventione* and Victorinus were known and read in Carolingian Francia and Germany: Alcuin used the *De inventione* as the principal source for his *Dialogus de rhetorica et de virtutibus*; Lupus of Ferrières wrote to Einhard asking to borrow the latter's copy of the *De inventione* and his *Explanationes in libros Ciceronis* (the Victorinus commentary);[30] and Paschasius Radbertus cites the anecdote about the painter Zeuxis from *De inventione* 2.1.1 at more than one point in his corpus.[31] But

---

28 Roger Ray assumed Bede's familiarity with the *De inventione*: see his "Bede's *Vera Lex Historiae*," *Speculum* 55, no. 1 (1980): 1–21 and "Bede and Cicero," *Anglo-Saxon England* 16 (1987): 1–15. For convincing counterarguments, see Gabriele Knappe, *Traditionen der klassischen Rhetorik im angelsächsischen England*, Anglistische Forschungen 236 (Heidelberg: Carl Winter, 1996), 151–55; Riesenweber, *Commenta in Ciceronis Rhetorica: Kommentar*, vol. 1, 60–64: "Die ersten *De inventione* Handschriften entstehen nach der Normannischen Eroberung Ende des 11. oder *Anfang des 12. Jahrhunderts*, also zu einer Zeit, als man auf dem Kontinent bereits dazu überging, eigene Kommentare zur ciceronianischen Rhetorik anzufertigen."

29 Gabriele Knappe, "Classical Rhetoric in Anglo-Saxon England," *Anglo-Saxon England* 27 (1998): 5–30; more generally see Knappe, *Traditionen*.

30 Lupus of Ferrières, *Lupi abbatis Ferrariensis epistolae* 1, in Monumenta Germaniae Historica, Epistolae Karolini Aevi 4, ed. Ernst Dümmler (Berlin: Weidmann, 1925), 8. Glosses and corrections to a *mutilus* of the *De inventione* in Lupus's hand survive in Paris, Bibliothèque nationale, ms lat. 7774A. See Élisabeth Pellegrin, "Les manuscrits de Loup de Ferrières," *Bibliothèque de l'École de chartes* 115 (1957): 5–31, at 11–12. On the manuscript histories of the *De inventione* and *Ad Herennium*, see Ruth Taylor-Briggs, "Reading between the Lines: The Textual History and Manuscript Transmission of Cicero's Rhetorical Works," in *The Rhetoric of Cicero in Its Medieval and Renaissance Commentary Tradition*, ed. Cox and Ward, 77–108.

31 Paschasius Radbertus, *Epitaphium Arsenii*, 1 prol., ed. Ernst Dümmler (Berlin: Verlag der königlichen Akademie der Wissenschaften, 1900), 18; Paschasius Radbertus, *Vita Adalhardi*, ch. 20, in Jacques-Paul Migne, ed.,

Carolingian historiography shows none of the hallmarks of rhetorical invention. There are no speeches or rhetorically inflected *descriptiones* in the histories of Einhard (c. 775–840 CE), Thegan (c. 800–850), Nithard, the Astronomer (c. 795–844), Frechulf of Lisieux (d. 850), or Paul the Deacon (c. 720–790). Nor, when we look at the comments on history-writing made by the authors of this period, is there any hint that the standard of plausibility was seen as applicable to historical writing. Indeed, there is no reason at all to think that the Ciceronian view of the role of *exaedificatio* and *inventio* in history-writing had any appreciable impact in the Early Middle Ages.

On the other hand, all three of the evidentiary criteria mentioned above — evidence for study of the *De inventione/Rhetorica ad Herennium,* specific authorial statements, and textual evidence for the deployment of rhetorical *inventio* — suddenly become prominent among a group of authors in northern France in the late tenth and early eleventh centuries. I have written about this development elsewhere at some length, and I will limit my remarks here.[32] In brief, two roughly contemporary historians — Dudo of Saint-Quentin (d. c. 1026) and Richer of Saint-Remi (d. after 998) revived the tradition of rhetorically inflected history-writing in the Latin West, composing narratives characterized by artificial speeches and descriptive passages, and in some cases the invention of historical details out of whole cloth.

Richer wrote his *Historia* (a four-book account of the West Frankish kings from 888–998) sometime between 991 and 998, and dedicated it to Gerbert of Aurillac, formerly schoolmaster at Rheims, and at that time archbishop of the see. He would go on to be appointed archbishop of Ravenna, and later pope, as

---

Patrologia Latina 120, cols. 1518C-D; Paschasius Radbertus, *Expositio in Mattheo libri* XII, ed. Beda Paulus, Corpus Christianorum, Continuatio Mediaevalis 56 (Turnhout: Brepols, 1984), prol., 6.

32 Justin Lake, "Truth, Plausibility, and the Virtues of Narrative at the Millennium," *Journal of Medieval History* 35, no. 3 (2009): 221–38. With the exception of my endorsement of Woodman's reading of Cicero's *De oratore*, which I have since reconsidered, I stand by the conclusions to this article.

Sylvester II, from 999–1003.³³ In the prologue to the *Historia*, Richer invokes the three virtues of narrative, writing that "I believe that the reader will be satisfied if I have rendered everything plausibly, clearly, and succinctly" ("probabiliter atque dilucide breviterque").³⁴ This appears to be the first occasion on which any medieval Latin historian makes an explicit reference to the *virtutes narrationis,* and it shows beyond any doubt that Richer conceived of his history as a rhetorical *narratio* in the Ciceronian sense. It is also plainly apparent from the text of the *Historia* that Richer practiced *inventio* on a large scale. Richer's most important source, the *Annals* of Flodoard of Rheims (which cover the years 919–966), is extant, and a comparison of the source text to the finished product shows that Richer gave himself considerable latitude to amplify, exaggerate, and even falsify the *Annals* when it served the needs of his narrative.³⁵ Finally, there is ample evidence that Richer had studied classical rhetoric, and particularly the *De inventione,* in detail. Richer's intellectual mentor (and possibly his teacher), Gerbert of Aurillac, was a key figure in shaping his understanding of history-writing.³⁶ Gerbert was a self-identified Ciceronian with a deep and nuanced understanding of classical rhetoric.³⁷ He served as

---

33 Richer of Saint-Remi, *Richeri historiarum libri IIII,* ed. Hartmut Hoffmann, Monumenta Germaniae Historica, Scriptores 38 (Hanover: Hahn, 2000). See Hartmut Hoffmann, "Die Historien Richers von Saint-Remi," *Deutsches Archiv für Erforschung des Mittelalters* 54 (1998): 445–532; Jason Glenn, *Politics and History in the Tenth Century: The Work and World of Richer of Reims* (Cambridge: Cambridge University Press, 2004); Justin Lake, *Richer of Saint-Rémi: The Methods and Mentality of a Tenth-Century Historian* (Washington, DC: The Catholic University of America Press, 2013).

34 Richer of Saint-Remi, *Historia,* prol.: "Satisque lectori fieri arbitror, si probabiliter atque dilucide breviterque omnia digesserim."

35 Lake, "Truth, Plausibility, and the Virtues of Narrative"; *Richer of Saint-Rémi,* 81–142. For the *Annals* see *Les Annales de Flodoard,* ed. Philippe Lauer, Collection de textes pour servir à l'étude et à l'enseignement de l'histoire (Paris: Alphonse Picard, 1905).

36 Pierre Riché, *Gerbert d'Aurillac, le pape de l'an mil* (Paris: Fayard, 1987); Patrizia Stoppacci, *Clavis Gerbertiana* (Florence: SISMEL, 2016).

37 See esp. ep. 158 in *Gerbert d'Aurillac: Correspondance, Les classiques de l'histoire de France au moyen âge,* 2 vols, ed. Pierre Riché and Jean-Pierre

master of the cathedral school of Rheims from 972–980, and again from 983–989, and after a brief and unsuccessful tenure as abbot of Bobbio (a position granted to him by Otto II of Germany), whose vast manuscript holdings must have inspired him, he set about assembling a rhetorical library at Rheims that would enable him to put instruction there on sounder footing.[38] Among the texts he obtained were the Victorinus commentary on the *De inventione*[39] (a text not available at Rheims prior to this), a rare copy of Cicero's *De oratore*,[40] Quintilian's *Institutio oratoria*,[41] and the *Declamationes maiores* attributed to Quintilian.[42]

The novel features of Richer's history — the invocation of the Ciceronian virtues of narrative in the prologue and the many freely composed speeches and descriptive passages — derive from an engagement with classical rhetoric, and in particular with the Ciceronian view of history as a branch of *narratio* subject to amplification via the techniques of rhetorical invention. Gerbert himself viewed the free composition of speeches as allowable even in synodal *acta*. He spent much of his tenure as archbishop of Rheims defending the legitimacy of the proceedings of the synod of Saint-Basle (June 17–18, 991), at which his predecessor, Arnulf, had been deposed and imprisoned.[43]

Callu (Paris: Les Belles Lettres, 1993), 2:392–95; Justin Lake, "Gerbert of Aurillac and the Study of Rhetoric in Tenth-Century Rheims," *Journal of Medieval Latin* 23 (2013): 49–85.

38 Ep. 44, *Correspondance*, ed. Riché and Callu, 1:106–9.
39 Bamberg, Staatsbibliothek, MS Class. 25. See Hartmut Hoffmann, *Bamberger Handschriften des 10. und des 11. Jahrhunderts*, Monumenta Germaniae Historica, Schriften 39 (Hanover: Hahn, 1995), 129–30.
40 Erlangen, Universitätsbibliothek, MS. 380. See Hoffmann, *Bamberger Handschriften*, 176–77.
41 Bamberg, Staatsbibliothek, MS. Class. 45. See Hoffmann, *Bamberger Handschriften*, 134–35.
42 Bamberg, Staatsbibliothek, MS. Class. 44. See Hoffmann, *Bamberger Handschriften*, 134.
43 *Acta concilii Remensis ad sanctum Basolum*, in *Die Konzilien Deutschlands und Reichsitaliens 916–1001*, ed. Ernst-Dieter Hehl, Monumenta Germaniae Historica, Concilia 6.2 (Hanover: Hahn, 2007), 380–469. See also Ferdinand Lot, *Études sur le règne de Hugues Capet et la fin du Xe siècle* (Paris:

Arnulf, an illegitimate son of King Lothar of West Francia (r. 954–986), had betrayed his oath of loyalty to Hugh Capet, the king who had appointed him archbishop in 989, by supporting the failed rebellion of his uncle Charles of Lotharingia.[44] When a papal legate convened a council at Mouzon in 995 to adjudicate the question of Arnulf's deposition, Gerbert redacted his own *acta* of the synod of Saint-Basle.[45] In the prologue to the *acta* he addresses the bishops who were present at Saint-Basle, asking them to correct any inaccuracies in his work, but it is clear that he intended it primarily for the Lotharingian bishops who had not been present in 991, and who questioned the validity of the oath of fidelity that Arnulf had sworn to Hugh Capet.[46] Surprisingly, Gerbert openly admits that he creatively reconstructed the speeches of the participants in composing his account of the synod:

> For I believe that a threefold method of interpretation should be employed, so that some things are translated word-for-word from one language into another, while in other cases the gravity of thought and dignity of expression will be shaped by the level of speech. In other cases, moreover, a single word may provide the opportunity for hidden things to be investigated and the sentiments [of the participants] to be brought more openly into the light. Even if I am unable to fully realize this goal, it is through these means that I will attempt to render the opinions of eminently learned men.[47]

É. Bouillon, 1903), 31–81; Claude Carozzi, "Gerbert et le concile de Saint-Basle," in *Gerberto, scienza, storia e mito. Atti del Gerberti Symposium 25–27 Iuglio 1983*, ed. Michel Tosi (Piacenza: Archivum Bobiense, 1985), 661–76.

44 Richer, *Historia*, 4.28–36; Ferdinand Lot, *Les derniers Carolingiens: Lothaire, Louis V, Charles de Lorraine (954–991)* (Paris: Émile Bouillon, 1891), 252–57.

45 *Acta concilii Remensis.*

46 *Acta concilii Remensis*, ch. 7, 399; Richer, *Historia*, 4.59.

47 *Acta concilii Remensis*, 392: "Siquidem triplici genere interpretationis utendum fore censeo, scilicet ut quaedam ad verbum ex alia in aliam transferantur linguam; in quibusdam autem sententiarum gravitas et eloquii dignitas dicendi genere conformentur; porro in aliis una dictio occasionem faciat et

The *triplex genus interpretationis* envisioned by Gerbert here consists of three elements: 1) translation from the Romance vernacular into Latin; 2) stylistic reworking of speech into a more elevated register—a clear reference to the three levels of style (*genera dicendi*) described in Book 4 of the *Rhetorica ad Herennium*; and 3) the imaginative generation of speech from words or phrases, which can mean nothing other than rhetorical *inventio*. Naturally, all three levels of *interpretatio* were subject to abuse by Gerbert, whose *acta* were not a neutral report of the proceedings of Saint-Basle, but a partisan document intended to win support for his occupancy of the see.

With Richer we have, for the first time, incontrovertible evidence of a medieval historian writing in accordance with the Ciceronian rules for *narratio probabilis*. At roughly the same time Dudo of Saint-Quentin was composing a prosimetrical survey of the history of the Norman dukes from their legendary origins to the end of the reign of Richard I (r. 942–996).[48] Dudo's *Gesta Normannorum* was initially undertaken at Richard's request, and continued after his death at the urging of his son and successor, Richard II (r. 996–1026), and Richard's half-brother, Raoul of Ivry. It was quite obviously intended to exalt the Norman dukes and give them a monumental history on a par with their West Frankish neighbors, but there is no consensus on how involved the Norman court was in its production or how it was meant to be read or performed.[49] Most relevant for this

---

abdita investigari et in lucem ipsos affectus manifeste proferri. Quae etsi ad plenum assequi non potuero, his tamen modis doctissimorum hominum sententias conabor interpretari."

48 Text in *De moribus et actis primorum Normanniae ducum*, ed. Jules Lair (Caen: Le Blanc-Hardel, 1865). The translation and commentary by Eric Christiansen are indispensable: *Dudo of St Quentin: History of the Normans* (Woodbridge: The Boydell Press, 1998).

49 The literature on Dudo is vast. See in particular Benjamin Pohl, *Dudo of St Quentin's "Historia Normannorum": History, Tradition, and Memory* (Woodbridge: Boydell and Brewer, 2015); Fraser McNair, "The Politics of Being Norman in the Reign of Richard the Fearless, Duke of Normandy (r. 942-966)," *Early Medieval Europe* 23, no. 3 (2015): 308–28, and Leah Shopkow, "The Carolingian World of Dudo of Saint-Quentin," *Journal of Medi-*

argument are Dudo's statements about history-writing, which are mostly found in the poems scattered throughout his work. The poetic preface to the third book is particularly important. Here Dudo beseeches God to endow him and his work with the most important qualities of style:

> Edifying my mind with the seven-fold nectar of the Spirit,
> My heart with the spark of rhetoric's flood,
> And my tongue with the three-part proposition,
> You will sprinkle them from the fount of health-giving knowledge,
> So that the narrative of this history, which we will reveal,
> Will be concise and plausible,
> And from this it will be clear to the discerning man.
> May the brevity of the partition shine out in the diction
> And may the explanation be entirely clear,
> Let the small number of characters be tied to the genre,
> And let the application of rhetoric
> Be derived from the facts and the theme.
> Now that the seven elements have been well learned
> As well as the rules and all the types of *status* [...].[50]

This passage is filled with *termini technici* of classical rhetoric, but three elements in particular stand out. First, Dudo asks that his history be clear (*apertus*), concise (*brevis*), and plausible (*probabilis*), that is, he asks that it manifest the three virtues of narrative. That "plausible" here is not merely a synonym for "true" is confirmed in a subsequent poem, an address by

---

eval History 15 (1989): 19–37. Dudo's history was written between 996 and 1020.

50 *De moribus*, 3, pref., 177–78: "Mentem septifidi nectare spiritus|et cor rhetorici fomite gurgitis|et linguam trimodo proloquio struens, asperges salubris fonte scientiae;|narratus brevis ut sitque probabilis|atque hinc exstet apertus homini scio huius historiae, quam reserabimus.|Partitus brevitas flamine splendeat,|in toto niteat quaeque solutio:|nectatur generi sic quoque paucitas| personae, exque datis atque negotio sumatur ratio rhetoricabilis."

Clio, the muse of history, in which she declares that it is her right "to hand down to posterity histories of a believable order" ("Iuris namque mei credibili ordine/rerum historias reddere posteris") — *credibilis* being a synonym for *probabilis*.[51] Second, Dudo asks that the "application of rhetoric" (*ratio rhetoricabilis*) be drawn from the facts and the theme ("exque datis atque negotio"). Here he appears to envision his task as taking the *data* and *negotia* that have been provided to him by his informants (in particular, members of the Norman ducal household) and applying to them the tools of rhetorical invention. Finally, he invokes the seven elements (*septem elementa*) needed to secure narrative plausibility according to Marius Victorinus: who (*quis*), what (*quid*), why (*cur*), where (*ubi*), when (*quando*), in what way (*quemadmodum*), and with what means (*cum quibus adminiculis*).[52] Naturally, the historian was rarely in a position to have accurate information about all of these aspects of a given event, especially if he were writing about the deeds of the distant past, as Dudo was in his first book. Hence, any complete accounting of the seven circumstantial elements would require the author to make assumptions about the kinds of things that were likely to have happened, even if they were not, strictly speaking, true.

Richer and Dudo's view of history as a *narratio* subject to amplification via the techniques of rhetorical invention represents something new, and it only could have come about through a close engagement with the triad of Ciceronian rhetorical texts mentioned above. There is other evidence from around the same time of a shift in the way in which history was conceptualized. Aimoin of Fleury, who was compiling a history of the Merovingian Franks at the same time that Richer was writing,

---

51 *De moribus*, 4, 211.
52 Victorinus, *Commenta in Ciceronis Rhetorica*, 1.21.29, ed. Riesenweber, 74–75: "Probabilis, inquit, erit narratio, si in ea fuerint illa omnia, quibus solet veritas inveniri: nam in his septem omnis ad fidem argumentatio continetur"; 1.26.37, 93: "Septem sunt quidem, ut diximus, elementa, unde omnis argumentatio capitur ad quamcumque rem: quis, quid, cur, quando, ubi, quemadmodum, quibus adminiculis."

studded his *Gesta Francorum* with freely invented speeches, just as Richer and Dudo had done.[53] His abbot and former schoolmaster, Abbo of Fleury (d. 1004), who commissioned the work, had studied the Victorinus commentary independently and evidently made it part of the curriculum at Fleury in the 970s and 980s.[54] There is, moreover, an astounding discussion of truth and plausibility in the *Carmen ad Rotbertum Regem*, a poem written by bishop Adalbero of Laon (the dedicatee of Dudo's history) and addressed to king Robert II (the Pious) of West Francia (r. 996–1031), who was also the presumed audience for Aimoin's *Gesta Francorum*.[55] The poem takes the form of dialogue between a bishop (Adalbero) and king (Robert) in which the former decries the dangerous changes to the social order of the kingdom that he sees taking place all around him. Particular scorn is reserved for the Cluniac order and their leader, Odilo, who is depicted — as part of a "world turned upside-down" motif — leading an army of monks into battle riding donkeys and camels, while knights wear monastic cowls and bishops plough the fields naked.[56] When Robert questions the reliability of these and similarly outlandish images, Adalbero claims to have invented them according to the standard of the plausible, while at the same time claiming that they are true:

---

[53] Aimoin of Fleury, *Gesta Francorum*, ed. André Duchesne, Historiae Francorum Scriptores coaetanei 3 (Paris: S. Cramoisy, 1641), 1–120; reprinted in Jacques-Paul Migne, ed., *Patrologia Latina* 139, cols. 627–798.

[54] For Abbo's rhetorical studies, see Aimoin of Fleury, *Vita Abbonis*, ch. 3, in *L'abbaye de Fleury en l'an mil*, Sources d'histoire médiévale 32, ed. Robert-Henri Bautier, Gillette Labory, et al. (Paris: Centre National de la Recherche Scientifique, 2004).

[55] For the *Carmen ad Rotbertum regem*, see *Adalbéron de Laon: Poème au roi Robert*, Les Classiques de l'histoire de France au Moyen Âge, ed. Claude Carozzi (Paris: Les Belles Lettres, 1979). For Aimoin's purpose in writing, see Karl Ferdinand Werner, "Die literarischen Vorbilder des Aimoin von Fleury," in *Medium Aevum Vivum: Festschrift für Walther Bulst*, ed. Hans Robert Jauss and Dieter Schaller (Heidelberg: Carl Winter: 1960), 69–103, at 95–96.

[56] *Carmen ad Rotbertum regem*, 37–44, 142–62.

Another tool (lit. "hammer") is available, the plausible case,
and here it is,
I have invented what I have set forth, not unmindful of
these things;
I speak to the present, and what I say is true.[57]

When Robert chides him for blurring the boundary between truth and fiction ("It is not right to call true what is not true"),[58] Adalbero replies that what he said is true, *even though it did not actually happen*: "Indeed, what I have said is true. You know that I have not departed from the truth [...]. You should know that everything did not happen this way, but it could have."[59]

Adalbero of Laon's astounding assimilation of plausibility to truth remains something of an outlier, but all of the late tenth-century texts surveyed above point in the same direction: to a self-conscious application of the doctrines and techniques of rhetorical invention based on an understanding of the *De inventione* and the Victorinus commentary. The most likely explanation for this development is the increasing attention devoted to invention as a branch of rhetoric in the second half of the tenth century, in contrast to the previous focus on style (*elocutio*), which in the Early Middle Ages was mostly a matter of learning the figures and tropes, and was as often as not subsumed under the teaching of grammar. This shift is evidenced both by an increase in copies of the *De inventione* and the increasing level of importance assigned to the text by teachers and authors.[60] One can compare, for example, the wholly derivative, and at one point erroneous, treatment of invention found in Alcuin's *Dialo-*

---

57 *Carmen ad Rotbertum regem*, 348–50: "Malleus alter adest, qui causa probabilis, hic est:| Inveni quod disposui, non immemor horum,| Eloquor in in presens et quod pronuncio verum."
58 *Carmen ad Rotbertum regem*, 351: "Quod non est verum, non est fas dicere verum."
59 *Carmen ad Rotbertum regem*, 352, 354: "En dixi verum, scis non excedere verum [...] Non sic gesta scias, sed cuncta geri potuisse."
60 Birger Munk Olsen, *L'étude des auteurs classiques latins aux XIe et XIIe siècles*, vol. 1 (Paris: Editions du Centre national de la recherche scientifique, 1982–1989), 127–29; Ward, *Ciceronian Rhetoric*, 90.

gus de rhetorica et virtutibus,⁶¹ composed c. 800, with the *De arte rhetorica* of Notker Labeo of St. Gall (c. 950–1022), a detailed and original treatise written with the explicit aim of showing the relevance of rhetoric — and particularly the manifold categories and subcategories of speech essential to rhetorical invention — to contemporary life.⁶² Notker, it is important to note, explicitly links history-writing and rhetoric, and states directly that all three virtues of narrative are found in historical works as well as speeches.⁶³

Familiarity with Cicero and Victorinus unites all the authors considered above. Notker knew the Victorinus commentary and used it as one of his chief sources.⁶⁴ Both Gerbert and Abbo studied the Victorinus commentary and introduced it to the authors whose works they inspired, Richer of Saint-Remi and Aimoin of Fleury respectively. Adalbero of Laon had clearly studied the *De inventione* and probably Victorinus as well, as evidenced by the content of the *Carmen* and the marginal glosses inserted by the author. It is harder to be certain of Dudo's rhetorical training, but he had clearly imbibed the doctrine that history was governed by the virtues of narrative, and his invocation of the seven elements (*septem elementa*) of plausible narrative is probably derived from Victorinus.

The evidence strongly suggests, therefore, that the turn of the first millennium was a hinge point in the composition of

---

61 See Wilbur Samuel Howell, *The Rhetoric of Alcuin & Charlemagne* (New York: Russell & Russell, 1965). Alcuin errs in using an inappropriate example to illustrate the *constitutio translativa* at lines 153–57.

62 The text of the *De arte rhetorica* is edited in *Notker der Deutsche: Die kleineren Schriften*, vols. 7 and 7A, ed. James C. King and Petrus W. Tax (Tübingen, 1996/2003). See also Samuel Jaffe, "Antiquity and Innovation in Notker's *Nova rhetorica*: The Doctrine of Invention," *Rhetorica* 3 (1985): 165–81, and Otto A.L. Dieter, "The Rhetoric of Notker Labeo," in *Papers in Rhetoric*, ed. Donald C. Bryant (Saint Louis, 1940).

63 *De arte rhetorica*, ed. King and Tax, 7:121, 17–18: "Iste tres partes orationis ab oratoribus acceptae, etiam apud hystoriographos inveniuntur"; p. 121, 23–26: Textus sive narratio in causis oratoriis et in libris hystoricis tres virtutes habet, sicut exordium: ut brevis sit [...] lucida [...] probabilis."

64 *Commenta in Ciceronis Rhetorica*, ed. Riesenweber, vol. 1, 66–67.

historiography in the Latin West. A century later, rhetorically inflected histories of the kind written by Richer, Dudo, and Aimoin became so common as not to attract any attention. The most pioneering studies on the role of rhetoric in medieval history-writing all focus primarily on works written in the twelfth century or later. [65] By this time no one seems to have thought that rhetorical amplification in a historical work with literary pretensions was a problem. Among classical historians there is evidence for an ongoing debate about the proper role of rhetoric in history. Polybius, for example, castigates Timaeus of Tauromenium for inserting "false rhetorical exercises" into his work,[66] while Lucian was keen to distinguish history from both panegyric and oratory.[67] In contrast, it is noteworthy how rarely medieval historians call attention to the distorting effects of rhetorical invention. William of Jumièges (c. 1000–1070) clearly felt some unease about Dudo of Saint-Quentin's *Gesta Normannorum*, which he was compelled to use as the principal source for the first four books of his own *Gesta Normannorum Ducum*, but he could not bring himself to criticize Dudo for his embellishments. He informs the reader, however, that he had excised material relating to the genealogy of Rollo (the shadowy founder of the Norman state) and a peculiar dream assigned to him by Dudo "since I deemed this material merely flattery that offered no semblance of anything honorable or useful."[68]

---

65 Partner, *Serious Entertainments*; Beer, *Narrative Conventions of Truth*; Morse, *Truth and Convention*; Otter, *Inventiones*.

66 Polybius, *Histories*, 12.25b4. https://penelope.uchicago.edu/Thayer/E/Roman/Texts/Polybius/12*.html.

67 Lucian, *De historia conscribenda*, 7–13, 45, 50. See also Melina Tamiolaki, "Lucian on Truth and Lies in Ancient Historiography: The Theory and Its Limits," in *Truth and History in the Ancient World: Pluralising the Past*, ed. Lisa Hau and Ian Ruffell (New York: Routledge, 2017), 267–83. For the Greek of Lucian see https://www.perseus.tufts.edu/hopper/text?doc=Perseus%3Atext%3A2008.01.0511, and for the English, http://lucianofsamosata.info/wiki/doku.php?id=home:texts_and_library:essays:the-way-to-write-history.

68 *The "Gesta Normannorum Ducum" of William of Jumièges, Orderic Vitalis, and Robert of Torigni*, ed. and trans. Elisabeth M.C. van Houts, Oxford Me-

Medieval historians tended to see partisanship and enmity, rather than rhetorical exuberance, as the real threats to historical truth. Adalbold of Utrecht (c. 970–1026), for example, in his biography of the German emperor Henry II, identified the risks to truth in history-writing as "hatred and earthly love, envy and hellish flattery."[69] Similarly, in the "Apology" that precedes the third book of his chronicle, Cosmas of Prague (c. 1045–1125) envisioned flattery as the reason that a historian might deviate from the truth and write what was false.[70] In the prologue to Book 4 of his *Gesta regum Anglorum*, William of Malmesbury (c. 1095–1143), meditating on the difficulties of writing contemporary history, noted that in the present evil age "an author will pass over the misdeeds that confront him out of fear, and for the sake of applause invents good deeds where there are none."[71] Similarly, in the general prologue to his *Chronicle*, William of Tyre (c. 1130–1186) wrote that historians were threatened by twin dangers, which beset them on both sides like Scylla and Charybdis:

> [...] they will either strive to produce a true account of events and stir up hostility in many quarters, or else conceal what happened in an effort to soften feelings of resentment, a course of action that is in no way blameless [...]. [Those who

---

dieval Texts 1 (Oxford: Clarendon Press, 1992), 6: "animadvertens ea penitus adulatoria, nec speciem honesti vel utilis pretendere."

69 Adalbold of Utrecht, *Vita Heinrici II imperatoris*, ed. Georg Waitz, Monumenta Germaniae Historica, Scriptores 4 (Hanover: Hahn, 1841), 683: "Sed scriptor veritatem tenere nequit, nisi haec quatuor aut potenter devitaverit aut aliquatenus a mente deposuerit: odium et carnalem dilectionem, invidiam et infernalem adulationem."

70 Cosmas of Prague, *Chronica Boemorum*, ed. Berthold Bretholz, Monumenta Germaniae Historica, Scriptorum rerum Germanicarum, Nova Series 2 (Berlin: Weidmann, 1923), 159–60: "Si autem a veritate deviantes aliter quam se res habent scripserimus, cum pene omnibus note sint cause, nihilominus adulationis et mendacii notam incidimus."

71 *William of Malmesbury: "Gesta regum Anglorum,"* 2 vols., ed. Roger Aubrey Baskerville Mynors, Rodney M. Thomson, and Michael Winterbottom (Oxford: Clarendon Press, 1998), vol. 1, 540: "scriptor obvia mala propter metum pretereat et bona, si non sunt, propter plausum confingat."

write history], therefore, will either fall short of their professional duty by showing inappropriate deference, or be compelled to bear the burden of enmity by pursuing the truth, which is the mother of hatred.[72]

If partiality and bias were seen as mortal threats to the truth value of history, the same cannot not be said of rhetorical expansion. When invoked by medieval historians, rhetoric and eloquence were typically shorthand for stylistic ornamentation — inevitably disclaimed by the author — rather than authorial license to expand upon events. In the prologue to his *Chronicle,* Gervase of Canterbury (c. 1140–1210) remarks on the differences between history, on the one hand, and chronicles and annals on the other, but he sees no threats to the truth from the stylistic pretensions of the authors of histories. They may employ "rhetorical flourishes" and proceed in a "roundabout and elegant" manner, but they nonetheless strive for truth in the same measure as the writers of more humble chronicles.[73] An interesting exception to this general rule is found in the *Encomium Emmae Reginae* (1041/1042), a tendentious history of the Danish conquest of England by Swein Forkbeard and his son Cnut, and the succession struggle following Cnut's death in 1035, written by a partisan of Cnut's Norman wife Emma.[74] In the pro-

---

72 *Willelmi Tyrensis Archiepiscopi Chronicon, Corpus Christianorum: Continuatio Mediaevalis,* vol. 63, ed. Robert Burchard Constantijn Huygens (Turnhout: Brepols, 1996), 97: "Aut enim rerum gestarum veritatem prosequentes multorum in se conflabunt invidiam, aut indignationis gratia leniende rerum occultabunt seriem, in quo certum est non deesse delictum...Aut igitur a sue professionis cadent officio obsequium prestantes indebitum, aut rei veritatem prosequentes, odium, cuius ipsa mater est, eos oportebit sustinere."

73 Gervase of Canterbury, *Chronica,* prol., in *The Historical Works of Gervase of Canterbury,* vol. 1, ed. William Stubbs (London: Longman and Co., 1879), 87: "Proprium est historici veritati intendere, audientes vel legentes dulci sermone et eleganti demulcere, actus, mores vitamque ipsius quam describit veraciter edocere, nichilque aliud comprehendere nisi quod historiae de ratione videtur competere."

74 See *Encomium Emmae reginae,* ed. and trans. Alistair Campbell (Cambridge: Cambridge University Press, 1998). See also Elizabeth M. Tyler,

logue to the *Encomium*, the author (a monk or cathedral canon of Saint-Omer), notes that falsehoods are sometimes inserted into histories "for the sake of adornment" (*ornatus gratia*):

> This quality, indeed, is required in history, that one should not deviate from the straight path of truth by any divergent straying, for when in writing the deeds of any man one inserts a fictitious element, either in error, or, as is often the case, for the sake of ornament, the hearer assuredly regards facts as fictions, when he has ascertained the introduction of so much as one lie. And so I consider that the historian should greatly beware, lest, going against the truth by falsely introducing matter, he lose the very name which he is held to have from his office.[75]

There is considerable irony at work here, since the *Encomium* contains a great many obvious fictions, though the degree to which the audience was meant to be complicit in this irony is an open question.[76] At the end of the first chapter — a fulsome account of the early years of Swein Forkbeard — the author responds preemptively to potential criticism that he was inventing

---

"Talking about History in Eleventh-Century England: The E*ncomium Emmae Reginae* and the Court of Harthacnut," *Early Medieval Europe* 13, no. 4 (2005): 359–83; Andy Orchard, "The Literary Background to the *Encomium Emmae Reginae*," *Journal of Medieval Latin* 11 (2001): 156–83; Eric John, "The *Encomium Emmae Reginae*: A Riddle and a Solution," *Bulletin of the John Rylands Library* 63 (1980–81): 58–94, and Felice Lifshitz, "The *Encomium Emmae Reginae*: A 'Political Pamphlet' of the Eleventh Century?," *Haskins Society Journal* 1 (1989): 39–50.

75 *Encomium Emmae reginae*, prol., 4–5, ed. Campbell: "Hoc enim in historia proprium exigitur, ut nullo erroris diverticulo a recto veritatis tramite declinetur, quoniam, cum quis alicuius gesta scribens veritati falsa quaedam seu errando, siue ut sepe fit ornatus gratia, interserit, profecto unius tantum comperta admixtione mendatii auditor facta uelut infecta ducit. Unde historicis magnopere cauendum esse censeo, ne veritati quibusdam falso interpositis contraeundo nomen etiam perdat, quod uidetur habere ex offitio."

76 See in particular Elizabeth M. Tyler, *England in Europe: English Royal Women and Literary Patronage c. 1000–1150* (Toronto: University of Toronto Press, 2017), 57–59, 65–70.

falsehoods "in order to court favor with anyone" (*alicuius amoris gratia*) by asking the reader to judge the truth or falsehood of his account for himself.[77]

The author of the *Encomium* wrote in a high style and was presumably trained in Ciceronian rhetoric, though we have no direct knowledge of his educational background. Nonetheless, his anguished meditation in the prologue about the problems of writing history is illuminating, however disingenuous this might be. The author, employing the same Scylla and Charybdis topos later found in William of Malmesbury, William of Tyre, and many other historians, claims to have felt hedged in by critics, who would either accuse him of *vana loquacitas* if his narrative was too prolix, or of concealing the very truth that needed to be revealed if he withheld too many details. The principal reason for invoking this commonplace seems to be to justify the imaginative narrative that follows; that is, the author can partially disguise, or at least justify, the liberties he is taking with the truth by invoking the danger of saying too little.

It is just possible, moreover, to read the passage about falsehoods introduced for the sake of ornament as a specific reference to Dudo of Saint-Quentin, who created a fictional Trojan genealogy for the Normans that the author of the *Encomium* does not replicate for the line of Cnut, Emma's Danish husband.[78] Dudo, more than anyone else, could be legitimately accused of purveying falsehoods *amoris gratia*. Finally, it is worth noting that in the closing words of the prologue the author declares that he will set about the *narrationis contextio*. Both words are important here; writing is often described using weaving metaphors in the Middle Ages. It is clearly implied that history

---

[77] *Encomium Emmae reginae*, 1.1, 10, ed. Campbell, lxxv: "At ne me credat aliquis hec falsa fingendo alicuius amoris gratia compilare: recte animadvertenti in subsequentibus patebit, utrum vera dixerim an minime."

[78] Campbell, ed., *Encomium Emmae reginae*, xxii, suspects that Emma recommended Dudo's history to the author of the *Encomium* as a model. Simon Keynes (in a supplementary introduction in the same volume, xl) doubts that the encomiast knew Dudo's work. See also Tyler, *England in Europe*, 126.

is an artificial construct, not simply a mirror of the events that it describes. This accords well with what John O. Ward has shown about the general consciousness of the artifice of historical composition in the twelfth century.[79] For there can be little doubt that by this time the Ciceronian view of history as literature that worked through "*exaedificatio* [...] in rebus et verbis" had become generally accepted by the literary elite of the Latin West.[80]

Just as Dudo could talk about applying a *ratio rhetoricabilis* and writing things of a *credibilis ordo* and simultaneously claim to be writing the truth, medieval authors from the eleventh century onward generally found no problem with rhetorical amplification as a tool of history. Only when *inventio* shaded into the wholesale invention of fictional people and events did problems arise. Hence the criticism leveled at Geoffrey of Monmouth's notorious pseudo-history by William of Newburgh and Gerald of Wales.[81] The problem, of course, from our perspective is that the line between an acceptable level of amplification and outright lying is not at all clear. Inventing words for a speech known to have been delivered was clearly an acceptable practice, for example, but what about adding in a speech that never took place? There was always a danger that the "tight box" of invention described by Lendon could become more capacious, as the historian allowed himself ever more liberty. If this danger was recognized in the eleventh and twelfth centuries, however, there is much less evidence to suggest it was a concern in the four centuries between the composition of Gregory of Tours's *Histories* and the works of Richer of Saint-Remi and Dudo of

---

79 John O. Ward, "Some Principles of Rhetorical Historiography in the Twelfth Century," in *Classical Rhetoric and Medieval Historiography*, ed. Ernst Breisach (Kalamazoo: Medieval Institute Publications, 1985), 103–65.

80 See Matthew Kempshall, *Rhetoric and the Writing of History, 400–1500* (Manchester: Manchester University Press, 2011); Ward, "Some Principles"; John O. Ward, "The Medieval Origins of Postmodern Practice," *Parergon* 14, no. 2 (1997): 101–28.

81 See in particular Ad Putter, "Latin Historiography after Geoffrey of Monmouth," in *The Arthur of Medieval Latin Literature*, ed. Siân Echard (Cardiff: University of Wales Press, 2011), 85–97.

Saint-Quentin. We should not, in other words, assume the same high level of rhetorical self-consciousness among all early medieval historians. At least among a certain group of authors, a true revolution in history-writing seems to have taken place around the turn of the first millennium. As a result of the increased copying of, and interest in, the *De inventione* and the Victorinus commentary, history increasingly came to be seen as an artificially constructed *narratio* subject to amplification through the inclusion of plausible, but not necessarily true, details.

Bibliography

Primary

Acta concilii Remensis ad sanctum Basolum. In *Die Konzilien Deutschlands und Reichsitaliens 916–1001,* Volume 2, edited by Ernst-Dieter Hehl, 380–469. Monumenta Germaniae Historica, Concilia 6.2. Hanover: Hahn, 2007.

Adalbero of Laon. *Carmen ad Rotbertum regem. Adalbéron de Laon: Poème au roi Robert.* Les Classiques de l'histoire de France au Moyen Âge. Edited by Claude Carozzi. Paris: Les Belles Lettres, 1979.

Adalbold of Utrecht. *Vita Heinrici II imperatoris.* Edited by Georg Waitz, 679–95. Monumenta Germaniae Historica, Scriptores 4. Hanover: Hahn, 1841.

Aimoin of Fleury. *Gesta Francorum.* In *Historiae Francorum Scriptores coaetanei,* Volume 3, edited by André Duchesne, 1–120. Paris: S. Cramoisy, 1641. Reprinted in Jacques-Paul Migne, ed., *Patrologia Latina* 139, cols. 627–798.

———. *Vita Abbonis.* In *L'abbaye de Fleury en l'an mil.* Sources d'histoire médiévale 32. Edited by Robert-Henri Bautier, Gillette Labory, et al. Paris: Centre National de la Recherche Scientifique, 2004.

Cicero. *De Inventione.* Edited and translated by H.M. Hubbell. *On Invention: The Best Kind of Orator.* Cambridge: Harvard University Press, 1949. DOI: 10.4159/DLCL.marcus_tullius_cicero-de_inventione.1949.

———. *De optimo genere oratorum.* Translated by James M. May and Jakob Wisse. *Cicero: On the Ideal Orator.* Oxford: Oxford University Press, 2001.

C. Marius Victorinus: Commenta in Ciceronis Rhetorica. Edited by Thomas Riesenweber. Bibliotheca Teubneriana. Berlin: De Gruyter, 2013. DOI: 10.1515/9783110313666.

Cosmas of Prague. *Chronica Boemorum.* Edited by Berthold Bretholz. Monumenta Germaniae Historica, Scriptorum rerum Germanicarum, Nova Series 2. Berlin: Weidmann, 1923.

Dudo of Saint-Quentin. *De moribus et actis primorum Normanniae ducum.* Edited by Jules Lair. Caen: Le Blanc-Hardel, 1865.

Translated by Eric Christiansen, *Dudo of St Quentin: History of the Normans*. Woodbridge: The Boydell Press, 1998.

Encomium Emmae reginae. Edited and translated by Alistair Campbell. Cambridge: Cambridge University Press, 1998.

Flodoard. *Annals. Les Annales de Flodoard*. Collection de textes pour servir à l'étude et à l'enseignement de l'histoire. Edited by Philippe Lauer. Paris: Alphonse Picard, 1905.

Gerbert of Aurillac. Letters. *Gerbert d'Aurillac: Correspondance*. 2 volumes. Edited by Pierre Riché and Jean-Pierre Callu. Les classiques de l'histoire de France au moyen âge. Paris: Les Belles Lettres, 1993.

Gervase of Canterbury. *Chronica. The Historical Works of Gervase of Canterbury*. Volume 1. Edited by William Stubbs. London: Longman and Co., 1879.

Lupus of Ferrières. Letters. *Lupi abbatis Ferrariensis epistolae 1*. In Monumenta Germaniae Historica, Epistolae Karolini Aevi 4. Edited by Ernst Duemmler. Berlin: Weidmann, 1925.

Notker Labeo. *De arte rhetorica. Notker der Deutsche: Die kleineren Schriften*, Volumes 7 and 7A. Edited by James C. King and Petrus W. Tax. Tübingen, 1996/2003.

Paschasius Radbertus. *Epitaphium Arsenii*. Edited by Ernst Dümmler. Berlin: Verlag der königlichen Akademie der Wissenschaften, 1900.

——. *Expositio in Mattheo libri XII*. Edited by Beda Paulus. 3 volumes. Corpus Christianorum, Continuatio Mediaevalis 56–56B. Turnhout: Brepols, 1984.

Paschasius Radbertus. *Vita Adalhardi*. In Jacques-Paul Migne, ed., *Patrologia Latina* 120, cols. 1507–1556.

Richer of Saint-Remi. *Historia. Richeri historiarum libri IIII*. Edited by Hartmut Hoffmann. Monumenta Germaniae Historica, Scriptores 38. Hanover: Hahn, 2000.

Thucydides. *History of the Peloponnesian War*. Translated by Richard Crawley. London: Longmans, Green, and Co., 1874.

William of Jumièges. *Gesta Normannorum Ducum. The "Gesta Normannorum Ducum" of William of Jumièges, Orderic Vitalis, and Robert of Torigni*. Volume 1. Oxford Medieval Texts. Edited and translated by Elisabeth M.C. van Houts. Oxford:

Clarendon Press, 1992. DOI: 10.1093/actrade/9780198222712.book.1.

William of Malmesbury. *Gesta regum Anglorum*. 2 volumes. Edited by Roger Aubrey Baskerville Mynors, Rodney M. Thomson, and Michael Winterbottom. Oxford: Clarendon Press, 1998.

William of Tyre. *Chronicle. Willelmi Tyrensis Archiepiscopi Chronicon*. Edited by Robert Burchard Constantijn Huygens. Corpus Christianorum: Continuatio Mediaevalis 63. Turnhout: Brepols, 1996.

Secondary

Beer, Jeanette. *Narrative Conventions of Truth in the Middle Ages*. Geneva: Droz, 1981.

Breisach, Ernst, ed. *Classical Rhetoric and Medieval Historiography*. Kalamazoo: Medieval Institute Publications, 1985.

Briscoe, John, and Tim J. Cornell, eds. *The Fragments of the Roman Historians*. Volume 1. Oxford: Oxford University Press, 2013.

Brunt, Peter A. "Cicero and Historiography." In *Studies in Greek History and Thought*, 181–209. Oxford: Clarendon Press, 1993.

Bryant, Donald C., ed. *Papers in Rhetoric*. Saint Louis: Washington University, 1940.

Cape, Robert W. "Persuasive History: Roman Rhetoric and Historiography." In *Roman Eloquence: Rhetoric in Society and Literature*, edited by William J. Dominik, 212–28. London: Routledge, 1997.

Carozzi, Claude. "Gerbert et le concile de Saint-Basle." In *Gerberto, scienza, storia e mito. Atti del Gerberti Symposium 25–27 Iuglio 1983*, edited by Michel Tosi, 661–76. Piacenza: Archivum Bobiense, 1985.

Cox, Virginia, and John O. Ward, eds. *The Rhetoric of Cicero in its Medieval and Renaissance Commentary Tradition*. Boston and Leiden: Brill, 2006. DOI: 10.1163/9789047404644.

Damon, Cynthia. "Rhetoric and Historiography." In *A Companion to Roman Rhetoric*, edited by William Dominik and Jon

Hall, 439–50. Malden: Wiley-Blackwell, 2007. DOI: 10.1002/9780470996485.ch32.

Dieter, Otto A.L. "The Rhetoric of Notker Labeo." In *Papers in Rhetoric*, edited by Donald C. Bryant, 27–33. Saint Louis: Washington University, 1940.

Echard, Siân, ed. *The Arthur of Medieval Latin Literature*. Cardiff: University of Wales Press, 2011.

Fornara, Charles William. *The Nature of History in Ancient Greece and Rome*. Berkeley: University of California Press, 1988.

Gill, Christopher, and T.P. Wiseman, eds. *Lies and Fiction in the Ancient World*. Liverpool: Liverpool University Press, 1993. DOI: 10.5949/liverpool/9780859893817.001.0001.

Glenn, Jason. *Politics and History in the Tenth Century: The Work and World of Richer of Reims*. Cambridge: Cambridge University Press, 2004.

Goffart, Walter. *The Narrators of Barbarian History (A.D. 550–800): Jordanes, Gregory of Tours, Bede, and Paul the Deacon*. Princeton: Princeton University Press, 1988.

Hau, Lisa, and Ian Ruffell, eds. *Truth and History in the Ancient World: Pluralising the Past*. New York: Routledge, 2017. DOI: 10.4324/9781315733463.

Hoffmann, Hartmut. *Bamberger Handschriften des 10. und des 11. Jahrhunderts*. Monumenta Germaniae Historica, Schriften 39. Hanover: Hahn, 1995.

———. "Die Historien Richers von Saint-Remi." *Deutsches Archiv für Erforschung des Mittelalters* 54 (1998): 445–532.

Holdsworth, Christopher, and T.P. Wiseman, eds. *The Inheritance of Historiography 350–900*. Exeter: University of Exeter Press, 1986. DOI: 10.5949/liverpool/9780859892728.001.0001.

Howell, Wilbur Samuel. *The Rhetoric of Alcuin & Charlemagne*. New York: Russell & Russell, 1965.

Jaffe, Samuel. "Antiquity and Innovation in Notker's *Nova rhetorica*: The Doctrine of Invention." *Rhetorica* 3 (1985): 165–81. DOI: 10.1525/rh.1985.3.3.165.

Jauss, Hans Robert, and Dieter Schaller, eds. *Medium Aevum Vivum: Festschrift für Walther Bulst*. Heidelberg: Carl Winter: 1960.

John, Eric. "The *Encomium Emmae Reginae*: A Riddle and a Solution." *Bulletin of the John Rylands Library* 63 (1980–81): 58–94. DOI: 10.7227/BJRL.63.1.4.

Kempshall, Matthew. *Rhetoric and the Writing of History, 400–1500*. Manchester: Manchester University Press, 2011.

Knappe, Gabriele. "Classical Rhetoric in Anglo-Saxon England." *Anglo-Saxon England* 27 (1998): 5–30. DOI: 10.1017/S0263675100004774.

———. *Traditionen der klassischen Rhetorik im angelsächsischen England*. Anglistische Forschungen 236. Heidelberg: Carl Winter, 1996.

Lake, Justin. "Gerbert of Aurillac and the Study of Rhetoric in Tenth-Century Rheims." *Journal of Medieval Latin* 23 (2013): 49–85. DOI: 10.1484/J.JML.1.103772.

———. *Richer of Saint-Rémi: The Methods and Mentality of a Tenth-Century Historian*. Washington, DC: The Catholic University of America Press, 2013.

———. "Truth, Plausibility, and the Virtues of Narrative at the Millennium." *Journal of Medieval History* 35, no. 3 (2009): 221–38. DOI: 10.1016/j.jmedhist.2009.05.003.

Lendon, J.E. "Historians without History: Against Roman Historiography." In *The Cambridge Companion to the Roman Historians*, edited by Andrew Feldherr, 41–61. Cambridge: Cambridge University Press, 2009. DOI: 10.1017/CCOL9780521854535.004.

Lifshitz, Felice. "The *Encomium Emmae Reginae*: A 'Political Pamphlet' of the Eleventh Century?" *Haskins Society Journal* 1 (1989): 39–50.

Lot, Ferdinand. *Études sur le règne de Hugues Capet et la fin du Xe siècle*. Paris: É. Bouillon, 1903.

———. *Les derniers Carolingiens: Lothaire, Louis V, Charles de Lorraine (954–991)*. Paris: Émile Bouillon, 1891.

Luce, T.J. Review of Anthony Woodman, *Rhetoric and Classical Historiography: Four Studies*. *Phoenix* 43, no. 2 (1989): 177. DOI: 10.2307/1088219.

Martínez Pizarro, Jaoquín. *A Rhetoric of the Scene: Dramatic Narrative in the Early Middle Ages*. Toronto: University of Toronto Press, 1989. DOI: 10.3138/9781487579753.

McNair, Fraser. "The Politics of Being Norman in the Reign of Richard the Fearless, Duke of Normandy (r. 942–966)." *Early Medieval Europe* 23, no. 3 (2015): 308–28. DOI: 10.1111/emed.12106.

Morse, Ruth. *Truth and Convention in the Middle Ages: Rhetoric, Representation, and Reality*. Cambridge: Cambridge University Press, 1991.

Northwood, Simon J. "Cicero's *De Oratore* 2.51–64 and Rhetoric in Historiography." *Mnemosyne* 61, no. 2 (2008): 228–44. DOI: 10.1163/156852507X195745.

Olsen, Birger Munk. *L'étude des auteurs classiques latins aux XIe et XIIe siècles*. 4 volumes. Paris: Editions du Centre national de la recherche scientifique, 1982–2014.

Orchard, Andy. "The Literary Background to the *Encomium Emmae Reginae*." *Journal of Medieval Latin* 11 (2001): 156–83. DOI: 10.1484/J.JML.2.304152.

Otter, Monika. *Inventiones: Fiction and Referentiality in Twelfth-Century English Historical Writing*. Chapel Hill: University of North Carolina Press, 1996.

Partner, Nancy. *Serious Entertainments: The Writing of History in Twelfth-Century England*. Chicago: University of Chicago Press, 1977.

Pellegrin, Élisabeth. "Les manuscrits de Loup de Ferrières." *Bibliothèque de l'École de chartes* 115 (1957): 5–31. DOI: 10.3406/bec.1957.449558.

Pohl, Benjamin. *Dudo of St Quentin's "Historia Normannorum": History, Tradition, and Memory*. Woodbridge: Boydell and Brewer, 2015.

Putter, Ad. "Latin Historiography after Geoffrey of Monmouth." In *The Arthur of Medieval Latin Literature*, edited by Siân Echard, 85–97. Cardiff: University of Wales Press, 2011.

Ray, Roger. "Bede and Cicero." *Anglo-Saxon England* 16 (1987): 1–15. DOI: 10.1017/S0263675100003835.

———. "Bede's *Vera Lex Historiae*." *Speculum* 55, no. 1 (1980): 1–21. DOI: 10.2307/2855707.

———. "The Triumph of Greco-Roman Rhetorical Assumptions in pre-Carolingian Historiography." In *The Inheritance of Historiography 350–900*, edited by Christopher Holdsworth and T.P. Wiseman, 67–84. Exeter: University of Exeter Press, 1986. DOI: 10.5949/liverpool/9780859892728.003.0007.

Riché, Pierre. *Gerbert d'Aurillac, le pape de l'an mil.* Paris: Fayard, 1987.

Riesenweber, Thomas. *Marius Victorinus, Commenta in Ciceronis Rhetorica: Prolegomena und kritischer Kommentar.* 2 volumes. Untersuchungen zur antiken Literatur und Geschichte, Bd. 120.1–2. Berlin: De Gruyter, 2015. DOI: 10.1515/9783110316483.

Schulz, Marie. *Die Lehre von der historischen Methode bei den Geschichtsschreibern des Mittelalters (VI.-XIII. Jahrhundert).* Berlin and Leipzig: W. Rothschild, 1909.

Shopkow, Leah. "The Carolingian World of Dudo of Saint-Quentin." *Journal of Medieval History* 15 (1989): 19–37. DOI: 10.1016/0304-4181(89)90031-6.

Shuttleworth Kraus, Christina, and Anthony Woodman, eds. *Latin Historians.* Oxford: Oxford University Press, 1997.

Simon, Gertrud. "Untersuchungen zur Topik der Widmungsbriefe mittelalterlicher Geschichtsschreibung bis zum Ende des 12. Jahrhunderts." *Archiv für Diplomatik* 4 (1958): 52–119 and 5/6 (1959/60): 73–153. DOI: 10.7788/afd.1960.56.jg.73.

Stoppacci, Patrizia. *Clavis Gerbertiana.* Florence: SISMEL, 2016.

Tamiolaki, Melina. "Lucian on Truth and Lies in Ancient Historiography: The Theory and Its Limits." In *Truth and History in the Ancient World: Pluralising the Past,* edited by Lisa Hau and Ian Ruffell. New York: Routledge, 2017.

Taylor-Briggs, Ruth. "Reading between the Lines: The Textual History and Manuscript Transmission of Cicero's Rhetorical Works." In *The Rhetoric of Cicero in Its Medieval and Renaissance Commentary Tradition,* edited by Virginia Cox and

John O. Ward, 77–108. Boston and Leiden: Brill, 2006. DOI: 10.1163/9789047404644_003.

Tosi, Michel, ed. *Gerberto, scienza, storia e mito. Atti del Gerberti Symposium 25–27 Iuglio 1983*. Piacenza: Archivum Bobiense, 1985.

Tyler, Elizabeth M. *England in Europe: English Royal Women and Literary Patronage c. 1000–1150*. Toronto: University of Toronto Press, 2017. DOI: 10.3138/9781442685956.

———. "Talking about History in Eleventh-Century England: The *Encomium Emmae Reginae* and the Court of Harthacnut." *Early Medieval Europe* 13, no. 4 (2005): 359–83. DOI: 10.1111/j.1468-0254.2005.00162.x.

Walsh, P.G. *Livy: His Historical Aims and Methods*. Cambridge: Cambridge University Press, 1961.

Ward, John O. *Ciceronian Rhetoric in Treatise, Scholion, and Commentary*. Typologie des sources du moyen âge occidental 58. Turnhout: Brepols, 1995.

———. "Cicero's *De inventione* and the *Rhetorica ad Herennium*: Commentaries and Contexts." In *The Rhetoric of Cicero in Its Medieval and Renaissance Commentary Tradition*, edited by Virginia Cox and John O. Ward, 3–69. Boston and Leiden: Brill, 2006.

———. "Some Principles of Rhetorical Historiography in the Twelfth Century." In *Classical Rhetoric and Medieval Historiography*, edited by Ernst Breisach, 103–65. Kalamazoo: Medieval Institute Publications, 1985.

———. "The Medieval Origins of Postmodern Practice." *Parergon* 14, no. 2 (1997): 101–28. DOI: 10.1353/pgn.1997.0012.

Werner, Karl Ferdinand. "Die literarischen Vorbilder des Aimoin von Fleury." In *Medium Aevum Vivum: Festschrift für Walther Bulst*, edited by Hans Robert Jauss and Dieter Schaller, 69–103. Heidelberg: Carl Winter, 1960.

Wiseman, T.P.. *Clio's Cosmetics: Three Studies in Greco-Roman Literature*. Leicester: Leicester University Press, 1979.

———. "Lying Historians: Seven Types of Mendacity." In *Lies and Fiction in the Ancient World*, edited by Christopher Gill and T.P.Wiseman, 122–46. Liverpool: Liverpool University Press, 1993. DOI: doi.org/10.5949/liverpool/9780859893817.003.0004.

Woodman, Anthony *Rhetoric and Classical Historiography: Four Studies*. London: Croom Helm, 1988.

5

The Literary Imaginary of the Past as the Truth of the Present: Occasional Literature in Twelfth-Century Constantinople

Ingela Nilsson

The relation between facts and fiction in literature has been debated for centuries, but it remains unresolved and under discussion to this day. The query concerns primarily the presence of the fictional in historiography, largely influenced and provoked by the work of Hayden White.[1] But, in the last decade or so, there has also been an increasing interest in the factual elements of fiction and the role of the empirical author for the reader's understanding of the fictional imaginary. The desperate quest to identify the "real person" behind the pseudonym Elena Ferrante, author of the successful *Neapolitan Novels* (2011–2015), may be seen as a symptom of this tendency, no longer accepting the theoretical distinction between the historical author, the

---

1 See Hayden White, *Metahistory: The Historical Imagination in Nineteenth-Century Europe* (Baltimore: John Hopkins University Press, 1973), and the essays collected in Hayden White, *The Content of the Form: Narrative Discourse and Historical Representation* (Baltimore: John Hopkins University Press, 1987), all published in the 1980s.

authorial persona, and the narrator.² This is an interesting development in metamodern concerns of the literary, because it reflects to some extent the way in which authorial personas of ancient and medieval literature have been understood as more or less directly corresponding to the empirical authors. Such attitudes have important consequences for the way in which we read texts, regardless of the period in which they were written.

I have previously been concerned with the way in which authors of the later Greek tradition, working in twelfth-century Constantinople, dealt with the narrative strategies of history writing and "novelistic" tendencies.³ Here I should like to return to the same period and socio-cultural context but expand my analysis to include not only explicitly historiographical texts. I wish to explore the concept of occasional literature as a useful way of defining and understanding literature that has an extraliterary end, inscribing itself as a link between the past and the present and placing itself in a position between the fictional and the factual. Such procedures presume an intellectual and cultural tradition that extends backward in time, making the connection to the past relevant to present society, along with a political and social system based on patronage that offers social and professional advancement as a reward for texts or other cultural

---

2 See, e.g., Mavis Himes, "Elena Ferrante and the Question of Authorial Anonymity," *Mavis Himes, PhD,* January 13, 2017, http://www.mavishimes.com/elena-ferrante-and-the-question-of-authorial-anonymity/, and Katherine Hill, "The Elana Ferrante in My Head," *The Paris Review,* January 29, 2020, https://www.theparisreview.org/blog/2020/01/29/the-elena-ferrante-in-my-head/.

3 See Ingela Nilsson, "Discovering Literariness in the Past: Literature vs. History in the Synopsis Chronike of Konstantinos Manasses," in *L'écriture de la mémoire: la littérarité de l'historiographie,* ed. Paulo Odorico, Panagiotes A. Agapetos, and Martin Hinterberger (Paris: Centre d'études byzantines, néo-helléniques et sud-est européennes, École des hautes études en sciences sociales, 2006), 15–31. See also Ingela Nilsson and Roger Scott, "Towards a New History of Byzantine Literature: The Case of Historiography," *Classica et Mediaevalia* 58 (2007): 319-32, on the literary aspects of Byzantine historiography, and, Ingela Nilsson, *Raconter Byzance: la littérature au XII*ᵉ *siècle* (Paris: Belles lettres, 2014) on narrative trends in twelfth-century Byzantium, including historiography.

expressions. For an author working in such a system, self-fashioning and self-promotion become important factors in gaining the attention and appreciation of patrons. Occasional literature therefore demands a strong and "individual" voice, or — as one would say in modern terms — careful "author branding." Before moving on to a case study drawn from twelfth-century Constantinople, I shall briefly sketch the theoretical background and outlines of this model.

The In-Between Position of Occasional Literature

The definition of literature in Byzantium has long been seen as problematic because it is largely a textual production with a seemingly non-literary purpose — a *Gebrauchsliteratur* based on imitation and therefore somehow less literary and less prestigious than previous and later examples.[4] It goes without saying that "literary" and "literature" in a medieval context mean something different from the modern notion, but that does not mean that Byzantine literature was devoid of artistic ambition and aesthetic concerns.[5] Instead, various rhetorical, stylistic, and narratological devices were employed by writers in order to produce texts that were both pleasing from a formal point of view and referential as to their content, which means that the message most often demanded a literary form which could also carry meaning in itself. This is where the use of ancient literature was crucial because the literary and linguistic forms inherited from the Greeks and Romans provided the Byzantines with meaningful ways of casting their texts.

---

[4] For a good summary of the problem, see Margaret Mullett, "No Drama, No Poetry, No Fiction, No Readership, No Literature," in *A Companion to Byzantium*, ed. Liz James (Oxford: Wiley-Blackwell, 2010), 227–38.

[5] See the brief but excellent introductions to literature and art in Charles Barber and Stratis Papaioannou, eds., *Michael Psellos on Literature and Art: A Byzantine Perspective on Aesthetics* (Notre Dame: Notre Dame University Press, 2017), 11–19, 247–61.

An apt way of describing literature and its functions in such a society is to define it as "occasional."[6] This is a concept that has been largely neglected in modern critical discourse, perhaps because of its traditionally low status. The occasional has often been seen as a discourse that has little or no aesthetic value in itself; that is, it merges with and reflects the occasion, lends its voice to someone else (e.g., a patron, a city, or a nation). It accordingly lacks the spontaneous and original voice that, according to romantic notions, defines "poetry proper." When, in the nineteenth century, political and social conditions changed and literary patronage largely disappeared from the public sphere, it fell into disrepute. An interesting reflection on the occasional was made at about this point in history, as Hegel considered its status between "poetry" and "reality" in his *Lectures on Aesthetics* (1835–1838). According to Hegel, occasional pieces (*Gelegenheitsgedichten*) express most amply the "living connection with the real world" (*die lebendige Beziehung zu dem vorhandenen Dasein*). The inferior position of occasional literature is due to this close connection between "the poetic" and "the real," an "entanglement" (*Verflechtung*) of poetry with life, by means of which it falls into a position of "dependence" (*Abhängigkeit*).[7]

---

6 Cf. Wolfram Hörandner, "Customs and Beliefs as Reflected in Occasional Poetry: Some Considerations," *Byzantinische Forschungen* 12 (1987): 235–47, at 236: "An occasional poem is either itself part of a process or of an object, or it describes a process (or object) or refers to them in any way whatsoever. For the modern reader these texts belong to literature; but originally, most of them were made for a special purpose. The German term, rather en vogue of late, is 'Gebrauchstexte', texts intended for use. Consequently, these poems are characterized in disposition and contents by their function." On this issue, see the excellent discussion in Krystina Kubina, *Die enkomiastische Dichtung des Manuel Philes. Form und Funktion des literarischen Lobes in der Gesellschaft der frühen Palaiologenzeit* (Berlin: De-Gruyter, 2020), esp. 163–87.

7 Georg W.F. Hegel, *Vorlesungen über die Ästhetik*, vol. 3 (Frankfurt am Main: Suhrkamp, 1970), 269–70. Hegel's interest in the occasional stemmed from his concern with art's relation to human existence (*Dasein*) and must therefore be seen in the wider perspective of his philosophical understanding of aesthetics. For a detailed discussion, see Gary Shapiro, "Hegel on the Meanings of Poetry," *Philosophy and Rhetoric* 8, no. 2 (1975): 88–107. Note also

Hegel's remarks are useful as a point of departure for a discussion of how this "entanglement" of poetry with life functions in practice. If we turn to modern literary criticism, historiography has generally been seen to have a closer relation to "facts" than poetry does, even if most scholars now would probably agree that historical narration does not reflect reality but rather presents it. To cite Roland Barthes, "reality" is but an unformulated meaning, "sheltering behind the apparent omnipotence of the referent."[8] Even though philosopher-scholars such as White, Hegel, and Barthes had different purposes with their studies, ranging from an interest in the philosophy of history to the narratological affiliation of "factography" and fiction, they were all in some way concerned with the entanglement of poetry and literature with reality. To some extent, one could argue that all literature is marked by this entanglement, in the sense that all artistic expression is based on some sort of human experience of the world. But through its generally referential character, occasional literature may be seen as more closely connected to a specific understanding of "reality" than literature in general. The reason is the fact that it is "occasioned" by specific events and/or needs to express a certain message of an often ideological character. In so doing, it employs and explores literary imaginaries that most often belong to the tradition on which the literature in question relies, which creates a link between the fictional imaginary of the past and the occasion at hand.

Since the literary text here is understood not as passive but as active and referential, a reader-response perspective becomes

---

Hayden White's discussion on Hegel's philosophy of history in *Metahistory*, 81–131.

8 Roland Barthes, "Historical Discourse," trans. Peter Wexler, in *Structuralism: A Reader*, ed. Michael Lane (London: Cape, 1970), 145–55, 154; first published as "Le discours de l'histoire," *Social Science Information* 6, no. 4 (1967): 65–75. Cf. Gérard Genette, *Fiction et diction: Précédé de, Introduction à l'architexte* (Paris: Seuil, 2004), 141–68, esp. 151–63, on the relation between fictional and factual narrative. Similar reasoning lies at the core of Hayden White's pioneering studies of historical imagination, showing how all historiography — ranging from annalistic chronicles to narrative histories — is imbued by narrative strategies that have close affinities with fiction.

necessary and is conditioned by the patronage system which offered occasions for literary performances.⁹ In her study of occasional poetry in the Renaissance, Jane Tompkins has described it as a kind of "public relations": "a source of financial support, a form of social protection, a means of securing a comfortable job, an instrument of socialization, a move in a complicated social game, or even a direct vehicle of courtship."¹⁰

Such a description suits also the circumstances under which Constantine Manasses (c. 1115–1175) and his peers worked, a setting in which a literary work was "not so much an object, therefore, as a unit of force whose power is exerted on the world in a particular direction."¹¹ In order to exert this power, writers needed to create a clearly recognizable voice as a means to communicate with both patron and audience, carrying a message that is relevant to them but yet keeping the writer's trademark. Such a voice can be achieved in various ways: linguistically, or stylistically, or narratologically.

Based on these considerations, my own understanding of occasional literature includes both commissioned works and self-promotional works produced in the hope of future commissions, written in either poetry or prose, for one specific occasion, in a short period or over a long period of time.¹² I should

---

9 On performance in Byzantium, see Margaret Mullett, "Rhetoric, Theory and the Imperative of Performance: Byzantium and Now," in *Rhetoric in Byzantium*, ed. Elizabeth Jeffreys (Aldershot: Ashgate Variorum, 2003), 151–71; Emmanuel C. Bourbouhakis, "Rhetoric and Performance in Byzantium," in *The Byzantine World*, ed. Paul Stephenson (London: Routledge, 2010), 175–87; and Przemyslaw Marciniak, "The Byzantine Performative Turn," in *Within the Circle of Ancient Ideas and Virtues: Studies in Honour of Professor Maria Dzielska*, ed. Kamilla Twardowska (Krakow: Historia Iagellonica, 2014), 423–30.

10 Jane P. Tompkins, "The Reader in History: The Changing Shape of Literary Response," in *Reader-Response Criticism: From Formalism to Post-Structuralism*, ed. Jane P. Tomkins (Baltimore: Johns Hopkins University Press, 1980), 201–32, at 208.

11 Ibid., 204.

12 Cf. Kubina, *Die enkomiastische Dichtung*, 235–38, on "Externe und interne Motivation," including uncommissioned poems ("ohne Bestellung"); also Emmanuel Bourbouhakis, *Not Composed in a Chance Manner: The Epi-*

like to underline that, in my view, both the occasional situation and writing on command privilege originality and encourage the challenging of conventions. In the following, I shall try to show how this works in a selection of works by the twelfth-century writer Constantine Manasses.[13]

Literature in Twelfth-Century Byzantium

Byzantine literature has long been known primarily for its imitation and continuation of the ancient Greek tradition, to the extent that it used to be seen rather as an inferior, decadent and distant relative of the noble Greeks. Such attitudes now belong in the past and Byzantine culture on the whole has been subject to a substantial revision, not the least in regard to its literary output. Rather than being imitative or static, it is characterized by an intense emulation and use of the Graeco-Roman heritage, including its Biblical and Patristic tradition. This use became particularly emphatic and to some extent charged in the twelfth century when the imperial family Komnenos had established a stable, financially and strategically successful empire, which at the same time was threatened from the outside: in the west by Normans and the Crusaders; in the east by the Seldjuk Turks.[14]

In the capital, Constantinople, there was now a court and an aristocracy in great need of three things. First, they needed an educational system that could produce functionaries for the administration of both the Church and the Empire, not only for the capital but for the entire East Roman expanse. Second, they needed an intellectual elite that could write occasional litera-

---

taphios for Manuel I Komnenos by Eustathios of Thessalonike (Uppsala: Acta Upsaliensis, 2017), 47* and 59*, on the specific occasions for performance in the twelfth century.

13 A fuller discussion of these issues can be found in Ingela Nilsson, *Writer and Occasion in Twelfth-Century Byzantium: The Authorial Voice of Constantine Manasses* (Cambridge: Cambridge University Press, 2021).

14 The best introduction to twelfth-century Byzantium remains Paul Magdalino, *The Empire of Manuel I Komnenos, 1143–1180* (Cambridge: Cambridge University Press, 1993). On Byzantine literature in the twelfth century, see also Nilsson, *Raconter Byzance*.

ture of different kinds — poems to celebrate a new-born prince or orations to announce and praise the victories of the emperor — for the new aristocracy that now had a central place next to the imperial court and acted as both patrons and audience of the rhetorical production. Third, there was a need for constant confirmation of one's own identity as Roman, Greek (in the cultural sense), and orthodox Christian. This would be particularly important in times like these, when the Byzantine world was threatened from both East and West. These three needs — education, occasional literature, and cultural confirmation — were filled by persons who could combine all three in their particular competence: a fairly large group of intellectuals who were active as teachers, rhetoricians, and poets. They often began their careers as teachers, either at one of the large schools in Constantinople or as private teachers, while also writing on commission for the court and the aristocracy. They could gain positions of different kinds within administration, as secretaries, notaries or higher functionaries, and a particularly successful career could end with an episcopate.

Interesting from a socio-cultural perspective is how the early career as a teacher offered opportunities to create networks that included influential families from the court and the aristocracy — networks that could later be used for a career as occasional writer, rhetorician, or historian. Former students could become not just potential clients but also mighty protectors. A case in point is Constantine Manasses, who is not among the better-known Byzantine authors and whose texts have not received much attention in the last century. He is a good example of someone who was active and successful for a long period — at least thirty years — and who wrote for a network of protectors who belonged to the imperial and aristocratic circles of Constantinople. Something that makes Manasses particularly apt for an investigation like this is his way of openly addressing in his texts his own position as teacher and writer, often in a manner that also reveals significant information on his patrons.

This "autobiographical" style of Manasses has rather frequently been read as offering insight into the "reality" of the author's feelings and personal life.[15] In contrast to such interpretations, I take an interest not primarily in Manasses the "empirical author," but in Manasses the "model author": the way in which he projected himself in his texts, using a voice that was recognizable to his audience.[16] This voice is significant for my understanding of occasional writing, since it is the central part of authorial self-fashioning. A study of all texts by Manasses that have come down to us reveals a surprisingly homogenous and consistent authorial persona. It is achieved on both linguistic and narrative levels, offering a coherent stylistic voice and a story that goes with it.

There are almost thirty preserved texts dating from the late 1130s or early 1140s to c. 1175. They span an entire career and offer a wide range of rhetorical and literary forms: from grammar exercises (schedography) and didactic poems to a large chronicle in verse and a series of orations dedicated to, among others, the emperor himself, Manuel I Komnenos (1143–1180). It is a varied production by an author who has often been dismissed as ingratiating and entertaining but who offers rich material for understanding better how occasional writing functioned in the twelfth century. Here I shall offer a small selection of passages in order to illustrate how Manasses employed the same style,

---

15 See esp. Catia Galatariotou, "Travel and Perception in Byzantium," *Dumbarton Oaks Papers* 47 (1993): 221–41, with the response by Margaret Mullett, "In Peril on the Sea: Travel Genres and the Unexpected," in *Travel in the Byzantine World*, ed. Ruth Macrides (Aldershot: Ashgate Variorum, 2002), 259–84, but note also Paul Magdalino, "In Search of the Byzantine Courtier: Leo Choirosphaktes and Constantine Manasses," in *Byzantine Court Culture from 829 to 1204*, ed. Henry Maguire (Cambridge: Harvard University Press, 1997), 141–65, at 162.

16 I rely here on the distinction made by Umberto Eco between empirical and model author; see, for example, Umberto Eco, *Six Walks in the Fictional Woods* (Cambridge: Harvard University Press, 1994), 15: "The model author […] is a voice that speaks to us affectionately (or imperiously, or slyly), that wants us beside it. This voice is manifested as a narrative strategy, as a set of instructions which is given to us step by step and which we have to follow when we decide to act as the model reader." This does not mean that the empirical and the model author are entirely separate unities; see further below.

the same motifs and the same imagery throughout his career, at the same time returning to some themes that concern his own activities as a writer.

The Authorial Voice and the Toils of Learning

Let us begin with a didactic poem that probably was written early in Manasses's career, when he was educating relatively young pupils in ancient Greek grammar and literature (late 1130s or early 1140s). It is a biography of the ancient author Oppian, consisting of fifty-two fifteen-syllable verses, the Byzantine so-called "political" verse.[17] The tradition of writing biographies of authors and poets goes back to antiquity and is accordingly part of a long tradition, but the twelfth century displays a particular interest in the authorial models of the past.[18] Manasses's poem presents a rather conventional biography, similar to other known tales of Oppian's life. It opens with his family and homeland: he was from the city of Nazarbos in Cilicia and his father Agesilaos was "filled with wisdom and learning | of the best and very highest kind."[19] This was in the time of Septimius Severus (193–211 AD), father of Marcus Antoninus, now better known as Caracalla (198–217). When the emperor came to Cili-

---

17 Aristide Colonna, "De Oppiani vita antiquissima," *Bollettino del Comitato per la preparazione della edizione nazionale dei classici greci e latini* 12 (1964): 33–40.

18 On authorial biographies in antiquity, see Mary R. Lefkowitz, *The Lives of the Greek Poets* (1981; rpt. Baltimore: Johns Hopkins University Press, 2012); this study focuses on the early period and does not include Oppian. On the twelfth-century interest in authorial personas of the past, see Eric Cullhed, "The Blind Bard and 'I': Homeric Biography and Authorial Personas in the Twelfth Century," *Byzantine and Modern Greek Studies* 38, no. 1 (2014): 49–67, and Aglae Pizzone, "The Autobiographical Subject in Tzetzes' Chiliades: An Analysis of Its Components," in *Storytelling in Byzantium: Narratological Approaches to Byzantine Texts and Images*, ed. Charálambos Messis, Margaret Mullett, and Ingela Nilsson (Uppsala: Uppsala University, 2018), 279–96.

19 Constantine Manasses, *Life of Oppian*, ll. 5–6: "σοφίας ὄντος τοῦ πατρὸς ἔμπλεω καὶ παιδείας | τῆς μείζονος καὶ μάλιστα καὶ τῆς ὑψηλοτέρας." Unless otherwise stated, all translations from Manasses's texts are my own.

cia to subdue his rivals, all local Cilician men took part in the campaign — only Oppian's father Agesilaos was missing: "For he spent his time, night and day, with books, | hunting down the best of all kinds of learning, | at the same time training his son for similar hunts."[20]

The emperor was annoyed, he sent for this "lover of wisdom" and had him exiled to the island of Melite (Malta). Oppian accordingly went to Malta with his father where he stayed until he was thirty, and it was there that he wrote first his treatise on fishing (*Halieutica*), then the one on hunting (*Cynegetica*) and finally the one of bird catching (*Ixieutica*). He also wrote other short books, notes the narrator, but time spared only those on hunting and fishing.[21] Oppian then went to Rome, where he met the new emperor, Antoninus (because Severus had passed away), and "handed over to him the books at which he had toiled (πονηθείσας)."[22] His feelings for the emperor appeared to be so great that he was awarded a wish, and his father was thus released from his exile. In addition, Oppian received one golden stater for each verse of his works.

The rest, says the narrator, he will disregard in order to avoid a long story, and with this the narrative as such is over. In its place, a list of "facts" (ὅτι) is presented: that they returned together to Nazarbos, but Oppian died in a plague that afflicted the city; that after his death, the people raised a statue of Oppian, inscribed with elegiac verses. Finally,

---

20 Ibid., ll. 16–18: "βίβλοις καὶ γὰρ ἐσχόλαζε νύκτωρ καὶ μεθ' ἡμέραν | θηρώμενος τὰ κάλλιστα πάντων τῶν μαθημάτων, | καὶ σκυλακεύων τὸν υἱὸν ἐς τὰς ὁμοίας θήρας."

21 Ibid., ll. 27–30. This corresponds to the modern situation, though the surviving work on hunting now is believed to be the work of a different Oppian. It opens with an invocation of Caracalla and the goddess Artemis, while the treatise on fishing has a dedication to Marcus Aurelius and his son Commodus. The treatise on bird-catching has survived only in an anonymous prose paraphrase, probably the same that Manasses used for his own descriptions of such hunting methods. See further below.

22 Ibid., l. 34: "καὶ βίβλους ἐνεχείρισεν αὐτῷ τὰς πονηθείσας."

that he [Oppian] suitably succeeds in pronouncing on every subject, | bringing the things he discusses in front of the readers' eyes | and, finally, that smoothness is abundant in his discourses, | enveloping clarity like a flower, | and that he also knows how to handle the density of thoughts, | which is difficult and extremely toilsome (ἐργῶδες) for rhetors.[23]

Despite this apparently simple and typical biography of Oppian, the text accordingly contains quite a few interesting references to the situation of a rhetor-writer, agreeing with points made by Manasses in other works. The life of Oppian is accordingly used as an imaginary of the past that can tell a truth of the present, as a metanarrative telling the story of the author himself.

First, is the description of Agesilaos studying night and day, so intensely that he misses the arrival of the emperor. This is a common motif not only in didactic poems, but also in other texts by Manasses. It is particularly prominent in his account of an embassy to the court of Tripoli, the so-called *Hodoiporikon* or *Itinerary*.[24] This is a narrative poem in four parts, describing how the poet-narrator is recruited for an expedition to the Crusader states with the aim of finding a new wife for the emperor, Manuel I Komnenos (1143–1180). His first wife has passed away in 1160/1161 after having given birth to two daughters, so Manuel needed a wife who could give him a male heir. Often read as a documentary or personal description of a journey to the Holy Land, the *Itinerary* may also be interpreted as a literary and rhetorical means of praising the qualities of the capital and the emperor, by describing the extreme longing that smites

---

23 Ibid., ll. 47–52: "ὅτι τυγχάνει προσφυῶς πάνυ τοι γνωματεύων, | τὰ πράγματα δ' ὑπόψια δείκνυσι παραβάλλων, | καὶ τελευταῖον ὡς πολὺ τὸ λεῖον ἐν τοῖς λόγοις, | ὃ τοῦ σαφοῦς σκευαστικὸν οἷά περ ἄνθος ἔχει, | ἠδ' οἶδε τὴν πυκνότητα τὴν τῶν ἐνθυμημάτων, | ὃ δυσχερὲς τοῖς ῥήτορσι καὶ παντελῶς ἐργῶδες."

24 Konstantin Horna, "Das Hodoiporikon des Konstantin Manasses," *Byzantinische Zeitschrift* 13, no. 2 (1904): 313–55; Κωνσταντῖνος Μανασσῆς, Ὁδοιπορικόν: κριτικὴ ἔκδοσις, μετάφρασις, σχόλια, ed. and trans. Konstantinos Chryssogelos (Athens: Sokele, 2017).

the writer-narrator who is forced to leave it behind.²⁵ The Holy Land is described as terribly hot and with bad food and foul water — the poet wonders how Jesus could even stand to live there. He falls ill and has to recover in Cyprus, where he finds a temporary sanctuary with one of his protectors. But even there, he finds himself far from the protecting environment of the capital: "For what is the dull flicker of the modest stars | compared with that all-feeding flame of the sun? | In comparison with the City of Constantine, | what's Cyprus in its totality and particulars?"²⁶ This image of the capital as the sun outshining the stars is reminiscent of the depiction of Emperor Manuel as the sun, employed in other texts by Manasses and imbuing the capital with imperial power. The narrator then focalizes his own experience of that power and compares it to his situation in Cyprus:

> Oh toil (μόχθος), oh education, oh learned men's books | with which from childhood I was senselessly stuffed; | oh torment of my body, oh these lengthy nights | which I spent in the company of books, | awake, not letting my eyes close for sleep, | isolated like a sparrow in my room, | or rather like an owl in the dark. | I live here in a land where literature is scarce, | I sit here idly, my lips are shackled, | I'm unemployed, immobile like a prisoner, | a rhetorician without a

---

25 Ingela Nilsson, "La douceur des dons abondants: Patronage et littérarité dans la Constantinople des Comnènes," in *La face cachée de la littérature byzantine: Le texte en tant que message immédiat*, ed. Paolo Odorico (Paris: Centre d'études byzantines, néo-helléniques et sud-est européennes, École des hautes études en sciences sociales, 2012), 179–93.

26 Constantine Manasses, *Itinerary*, ll. 2.87–90: "τί γὰρ ταπεινῶν ἀστρίων ἀμαυρότης | πρὸς τὴν τὸ πᾶν βόσκουσαν ἡλίου φλόγα; | ἢ τί πρὸς αὐτὴν τὴν Κωνσταντίνου πόλιν | ἡ Κύπρος ἡ σύμπασα καὶ τὰ τῆς Κύπρου." Translation by Willem J. Aerts, "A Byzantine Traveller to one of the Crusader States," in *East and West in the Crusader States: Contexts — Contacts — Confrontations III*, ed. Krijnie Ciggaar and Herman Thuele (Leuven: Peeters, 2003), 165–221, here modified. Cf. *Itinerary*, 2.154–55 on Constantinople as "eye of the world, ornament of the globe, | wide-shining star and lantern of this earth."

tongue, with no liberty of speech, | a rhetorician without a voice, without his exercise.[27]

The suffering intellectual is familiar from other Komnenian authors, but Manasses offers a decisive twist of the motif: the toils of learning, being part of Constantinopolitan life, are contrasted with the province, void of learning and, most importantly, without a function for a Constantinopolitan rhetorician. The home that he remembers was filled with laborious reading of books of the past, highly relevant in the present: the allusions used in the poem suggest both classical and biblical literature.[28] The narrator continues to describe the fate of such a voiceless orator, likening his situation to that of a garden without water, to crickets wasting away in the winter, to a singing bird trapped in a cage. The only remedy to his ailments is to return to the capital, where he has a function and can exercise his craft. Such descriptions put the focus on the writer rather than the emperor, and the *Itinerary* can thus be used as a way of better understanding the situation of a writer on commission — a cricket, a singing-bird — and his relation to the emperor and his protective wings. The praise of the imperial capital becomes, at the same time, a praise of not only the emperor but also of his eulogist, the writer-narrator, and his skills — his grasp of ancient imagery.

---

27 Constantine Manasses, *Itinerary*, 2.91–102: "ὦ μόχθος, ὦ μάθησις, ὦ σοφῶν βίβλοι, | αἷς συνεσάπην ἀνοήτως ἐκ νέου· | ὦ σώματος κάκωσις, ὦ νυκτῶν δρόμοι, | ἃς ἀνάλωσα ταῖς βίβλοις ἐντυγχάνων, | ἄϋπνος, οὐ βλέφαρα κάμπτων εἰς ὕπνον, | ὥσπερ μονάζων στρουθὸς ἐν δωματίῳ, | ἢ μᾶλλον εἰπεῖν, ἐν σκότει νυκτικόραξ. | εἰς γῆν παροικῶ τὴν σπανίζουσαν λόγων· | ἀργὸς κάθημαι, συμπεδήσας τὸ στόμα, | ἀεργός, ἀκίνητος ὡς φυλακίτης, | ῥήτωρ ἄγλωσσος οὐκ ἔχων παρρησίαν, | ῥήτωρ ἄφωνος οὐκ ἔχων γυμνασίαν."

28 The Itinerary opens with the narrator reading Athenaeus in bed, probably a programmatic reference to yet another ancient author who was concerned with the Greek heritage. In the passage cited above, there is an allusion to Psalm 102:6 ("I am like a desert owl of the wilderness, | like an owl of the waste places"). This way of mingling "pagan" and biblical references is typical for Byzantine literature.

The toil and labor that is thematized in these passages, often in terms of μόχθος or πόνος or one of their many synonyms, recurs in Manasses's works in relation to both education and the production of commissioned work. A good example of the latter may be found in the large verse chronicle for which Manasses is most known, the *Synopsis Chronike*, written in the 1140s for one of the most important women patrons of the twelfth century, sebastokratorissa Irene.[29] It accordingly belongs rather early in Manasses's career and may have influenced his future commissions and networks. In the introductory verses to the chronicle, the author describes his task as follows:

> Since you, as a foster child of learning (τροφίμη λόγου), have desired | that a comprehensible and clear narrative should be composed for you, | teaching ancient history in a plain manner | — who reigned from the beginning and how far they reached, | over whom they ruled and for how many years — | I will take on the burden of this toil, | even though it is a difficult and burdensome task, involving much work (ἐργῶδες); | for I am compensated for my efforts in this writing (τοὺς ἐν τοῖς λόγοις μόχθους) | by the size of your gifts and your generosity, | and the burning heat of my toil and travail | is cooled by your gifts, frequently bestowed.[30]

---

29 *Constantini Manassi Breviarium Chronicum*, ed. Odysseus Lampsidis (Athens: Apud Institutum Graecoromanae, 1996). On Irene, see Elizabeth Jeffreys, "The Sebastokratorissa Irene as Patron," in *Female Founders in Byzantium and Beyond*, Wiener Jahrbuch für Kunstgeschichte 60/61 2011/2012, ed. Lioba Theis, Margaret Mullett, Michael Grünbart, Galina Fingarova, and Mattew Savage (Vienna: Boehlau, 2014), 175–92.

30 *Synopsis Chronike*, 7–17: "ἐπεὶ γοῦν ἐπεπόθησας οἷα τροφίμη λόγου / εὐσύνοπτόν σοι καὶ σαφῆ γραφὴν ἐκπονηθῆναι, | τρανῶς ἀναδιδάσκουσαν τὰς ἀρχαιολογίας | καὶ τίνες ἦρξαν ἀπ' ἀρχῆς καὶ μέχρι ποῦ προῆλθον | καὶ τίνων ἐβασίλευσαν καὶ μέχρις ἐτῶν πόσων, | ἡμεῖς ἀναδεξόμεθα τὸ βάρος τοῦ καμάτου, | κἂν δυσχερές, κἂν ἐπαχθὲς τὸ πρᾶγμα, κἂν ἐργῶδες· | παραμυθοῦνται γὰρ ἡμῶν τοὺς ἐν τοῖς λόγοις μόχθους | αἱ μεγαλοδωρίαι σου καὶ τὸ φιλότιμόν σου, | καὶ τὸν τοῦ κόπου καύσωνα καὶ τῆς ταλαιπωρίας | αἱ δωρεαὶ δροσίζουσι κενούμεναι συχνάκις." Cf. translation by Michael Jeffreys, "The Nature and Origin of Political Verse," *Dumbarton Oaks Papers* 28 (1974): 141–95, 158.

This kind of introduction functions as a sort of reminder or perhaps repetition of the agreement that had most likely been made between the commissioner and the writer. In order to underline the learning and writing involved in the process, the word *logos* is used twice (first in singular, then in plural), the meanings of which in Byzantine Greek span from the original "word," "tale" and "reason" to "oratory," "writing," "learning," and "literature."

This situation of patronage brings us back to the *Life of Oppian* and the tale of how Oppian went to Rome and handed over his works to the emperor Caracalla. This story has a clear parallel in contemporary patronage situations and Manasses's relation to Irene and other patrons. In Manasses's poem, Oppian went to Rome to see the emperor and "handed over to him the books he had toiled at (βίβλους [...] τὰς πονηθείσας)." Even the choice of verb (πονέω) for his production of books thus recalls the vocabulary of such toilsome writing on command or for powerful persons, as it is in the case of Irene cited above. It is clear from both texts that πόνος and λόγος — "hard work" and "literature" — belong together. For this hard work and its result, the emperor awarded Oppian with a wish and a gold coin for each of the verses he had written. This is another parallel to the patronage situation in which Manasses and his students found themselves: they were probably awarded much less for their texts, but Oppian provided an example of how an author of the past had worked for the emperor, just as many did now in the twelfth century.

Such a system demanded good relations with both peers and patrons, and sometimes the line between the two is difficult to draw since, as we shall see, the relation between writer and addressee tends to be described in terms of similarity. Education and learning had a high status, also for individuals of noble birth. Sebastokratorissa Irene, who may have been of non-Byzantine birth but who married into the imperial family, needed simple teaching in the Graeco-Roman heritage. That is why she was still a "foster child of learning" (τροφίμη λόγου) in adulthood. By contrast, those who were born into the imperial family, and especially the boys, had been taught from a young age by teachers like Manasses.

The Authorial Voice and the Characterization of the Addressee

This brings us to the final paragraph of the *Life of Oppian* on the skills and advantages of the ancient author. These lines tie in with the activities of a rhetor and offer some technical advice to the reader or listener, presumably a student, as regards the composition of such discourse. Oppian is useful because he offers suitable topics presented in a smooth and clear form, even "dense" thoughts are handled with skill — something even rhetors struggle with and students therefore need to learn. This comment is useful to have in mind as one moves on to the later phase of Manasses's career and a series of orations that he wrote for patrons and "friends" in the 1160s and 1170s. What is rather striking in these orations is not only the careful self-representation of the author-narrator, which is only to be expected, but also the elaborate characterization of the addressee. This particular technique could be seen as central to the "poetics of patronage" that shaped literature produced within socio-cultural systems based on commission and symbolic power.

My approach here focuses on the writer and the text, rather than the patron or the system. I have been inspired by Margaret Mullett's writer-centered approach, based on the observation that Komnenian writers did not write for only one patron, but rather accepted patronage where they could find it.[31] But in order to offer a more nuanced definition of what patronage in the twelfth century is and means, I have adapted the anthropological-semiotic model proposed by the musicologist Claudio Annibaldi for the case of musical patronage in the early modern

---

[31] Margaret Mullett, "Aristocracy and Patronage in the Literary Circles of Comnenian Constantinople," in *The Byzantine Aristocracy: IX to XIII Centuries*, ed. Michael Angold (Oxford: British Archaeology Report, 1984), 173–97.

period.³² According to Annibaldi's model, music was intended "to symbolise and represent the social status of the patron commissioning it."³³ This assumption, which is based on the workings of hierarchy and convention, has two implications that are just as relevant for the Byzantine situation (i.e., if "music" may simply be exchanged for "rhetoric"). First, the relationship between rhetorician and patron is conceived as the interplay between the rhetorical event (produced by the rhetorician and commissioned by the patron) and the world "in the presence of which those events took place" — a world "composed of anyone capable of correlating the events in question to the social rank of the individuals or institutions promoting them."³⁴ Second, "the object of the relationship between [rhetorician] and patron is to be identified not as the composition of the [text] (as customarily thought), but as a performance, even an entirely improvised performance"; an extension of the writer's professional duties "to any activity required to realise a [rhetorical] performance appropriate to his patron's rank."³⁵

This can be more or less directly transferred to the twelfth-century situation. The relationship between writer and patron is, in practice, an interplay between the occasion at which a text is performed and the surrounding circle of aristocrats and peers. Moreover, the object of that interplay is the occasional, or performative, aspects of the text. But the question is still what patronage means, that is, in what way music, or indeed rhetoric, "actually symbolised the rank of the individual or institution commissioning it."³⁶ This is an aspect of patronage that has often been overlooked, but Annibaldi's model with its semiotic

---

32 See Claudio Annibaldi, "Towards a Theory of Musical Patronage in the Renaissance and Baroque: The Perspective from Anthropology and Semiotics," *Recercare* 10 (1998): 173–82, which offers a summary in English of the theoretical model presented in the introduction to his *La musica e il mondo: mecenatismo e committenza musicale in Italia tra Quattro e Settecento* (Bologna: Il Mulino, 1993), 9–42.
33 Annibaldi, "Towards a Theory," 173–74.
34 Ibid., 174.
35 Ibid. Brackets indicate my revisions of Annibaldi's text.
36 Ibid., 174.

focus forces us to offer an answer: the performance of the text, along with the text itself (its functions and form), demonstrate the "artistic sensibility and connoisseurship"[37] of the patron. In Byzantine terms it demonstrates their *paideia*. An advantage of Annibaldi's model is also that it focuses on the product, whether music or text, as an expression of a cultural and semiotic relationship rather than a factual relationship between people. There are two ways, he argues, of using commissioned works to represent the social status of the patron, and thus two kinds of patronage, based on "metaphoric" and "metonymic" relationships, that is "similarity" and "contiguity."[38] The latter is the means by which "conventional patronage" achieves its end. The work symbolizes the rank of patron "through reference to repertoires traditionally associated with the élite class" and thus, in the case of Byzantium, proves to be a sort of rhetorical "accessory of the élite itself."[39] In turn, "humanistic patronage" symbolizes the rank of its patron through the display of his artistic sensibility, and it achieves its end by "similarity," "by displaying compositional qualities that parallel the sophisticated tastes of the class in question."[40]

The social status of the patron in twelfth-century Byzantium can certainly be said to reflect these semiotic aspects. Contiguity tends to mark more conventional pieces written for the emperor or other members of the imperial court (e.g., *encomia* of the emperor brimming with topoi) while similarity characterizes pieces written for patrons with whom the writer has a more personal relationship.[41] In the case of Manasses, the dis-

---

37 Ibid.
38 Ibid., 175, drawing on Roman Jakobsen's distinction of linguistic communication in those terms.
39 Annibaldi, "Towards a Theory," 176. Cf. Floris Bernard, *Writing and Reading Byzantine Secular Poetry, 1025–1081* (Oxford: Oxford University Press, 2014), 291–332, and his approach to patronage influenced by Pierre Bordieu's concept of "cultural capital."
40 Annibaldi, "Towards a Theory," 176.
41 These cultural-semiotic relationships are to some extent a reflection of factual relationships, in the sense that the emperor and his close family were more distant from the writer (both ideologically and physically). Moreover,

tance kept between the writer-observer and the object of praise in the ekphrasis *Description of a Crane Hunt* and the encomiastic oration *To Emperor Manuel Komnenos* is an expression of contiguity,[42] while I shall focus on cases of similarity in the following. But first a final theoretical consideration of the presence of a "factual" addressee in a text, that is, a historical person who is known also from other documentation, such as Sebastokratorissa Irene or Manuel Komnenos. Such a presence does not necessarily indicate that he or she was a patron, nor does the characterization of the addressee necessarily reflect the "real" person. While many literary scholars would now agree that the empirical author is not exactly the same as the authorial persona, which may vary considerably from work to work, there has been less discussion of the persona of the addressee. In the case of patronage, it has often been assumed that commissioned texts mirror the wishes and attitudes of the addressees (i.e., patrons) rather than the writer themselves, and that such works should be read as social documents rather than literary works.

James Zetzel challenged this idea by arguing for a "poetics of patronage" that includes the construction of an addressee-patron just as carefully wrought as the persona of the poet.[43] Based on examples from Roman poets of the first century BCE, Zetzel showed how the choice of addressee is not necessarily a function of the relationship between the poet and the person addressed; that is, it does not have to mirror a personal relationship but "can be seen as a correlate of both the subject and the style of the poem."[44] The addressee, which may or may not reflect a real person, is "an element in a work of art" and the rela-

---

the generosity and philanthropy of the emperor was part of his imperial virtues and therefore different from the goodwill of aristocrats.

42 See E. Kurtz, "Eshje dva neizdannyh proizvedenija Konstantina Manassii," *Vizantijskij Vremennik* 12 (1906): 69–98. For an analysis, see Nilsson, *Writer and Occasion*, ch. 2.

43 James E.G. Zetzel, "The Poetics of Patronage in the Late First Century B.C.," in *Literary and Artistic Patronage in Ancient Rome*, ed. Barbara K. Gold (Austin: University of Texas Press, 1982), 87–102.

44 Ibid., 88.

tionship between the writer and the patron, as described in the work, becomes a vehicle for discussing the role of the poet in society.[45] Such an approach seems very useful when we consider twelfth-century texts, in which the writer-patron relationship is often implicitly or explicitly in focus. Combined with Annibaldi's model of relations marked by contiguity vs. similarity, Zetzel's analysis of the addressee thus offers a fruitful way of dealing with patronage from a text-centered perspective. With this in mind, we can turn back to the texts of Manasses.

By the end of the 1160s, Manasses wrote an encomium of a certain Michael Hagiotheodorites, an influential functionary and logothete of the drome (i.e., a position of high standing close to the emperor) in 1166–1170.[46] Hagiotheodorites's administrative position as logothete, as well as his being director of the imperial orphanage (*orphanotrophos*), entailed both wealth and opportunities for patronage.[47] This is indicated not only by the encomium of Hagiotheodorites by Manasses, but also noted in other orations. In addition to dispensing charity directly and through the emperor, he was also known as a skilled writer and rhetorician, which manifested both in imperial administration and in skillfully composed iambic poetry.[48] Manasses is careful to underline this in his encomium, which opens with a story from classical antiquity, introduced with a pun on the multiple meaning of the word *logos* as both story/tale and oration: "This is a Hellenic story (Λόγος οὗτος ἑλλήνιος); the Hellenes were remarkably clever, so may the story (λόγος) not be unprofitable. May this Hellenic story open my oration (τοῦ λόγου λόγος)."[49]

---

45 Ibid., 95.
46 Konstantin Horna, "Eine unedierte Rede des Konstantin Manasses," *Wiener Studien* 28 (1906): 171–204, at 193–94. Hagiotheodorites is not named in the title of the oration, but he can be identified thanks to its content.
47 Magdalino, *The Empire of Manuel I Komnenos*, 256–57.
48 Horna, "Eine unedierte Rede," 194. See also Magdalino, *The Empire of Manuel I Komnenos*, 257, 314.
49 Constantine Manasses, *Encomium of Michael Hagiotheodorites*, ll. 1–2: "Λόγος οὗτος ἑλλήνιος· περιττοὶ τὴν σύνεσιν Ἕλληνες· εἴη ἂν οὖν ὁ λόγος οὐκ ἄχρηστος. ἀρχέτω δή μοι τοῦ λόγου λόγος ἑλλήνιος." Here probably

The story tells of the ancient artists Apelles and Lysippus, intended to illustrate the writer's own situation. He has been writing for the wrong persons, but has now been advised by a friend to turn instead to the addressee, "the noble logothete." The "Hellenic" story, possibly made up by Manasses himself but taking the form of an ancient imaginary, is accordingly used as a means to explain the present occasion.

The encomium is a highly interesting example of the complicated navigation of a patronage system, but what interests me here is the way in which the addressee is characterized as a peer of the writer. As already noted, Hagiotheodorites was known for his rhetorical and literary skills, on which Manasses comments as follows:

> There is never a lack of trophies set up by the emperor (for neither does heaven lack stars, nor the sea water or the sun beautiful light); these triumphs, these famous victories must be made known to the city of Byzantion, the sun among towns, the beauty of the earth, the eye of the universe. Here the logothete writes beautifully and declaims, he displays the graces of the sophistic art that reared him, attracts with melodious writings and delights with beautifully articulated sounds, like the reeds under the lyre.[50]

The glory of Constantinople is here connected to the "cherished sophistic art" inherited from the Graeco-Roman tradition, employed for occasional rhetoric in the service of the empire. The rhetor-narrator then goes on to describe a grammar contest ar-

---

an allusion to Aelian, *Poikile historia* 13 ("Λόγος οὗτος Ἀρακάδιος"), and Horna, "Eine unedierte Rede," 187.

50 Constantine Manasses, *Encomium of Michael Hagiotheodorites*, ll. 253–60: "Οὐκ ἐπιλείπουσί ποτε τρόπαια τῷ αὐτοκράτορι κατορθούμενα (οὐ γὰρ οὐρανῷ ἐλλείπουσιν ἄστρα οὐδὲ ὕδωρ θαλάσσῃ οὐδὲ ἡλίῳ κάλλος φωτός)· ταῦτα δὴ τὰ τροπαιουχήματα, ταύτας τὰς νίκας καὶ περιδόξους χρὴ μαθεῖν καὶ τὴν Βύζαντος, τὸν ἥλιον τῶν χωρῶν, τὸ κάλλος τῆς γῆς, τὸν ὀφθαλμὸν τοῦ παντός. ἐνταῦθα ὁ λογοθέτης εἰς κάλλος γράφει καὶ ῥητορεύει καὶ τὰς τῆς θρεψαμένης σοφιστικῆς ἐπιδείκνυσι χάριτας καὶ εὐκελάδοις ἕλκει γραφαῖς καὶ καλλιστόμοις τέρπει φωναῖς, ὡς οἱ ὑπολύριοι δόνακες."

ranged at the court,⁵¹ an event at which both the logothete and the emperor is present:

> At one occasion a contest is arranged for the foster children of grammar (παισὶ τροφίμοις γραμματικῆς) in the presence of the emperor; and traps preying on their minds are hidden for them and treacherous nets for their intellects are disguised, like the traps for airborne birds, which bird-catchers contrive with lime and decoy birds and snares. Then indeed the logothete discloses his art and fills all around the palace with his voice and prepares snares for the young boys. One would then see his skill in the sophistic art (σοφιστικῆς δεξιότητα) and praise his intelligence and admire his skillful contrivance. One of the young boys was caught by the tip of his wing, another was captured by the neck, one had bitter fetters bound around his back, another yet was fluttering his wings as if to fly away but was also caught; no one could get entirely out of the trap.⁵²

Such occasions are filled with charm, comments the rhetor before moving on to excessively praise the addressee in all other kinds of literary activities, finding him superior even to

---

51 Such events are known to have taken place in the eleventh and twelfth centuries: see Bernard, *Writing and Reading Byzantine Secular Poetry, 1025–1081*, 259–66 and Timothy S. Miller, "Two Teaching Texts from the Twelfth-Century Orphanotropheion," in *Byzantine Authors: Literary Activities and Preoccupations*, ed. John William Nesbitt (Boston and Leiden: Brill, 2003), 9–20.

52 Constantine Manasses, *Encomium of Michael Hagiotheodorites*, ll. 264–74: "ἵσταταί ποτε καὶ παισὶ τροφίμοις γραμματικῆς ἐν ὀφθαλμοῖς βασιλέως ἀγών· καὶ κρύπτονται τούτοις παγίδες νόας θηρεύουσαι καὶ ὑπορύττονται θήρατρα φρενῶν δολωτήρια, καθάπερ ἀεροπόροις ὀρνέοις ἐπιβουλαί, ἃς τεχνάζονται ἰξευταὶ καὶ παλευταὶ καὶ βροχοποιοί. τότε δὴ τότε τὴν ἑαυτοῦ τέχνην ὁ λογοθέτης παραγυμνοῖ καὶ περιλαλεῖ τὰ ἀνάκτορα καὶ ἑτοιμάζει βρόχους τοῖς μείραξιν. ἴδοι τις ἂν τότε σοφιστικῆς δεξιότητα καὶ ἐπαινέσεται τὸ εὐσύνετον καὶ θαυμάζεται τὸ εὐμήχανον· ὁ μὲν τῶν μειράκων ἄκρας ἑάλω τῆς πτέρυγος, ὁ δ' ἐκ μέσης ἐζωγρήθη δειρῆς, τοῦ δὲ νῶτον δέσμη περιέσχε πικρά, ὁ δὲ πτερύσσεται μὲν ὡς ὑπερπετασθησόμενος, ἠγρεύθη δὲ καὶ αὐτός· καὶ παντελῶς οὐδεὶς τὴν παγίδα ἐξήλυσεν."

Herodotus, Xenophon, Sappho, and Anacreon. While these latter similes are rather conventional when praising literary skills, the passage describing the grammar contest is more "personal" in the sense that it describes an event to which the narrator was presumably an eyewitness. The contest is brought up as a way of underlining the intellectual capacities of the addressee, that is, the focus is not on the contest as such, but on the characterization of the logothete. As noted above, such a characterization of the addressee creates a relation between the author and his addressee that is based on metaphorical similarity, potentially flattering for the addressee and accordingly potentially useful for the author. The very foundation of this characterization is the use and the "re-presentation" of the *paideia* of the past.

The description of the logothete is strongly reminiscent of another contest described in the *Funerary Oration on the Death of Nikephoros Komnenos* (c. 1173).[53] Nikephoros was a member of the imperial family and grandchild of the prominent historian Anna Komnene (c. 1083–1153), something that is underlined in the funeral lament.[54] After the traditional praise of Nikephoros's parents and grandparents, the turns come to Nikephoros's skills in rhetoric, poetry and grammar. The role played by Nikephoros is the same that we saw being played by Hagiotheodorites in the passage above, where they both function as some sort of game leaders, "setting traps" in grammar for the students:

> The moment had come when boys gather to wrestle with each other, those whom the [...] grammar has bred and made suckle the breast of schedographic foresight and now

---

53 E. Kurtz, "Evstafija Fessalonikijskago i Konstantina Manassii monodii na konchiny Nikifora Komnina," *Vizantijskij Vremennik* 17 (1910): 283–322.

54 Considerable space is devoted to Anna and her husband Bryennios (*Funerary Oration on the Death of Nikephoros Komnenos*, 120–69), elaborately praising Anna as a female intellectual and poet equal to her husband in intelligence and learning. She is a Theano and a Sappho, but also a Hypatia and a Cleopatra, combining in her person not just philosophical and poetic capacities, but also a simple yet imperial character. On this passage see Leonora Alice Neville, *Anna Komnene: The Life and Work of a Medieval Historian* (Oxford: Oxford University Press, 2016), 118.

send to the palace to fight like brave athletes in speechmaking (γενναίους ἀθλευτὰς λογικῶς) before the emperor, who is acting as prize giver and game master. And then the command of the emperor to Komnenos — the child soldiers of words (οἱ τοῦ λόγου πυγμάχοι παιδίσκοι) were watching his tongue, as though it were the judge of their strength. But what wisdom, what sweetness, what labyrinth of word-traps! How beautiful was there the surface, how cunning was there the depth; the bait was attractive to the eye and the hidden hook strong! The child was gaping, bewitched by what he saw, the trap immediately caught him. So capable was he [Nikephoros] of skillfully arranging a web of words and sneakily hide a combination of industrious nets, and the praised fallacy [...] and device the most efficient hunting implements.[55]

Again, the description underlines the capacities of the addressee and helps characterize him in terms of similarity with the writer. They are both in control of grammar, though they play different roles at the court. In this passage, the kind of traps that are intended are also explained. This is the art of schedography, a grammar exercise that was popular in the twelfth century and

---

55 Constantine Manasses, *Funerary Oration on the Death of Nikephoros Komnenos*, ll. 453–66: "Ἐνειστήκει καιρός, καθ' ὃν συνίασι παῖδες ἀλλήλοις συμπλακησόμενοι, οὓς ἡ πρ [...] γραμματικὴ ὠδινήσασα καὶ σχεδικῆς προνοίας οὖθαρ θηλάσαι ποιήσασα εἰς τὰ βασίλεια πέμπει γενναίους ἀθλευτὰς λογικῶς ἀγωνιουμένους ὑπὸ βραβευτῇ καὶ γυμνασιάρχῃ τῷ αὐτοκράτορι. καὶ τηνικαῦτα τὸ νεῦμα τοῦ βασιλέως ἐπὶ τὸν Κομνηνόν· καὶ οἱ τοῦ λόγου πυγμάχοι παιδίσκοι πρὸς τὴν ἐκείνου γλῶτταν ἑώρων ὡς τῆς αὐτῶν ἰσχύος χρηματίζουσαν βασανίστριαν. ἀλλὰ τῆς σοφίας ἐκείνου, ἀλλὰ τῆς μελιχρότητος, ἀλλὰ τοῦ λαβυρίνθου τῶν δόλων τῶν λογικῶν. ὡς καλὸν ἐκεῖ καὶ τὸ ἐπιπόλαιον, ὡς εὐφυὲς ἐκεῖ καὶ τὸ κατὰ βάθους, καὶ τὸ κατ' ὄψιν δέλεαρ ἑλκτικὸν καὶ τὸ λανθάνον ἄγκιστρον κραταιόν. ἐπέχαινε μὲν ὁ παιδίσκος τῷ φαινομένῳ θελγόμενος, ἡ δὲ παγὶς εὐθέως συνεῖχεν αὐτόν. οὕτως ἦν ταχὺς λογικὴν πλεκτάνην εὖ διαθέσθαι καὶ τεχνικῶν ἀρκύων ὑπορύξαι πλοκὴν ἐπαινούμενόν τε ψεῦδος [...] καὶ θήρατρα μηχανήσασθαι δεξιώτατα." The text of the manuscript is damaged, and I rely on the edition by Kurtz for my understanding of the passage.

that Manasses, among many others teachers, composed.[56] The aim of the exercise was to practice ancient Greek grammar and orthography by exposing the students to various "mistakes" that they were supposed to correct. Again, we are dealing with a representation of *paideia*, where the *schede* are exposing the students to ancient grammar just like the author is exposing his audience to the forms, characters and imaginaries of ancient literature.

The praise of Nikephoros goes on. His rhythm and cadence in all metric varieties was amazing, and he was superior to Archilochus as well as to Ion of Achaea and "the poet of Cilicia" (probably Aratus, but perhaps Oppian), superior to his contemporaries and receiving the praise of the emperor. Nowhere in the oration is it explicitly stated that Nikephoros was Manasses's patron, nor that he had been one of his proud teachers. Eustathios of Thessaloniki too, in his monody on Nikephoros Komnenos, praises his intellectual capacities and mentions the grammar competition.[57] Does this mean that both authors had witnessed the same or similar events at the court, and that they did so in their capacity as teachers? Not necessarily. That specific setting may have been a construction, just like the characterization of the deceased. It is, however, likely that Nikephoros, who was born c. 1143 and probably went to school in the 1150s and 1160s, had encountered both Eustathios and Manasses during his years of education in Constantinople. Moreover, the way in which Manasses inserts personal experiences of not only Nikephoros himself, but also of his mother, seems to indicate a familiarity and "friendship" that probably should be defined in terms of patronage. But regardless of exactly how the relation between

---

56 For a basic definition of schedograhy, see Panagiotis A. Agapitos, "Grammar, Genre, and Patronage in the Twelfth Century: A Scientific Paradigm and Its Implications," *Jahrbuch der Österreichischen Byzantinistik* 64 (2014): 1–22, at 4–5. For the schede by Manasses, see Ioannis D. Polemis, "Fünf unedierte Texte des Konstantinos Manasses," *Rivista di Studi Bizantino e Neoellenici* 33 (1996): 279–92.
57 Kurtz, "Evstafija Fessalonikijskago i Konstantina Manassii monodii," 290–302.

Manasses and Nikephoros looked, the text itself offers an image of a writer-patron relation that is based on some kind of teacher-student relation in early years. This relation is clearly based on similarity, with the student eventually becoming more or less the teacher's peer.

These two passages describing grammar competitions are interesting in several ways. First of all, they offer a unique insight into the educational system of twelfth-century Constantinople, preparing the pupils for performance in the presence of the emperor. Moreover, they show that Manasses had a position in that system, perhaps as teacher at the imperial orphanage, the so-called *Orphanotropheion*.[58] At the same time, the two texts are important sources for the understanding of relations between different agents within a culture based on patronage. As a teacher who was involved in the education of young aristocrats and members of the imperial family, one was similarly involved in the education of future patrons and commissioners. Being a teacher was accordingly also a means to securing one's future career as a poet and rhetorician. More importantly, the key to success was the mastering of the linguistic and literary past and the capacity to make it relevant in the present.

The Creative Force of the Occasion, the Strong Voice of Its Producers

To conclude, I should like to return to the didactic poem on Oppian and its closing verses, which discuss Oppian's stylistic and rhetorical advantages. In light of what was noted above — that Oppian is represented as a poet who laboriously writes for the emperor, just like Manasses himself — these verses gain a particular importance. Not only because Manasses was a rhetorician, but also because one of his recurring devices was the use of ekphrastic discourse, that is the rhetorical description that brings before the eyes of the reader/listener the object depict-

---

58 Cf. Polemis, "Fünf unedierte Texte," 280–81, arguing that Manasses was a teacher at the Patriarchal School in Constantinople.

ed.[59] This strategy comes to the fore in the descriptions of the grammar contests in which students were involved. The imagery employed for describing the toils of the grammar students, as a struggle for life or death in the manner of bird catching, makes the scene vivid and dramatic. The same representations are used extensively in two independent ekphraseis by Manasses, the *Description of a Crane Hunt* and the *Description of the Catching of Finches,* while the bird imagery is prevalent in several of his texts. Such imagery goes back to the treatise on bird catching by Oppian, or rather to the anonymous prose paraphrase that was circulating in Byzantine times and that Manasses probably used as a model for his own descriptions.[60] This means that Oppian's hunting descriptions played an important role throughout Manasses's career as an important ancient model for Byzantine students, teachers, and professional writers on commission. The characterization of Oppian as a peer of Manasses's authorial persona was perfectly in line with such hypertextual procedures,[61] in which the ancient texts were used not only as linguistic and literary resources, but also for metanarrative purposes.

---

59 On the ekphrasis in the Greek tradition, see the standard work by Ruth Webb, *Ekphrasis, Imagination and Persuasion in Ancient Rhetorical Theory and Practice* (Farnham: Ashgate, 2009). On Manasses's use of ekphrasis, see Ingela Nilsson, "Narrating Images in Byzantine Literature: The Ekphraseis of Konstantinos Manasses," *Jahrbuch der Österreichischen Byzantinistik* 55 (2005): 121–46, and Ingela Nilsson, "Constantine Manasses, Odysseus and the Cyclops: On Byzantine Appreciation of Pagan Art in the Twelfth Century," *Byzantinoslavica* 69 (2011): 123–36.

60 See above, n. 21. This was probably noted also by readers of Manasses; one of the manuscripts of his *Life of Oppian,* Marc. F. a. 479, has Manasses's poem copied after Oppian's *Cynegetica.*

61 I deliberately use the term "hypertextual" rather than "intertextual," relying on Genette's model of literature as "palimpsestuous," that is, consisting of several layers of complex transtextual relationships. See Gérard Genette, *Palimpsests: Literature in the Second Degree,* trans. Channa Newmand and Claude Dubinsky (Lincoln: University of Nebraska Press, 1997); for this approach and Byzantine literature, see Ingela Nilsson, "The Same Story but Another: A Reappraisal of Literary Imitation in Byzantium," in *Imitatio — Aemulatio — Variatio,* ed. Elisabeth Schiffer and Andrea Rhoby (Vienna: Österreichische Akademie der Wissenschaften, 2010), 195–208.

This way of creating a clear and consistent authorial voice with the help of recurring motifs, stylistic, and narrative devices is central to my understanding of occasional literature. Not all texts discussed here would traditionally be seen as "occasional" in the strict sense, but they all have an extraliterary aim, that is, they are "occasioned" by a specific event or patron, and they were all performed at one or several occasions. In that capacity, they offered a connection between that "real" event (i.e., the present) and its hypotextual reality (the past). Thus bringing in a variety of "fictional" hypotexts, imageries, and discourses, the occasional pieces of Manasses would have a two-fold function: to display and promote the author himself and his production and, at the same time, to challenge the conventions of rhetorical composition based on prestigious models of the past. Writing on commission thus privileged originality and demanded a certain blurring of fictional and factional strategies, all in order to present the narrator and his addressee in a convincing and historically grounded manner.

Relying on historical details inserted in such texts may therefore lead us astray if we are after the truth of the empirical author or addressee — just like the Neapolitan novels by Ferrante. But treated with methodological respect, the texts reveal significant information about the sociocultural circumstances of their creation and the considerable skill of their authors. In this respect, the distinction between the empirical and the model author turns out to be less clear than the theoretical model adapted here may imply: the situation of the empirical author certainly affected the expression of the model author, so that they sometimes cannot be distinguished. The study of occasional literature also displays how the line between the fictional and the factual never is straightforward in literary compositions. The question is not so much about genre (as in historiography vs. novel), but rather about immediate as well as wider, socio-cultural functions. The need to connect a present event to a historical past, and thus to underline the truthfulness of both by means of fictional strategies or ancient imaginaries, was more important in twelfth-century Byzantium than any modern concern with the fictional text as a lie. And perhaps that insight can help us to understand better not only the texts by Constantine Manasses, but also literary production at large, including the authorship of Elena Ferrante.

Bibliography

Primary

Constantine Manasses, *Funeral Lament on the Death of Nikephoros Komnenos*. In E. Kurtz, "Evstafija Fessalonikijskago i Konstantina Manassii monodii na konchiny Nikifora Komnina." *Vizantijskij Vremennik* 17 (1910): 283–322.

Constantine Manasses. *Itinerary*. Edition and translation in Willem J. Aerts, "A Byzantine Traveller to One of the Crusader States." In *East and West in the Crusader States: Contexts — Contacts — Confrontations III*, edited by Krijnie Ciggaar and Herman Thuele, 165–221. Leuven: Peeters, 2003.

Constantini Manassi Breviarium Chronicum. Edited by Odysseus Lampsidis. Athens: Apud Institutum Graecoromanae, 1996.

Κωνσταντίνος Μανασσής, *Οδοιπορικόν: κριτική έκδοση, μετάφραση, σχόλια*. Edited and translated by Konstantinos Chryssogelos. Athens: Sokele, 2017.

Synopsis Chronike. Translated in Michael Jeffreys, "The Nature and Origin of Political Verse." *Dumbarton Oaks Papers* 28 (1974): 141–95. DOI: 10.2307/1291358.

Secondary

Agapitos, Panagiotis A. "Grammar, Genre, and Patronage in the Twelfth Century: A Scientific Paradigm and Its Implications." *Jahrbuch der Österreichischen Byzantinistik* 64 (2014): 1–22. DOI: 10.1553/joeb64s1.

Angold, Michael, ed. *The Byzantine Aristocracy: IX to XIII Centuries*. Oxford: British Archaeology Report, 1984. DOI: 10.30861/9780860542834.

Annibaldi, Claudio. *La musica e il mondo: Mecenatismo e committenza musicale in Italia tra Quattro e Settecento*. Bologna: Il Mulino, 1993.

———. "Towards a Theory of Musical Patronage in the Renaissance and Baroque: The Perspective from Anthropology and Semiotics." *Recercare* 10 (1998): 173–82.

Barber, Charles, and Stratis Papaioannou, eds. *Michael Psellos on Literature and Art: A Byzantine Perspective on Aesthetics.* Notre Dame: Notre Dame University Press, 2017. DOI: 10.1353/cjm.2018.0021.

Barthes, Roland. "Historical Discourse." Translated by Peter Wexler. In *Structuralism: A Reader,* edited by Michael Lane, 145–55. London: Cape, 1970.

———. "Le discours de l'histoire." *Social Science Information* 6, no. 4 (1967): 65–75. DOI: 10.1177/053901846700600404.

Bernard, Floris. *Writing and Reading Byzantine Secular Poetry, 1025–1081.* Oxford: Oxford University Press, 2014. DOI: 10.1093/acprof:oso/9780198703747.001.0001.

Bourbouhakis, Emmanuel C. *Not Composed in a Chance Manner: The Epitaphios for Manuel I Komnenos by Eustathios of Thessalonike.* Uppsala: Acta Upsaliensis, 2017.

———. "Rhetoric and Performance in Byzantium." In *The Byzantine World,* edited by Paul Stephenson, 175–87. London: Routledge, 2010. Ciggaar, Krijnie, and Herman Thuele, eds. *East and West in the Crusader States: Contexts — Contacts — Confrontations III.* Leuven: Peeters, 2003.

Colonna, Aristide. "De Oppiani vita antiquissima." *Bollettino del Comitato per la preparazione della edizione nazionale dei classici greci e latini* 12 (1964): 33–40.

Cullhed, Eric. "The Blind Bard and 'I': Homeric Biography and Authorial Personas in the Twelfth Century." *Byzantine and Modern Greek Studies* 38, no. 1 (2014): 49–67. DOI: 10.1179/03 07013113Z.00000000035.

Eco, Umberto. *Six Walks in the Fictional Woods.* Cambridge: Harvard University Press, 1994.

Galatariotou, Catia. "Travel and Perception in Byzantium." *Dumbarton Oaks Papers* 47 (1993): 221–41. DOI: 10.2307/1291679.

Genette, Gérard. *Fiction et diction: précédé de, Introduction à l'architexte.* Paris: Seuil, 2004.

———. *Palimpsests: Literature in the Second Degree.* Translated by Channa Newman and Claude Dubinsky. Lincoln: University of Nebraska Press, 1997.

Gold, Barbara K., ed. *Literary and Artistic Patronage in Ancient Rome*. Austin: University of Texas Press, 1982.

Hegel, Georg W.F. *Vorlesungen über die Ästhetik*. Volume 3. Frankfurt am Main: Suhrkamp, 1970.

Hill, Katherine. "The Elana Ferrante in My Head." *The Paris Review*, January 29, 2020. https://www.theparisreview.org/blog/2020/01/29/the-elena-ferrante-in-my-head/.

Himes, Mavis. "Elena Ferrante and the Question of Authorial Anonymity." *Mavis Himes, PhD*, January 13, 2017. http://www.mavishimes.com/elena-ferrante-and-the-question-of-authorial-anonymity/.

Hörandner, Wolfram. "Customs and Beliefs as Reflected in Occasional Poetry: Some Considerations." *Byzantinische Forschungen* 12 (1987): 235–47.

Horna, Konstantin. "Das Hodoiporikon des Konstantin Manasses." *Byzantinische Zeitschrift* 13, no. 2 (1904): 313–55. DOI: 10.1515/byzs.1904.13.2.313.

———. "Eine unedierte Rede des Konstantin Manasses." *Wiener Studien* 28 (1906): 171–204.

James, Liz, ed. *A Companion to Byzantium. Companions to the Ancient World*. Oxford: Blackwell, 2010. DOI: 10.1002/9781444320015.

Jeffreys, Elizabeth, ed. *Rhetoric in Byzantium*. Aldershot: Ashgate Variorum, 2003.

———. "The Sebastokratorissa Irene as Patron." In *Female Founders in Byzantium and Beyond, Wiener Jahrbuch für Kunstgeschichte* 60/61 2011/2012, edited by Lioba Theis, Margaret Mullett, Michael Grünbart, Galina Fingarova, and Mattew Savage, 175–92. Vienna: Boehlau, 2014.

Jeffreys, Michael. "The Nature and Origin of Political Verse." *Dumbarton Oaks Papers* 28 (1974): 141–95. DOI: 10.2307/1291358.

Kubina, Krystina. *Die enkomiastische Dichtung des Manuel Philes. Form und Funktion des literarischen Lobes in der Gesellschaft der frühen Palaiologenzeit*. Berlin: DeGruyter, 2020. DOI: 10.1515/9783110634839.

Kurtz, E. "Eshje dva neizdannyh proizvedenija Konstantina Manassii." *Vizantijskij Vremennik* 12 (1906): 69–98.

———. "Evstafija Fessalonikijskago i Konstantina Manassii monodii na konchiny Nikifora Komnina." *Vizantijskij Vremennik* 17 (1910): 283–322.

Lane, Michael, ed. *Structuralism: A Reader*. London: Cape, 1970.

Lefkowitz, Mary R. *The Lives of the Greek Poets*. 1981; rpt. Baltimore: Johns Hopkins University Press, 2012.

Macrides, Ruth, ed. *Travel in the Byzantine World*. Aldershot: Ashgate Variorum, 2002.

Magdalino, Paul. "In Search of the Byzantine Courtier: Leo Choirosphaktes and Constantine Manasses." In *Byzantine Court Culture from 829 to 1204*, edited by Henry Maguire, 141–65. Cambridge: Harvard University Press, 1997.

———. *The Empire of Manuel I Komnenos, 1143–1180*. Cambridge: Cambridge University Press, 1993.

Maguire, Henry, ed. *Byzantine Court Culture from 829 to 1204*. Cambridge: Harvard University Press, 1997.

Marciniak, Przemyslaw. "The Byzantine Performative Turn." In *Within the Circle of Ancient Ideas and Virtues: Studies in Honour of Professor Maria Dzielska*, edited by Kamilla Twardowska, 423–30. Krakow: Historia Iagellonica, 2014.

Messis, Charálambos, Margaret Mullett, and Ingela Nilsson, eds. *Storytelling in Byzantium: Narratological Approaches to Byzantine Texts and Images*. Uppsala: Uppsala University, 2018.

Miller, Timothy S. "Two Teaching Texts from the Twelfth-Century Orphanotropheion." In *Byzantine Authors: Literary Activities and Preoccupations*, edited by John William Nesbitt, 9–20. Boston and Leiden: Brill, 2003.

Mullett, Margaret. "Aristocracy and Patronage in the Literary Circles of Comnenian Constantinople." In *The Byzantine Aristocracy: IX to XIII Centuries*, edited by Michael Angold, 173–97. Oxford: British Archaeology Report, 1984.

———. "In Peril on the Sea: Travel Genres and the Unexpected." In *Travel in the Byzantine World*, edited by Ruth Macrides, 259–84. Aldershot: Ashgate Variorum, 2002.

———. "No Drama, No Poetry, No Fiction, No Readership, No Literature." In *A Companion to Byzantium*, edited by Liz James, 227–38. Oxford: Blackwell Companions to the Ancient World, 2010.

———. "Rhetoric, Theory and the Imperative of Performance: Byzantium and Now." In *Rhetoric in Byzantium*, edited by Elizabeth Jeffreys, 151–71. Aldershot: Ashgate Variorum, 2003.

Nesbitt, John William, ed. *Byzantine Authors: Literary Activities and Preoccupations*. Boston and Leiden: Brill, 2003.

Neville, Leonora Alice. *Anna Komnene: The Life and Work of a Medieval Historian*. Oxford: Oxford University Press, 2016. DOI: 10.1093/acprof:oso/9780190498177.001.0001.

Nilsson, Ingela. "Constantine Manasses, Odysseus and the Cyclops: On Byzantine Appreciation of Pagan Art in the Twelfth Century." *Byzantinoslavica* 69 (2011): 123–36.

———. "Discovering Literariness in the Past: Literature vs. History in the Synopsis Chronike of Konstantinos Manasses." In *L'écriture de la mémoire: la littérarité de l'historiographie*, edited by Paulo Odorico, Panagiotes A. Agapetos, and Martin Hinterberger, 15–31. Paris: Centre d'études byzantines, néo-helléniques et sud-est européennes, École des hautes études en sciences sociales, 2006.

———. "La douceur des dons abondants: Patronage et littérarité dans la Constantinople des Comnènes." In *La face cachée de la littérature byzantine: Le texte en tant que message immédiat*, edited by Paolo Odorico, 179–93. Paris: Centre d'études byzantines, néo-helléniques et sud-est européennes, École des hautes études en sciences sociales, 2012.

———. "Narrating Images in Byzantine Literature: The Ekphraseis of Konstantinos Manasses." *Jahrbuch der Österreichischen Byzantinistik* 55 (2005): 121–46. DOI: 10.1553/joeb55s121.

———. *Raconter Byzance: la littérature au XIIe siècle*. Paris: Belles lettres, 2014.

———. "The Same Story But Another: A Reappraisal of Literary Imitation in Byzantium." In *Imitatio — Aemulatio — Variatio*, edited by Elisabeth Schiffer and Andrea Rhoby, 195–208. Vienna: Österreichische Akademie der Wissenschaften, 2010.

———. *Writer and Occasion in Twelfth-Century Byzantium: The Authorial Voice of Constantine Manasses.* Cambridge: Cambridge University Press, 2021.

Nilsson, Ingela, and Roger Scott. "Towards a New History of Byzantine Literature: The Case of Historiography." *Classica et Mediaevalia* 58 (2007): 319–32. DOI: 10.4324/9781351219464-5.

Odorico, Paolo, ed. *La face cachée de la littérature byzantine: le texte en tant que message immédiat.* Paris: Centre d'études byzantines, néo-helléniques et sud-est européennes, École des hautes études en sciences sociales, 2012.

Odorico, Paolo, Panagiotes A. Agapetos, and Martin Hinterberger, eds. *L'écriture de la mémoire: la littérarité de l'historiographie.* Paris: Centre d'études byzantines, néo-helléniques et sud-est européennes, École des hautes études en sciences sociales, 2006.

Pizzone, Aglae. "The Autobiographical Subject in Tzetzes' Chiliades: An Analysis of Its Components." In *Storytelling in Byzantium: Narratological Approaches to Byzantine Texts and Images,* edited by Charálambos Messis, Margaret Mullett, and Ingela Nilsson, 279–96. Uppsala: Uppsala University, 2018.

Polemis, Ioannis D. "Fünf unedierte Texte des Konstantinos Manasses." *Rivista di Studi Bizantino e Neoellenici* 33 (1996): 279–92.

Shapiro, Gary. "Hegel on the Meanings of Poetry." *Philosophy and Rhetoric* 8, no. 2 (1975): 88–107. https://www.jstor.org/stable/40236923.

Schiffer, Elisabeth, and Andrea Rhoby, eds. *Imitatio—Aemulatio—Variatio.* Vienna: Österreichische Akademie der Wissenschaften, 2010.

Stephenson, Paul, ed. *The Byzantine World.* London: Routledge, 2010. DOI: 10.4324/9780203817254.

Theis, Lioba, Margaret Mullett, Michael Grünbart, Galina Fingarova, and Mattew Savage, eds. *Female Founders in Byz-*

antium and Beyond. Wiener Jahrbuch für Kunstgeschichte 60/61 2011/2012. Vienna: Boehlau, 2014.

Tomkins, Jane P., ed. *Reader-Response Criticism: From Formalism to Post-Structuralism*. Baltimore: Johns Hopkins University Press, 1980.

———. "The Reader in History: The Changing Shape of Literary Response." In *Reader-Response Criticism: From Formalism to Post-Structuralism*, edited by Jane P. Tomkins, 201–32. Baltimore: Johns Hopkins University Press, 1980.

Twardowska, Kamilla, ed. *Within the Circle of Ancient Ideas and Virtues: Studies in Honour of Professor Maria Dzielska*. Krakow: Historia Iagellonica, 2014.

Webb, Ruth. *Ekphrasis, Imagination and Persuasion in Ancient Rhetorical Theory and Practice*. Farnham: Ashgate, 2009.

White, Hayden. *Metahistory: The Historical Imagination in Nineteenth-Century Europe*. Baltimore: John Hopkins University Press, 1973.

———. *The Content of the Form: Narrative Discourse and Historical Representation*. Baltimore: John Hopkins University Press, 1987.

Zetzel, James E.G. "The Poetics of Patronage in the Late First Century B.C." In *Literary and Artistic Patronage in Ancient Rome*, edited by Barbara K. Gold, 87–102. Austin: University of Texas Press, 1982.

6

Romance, Legend, and the Remote Past: Historical Framing in Late Medieval Icelandic Sagas

Ralph O'Connor

This chapter concerns the Old Norse prose narratives composed in Iceland and Norway and known as sagas, *sögur*.[1] Saga-writing in the Norse world began, as far as we know, in the twelfth century and continued, in Iceland, until the early twentieth. It was rooted in an adaptation of indigenous oral storytelling and commemorative traditions within a Christian literate framework. Many sagas seem designed for hearing as well as for reading, aligning them with other European forms such as epic and romance. Analogous vernacular prose traditions had already emerged elsewhere in Europe, notably the prose sagas of Ireland and Gaelic Scotland written from the seventh century onward. A comparative assessment of the making and reception of the

---

1 A paper drawing on this chapter was presented in seminars at St. Andrews's Strathmartine Institute and Aberdeen's Centre for Scandinavian Studies in May 2018. I am grateful to the participants for their insightful comments, and to Paul Bibire and Catalin Taranu for helpful discussion during the gestation period. Note regarding references: in this chapter, Icelandic authors' names are cited (and alphabetized in the bibliography) with the first name taking priority, as is customary in Iceland where very few people have surnames. I am grateful to the Leverhulme Trust for funding this research.

two major saga-writing traditions would be rewarding, but for reasons of space this chapter will focus on the Norse-Icelandic tradition. I will not comment on the usefulness of sagas as historical sources for our own histories of early Scandinavia. Instead, I will explore to what extent they were framed as history by the people who wrote and transmitted them in the Middle Ages.

As a written form, the Norse-Icelandic saga arose within the cultural ferment often called the twelfth-century Renaissance. It was one among several forms representing past events, emerging alongside hagiography, chronicles, and national histories. The most ambitious of these other genres in the North was the *Gesta Danorum* (*The History of the Danes*), an elaborate Latin prosimetrum account of Danish rulers from mythical times to the twelfth century written around 1200 by the Danish scholar Saxo Grammaticus, drawing on Icelandic oral narratives about the legendary past.[2] To begin with, writings by Icelanders about their own history, starting with the island's ninth-century settlement, took other forms than sagas. For example, the early twelfth-century scholar Ari Þorgilsson is credited with the authorship of a brief history in Norse prose entitled *Íslendingabók* (*The Book of Icelanders*) and of a now-lost early version of *Landnámabók* (*The Book of Settlements*), which survives in later recensions as a systematic account of settler families and land claims interspersed with saga-like anecdotes.[3]

What distinguished sagas from chronicles and national histories was their narrative focus, gripping an audience's attention as well as informing and edifying them. Like Gaelic sagas, and epic and romance generally, most Norse-Icelandic sagas focus their main storylines on a few leading protagonists and a distinct sequence of events, despite often having very large casts of characters and multi-generational preludes and postludes.

---

2   Saxo Grammaticus, *Gesta Danorum: The History of the Danes*, ed. Karsten Friis-Jensen, trans. Peter Fisher, 2 vols. (Oxford: Clarendon Press, 2015).

3   *Íslendingabók, Landnámabók*, ed. Jakob Benediktsson, Íslenzk fornrit 1 (Reykjavik: Hið íslenzka fornritafélag, 1986–1988).

Only rarely did individual sagas attempt the panoramic scope of a chronicle or national history: that ambition was normally reserved for saga compilations.[4]

Modern scholars group sagas by type of protagonist and chronological setting.[5] The oldest sagas extant, from c. 1150–1200, include translated biographies of saints of the early Church (*heilagra manna sögur*), translated antiquity sagas about Greek, Roman, and biblical history (sometimes unhelpfully labeled "pseudo-historical sagas"), and original biographies of Scandinavian rulers, initially those of the tenth, eleventh, and twelfth centuries (*konungasögur*, kings' sagas). Increasingly, kings' sagas were combined into regnal sequences about, for example, the earls of Orkney or the kings of Norway—most famously the early thirteenth-century *Heimskringla*, usually attributed to Snorri Sturluson. By 1250, saga-writing embraced a wider range of subject matter, including prominent Icelanders of the Viking Age (*Íslendingasögur* or family sagas) and of the twelfth and thirteenth centuries (*samtíðarsögur* or contemporary sagas),[6] as well as sagas about a more remote Scandinavian and European past (*fornaldarsögur*, legendary sagas). In Norway and Iceland, the same period saw the first Norse adaptations of Continental European vernacular narratives: individual translated romances and *chansons de geste* (translated *riddarasögur* or knights' sagas) and the three great compilations *Strengleikar* (*Stringed Instruments*, translating Marie de France's *lais*), *Karlamagnús*

---

4   Some larger-scale narratives were given the title *saga* only by nineteenth-century editors, such as *Gyðinga saga*, *Veraldar saga*, *Sturlunga saga*, and *Guta saga*.

5   For discussion and bibliography on individual sagas and groups, and scholarly consensus about dating (a very tricky business), see Phillip Pulsiano and Kirsten Wolf, eds., *Medieval Scandinavia: An Encyclopedia* (New York: Garland, 1993), and Rory McTurk, ed. *A Companion to Old Norse-Icelandic Literature and Culture* (London: Blackwell, 2005). The best substantial English-language overview is Sverrir Tómasson, "The Middle Ages: Old Icelandic Prose," in *A History of Icelandic Literature*, ed. Daisy Neijmann (Lincoln: University of Nebraska Press, 2006), 64–173.

6   This grouping includes *biskupa sögur* (bishops' sagas) and the sagas brought together in the compilation *Sturlunga saga*.

saga (*The Saga of Charlemagne,* translating several *chansons de geste*), and *Þiðreks saga af Bern* (*The Saga of Theodoric of Verona,* translating north German legends). By 1300 Icelanders were writing their own romance-like adventure sagas set all around the known world (indigenous *riddarasögur*). These became the most popular of all the sagas.

Saga-writing thus absorbed several genres that scholars typically prefer to separate out into historical and fictional forms. The earliest examples are rooted in European historical genres such as royal biography and hagiography, but as the thirteenth century wore on, other genres which we usually distinguish from history-writing fed into the mix: epic, romance, *lai, fabliau*. Individual sagas and saga groups are placed by modern scholars at different positions on an agreed spectrum of intended veracity.[7] At one end are *konungasögur*, antiquity sagas and *samtíðarsögur*, typically seen as "historiography in a broader sense."[8] At the other end, generally viewed as fiction, are the sagas commonly linked with romance or fairytale: *riddarasögur*, the more romantic *fornaldarsögur* (a subgroup bearing the German label *Abenteuersagas,* adventure sagas), and a subset of allegedly late family sagas. In the middle of the spectrum sit the allegedly earlier examples of the family sagas and *fornaldarsögur*: the so-called "classical" family sagas, including *Brennu-Njáls saga* (*The Saga of Burnt Njáll*) and *Egils saga Skalla-Grímssonar* (*The Saga of Egill Skalla-Grímsson*), and the subgroup of *fornaldarsögur* known as *Heldensagas* (heroic sagas), which includes *Völsunga saga* (*The Saga of the Volsungs*) and *Hervarar saga ok Heiðreks*

---

7 For more detail on these trends, see Ralph O'Connor, "History and Fiction," in *The Routledge Research Companion to the Medieval Icelandic Sagas,* ed. Ármann Jakobsson and Sverrir Jakobsson (London: Routledge, 2017), 88–110.

8 Stefanie Würth, "Historiography and Pseudo-History," in *A Companion to Old Norse-Icelandic Literature and Culture,* ed. Rory McTurk (London: Blackwell, 2005), 161. Saga scholars frequently use "historiography" to denote what I call here history or history-writing. Conversely, many historians of medieval Europe use "historiography" to refer to scholarly debates and interventions rather than to a literary form. I am indebted to Lesley Abrams for this observation.

konungs (*The Saga of Hervör and King Heiðrekr*).[9] These are often viewed as essentially fictional but rooted in traditions that medieval audiences treated as historical. The "classical" family sagas, in particular, have been analyzed in ways which take seriously both their creative aspects and their contemporary historical function. Aided by the recent momentum of cultural memory studies, this is becoming a dominant view, sometimes applied to a few of the allegedly oldest *fornaldarsögur* as well.[10]

The placement of individual sagas on this history-fiction spectrum largely corresponds to consensus about their date of composition, itself based on assumptions that imaginative freedom and experimentation increased as the genre developed: older sagas are more historical, younger sagas more fictional. Hard evidence for dating is usually so scanty that a saga's perceived density of information or degree of inventiveness can become the deciding factor in its dating. This developmental logic has resulted in the dubious assignment of more folktale-like family sagas to a later, so-called "post-classical" period, and in the assumption that the tragic, formally unwieldy *Heldensagas* must be earlier than the cheerier and more smoothly shaped

---

9 The third of the German subgroups, *Wikingersagas* (Viking sagas), is rather miscellaneous.

10 On this view of family sagas, see Preben Meulengracht Sørensen, *Saga and Society: An Introduction to Old Norse Literature*, trans. John Tucker (Odense: Odense University Press, 1993), and Preben Meulengracht Sørensen, *Fortælling og ære: studier i islændingesagaerne* (Aarhus: Aarhus Universitetsforlag, 1993). See also Margaret Clunies Ross, *Prolonged Echoes: Old Norse Myths in Medieval Northern Society*, Vol. 2: *The Reception of Norse Myths in Medieval Iceland* (Odense: Odense University Press, 1998), 44–96, and Vésteinn Ólason, "The Icelandic Saga as a Kind of Literature with Special Reference to Its Representation of Reality," in *Learning and Understanding in the Old Norse World: Essays in Honour of Margaret Clunies Ross*, ed. Kate Heslop, Judy Quinn, and Tarrin Wills (Turnhout: Brepols, 2007), 27–48. For applications to certain *fornaldarsögur*, see Elizabeth Ashman Rowe, *Vikings in the West: The Legend of Ragnarr Loðbrók and His Sons* (Vienna: Fassbaender, 2012), and Annette Lassen, "*Origines Gentium* and the Learned Origin of *Fornaldarsögur Norðurlanda*," in *The Legendary Sagas: Origins and Development*, ed. Ármann Jakobsson, Annette Lassen, and Agneta Ney (Reykjavik: University of Iceland Press, 2012), 35–58, with further references.

and more romance-oriented *Abenteuersagas,* even though both subgroups of *fornaldarsögur* appear simultaneously in the manuscript record.[11] Given that the first known Norse translation of a romance is conventionally dated to the 1220s (*Tristrams saga ok Ísöndar,* adapting Thomas of Brittany's *Tristan*), this logic should be treated with caution.

This developmental model is not restricted to Nordic literary history. A similar progress from (pseudo)history to fiction is often applied to Gaelic sagas.[12] Similarly, critics of medieval French and German literature plot increasing fictionality from histories through *romans d'antiquité* to the courtly romances in which narrative was finally "emancipated" from historical veracity.[13] As was explored in the introduction to this volume, this model is reinforced by scholars' continued use of overly narrow definitions of history-writing in which epic and especially romance are treated *a priori* as history's "Other," maintaining old polarities of "history vs. literature."

By contrast, this chapter analyses texts whose freer use of imaginative and entertaining techniques did not necessarily constitute a departure from history in their terms. Because sagas straddle the assumed boundary between historical and imaginative writing, they provide a useful corpus with which to re-examine that boundary and expand the range of literary genres

---

[11] On this point, see Ármann Jakobsson, "The Earliest Legendary Saga Manuscripts," in *The Legendary Sagas,* eds. Jakobsson, Lassen, and Ney, 21–32.

[12] Donnchadh Ó Corráin, "Irish Origin Legends and Genealogy: Recurrent Aetiologies," in *History and Heroic Tale: A Symposium,* ed. Preben Meulengracht Sørensen, Tore Nyberg, Iorn Pio, and Aage Trommer (Odense: Odense University Press, 1985), 85–86.

[13] See, for example, G.T. Shepherd, "The Emancipation of Story in the Twelfth Century," in *Medieval Narrative: A Symposium,* ed. Hans Bekker-Nielsen, Peter Foote, Andreas Haarder, and Preben Meulengracht Sørensen (Odense: Odense University, 1979), 44–57; D.H. Green, *The Beginnings of Medieval Romance: Fact and Fiction, 1150–1220* (Cambridge: Cambridge University Press, 2002), esp. 176–80; and Peter Ainsworth, "Legendary History: *historia* and *fabula,*" in *Historiography in the Middle Ages,* ed. Deborah Mauskopf Deliyannis (Boston and Leiden: Brill, 2003), 387–416.

which could be historical genres too.¹⁴ Against the theoretical backdrop articulated in this volume's introduction, and following in the spirit of Ruth Morse's and Nancy Partner's seminal analyses of the inventive dimension of medieval European writing about the past, I will suggest that the creative freedom enjoyed by saga-writers indicates that the limits of truthfulness in historical writing were often broader than we assume, especially in histories of the remote past. Here Isidore of Seville's neat division between *historia, argumentum,* and *fabula* dissolves:¹⁵ the typical saga told a true story about a past too distant to be represented without abundant invention, a need which increased (with greater demands on the audience's credulity) the further away in space or time the events were situated in relation to the narrator and audience.

This is a complex matter requiring a wide range of supporting evidence. In particular, a fuller account would need to attend to reception as well as inscription and intention, and to the spectrum of cognitive positions that individual audience members might occupy between, or even independent from, the poles of credulity and skepticism. But authorial intention is a useful starting point. However inappropriate a crude "history or fiction" binary may be from our perspective, and however multifaceted the purposes of sagas were, I will argue that these texts were framed by their authors and redactors in ways which invited audiences to treat their contents as historical. How that

---

14 Compare Catalin Taranu, *The Bard and the Rag-Picker: Vernacular Verse Histories in Early Medieval England and Francia* (London: Routledge, 2021) and Taranu's chapter in this volume.

15 Nancy F. Partner, *Serious Entertainments: The Writing of History in Twelfth-Century England* (Chicago: University of Chicago Press, 1977), and Ruth Morse, *Truth and Convention in the Middle Ages: Rhetoric, Representation, and Reality* (Cambridge: Cambridge University Press, 1991). Isidore's scheme is discussed in the Introduction to this volume. My approach to accounts of the remote past draws on Lars Boje Mortensen, "The Status of the 'Mythical' Past in Nordic Latin Historiography (c. 1170–1220)," in *Medieval Narratives between History and Fiction: From the Centre to the Periphery of Europe, c. 1100–1400,* ed. Panagiotis A. Agapitos and Lars Boje Mortensen (Copenhagen: Museum Tusculanum, 2012), 103–40.

invitation was taken must remain a question for another day. I will focus on framing devices in saga beginnings and endings, primarily in the sagas commonly viewed as fictional.

Story and *fræði* in the Family Sagas

My own previous work in this vein has focused on narrators' overt protestations of veracity or good faith, especially in prologues or epilogues. These declarations often appear in romances (Chrétien's *Cligès*) and romance-like sagas (*fornaldarsögur*, indigenous *riddarasögur*).[16] The difficulty is that, when they appear in works generally considered today to be fiction, they are seldom taken seriously. Consequently, other kinds of evidence are needed. Further evidence of historical intent may be found in the passages of historical information or *fræði* placed at sagas' beginnings and endings to provide a context, outside the story proper, from which the narrative is seen to emerge.

Such passages need not closely resemble chronicles to indicate historical intent. Even national histories, which sometimes use synchronisms or dates to locate their narratives within universal history, were not required to do so. Several national histories keep their reference points local: Saxo's *History of the Danes* is structured around events internal to the history itself, making little or no reference to the world beyond, and Geoffrey of Monmouth's *History of the Britons* (or *History of the Kings of Britain*) is only slightly more forthcoming on this front.[17] In individual sagas, whose subjects were families and individuals rather than nations, local context was often felt sufficient without compromising the story's veracity.

As I will show, these historical anchorage points appear not only in sagas conventionally pigeonholed as (pseudo-)historical, but also in those seen as fictional. I begin with the so-called

---

16 See, for example, Ralph O'Connor, "History or Fiction? Truth-Claims and Defensive Narrators in Icelandic Romance-Sagas," *Mediaeval Scandinavia* 15 (2005): 1–69.

17 On this aspect of Saxo, see his *Gesta Danorum*, 1:19–20, n. 1.

"classical" family sagas, whose information-heavy beginnings and endings are widely acknowledged as signs of historical intent. I will then examine sagas where historical underpinnings might seem less of a priority, the "post-classical" family sagas, *fornaldarsögur* and *riddarasögur*.

Any newcomer to the "classical" family sagas is immediately struck by the thicket of genealogical and political information they have to penetrate before the main storyline begins. In 1973 Kathryn Hume showed how important these deposits of information were in connecting sagas' events to their audience, whose members might claim descent from saga protagonists. They give the impression of fully fledged stories emerging organically from a web of historical and genealogical tradition. A specific sequence of events or biography is pulled out of that background weave, spun into a memorable narrative, and, in some cases, brought to a close by returning to the shared matrix of historical tradition. These beginnings and endings are written in an enumerative rather than dramatic style, consisting of condensed summaries of information rather than developed narrative. But Hume argued that the personal connection they underline would have had a deep emotional resonance for their audiences and was an intrinsic aspect of saga aesthetics.[18] What this means, although Hume did not express it as such, is that the putative historicity of the events depicted was part of their emotional appeal as stories. Engaging an audience's emotions and providing an audience with information were two sides of the same saga, not purposes hived off into different genres. These information-heavy preambles may introduce thematic concerns, belying the common assumption that thematic and chronological forms of organization belonged to fictional and chronological genres respectively.[19]

---

18 Kathryn Hume, "Beginnings and Endings in the Icelandic Family Sagas," *Modern Language Review* 68, no. 3 (1973): 593–606; see also Vésteinn Ólason, *Dialogues with the Viking Age: Narration and Representation in the Sagas of the Icelanders*, trans. Andrew Wawn (Reykjavik: Heimskringla, 1998), 84–87.
19 An assumption articulated in Ainsworth, "Legendary History," 402–3.

A good example of this interplay of information and narrative is found in the early family saga *Egils saga Skalla-Grímssonar*, a substantial biography of the warrior-poet Egill Skalla-Grímsson. It begins with genealogical information about Egill's Norwegian ancestors, hinting that his grandfather was a werewolf with troll blood in his veins and preparing us for trouble later on.[20] Then, opening a connected narrative sequence, comes an account of King Haraldr Fairhair's aggressive takeover of much of Norway, a backstory grounding many family sagas.[21] Out of this linked genealogical and political background the events of the saga proper unfold: Egill's father and grandfather become embroiled in these events and emigrate to Iceland, where Egill is born. After a long narrative of Egill's career, once he is too old to do more mighty deeds and his son Þorsteinn emerges from his shadow, the narrative surface becomes less continuous. Connections between episodes loosen and the narrator prepares to reinsert the story into its historical matrix by listing Egill's descendants through Þorsteinn.[22] The last two chapters take leave of Egill's family in retrospective gestures. First comes an anecdote documenting the exhumation and reburial of Egill's bones after Christianization, during which Skapti Þorarinsson tries to smash Egill's massive skull with an axe: "it turned white, but was not dented or broken." A touch of experimental archaeology thus authenticates the saga's testimony of Egill's resilience and larger-than-life character. Finally, the narrator reflects on the prestige of Egill's dynasty, name-checking prominent kin mentioned elsewhere and emphasizing, again, the family's strange mixture of opposing hereditary traits which intimately informs the saga's storyline.[23]

---

20 *Egils saga I*, 3–4. *Egils saga Skalla-Grímssonar*, ed. Bjarni Einarsson, Bind I, A-redaktionen, Editiones Arnamagnæanæ A 19 (Copenhagen: Reitzel, 2001), 3–4.
21 Ibid., 4–7.
22 Ibid., 154–55.
23 Ibid., 184–86: "huitnaði [firer en] ecki dalaði ne sprack." All translations from sagas are my own unless otherwise indicated. As far as typography

The density of these passages of historical anchorage varies greatly from one family saga to another, as does the closeness of their "fit" with other extant historical authorities, *Landnámabók* and sagas of Norwegian kings. Some family sagas lack any opening orientation except the names of the initial protagonists but provide a mass of information at the end, such as *Þorsteins þáttr stangarhǫggs* (*The Tale of Þorsteinn Staff-Struck*).[24] Other sagas offer very little at either end, such as *Valla-Ljóts saga* (*The Saga of Valla-Ljótr*).[25] Its opening simply introduces Sigurðr Karlsson, his immediate family and another man named Torfi, followed by a chronological marker which also introduces a character, Guðmundr, well known from other sagas, and often portrayed negatively: "At that time Eyjólfr lived at Mǫðruvellir, and Guðmundr his son was there with him." It ends even more briefly: "Ljótr was considered a very great chieftain, and with that his dealings with Guðmundr the Powerful concluded. Guðmundr kept his honor right up to his dying day, and here ends this saga."[26] This closing gesture returns the audience to the contested backstory of Guðmundr mentioned at the opening, a back-history which *Valla-Ljóts saga* has now adjusted. Evidently, detailed external or even internal orientation by reigns or events was not necessary to sagas set in settlement-era Iceland. The mere mention of a prominent family could anchor a saga in time and place.

Whether laconic or expansive, the "classical" family sagas follow a pattern by which dramatic narrative visibly emerges from, or subsides into, a surrounding matrix of historical in-

---

allows, my quotations from texts in Norse and other languages follow the orthography and punctuation of the editions quoted.

24 *Austfirðinga sǫgur*, ed. Jón Jóhannesson, Íslenzk fornrit 11 (Reykjavík: Hið íslenzka fornritafélag, 1950), 69, 78–79.

25 This saga belies Hume's claim ("Beginnings and Endings," 596) that no (classical) family saga has both a brief introduction and a brief conclusion. *Gunnars saga Þiðrandabana* is another example.

26 *Eyfirðinga sǫgur*, ed. Jónas Kristjánsson, Íslenzk fornrit 9 (Reykjavík: Hið íslenzka fornritafélag, 1956), 233: "Þá bjó Eyjólfr á Mǫðruvǫllum, ok Guðmundr, sonr hans, var þar með honum"; 260: "þótti Ljótr inn mesti hǫfðingi, ok lýkr þar viðskiptum þeira Guðmundar ins ríka. En Guðmundr helt virðingu sinni allt til dauðadags, ok lýkr þar þessi sǫgu".

formation — although that, too, may have been invented. The mirror-image of this symbiotic relationship appears in *Landnámabók*, whose main purpose was to provide information about family history and land claims. Here, information frequently flowers into saga-like anecdotes. To understand the settlement claims of Uni Garðarson's family it is not necessary to know how Tjǫrvi, nephew of Hróarr, carved rude pictures on the lavatory wall about the married woman he loved, or how he made an incriminating verse about this which got him and Hróarr killed. But it helps to explain Tjǫrvi's nickname (*enn háðsami*, "Mocker")[27] — and it's a good story.

Both family sagas and settlement accounts show that dramatic narrative was a natural outgrowth of thinking about the past. Storytelling was not distinct from *fræði* (information), but rather functioned as a way of presenting that information.[28] There is nothing especially unique or surprising in this. A similar ebb and flow between information about the past and dramatization of that past is visible in texts from other cultures in which genealogy loomed large as a vehicle of cultural memory, such as the Old and Middle Gaelic sagas of Ireland and Scotland.[29] As to audience response, Vésteinn Ólason's inference seems reasonable: "the most important function of the introduction is to establish

---

27 *Íslendingabók, Landnámabók*, ed. Jakob Benediktsson, 301–2.
28 Meulengracht Sørensen, *Saga and Society*, 107–8, and Meulengracht Sørensen, *Fortælling og ære*, 33–51. The Gaelic word *senchas* similarly encapsulates both information and narrative, meaning "traditional information about the past in narrative form."
29 On this point see Ó Corráin, "Irish Origin Legends," 56, and for some especially relevant texts, see Dan M. Wiley, ed., *Essays on the Early Irish King Tales* (Dublin: Four Courts, 2008), and *Corpus genealogiarum Hiberniae*, ed. Michael A. O'Brien (Dublin: Dublin Institute for Advanced Studies, 1976), 139–54. Parallels between the two saga-writing traditions in this respect have been discussed by Erich Poppe, "Narrative History and Cultural Memory in Medieval Ireland: Some Preliminary Thoughts," in *Medieval Irish Perspectives on Cultural Memory*, ed. Jan Erik Rekdal and Erich Poppe (Münster: Nodus, 2014), 135–76 and *Of Cycles and Other Critical Matters: Some Issues in Medieval Irish Literary History and Criticism*, E. C. Quiggin Memorial Lectures 9 (Cambridge: Department of Anglo-Saxon, Norse and Celtic, 2008).

the impression that a reader or listener will be engaging with a truthful narrative about important people. In this way it sets the tone and, as it were, tunes the receiver."[30] By implication, if similar informational strategies occur in other kinds of sagas, they too may be intentionally veracious.

Once the narrative contours of an individual saga gained currency, it became part of the matrix of *frœði* on which later compositions drew.[31] This procedure underpins the tendency of sagas of all kinds to allude to other sagas, sometimes as repositories of further information about something mentioned briefly in the story.[32] Saga literature thus participates fully in the agglutinative, gravitational tendency of medieval narrative, whose authors, like genealogists and lawyers, forged causal or familial connections between existing traditions, authenticating their narratives by linking them to a nebulous body of hearsay and text. These information-heavy beginnings and endings bear comparison with the common medieval urge to compose sequels and prequels, and to connect separate narratives into "cycles."[33] To liken this cyclic urge to the consciously fictive sequel-spawning of modern films and novels underscores the creativity involved, but does no justice to its essentially historical attitude.[34]

Hume's study is restricted to the "classical" family sagas, supposedly composed before about 1280. By the fourteenth century, Icelanders under Norwegian and then Danish rule are often thought to have turned away from their own history to the

---

30 Vésteinn Ólason, *Dialogues*, 87.
31 Meulengracht Sørensen, *Fortælling og ære*, 33–51.
32 See William Manhire, "The Narrative Functions of Source-References in the Sagas of Icelanders," *Saga-Book of the Viking Society* 19 (1974–1977): 170–90, supplemented by Slavica Ranković, "Authentication and Authenticity in the Sagas of Icelanders and Serbian Epic Poetry," in *Medieval Narratives between History and Fiction*, ed. Agapitos and Mortensen, 199–234.
33 Poppe, *Of Cycles*.
34 Of course, the fictionality of modern novels and films can be far from simple: for example, the fuzzy boundary between veracious and fictitious life-writing has been a site of authorial play and divergent reception ever since the seventeenth century.

escapist thrills of romance and fantasy. Our understanding of the *fornaldarsögur* and *riddarasögur* still owes much to this notion of literary decline under foreign domination, even though today the results are viewed more sympathetically and with a stronger political dimension. Those latecomers to the saga-writing tradition are, in turn, thought to have influenced later family sagas, resulting in the "post-classical" family sagas. Like the *fornaldarsögur* and *riddarasögur,* these are frequently seen as fiction[35] because of their freer use of wondertale motifs, and because they are thought to be less interested in the socio-legal intricacies of Saga-Age Iceland and more interested in superhero derring-do. Here is not the place to enter the debate about the differences between "classical" and "post-classical" family sagas, except to say that these have been overstated. Examples of both kinds were probably composed alongside each other in the thirteenth and fourteenth centuries and later, rather than folding into a developmental succession from early to late.[36] My use of the categories "classical" and "post-classical" merely reflects common scholarly usage, and the quotation marks are intentional.

If, as most agree, "post-classical" family sagas heave closer to romance than to the historical mode of the "classical" sagas, we might expect gestures of historical anchorage to dwindle away. In fact, they persist, as the following examples show. An extreme case of these sagas' allegedly fabulous tendencies is *Bárðar saga Snæfellsáss* (*The Saga of Bárðr the Snæfell-God*), about the son of an Arctic giant and a mother of troll descent. After living among humans, he moves into a cave in the Icelandic glacier Snæfellsjökull and becomes a local guardian spirit or *áss*. The opening paragraphs introduce the giants who inhabited the ancient Arctic wastes: "There was a king named Dumbr [Mist]; he ruled over the ocean gulfs which run southeast from Risaland

---

35 Vésteinn Ólason more cautiously notes that these sagas still "pretend to be history": see his "The Fantastic Element in Fourteenth Century *Íslendingasögur*: A Survey," *Gripla* 18 (2007): 7–22.
36 See Daniel Sävborg, "Den 'efterklassiska' islänningasagan och dess ålder," *Journal of English and Germanic Philology* 127 (2012): 19–57.

[Giantland]."³⁷ To us this may sound more like myth than history, but giants were not imaginary beings. Their origins and diminution fascinated historians, from Saxo around 1200 to Arngrímur Jónsson around 1600.³⁸ Árngrímur used *Bárðar saga* as a sourcebook on Arctic geography, and the saga itself localizes the giants' habitations and political dealings, moving from conjectural to recorded history when Bárðr's giant foster-father Dofri also fosters the future king Haraldr Fairhair.³⁹ This last anecdote derives from *Hálfdanar þáttr svarta ok Haralds hárfagra* (*The Tale of Hálfdan the Black and Haraldr Fairhair*), a legendary-historical account preserved in the prestigious manuscript *Flateyjarbók* which compiled the histories of Norwegian kings from ancient times to the twelfth century.⁴⁰ Later episodes of *Bárðar saga* are grafted onto the legend-encrusted biographical saga of the missionary king Óláfr Tryggvason, also in *Flateyjarbók*.⁴¹ Other historical resources exploited included *Landnámabók*, quoted very extensively,⁴² and local folklore about Snæfellsnes placenames. From this tapestry of written and oral sources, the saga author's mythopoietic imagination could take

---

37 This version of the opening is in *Harðar saga*, ed. Þórhallur Vilmundarson and Bjarni Vilhjálmsson, Íslenzk fornrit 13 (Reykjavik: Hið íslenzka fornritafélag, 1991), 101: "Dumbr hefir konungr heitit; hann réð fyrir hafsbotnum þeim, er ganga af Risalandi í landsuðr."
38 Saxo, *Gesta Danorum*, 1.18, 40; Arngrímur Jónsson, *Opera latine conscripta*, ed. Jakob Benediktsson, 4 vols., Bibliotheca Arnamagnæanæ 9–12 (Copenhagen: Munksgaard, 1950–1957), 2:30–46.
39 *Harðar saga*, ed. Þórhallur Vilmundarson and Bjarni Vilhjálmsson, 104.
40 On this manuscript, see Elizabeth Ashman Rowe, *The Development of Flateyjarbók: Iceland and the Norwegian Dynastic Crisis of 1389* (Odense: University Press of Southern Denmark, 2005).
41 Annette Lassen, "The Old Norse Contextuality of *Bárðar saga Snæfellsáss*: A Synoptic Reading with *Óláfs saga Tryggvasonar en mesta*," in *Folklore in Old Norse — Old Norse in Folklore*, ed. Daniel Sävborg and Karen Bek-Pedersen (Tartu: University of Tartu Press, 2014), 102–19.
42 *Harðar saga*, ed. Þórhallur Vilmundarson and Bjarni Vilhjálmsson, 109–11, 120–21, 131–32, 137, and 170–72.

wing, producing a layered settlement history for its troll-like protagonist.[43]

Most "post-classical" family sagas are about human beings, so their openings appear less outlandish. *Grettis saga* (*Grettir's Saga*), the longest and best-known, begins with a complex weave of genealogical information, resumes of ancestral adventures in the British and Irish isles, and a notice about Haraldr Fairhair's expansionism, all presented as historical context.[44] Reinforcing the saga's commemorative function, it closes with a retrospective passage akin to the reflections on Egill's bones and family which conclude *Egils saga*. The historian Sturla Þórðarson is said to have judged that Grettir was the most distinguished outlaw in history by virtue of how long he survived in the wilds, his monster-fighting abilities, and the prestigious circumstances in which his killing was avenged (in Byzantium).[45] Whether or not these reflections were really Sturla's, the implication is that these facts make Grettir's career worth telling. Intriguingly, two of these three alleged facts about Grettir relate to parts of his saga usually seen as pure fiction: monster fights on the one hand, and the romanticized, *Tristan*-influenced Byzantine episode on the other.[46]

Many other "post-classical" sagas employ close-packed information about settlers' genealogies related to or copied from *Landnámabók* as starting points for their own compositions.[47]

---

43 See Ármann Jakobsson, "History of the Trolls? *Bárðar saga* as an Historical Narrative," *Saga Book of the Viking Society* 25 (1998): 53–71, and Sävborg and Bek-Pedersen, eds. *Folklore in Old Norse — Old Norse in Folklore*.

44 *Grettis saga*, ed. Guðni Jónsson, Íslenzk fornrit 7 (Reykjavik: Hið íslenzka fornritafélag, 1936), 3–36.

45 Ibid., 289–90. Similar claims conclude *Harðar saga*, ed. Þórhallur Vilmundarson and Bjarni Vilhjálmsson, 97, xliv–lxvii.

46 The monsters' fabulous nature is argued by Kathryn Hume, "From Saga to Romance: The Use of Monsters in Old Norse Literature," *Studies in Philology* 77 (1980): 6–7.

47 Examples not discussed below include *Harðar saga* and *Gull-Þóris saga*: *Harðar saga*, ed. Þórhallur Vilmundarson and Bjarni Vilhjálmsson, 3–7, 175–82.

Their source material is not cut and pasted, but reworked, as in *Landnámabók* itself. For example, the opening genealogy of King Haraldr in *Flóamanna saga* (*The Saga of the People of Flói*) has been amplified from its main source, the *Sturlubók* recension of *Landnámabók*, by tracing the ancestry of Haraldr's great-grandmother right back to the euhemerized king Óðinn "who ruled over Ásgarðr" via Ragnarr loðbrók and Sigurðr the Dragon-Slayer. One text of this saga also closes with a long genealogy linking its hero to Jón Hákonarson, the fourteenth-century patron of the saga's oldest known manuscript.[48]

In *Kjalnesinga saga* (*The Saga of the People of Kjalarnes*), the central story of the otherwise unattested Irish Christian settler Andríðr and his son Búi is anchored historically in an account of a better-known Irish Christian settler from the Hebrides named Örlygr, also mentioned, with divergent details, in *Landnámabók*.[49] Both saga and settlement history specifically note the iron church bell and lectionary which Örlygr brings to Iceland, and the saga ends by reinserting the story into its physical environment: first the heathen period in which Búi died, then the Christian period of the late thirteenth century.

> The church that Örlygr had had built was still standing at Esjuberg then [when Búi was buried] [...]. The same iron bell was hanging in front of the church at Esjuberg when bishop Árni Þorláksson headed the church [...] and it was worn through by rust. Bishop Árni also had the same lectionary brought south to Skálholt and had all the pages prepared and fixed into its binding, and it contains Irish letters.[50]

---

48 *Harðar saga*, ed. Þórhallur Vilmundarson and Bjarni Vilhjálmsson, 231–38 (231: "er réð fyrir Ásgarði"), 326–27. The oldest known manuscript is *Vatnshyrna*, now lost. Compare the similarly grandiloquent genealogical claims concluding *Króka-Refs saga* (ibid., 160).

49 *Kjalnesinga saga*, ed. Jóhannes Halldórsson, Íslenzk fornrit 14 (Reykjavík: Hið íslenzka fornritafélag, 1959), 3–5; *Íslendingabók, Landnámabók*, ed. Jakob Benediktsson, 52–55, 168–77.

50 *Kjalnesinga saga*, ed. Jóhannes Halldórsson, 43–44: "Þá stóð enn kirkja sú at Esjubergi, er Örlygr hafði látit gera [...]. Sú in sama járnklukka hekk þá fyrir kirkjunni á Esjubergi, er Árni biskup réð fyrir stað, Þorláksson, [...]

Búi's descendants are not named, but the saga adds that *mikil ætt* "a great lineage" is descended from him. This is a common referential shortcut found in "classical" as well as "post-classical" family sagas.[51] But the fact of his lineage is insisted on, as are the alleged physical relics of Irish Christianity's brief toehold in southwest Iceland decades before the island's official conversion.

Other "post-classical" family sagas anchor themselves in the authoritative sagas of Norwegian kings. The complete recension of *Þórðar saga hreðu* (*The Saga of Þórðr the Quarrelsome*) constructs a Norwegian prelude for its protagonist by narrating versions of episodes in kings' sagas, including an amplified rendition of the killing of King Sigurðr Snake by Klyppr Þórðarson — here aided by his otherwise-unattested brother Þórðr, the saga's hero, who subsequently emigrates to Iceland.[52] Þórðr's own prestige is enhanced by his service at the court of King Gamli, on whom the audience will find more information "in the sagas of the kings of Norway."[53] The divergent, incomplete recension of *Þórðar saga* has a different but equally referential prelude, including Gamli but not Sigurðr, and begins with a genealogy of Þórðr's grandfather Hörða-Kári and an account (close to *Landnámabók*) of his grandson Úlfljótr, the man credited with introducing Iceland's first lawcode.[54] This recension ends by listing the descendants of Þórðr and his foster son Eiðr down to the fourteenth century, linking the hero once again to the patron of the saga's earliest known manuscript, Jón Hákonarson, via his wife Ingileif.[55] Both recensions embody different inflections of

---

ok var þá slitin af ryði. Árni biskup lét ok þann sama plenarium fara suðr í Skálholt ok lét búa ok líma öll blöðin í kjölinn, ok er irskt letr á."

51 Such as *Hallfreðar saga*, ed. Bjarni Einarsson (Reykjavik: Stofnun Árna Magnússonar, 1977), 111,*Gunnars saga Keldugnúpsfífls* in *Kjalnesinga saga*, ed. Jóhannes Halldórsson, 343 (and n. 1), 363, 378–79. Several "classical" sagas end without any reference to protagonists' descendants.

52 *Kjalnesinga saga*, ed. Jóhannes Halldórsson, 165–68.

53 Ibid., 165: "í sögum Nóregskonunga."

54 Ibid., 229–32. Cf. *Íslendingabók, Landnámabók*, ed. Jakob Benediktsson, 311–15 (*Hauksbók* recension).

55 *Kjalnesinga saga*, ed. Jóhannes Halldórsson, 224–26 and 245–47 (*Vatnshyrna* again).

the desire to embed a saga's events in a recognized historical background. Other gestures of historicity include physical testimony of Þórðr's building skills — a hall in Hrafnagil which "still stands today" — in both recensions. The complete recension even ends with an oblique truth-claim hinting at the existence of competing accounts: "we have not heard anything further truthfully told about him."[56]

Historical Anchorage in the Distant Past: The *fornaldarsögur*

The examples discussed above show that "classical" and "postclassical" family sagas alike locate their narratives in historical time and space. This need not seem surprising. These were sagas about Icelanders, for Icelanders. The personal connection is obvious, even if the story might look doubtful. But similar historical anchorages are used in the *fornaldarsögur,* which are set much further away in space and time, usually in Scandinavia or northern Europe and usually before the period during which Iceland was settled.[57] Many of their preludes or postludes are brief, but even the shorter ones provide much more information than one needs to enjoy the story purely as a story.

The legendary kings named in most *fornaldarsaga* openings are, as Ruth Righter-Gould pointed out in 1980, not recognized as historical today. But Righter-Gould was wrong to suggest that such "fictitious" figures undermined the sagas' credibility for medieval audiences,[58] unless the early portions of *Heimskringla* or Saxo's *History of the Danes* are also regarded as fictional. While some may have doubted, medieval audiences were often prepared to take such legendary information on trust.

A detailed example of this attitude occurs in one of the first legendary sagas to appear in the manuscript record, *Hervarar*

---

56 Ibid., 224, 246 ("enn stendr í dag"); ibid., 226 ("Höfum vér ekki fleira heyrt með sannleik af honum sagt.")
57 There is no clear north-south divide between *fornaldarsögur* and *riddarasögur*.
58 Ruth Righter-Gould, "The 'Fornaldar sögur Norðurlanda': A Structural Analysis," *Scandinavian Studies* 52 (1980): 425–26.

saga ok Heiðreks (*The Saga of Hervör and Heiðrekr*). The only surviving complete recension ("U") of this complex narrative begins with a chronicle-like prelude tracing Hervör's ancestry back six generations to the remote period *before* the arrival of the euhemerized king Óðinn in Scandinavia, when giants and humans interbred. This prelude intersperses genealogical and geographical information with anecdotes, as in *Landnámabók*. At the end, after a climactic battle involving Hervör's grandchildren, the storyline thins out into a chronicle, listing the next twenty generations of Swedish rulers with occasional synchronisms linking their reigns with famous Norwegian kings.[59] Altogether, the U-recension weaves together regnal lists, genealogical traditions and historicized myths into a geographical and chronological panorama of the Old North from its first inhabitants to the twelfth century, a feat paralleled only by Saxo's *History of the Danes*. But this is a saga, not a national history. The panorama's two ends, prehistoric and recent, are foreshortened and placed in the background. Against this context, the three generations represented by Hervör, Heiðrekr and his offspring stand out in strongly characterized relief.

As Alaric Hall has shown, the detail of the U-recension's historical framework makes it unusual among the *fornaldarsögur*.[60] The incomplete R- and H-recensions share a briefer prelude tracing Hervör's ancestry back three generations,[61] and we cannot tell whether they originally contained the chronicle-like closing sequence. It has been suggested that the relative lengths of the recensions' preludes indicate degrees of intended veracity. Hall calls the U-recension's approach "a complete change [...] from *fornaldarsaga* conventions" and implies that its story, uniquely among the *fornaldarsögur*, is thus provided with "a

---

[59] *Saga Heiðreks konungs ins vitra*, ed. and trans. Christopher Tolkien (London: Thomas Nelson, 1960), 66–68, 59–61. The U-recension survives only in post-medieval copies but is clearly medieval.

[60] Alaric Hall, "Changing Style and Changing Meaning: Icelandic Historiography and the Medieval Redactions of *Heiðreks saga*," *Scandinavian Studies* 77 (2005): 1–30.

[61] *Saga Heiðreks*, ed. and trans. Tolkien, 1–10.

historical context." For Karl G. Johansson, the R-recension's shorter prelude suggests a "fictional function."[62] But three generations is not bad going. We should not make the extreme case of the U-recension a yardstick of intended historicity, any more than we should call Saxo's *History of the Danes* "more historical" than the earlier chronicles whose prehistory it amplified, such as *The Chronicle of Lejre*. As seen with the diverse family saga preludes, historical intention is not reducible to length alone. The historical claims of the R-recension, and of shorter *fornaldarsögur* with briefer preludes, cannot be dismissed for this reason. Instead, the logic can be turned on its head. By moving in the generic direction of a chronicle, the U-recension confirms just how seriously "mythical" beings could be taken as the subjects of histories. It provides a striking marker of the historicity of legendary matter in general, and thus a helpful backdrop against which the briefer framing passages of other legendary sagas can be viewed.

In terms of scope, the closest equivalent to the U-recension of *Hervarar saga* among other legendary sagas is *Völsunga saga*. Usually treated today as a discrete narrative, in its only surviving medieval manuscript it functions as a legendary-historical prelude to *Ragnars saga loðbrókar* (*The Saga of Ragnarr Furry-Trousers*).[63] Once again a protagonist's genealogy is traced back to the beginnings of human history. Here the connection with Icelanders was more direct: Ragnarr and his sons were claimed as ancestral figures by at least three Icelandic settler families, one of which is named in *Ragnars saga* as well as *Landnámabók*.[64]

---

62 Hall, "Changing Style," 12; Karl G. Johansson, "Narratives and Narrators on the Move: Some Examples of Change and Continuity in the Tradition of Fantastic Fiction," in *The Legendary Sagas*, ed. Jakobsson, Lassen, and Ney, 357.

63 This is clearest in *Vǫlsunga saga ok Ragnars saga loðbrókar*, ed. Magnus Olsen (Copenhagen: Møller, 1906–1908), 110–11, where both sagas are printed together as in the manuscript NKS 1824b 4to.

64 *Fornaldar sögur Norðurlanda*, ed. Guðni Jónsson, 4 vols. (Reykjavik: Íslendingasagnaútgáfan, 1950), 1.280, and *Íslendingabók, Landnámabók*, ed. Jakob Benediktsson, 239–42 (see also 214 and cxxx). On Icelanders tracing

Ragnarr and his sons feature as protagonists or genealogical anchorage points in several sagas, as does the father of Ragnarr's second wife Áslaug, Sigurðr the Dragon-Slayer, who is also the hero of several eddic poems. In its extant form, *Völsunga saga* draws directly on those poems to fill out the pedigree of Ragnarr's sons with memorable narrative and poetry.[65] Beginning with Sigi, rumored to be Óðinn's son, it covers five generations of Áslaug's ancestors in increasing detail, culminating in a loosely structured epic treatment of Sigurðr and his contemporaries. The saga ends abruptly, leading directly into *Ragnars saga* in which Áslaug, Ragnarr and his sons occupy the limelight.

Most critics treat *Völsunga saga* as a narrative expression of mythic or ideological truths, which it certainly is. Nevertheless, in its extant form it makes no sense to see it as fiction, despite its numerous fantastic episodes and its failure even to euhemerize the genealogy's alleged apical figure, Óðinn, who keeps uncannily intervening in the affairs of the Völsungs down the centuries. Óðinn's identity seems deliberately ambiguous. The saga does not narrate his life, beginning instead with Sigi. But the adventures of later Völsungs are presented as essential background to the story of Ragnarr and his sons, making the Völsungs part of the web of history and genealogy into which leading Icelanders slotted their families. Sigurðr's perceived historicity in medieval Iceland is confirmed by brief notices in annalistic chronicles, genealogies and other legendary histories.[66] Some of the legends told about Sigurðr in *Völsunga saga* were treated as history, as is implied by an episode in the longest recension of *Óláfs saga Tryggvasonar*—a major reference-point for medieval Icelandic historians—where the Norwegian missionary

---

descent from Ragnarr's sons, see Clunies Ross, *Prolonged Echoes 2*, 92, and Rowe, *Vikings in the West*, esp. 219–44.

65 Whether *Völsunga saga* was originally composed as a prelude to *Ragnars saga* is unknown.

66 Elizabeth Ashmann Rowe, "*Quid Sigvardus cum Christo?* Moral Interpretations of Sigurðr Fáfnisbani in Old Norse Literature," *Viking and Medieval Scandinavia* 2 (2006): 176–77.

king hears some of these stories and credits them as true.[67] One late annalistic reference to Sigurðr helps explain how the implausible feats attributed to him and his contemporaries in sagas could be credited. The 1405 annal in *Lögmannsannáll* mentions that an Icelander visiting "Affrica" saw such secular relics as the hilt of Sigurðr's ten-foot-long sword and an enormous tooth of Starkaðr the Old.[68] Some scholars doubt that such claims could have been intended or taken seriously,[69] but this is a modern qualm. The giant stature of former humans was authorized by the Old Testament and was a commonplace for medieval and early modern historians.[70]

Both these *fornaldarsögur* belong to the allegedly early subgroup known as *Heldensagas*. Both draw openly on older heroic poetry and oral Germanic tradition, so their function as legendary history has been taken seriously by some scholars, like that of the first saga of *Heimskringla*, *Ynglinga saga* (*The Saga of the Ynglings*), set in a similarly distant past.[71] A few critics have even proposed that the first *fornaldarsögur* emerged directly from Latin *origo gentis* history-writing like Saxo's, a comparison worth developing further.[72] Legendary sagas with looser links to earlier heroic tradition, especially the quest-based *Abenteuersa-*

---

67 *Óláfs saga Tryggvasonar en mesta*, ed. Ólafur Halldórsson, 3 vols. (Copenhagen: Munksgaard and Reitzel, 1958–2000), 3.38 (conclusion of *Norna-Gests þáttr*). Rowe, distinguishing between the historicity of saga characters and that of stories featuring them, calls this passage and the stories quoted "pure fiction" (Rowe, "*Quid Sigvardus cum Christo?*" 176), but this is not how they are presented in *Óláfs saga*.

68 *Islandske annaler indtil 1578*, ed. Gustav Storm (Christiania: Grøndahl, 1888), 288 (see 246–47 for Ragnarr and his sons). On this see Rowe, "*Quid Sigvardus cum Christo?*" 176–77.

69 Stephen A. Mitchell, *Heroic Sagas and Ballads* (Ithaca: Cornell University Press, 1991), 136.

70 See n. 38 above for examples by Saxo and Arngrímur Jónsson.

71 See, for example, Klaus von See, *Europa und der Norden im Mittelalter* (Heidelberg: Winter, 1999), 397–408 (on what he calls *Vǫlsunga ok Ragnars saga*); *Vǫlsunga saga: The Saga of the Volsungs*, ed. and trans. Kaaren Grimstad (Saarbrücken: AQ-Verlag, 2000), 16–20, and Hall, "Changing Style" (on the U-recension of *Hervarar saga*).

72 Lassen, "*Origines Gentium*," with further references.

gas, are assumed to be a secondary development in a fictional direction, drawing more on romance and fairytale. Whether secondary or simultaneous, the same contrast is widely perceived: the *Heldensagas* depict a past which was distant but understood as real, but the *Abenteuersagas* depict a past in which nobody was expected to believe. Romance and fairytale step in where history fears to tread.

If this view were accurate, we would expect details of historical anchorage found in family sagas and *Heldensagas* to be absent from the more romanticized *fornaldarsögur*. Romance openings, according to Hume, are extremely economical: the protagonist is introduced and "we are told his homeland, parentage, and rank, but nothing more unless it is relevant to his adventures."[73] This is certainly true of some romances, although the frequent mention of a well-known, putatively historical ruler like Arthur does anchor their storylines, however briefly. More importantly, strong romance influence on the *fornaldarsögur* did not remove the need for a thickly described historical context. Here we find the same patterns as seen earlier: a saga emerges from a matrix of dynastic or regional history, or as a dynastic appendage to an existing text. The chunks of information are typically briefer than in the longest family saga or *Heldensaga* preludes, but no inverse correlation between romance and history is visible here.

One example is the late adventure saga *Sörla saga sterka* (*The Saga of Sörli the Strong*), surviving in post-medieval manuscripts and full of borrowings from French courtly terminology. It is a true "Viking romance." Its opening functions primarily to introduce the hero and his father. But it gives more information than such a function strictly requires. Before introducing Sörli and his siblings, it begins:

> At the time when King Hálfdan Brana's-Fosterling ruled Sweden the Cold, which he conquered from Agnarr the Wealthy, and had placed his kinsman-by-marriage Astró as ruler of

---

73 Hume, "Beginnings and Endings," 595.

England and had made him its duke, a king named Erlingr ruled over Oppland. He ruled one third of Norway, while King Haraldr Valdimarsson ruled two-thirds of the realm. King Erlingr was thought a great and very wealthy ruler, because he had served King Knútr the Great for a long time and had been enriched by him with much wealth, possessions and fine treasures. The king's queen was named Dagný, descended from the Æsir.[74]

Several of these people later play important roles in the story, but it is not strictly necessary for them all to be introduced together like this: their appearance here suggests a need to provide a historical backdrop. Contrary to Hume's principle, several of these historically specific details play no role in the plot itself: the fact that Hálfdan ruled Sweden the Cold, Astró's ducal title, the origins of Erlingr's wealth, or Dagný's descent from the Æsir.[75] The opening sentence also positions *Sörla saga* as a sequel to a now-lost version of *Hálfdanar saga Brönufóstra,* displaying the cyclic impulse already mentioned.[76] The saga's conclusion conforms

---

74 *Fornaldar sögur,* ed. Guðni Jónsson, 3.369: "Í þann tíma, sem Hálfdan konungr Brönufóstri stýrði Svíþjóð inni köldu, er hann vann af Agnari inum auðga, en setti Astró, mág sinn, yfir England ok gerði hann hertuga þar yfir, réð sá konungr Upplöndum, er Erlingr hét. Hann stýrði þriðjungi Noregs, en Haraldr konungr Valdimarsson tveim hlutum ríkis. Erlingr konungr þótti höfðingi mikill ok stórauðigr, því at hann hafði lengi verit með Knúti konungi inum ríka ok hafði öðlazt af honum mikinn auð, fé ok góða gripi. Drottning konungs hét Dagný, komin af Æsum." These details vary in the extant manuscripts, as shown by Silvia Hufnagel, "Sörla saga sterka: Studies in the Transmission of a fornaldarsaga," PhD diss., University of Copenhagen, 2012. One scribe went out of his way to disagree with another version's claim, in the postlude, that Sörli was the grandfather of Ragnarr loðbrók (ibid., 152). I am grateful to Silvia Hufnagel for giving me a copy of her PhD dissertation.

75 Erlingr's too, in one manuscript: Silvia Hufnagel, "Sörla saga sterka and Rafn's Edition," in *Á austrvega: Saga and East Scandinavia: Preprint Papers of the 14th International Saga Conference,* ed. Marco Bianchi, Fredrik Charpentier Ljungqvist, Agneta Ney, and Henrik Williams, 398–404 (Gävle: Gävle University Press, 2009), 403.

76 In the extant *Hálfdanar saga Brönufóstra,* Hálfdan does not encounter Agnarr or any ruler of Sweden the Cold, but rules Denmark and then England.

to romance expectations with its glamorous triple wedding but violates those expectations when the name of the hero's bride is said to be unknown to the storyteller.[77] This admission of ignorance, a gesture common in other kinds of sagas, strengthens the impression, if not necessarily the reality, of a narrator passing on a tradition and scrupulously refusing to invent a name if none is recorded.[78]

Hálfdanar saga Eysteinssonar (*The Saga of Hálfdan Eysteinsson*) is essentially a bridal-quest romance: its hero falls in love with the white hand of a mysterious visitor whom he seeks and eventually marries. It, too, begins and ends with a plethora of historical and genealogical data, even drawing a direct link between its protagonists and one Icelandic settler family. Its first recension begins by sketching the genealogy of the hero's father Eysteinn around familiar legendary-historical landmarks:

> There was a king named Þrándr; Trondheim in Norway is named after him. He was the son of Óðinn's son Sæming, who ruled over Hálogaland. Sæming married Nauma after whom Namdal is named. Þrándr was a great ruler. His wife was called Dagmær, sister of Svanhvít whom Hrómundr Gripsson married. One of their sons was called Eysteinn, and the other Eiríkr the Far-Traveler who discovered the Field of the Undying, but his mother's name is not known. Eysteinn married, taking Sigurðr Hart's daughter Ása as his wife. Her mother was Áslaug, daughter of Sigurðr Snake-in-the-Eye. With her Eysteinn acquired Finnmark, Valdres, Totn and Hadaland. He was a powerful and firm ruler.[79]

His dragon-ship, however, is prominent in the extant saga, as in *Sörla saga*.

77 *Fornaldar sögur*, ed. Guðni Jónsson, 3:409.

78 On this authenticating strategy generally, see Manhire, "Narrative Functions," 183–37, and Ranković, "Authentication," 220–23.

79 *Hálfdanar saga Eysteinssonar*, ed. Franz Rolf Schröder (Halle: Niemeyer, 1917), 90–91: "Þrándr hefir konungr heitit; við hann er kendr Þrándheimr í Nóregi; hann var sonr Sæmings konungs, sonar Óðins, er réð fyrir Hálogalandi. Sæmingr átti Naumu, er Naumudalr er við kendr. Þrándr var mikill hǫfðingi; hans kona hét Dagmær, systir Svanhvítar, er Hrómundr Gripsson

Hrómundr Gripsson stars in another *fornaldarsaga* whose historicity was debated in medieval Iceland: a famous description of storytelling at a twelfth-century wedding in *Þorgils saga ok Hafliða* mentions that some people called Hrómundr's saga an entertaining lie (*lygisaga*), but that others reckoned him one of their ancestors.[80] *Landnámabók* mentions him as a rather important ancestor: he was the grandfather of Ingólfr Árnason, the first Norseman to establish a lasting settlement in Iceland.[81] Eiríkr the Far-Traveler was a legendary Norwegian prince credited with preparing Norway for its subsequent Christianization: his eastern adventures are described in *Eiríks saga víðförla,* which functions as a prelude to Óláfr Tryggvason's biography in *Flateyjarbók*.[82] Finally, Eysteinn's queen Ása is made a direct descendant of both Ragnarr loðbrók and Sigurðr the Dragon-Slayer, thus giving Eysteinn's son Hálfdan, the saga's hero, a double dose of Óðinnic ancestry. These ten short sentences pack in a wealth of significant historical context.

Like several family sagas, the first recension of *Hálfdanar saga Eysteinssonar* has a leisurely, information-rich ending, gradually thinning out into condensed notices about what the main characters and their descendants did later. Like the prelude, this postlude hooks onto legendary traditions beyond the story proper, whether taking place simultaneously with the saga's action or long afterwards: Valr's and Raknarr's activities in

---

átti; þeirra son hét Eysteinn, en annarr Eiríkr enn víðǫrli, er fann Ódáinsakr; hans móðir er ekki nefnd. Eysteinn giptiz ok fekk dóttur Sigurðar hjartar, er Ása hét; hennar móðir var Áslaug, dóttir Sigurðar orms-í-auga. Eysteinn fekk með henni Finnmǫrk ok Valdres, Þótn ok Haðaland; hann var ríkr ok stjórnsamr." The saga's opening and closing genealogies are more detailed in the second recension and include a link to *Fertrams saga ok Platós,* a late *riddarasaga* (ibid., 57–59).

80 *Þorgils saga ok Hafliða,* ed. Ursula Brown (London: Oxford University Press, 1952), 17–18. For discussion, see O'Connor, "History or Fiction?," 133–41, with further references. See also Anatoly Liberman, *The Saga Mind and the Beginnings of Icelandic Prose* (Lewiston: Edwin Mellen, 2018).

81 *Íslendingabók, Landnámabók,* ed. Jakob Benediktsson, 38–40. I am grateful to Paul Bibire for reminding me of this.

82 Rowe, *Development of Flateyjarbók,* 152–99.

the Arctic wilderness (allegedly summarized from a lost "great saga" of Valr),[83] Göngu-Hrólfr's marriage to the granddaughter of Earl Skúli (told fully in *Göngu-Hrólfs saga*), Oddr the Showy's settlement in Iceland (told in more detail in *Landnámabók*), the waterfall expedition of Oddr's son Gold-Þórir (told fully in *Gull-Þóris saga*).[84] Once again, dramatic narrative resolves into information and implied narrative, and listeners are directed elsewhere for more details.

Even the uproarious *Bósa saga ok Herrauðs* (*The Saga of Bósi and Herrauðr*) follows suit. Its main plot is tightly structured, but its margins are awash with data. The prelude locates its storyline at the time of the legendary Danish ruler Haraldr Wartooth,[85] whose fall at the Battle of Brávellir was a defining event in Scandinavian legendary history. The protagonists fight in this battle, too, but it is a mere digression in the saga's plot, where interested listeners or readers are referred to a now-lost "saga of Sigurðr Hring" for more details.[86] The saga's opening also mentions Herrauðr's uncles Náttfari and Dagfari (Nightfarer and Dayfarer). Their names sound suspiciously made-up, symbolic of some role they might play in the saga, but they turn out to be quotidian details from, or mimicking, a received tradition. They play no role except to summon the protagonists to Brávellir, where they themselves are killed. Other details in the prelude — the fact that Herrauðr's father's paternal half-brother was Gautrekr the Generous (another celebrated legendary king and the protagonist of *Gautreks saga*), King Óðinn's Asian origins — bolster both Herrauðr's prestige and the story's historical and intertextual anchorage. So, too, do the closing genealogical notices about Bósi's son Sviði the Bold (mentioned in two other legendary sagas), and his grandson Vilmundr the Outsider (hero of *Vilmundar saga viðutan*), and the final anecdote about

---

83 *Hálfdanar saga*, ed. Schröder, 133–39 (136: "mikil saga"). On the Raknarr-Valr story, also mentioned in other texts, see ibid., 42–52.
84 See also *Íslendingabók, Landnámabók*, ed. Jakob Benediktsson, 154.
85 *Die "Bósa-saga" in zwei Fassungen*, ed. Otto Luitpold Jiriczek (Strassburg: Trübner, 1893), 3.
86 Ibid., 33–34 ("í sögu Sigurðar hrings").

how Ragnarr loðbrók came to marry Herrauðr's daughter Þóra and earned his own nickname. This last has been drawn from the extant *Ragnars saga loðbrókar*, thus positioning *Bósa saga* as part of the backstory to the more authoritative *Ragnars saga*.[87]

The historical pretensions of this most rollicking of sagas are completed by the fact that its historical prelude (in most of its medieval manuscripts) is preceded by a short prologue defending its truthfulness against those who would dismiss it as mere "nonsense" (*lokleysa*),[88] suggesting that historicity and entertainment need not be mutually exclusive. A similar juxtaposition of close-packed historical and geographical data with a rhetorical defense of the saga's historicity concludes the heavily romance-influenced *Göngu-Hrólfs saga* (*The Saga of Hrólfr the Walker*). Indeed, this sequence follows hard on the heels of the extravagant triple wedding which ends the story proper, as if to reaffirm its grounding in the real world and not the world of fantasy, despite its chivalric trappings.[89]

So far, I have been arguing that these framing devices demonstrate the writer's intention of appearing, however disingenuously, as a historian. One possible objection is that many of these framing passages could be seen as using the sober rhetoric of historical fact to top and tail an essentially fictional story which nobody was expected to believe, and that any intelligent audience would know that the point where the information-heavy prelude stopped and the main storyline powered up marked a transition into a world of fantasy. This would be an excessively crude way of conceptualizing how "belief" in a story's veracity is likely to have operated on the ground, as if it could be switched on and off at discrete moments in the text. In any case, in terms of plausibility or "sobriety" these passages are not so easily hived off from the stories they surround. They are often as fantastic as the main storylines, sometimes more so. I here gather and recall a few examples. The most obviously romantic episode

---

87 Ibid., 62–63.
88 Ibid., 3, n. 1.
89 *Fornaldar sögur*, ed. Guðni Jónsson, 3:277–79.

in any family saga, *Grettis saga*'s Tristanesque conclusion in Byzantium, is highlighted in the postlude as one of the historical facts making Grettir memorable, as are his monster-fights which some see as a hallmark of fictionality. By far the weirdest happening in *Gull-Þóris saga*, its protagonist's transformation into a dragon, is reserved for the saga's postlude summarizing local historical traditions. The chronicle-like prelude to the U-text of *Hervarar saga* is packed with phenomena we would see as fantasy, all presented as historical and genealogical information. The densest concentration of extracts from *Landnámabók* and place-name legends in any family saga is found in the most fantastic of all, *Bárðar saga*. And the longer recension of *Gísla saga* displays a greater desire to position the saga's events against a historical and genealogical background, but also contains a much stronger supernatural component than the better-known shorter recension.[90]

The inclusion of these romantic or uncanny events cannot be reduced to the entertainment function of fictional prose, because in these passages the events' entertainment value is rarely exploited. All of them explicitly form part of a discourse of information, *fræði*, which stands behind the storyline. In some sagas — *Bósa saga* is a contender — the entire saga is woven through with a burlesque tone that, some have argued, extended to the saga's claim to narrate history.[91] But, if so, we cannot assume that everyone in the audience would have seen it in this way, even if they enjoyed the passages of generic parody. Taken as a whole in the sagas explored so far, these framing passages show how far the limits of putative historical truthfulness could be stretched, even in summaries of information. So, what is

---

90 *Vestfirðinga sǫgur*, ed. Björn K. Þórólfsson and Guðni Jónsson, Íslenzk fornrit 6 (Reykjavik: Hið íslenzka fornritafélag, 1943), 3–118; *Membrana Regia Deperdita*, ed. Agnete Loth, Editiones Arnamagnæanæ A 5 (Copenhagen: Munksgaard, 1960), 3–80.

91 Vésteinn Ólason, "The Marvellous North and Authorial Presence in the Icelandic *Fornaldarsaga*," in *Contexts of Pre-Novel Narrative: The European Tradition*, ed. Roy Eriksen (Berlin: de Gruyter, 1994), 103–34. For discussion, see O'Connor, "History or Fiction?"

often thought to be "story emerging from history," or "history giving birth to fiction," is really a dramatic historical *narrative* arising from a summary of historical *information*—one kind of historical discourse yielding to another, then back again. The artfulness of the core storyline does not, in itself, falsify its claim to be history.

Historical Anchorage in Norse-Icelandic Romance

What of the sagas closest to romance, the *riddarasögur*? The saga-groups discussed so far all offer some ancestral connection to activate the audience's personal or familial investment in their literal truthfulness: settler families, local rulers, Viking prehistory. But in stories set beyond Scandinavia, we might assume that there was no longer any need to maintain the pretense of, or belief in, historical veracity. This assumption may seem confirmed by the fact that several *riddarasögur* translate courtly romances, and that like their sources, most translated *riddarasaga* openings lack the fine-grained historical detail seen in many family sagas and *fornaldarsögur*.

But the contrast is not straightforward. For one thing, these translations' source-texts straddle the history-fiction boundary as understood today: they include *chansons de geste* as well as romances, *lais,* and one *fabliau*. And whatever the source-genre, comparisons of the opening and closing sequences of translated *riddarasögur* with those of their sources suggest a desire to align these narratives with the essentially historical expectations of the saga genre. Besides the removal of allegorical and figurative passages and the reduction of internal monologues, Geraldine Barnes has noted the addition of genealogical details in the conclusions of *Parcevals saga* (translating Chrétien's *Perceval*) and *Flóres saga ok Blankiflúr* (translating *Floire et Blanchefleur*), fixing the story firmly within dynastic and temporal contexts, and a tendency to transform a source's self-conscious authorial persona into the impersonal voice of a tradition-bearer handing down a story. For Barnes, these features move the translated *riddarasögur* away from what she sees as the "fictional mode" of their sources and towards the "historical mode" of the family sagas.[92] The late Christopher Sanders discerned a similar move in the direction of history-writing in *Bevers saga* (translating *Boeve de Hametoun*).[93]

The beginnings and endings of translated *riddarasögur* may be concise, but they ensure that the audience either understands the story's historical setting or, at least, grasps its commemorative intention. Barnes's observations about *Ívens saga* and its source, Chrétien's *Yvain*, deserve reiterating here. *Yvain* begins: "Arthur, the good King of Britain, he whose prowess teaches us that we should be brave and courteous, held a rich and kingly court on the feast-day, which costs so much, that we call Pentecost. The king was at Carduel in Wales."[94]

Arthur's name and title are treated as sufficient orientation for the audience, and the story's exemplary aspect comes uppermost. Whether this amounts to a fictional gesture, as is often assumed, is another question. But Norwegian and Icelandic audiences could not be expected to know all about Arthur and his reputation, so more details are needed. *Ívens saga* thus begins:

> The excellent King Arthur ruled England, as is known to many. After a time, he became king of Rome. He was the most illustrious of the kings who had lived on this side of the ocean, and the most popular apart from Charlemagne. He had the bravest knights in Christendom. It happened one

---

[92] Geraldine Barnes, "Authors, Dead and Alive, in Old Norse Fiction," *Parergon*, New Series 8, no. 2 (1990): 5–22.

[93] Christopher Sanders, "*Bevers saga* in the Context of Old Norse Historical Prose," in *Sir Bevis of Hampton in Literary Tradition*, ed. Jennifer Fellows and Ivana Djordjević (Cambridge: Brewer, 2008), 51–66.

[94] Chrestien de Troyes, *Yvain (Le Chevalier au lion)*, ed. Wendelin Foerster and Thomas B.W. Reid (Manchester: Manchester University Press, 1974), 1: "Artus, li buens rois de Bretaingne, | La cui proesce nos ansaingne, | Que nos soiiens preu et cortois, | Tint cort si riche come rois | A cele feste, qui tant coste, | Qu'an doit clamer la pantecoste. | Li rois fu a Carduel an Gales." "Carduel" may refer to Carlisle in Cumbric-speaking North Britain.

time that he had, as usual, gathered all his friends and held great festivities at Pentecost, which we call Whitsun.⁹⁵

This prelude hardly matches those of many family sagas, but it does provide anchorage.⁹⁶ By drawing on Geoffrey of Monmouth's narrative about Arthur's Roman conquests and invoking the *imperium* of Charlemagne, it locks the story more explicitly into European history as well as providing calendrical orientation.

Even more detail is found in the *fabliau* adaptation *Möttuls saga* (*The Saga of the Mantle*). Its substantial "translator's prologue" opens with a detailed description of how magnificent Arthur was, followed by a declaration of the reliability of this information:

This is attested by truthful narratives (*sannar sögur*) about him and much reliable information (*góð frœði*) recorded by worthy clerks (*klerkar*) about his many deeds [...]. This book tells about a curious and amusing incident which took place [...]. And this true account (*þvílík sannindi*), which came to me in French, I have translated into Norse for you listeners as entertainment and diversion *(til gamans ok skemtanar)*, since the worthy King Hákon asked me [...].⁹⁷

---

95 *Norse Romance II: Knights of the Round Table*, ed. and trans. Marianne E. Kalinke (Cambridge: Brewer, 1999), 38 (translation adapted from hers): "Hinn ágæti kóngr Artúrus réð fyrir Englandi, sem mörgum mönnum er kunnigt. Hann var um síðir kóngr yfir Rómaborg. Hann <er> þeira kónga frægastr er verit hafa þann veg frá hafinu ok vinsælastr annarr en Karlamagnús. Hann hafði þá röskustu riddara er í váru kristninni. Þat var einn tíma sem jafnan, at hann hafði stefnt til sín öllum sínum vinum ok helt mikla hátíð á pikkisdögum, er vér köllum hvítasunnu."

96 Barnes, "Authors, Dead and Alive," 9–10, who also notes the removal of Chrétien's irony.

97 *Norse Romance II*, ed. and trans. Kalinke, 6 (translation adapted from hers): "Þat vátta honum sannar sögur ok margskonar góð fræði er ger váru af dýrum klerkum um mart hans athæfi [...]. Nú segir þessi bók frá einum kynligum ok gamansamligum atburð er gerðiz [...]. En þvílík sannindi sem valskan sýndi mér þá norræna<ða> ek yðr áheyrendum til gamans ok skemtanar svá sem virðuligr Hákon kóngr [...] bauð."

The stance of telling a true story, of drawing entertainment from reliable information, may seem already implicit in the Old French *Lai du cort mantel*. But it is made explicit in the Norse, perhaps to compensate for the brevity of historical context otherwise given in this text, offered within a genre where more anchorage was often expected. The Icelandic adaptation places equal emphasis on the entertaining and veracious aspects of the text, as if to remind audiences, including potential skeptics or those who fear boredom, that stories can be both true and enjoyable. We, perhaps, need more reminding of this than they did.

An increased emphasis on commemorative purposes in Norse adaptations of Continental narratives is clearest in the Old Norwegian adaptation of the *lais* of Marie de France, *Strengleikar*, again perhaps to compensate for a lack of historical detail in the originals which would have struck any translator versed in the saga tradition. Geographical and historical reference points in Marie's *lais* are often perfunctory, sometimes lacking altogether; they are usually seen as intentionally fictional. But Marie's general prologue and introductions to individual *lais* insist on their veracity and commemorative function, something which modern scholars either ignore or treat apologetically as Marie's sop to a conservative audience.[98] The Norwegian translation amplifies Marie's emphasis on historicity and commemoration as well as exemplarity. Its general prologue, added to Marie's own, opens with the announcement that the narrator has inquired into "the deeds (*athæfi*) of those who lived in former times."[99] *Athæfi* is the first word, mirroring the use of *gesta*

---

98 Green, *Beginnings*, 180–81; Glyn S. Burgess, "Introduction," in Marie de France, *Lais*, ed. Alfred Ewert (Bristol: Bristol Classical Press, 1995), xvi–xvii. The most sophisticated recent account of Marie's writings taken as a whole (R. Howard Bloch, *The Anonymous Marie de France* [Chicago: University of Chicago Press, 2003]) discusses her emphasis on commemoration solely in terms of a desire to preserve stories previously recounted, evading the equally significant issue of those stories' claimed veracity.

99 *Strengleikar: An Old Norse Translation of Twenty-One Old French Lais*, ed. and trans. Robert Cook and Mattias Tveitane (Oslo: NHKI, 1979), 4: "<A>t hæve þeirra er i fyrnskunni varo."

(deeds) in larger histories' titles and recalling Isidore's definition of *historia* as an account of "true things that were done," *res verae quae factae sunt*.

The Norwegian prologue next highlights the stories' linked exemplary, entertaining, and informative functions: they were written as everlasting commemoration (*áminningar*), as entertainment, and as a source of great learning (*margfrœði*) for posterity, so that all may amend and illuminate their lives with knowledge of past events; and so that what happened in the distant past will not be hidden in later times when such great deeds are rarer.[100] The Norwegian prologue to *Equitan* reinforces Marie's own commemorative gesture by placing even more emphasis on the events themselves than does Marie:

> concerning the events that took place in that country — in order that they be known to posterity and not be lost to strangers — [scholars] had them written for the sake of commemoration (*til áminningar*) in lays accompanied by stringed instruments, and made into entertainment (*til skemtanar*). There were many of these events that we should not forget when we are trying to make a book of lays.[101]

Jürg Glauser's suggestion that the narrator of this prologue "reflects minutely over moments in which putatively factual events enter the space of fiction" makes sense only if fiction is seen as the only possible kind of entertainment.[102] Whatever we might

---

100 Ibid., 4 (translation adapted from theirs): "til ævenlægrar aminningar til skæmtanar. og margfrœðes viðr komande þioða at huerr bœte ok birte sitt lif. af kunnasto liðenna luta. Oc at æigi lœynizsk þat at hinum siðarstom dogum er gærðozk i andværðom."

101 Ibid., 66: "um atburði þa er jnnanlandz gærðuzt at kunnigir skylldo vera viðrkomandom ok æigi glœymazt okunnom þa leto þæir rita til aminningar. i strænglæika lioð ok af þæim gera til skemtanar ok varo mioc margir þæir atburðir er oss samer æigi at glœyma. er viðr læitom lioða bok at gera." Compare Marie, *Lais*, 26.

102 Jürg Glauser, "Staging the Text: On the Development of a Consciousness of Writing in the Norwegian and Icelandic Literature of the Middle Ages," in *Along the Oral-Written Continuum: Types of Texts, Relations and Their Im-*

call Marie's *lais* today, their translator(s) presented them as entertaining histories.

We come finally to my hardest case, the indigenous *riddarasögur*. The translated *riddarasögur* could be seen as veering in a historical direction because they took prestigious written sources literally. As one version of *Göngu-Hrólfs saga* puts it, "it is difficult to contradict what previous scholars (*fræðimenn*) have composed."[103] But the indigenous *riddarasögur* are largely invented. For those who first composed each one, little constraint was imposed by pre-existing traditions. Hume's paradigmatic example of a romance-opening comes from *Valdimars saga*, which appears totally uninterested in historical context and reaches the customary enumeration of the protagonist's qualities by its fourth sentence: "There was a king named Filipus and he ruled Germany. He and his wife had two children. His son was named Valdimar and his daughter Marmoria. Valdimar was big, strong and handsome [...]." The equally brief ending mentions that the hero and his queen had many children, but no one is named.[104] No concerted attempt is made to locate these characters against a background of recognizable German or European history, to define them in any terms except those internal to the story.

The saga's meaning is thus located entirely in the plot itself, and in the moral or exemplary patterning visible therein. Indigenous *riddarasögur* play variations on plot patterns from international popular tales, romances, saints' legends, and northern folklore — often in highly creative ways, but almost always leading inevitably to the hero's wedding and successful acquisition of power. As Paul Bibire puts it, these sagas present

---

plications, ed. Leidulf Melve, Else Mundal, and Slavica Ranković (Turnhout: Brepols, 2010), 333–34.

103 *Fornaldar sögur*, ed. Guðni Jónsson, 3:231.

104 *Late Medieval Icelandic Romances*, ed. Agnete Loth, 5 vols., Editiones Arnamagnæanæ B 20–4 (Copenhagen: Munksgaard, 1962–1965), 1:53: "<F>ilipus hefer kongr heitet. hann red fyrir Saxlandj. hann atte vid sinnj drottningu tuau barn. son hans het Ualldjmar en Marmoria dotter. Valldjmar var stor ok sterkr ok vænn"; ibid., 77–78; Hume, "Beginnings and Endings," 595.

idealized "rituals of human achievement."[105] Like several others, *Valdimars saga* identifies itself as an *æfintýr*, a term frequently used of a self-standing *exemplum* or moral tale in late medieval Iceland (it is analogous to French *aventure*, from which it was borrowed via Middle Low German *eventūr*, and also means "episode" or "adventure").[106] Shared manuscript attestation and common narrative strategies suggest that the writing of *exempla* and of romance sagas were closely intertwined. Their functions overlap: the extant *exemplum*-collections entertain as well as edify, while the engaging storylines of many *riddarasögur* map idealized patterns of behavior for audiences to imitate or avoid.[107] Consequently, we may suspect that indigenous *riddarasögur* must have been intended as fiction. Perhaps some were.

However, the relationship between exemplarity and fictionality is not straightforward, and deserves fuller discussion than space allows here. With obvious exceptions like animal-fables — relatively rare in medieval Icelandic *exempla*-collections — *exempla* in medieval Europe were generally assumed to be taken from history, while providing moral examples was seen as one of the main reasons for writing history in the first place.[108] Exemplary narratives occur not only in *riddarasögur* but also in kings' sagas, contemporary sagas, family sagas and

---

105 Paul Bibire, "From *riddarasaga* to *lygisaga*: The Norse Response to Romance," in *Les Sagas de chevaliers (Riddarasögur)*, ed. Régis Boyer, Serie Civilisations 10 (Toulon: Sorbonne, 1985), 74.

106 *Late Medieval Icelandic Romances*, ed. Loth, 1.78. On *aventure*, see Bloch, *Anonymous Marie*, 26-29. On *æfintýr* and *exempla*, see Shaun F.D. Hughes, "The Old Norse Exempla as Arbiters of Gender Roles in Medieval Iceland," in *New Norse Studies: Essays on the Literature and Culture of Medieval Scandinavia*, ed. Jeffrey Turco, Islandica 58 (Ithaca: Cornell University Press, 2015), 268-80 (including notes). I am grateful to Shaun Hughes for sending me a copy.

107 Jürg Glauser, *Isländische Märchensagas: Studien zur Prosaliteratur im spätmittelalterlichen Island*, Beiträge zur nordischen Philologie 12 (Basel: Helbing and Lichtenhahn, 1983), and Geraldine Barnes, "Romance in Iceland," in *Old Icelandic Literature and Society*, ed. Margaret Clunies Ross (Cambridge: Cambridge University Press, 2000), 266-86.

108 Morse, *Truth and Convention*, 86-87, 94-95.

universal-history compilations.[109] In these contexts they claim to be true stories, even if they are manifestly invented, so the fact that a *riddarasaga* may be labeled *æfintýr* or has an exemplary air does not necessarily indicate the intention of departing from history. We may suspect a fictional agenda behind the failure to embed a clearly exemplary saga within externally documented history, as with *Valdimars saga*. Certainly, it does not invite the same degree of audience investment in the historicity of its plot as do most of the sagas discussed earlier in this chapter. But it is worth noting that, merely by providing characters' names, parents and geographical whereabouts, even the pared-down *Valdimars saga* is more open to reception as history than is the kind of *exemplum* which weaves a story around a nameless and unlocalized protagonist.

Nor is *Valdimars saga* as typical of indigenous *riddarasögur* as Hume suggests. Some of them display similar economy, but several boast opening sequences containing precisely the kind of detailed historical and geographical anchorage which the translated *riddarasögur* generally lack. Instead of the communally shared web of genealogy and regional history invoked by sagas with northern settings, *riddarasaga* context is typically provided by universal history, mediated through encyclopedic texts and translated histories of famous classical, biblical, or medieval rulers.[110] As in the *romans d'antiquité* or Geoffrey's *History of the Kings of Britain*, the largely invented stories of the indigenous *riddarasögur* are grafted onto that authoritative stock. Thus, in manuscripts like the now-lost fourteenth-century *Ormsbók*, translated sagas of antiquity (*Trójumanna saga* and *Breta sögur*) appear alongside *riddarasögur*, swapping historical reference

---

109 Ármann Jakobsson, *A Sense of Belonging: Morkinskinna and Icelandic Identity, c. 1220*, trans. Fredrik Heinemann (Odense: University Press of Southern Denmark, 2014); Svanhildur Óskarsdóttir, "Writing Universal History in Ultima Thule: The Case of AM 764 4to," *Mediaeval Scandinavia* 14 (2004): 185–94. On *exemplum*-collections, see Hughes, "Old Norse Exempla."

110 The fundamental study is Geraldine Barnes, *The Bookish Riddarasögur: Writing Romance in Late Medieval Iceland* (Odense: University Press of Southern Denmark, 2014).

points and literary techniques in a Horatian blend of entertainment and edification.[111]

A typical example of what Barnes calls the "bookish *riddarasögur*" is the first recension of *Dínus saga dramblát*a (*The Saga of Dínus the Haughty*). In contrast to *Valdimars saga*, this saga takes twenty-six lines in a modern edition to get from the beginning of the world to the era of the protagonist's father, and longer still to reach the protagonist. Its encyclopedic prelude begins with the broadest possible backdrop: "We find it written in ancient books of learning (*fræðibókum*) that the world is divided into three parts or *partes*: the first, in the south, is named Asia, the western one Africa, and the northern region is called Europe. In Europe there are excellent and famous realms, and everything in them is beautiful and lush."[112] The narrative then zooms in on Egypt, then Alexandria and its history within the six-age scheme (Alexander the Great, St. Catherine of Alexandria, changes in kingship practice), before introducing the hero's parents.[113] The second recension abbreviates the saga proper but amplifies its historical prelude, borrowing from *Alexanders saga*.[114]

A more elaborate world-historical prelude opens *Adonías saga*, set in Syria and contextualized with a long summary of ancient Near Eastern migrations and conquests linked to the prestigious antiquity sagas *Trójumanna saga* and *Alexanders*

---

111 For different assessments of this blend, see Sanders, "*Bevers saga*," and Stefanie Würth, "The Common Transmission of *Trójumanna saga* and *Breta sögur*," in *Beatus Vir: Studies in Early English and Norse Manuscripts in Memory of Phillip Pulsiano*, ed. A.N. Doane and Kirsten Wolf (Tempe: Arizona Center for Medieval and Renaissance Studies, 2006), 297–328.
112 *Dínus saga dramblát*a, ed. Jón Jóhannesson (Reykjavik: Háskóli Íslands, 1960), 3: "Suo finst j fornumm fræde bökumm skriffad, ad heiminum sie skifft j þria hlute edur parta, og heiter hann firste sudur Hasia, enn hinn vestre Affricha, enn nordur älfann er kóllud Euröpä. J Europa eru agiætlig rijke, og frægdarlig og j þui er øll frigd og blöme"; translation drawing on Barnes, *Bookish Riddarasögur*, 53–54.
113 *Dínus saga*, ed. Jón Jóhannesson, 3–5.
114 Ibid., 97–98.

saga.¹¹⁵ *Ectors saga* presents itself more straightforwardly as a supplement to *Trójumanna saga*, claiming to tell of a descendant of King Priam of Troy, named Ector after Priam's famous son. Its prelude mentions the dispersal of Priam's kindred after the Trojan War and their founding of new nations and dynasties, one of which, in Norse-Icelandic mythography, was the euhemerized Æsir themselves. One such migrant was Karnotius, who returned to Turkey and recaptured the lands Priam had ruled, upstaging all those "new Troys" founded by better-known Trojan migrants such as Brutus in Geoffrey of Monmouth and *Breta sögur*.¹¹⁶ The son of this second Priam is thus a second Hector. Trojan allusions multiply: Ector is said to resemble Alexander (Paris) of Troy, and is given Hercules's sword and a shield that once belonged to Achilles "as it says in *Trójumanna saga*."¹¹⁷ At the end, the saga's credibility is defended by appealing to *Trójumanna saga* and to the authority of Gautier de Châtillon—presented as the saga-author's chief source—who had called Ector "the equal of Alexander the Great." Last comes a grand chronological gesture, an actual date, invoked with heavy-handed defensiveness: "So we must not doubt this tale (*ævintýr*) about that great battle. It took place on July 1, 377 years before the Passion

---

115 *Late Medieval Icelandic Romances*, ed. Loth, 3:74–77. In one manuscript, this prelude is itself preceded by a prologue (ibid., 3:69–74) which recommends the moral usefulness of such acts of information-gathering and commemoration—paradoxically, by summarizing two of Æsop's fables, here labeled explicitly as fiction ("fabulas") in contrast with the saga proper. On the saga's exemplary dimension, see Sverrir Tómasson, "The 'fræðisaga' of Adonias," in *Structure and Meaning in Old Norse Literature: New Approaches to Textual Analysis and Literary Criticism*, ed. John Lindow, Lars Lönnroth, and Gerd Wolfgang Weber (Odense: Odense University Press, 1986), 378–93, and Barnes, *Bookish Riddarasögur*, 96–100.

116 On Arthurian aspects of this saga, see Marianne E. Kalinke, "*Ectors saga*: An Arthurian Pastiche in Classical Guise," *Arthuriana* 22, no. 1 (2012): 64–90.

117 *Late Medieval Icelandic Romances*, Loth, ed., 1:81–86: "suo sem s(egir) ij Troiomanna sogu."

of the Savior of the world. And here we bring these episodes to a close."[118]

Antiquity sagas and universal history here function as intertextual reference points to ground the narratives historically. But other sagas and more local traditions, too, could be used as background history for *riddarasögur*, albeit usually more briefly. Thus *Samsons saga fagra* (*The Saga of Samson the Fair*), which divides its action between the Arthurian world and the Arctic realm of Giantland (given solidity by Classical learning on monstrous races), ends with a fact-packed postlude which positions *Samsons saga* as a prequel to both the Arthurian *fabliau*-adaptation *Möttuls saga* (explaining the origin of that saga's magical cloak) and the indigenous crusader-romance *Bærings saga*, whose protagonist is Samson's grandson.[119] The fact that this saga's Arthurian information conflicts with Geoffrey's *History* and Continental romances simply shows how flexible such reference points could be. It does not prevent them functioning as historical anchorage.

Arthur's reign anchors the opening of the longer recension of *Sigurðar saga þögla* (*The Saga of Sigurðr the Silent*) "in the days of the famous King Arthur of Britain," and its heroine is introduced as the daughter of the protagonists of *Flóres saga ok Blankiflúr*, with a specific reference to their saga and to details of its storyline. *Sigurðar saga* thus becomes a sequel to *Flóres saga*, with an unpleasantly sadistic twist on the latter's bridal-quest pattern.[120] This genealogical connection was taken seriously by at least one post-medieval scribe,[121] and this saga, too, ends by tracing the protagonist's descendants down two more genera-

---

118 Ibid., 1:185–86: "Megum uer þuij eigi mistrua þessu ęuinntyre vm þann mikla bardaga. var hann hinn fyrsta kalendas uilij mana(dar) og uor(u) þaa til pijninngar heimsins lausnara. ccc. vetra siotigir og .uij. uetur og latum uer nu hier nidr falla þessa atburde."
119 *Samsons saga fagra*, ed. John Wilson (Copenhagen: Jörgensen, 1953), 46–47.
120 On sequel- and prequel-formation in other *riddarasögur*, see Marianne E. Kalinke, *Stories Set Forth with Fair Words: The Evolution of Medieval Romance in Iceland* (Cardiff: University of Wales Press, 2017), 142–61.
121 Reykjavik, *National Library of Iceland*, Lbs 4412 4to (c. 1850), fol. 72v.

tions.¹²² Similarly, the legendary Northern warlord Hildibrandr, a protagonist of the *fornaldarsaga Ásmundar saga kappabana*, is claimed as a protagonist's grandson at the end of *Sigurðar saga fóts* (*The Saga of Sigurðr Foot*),¹²³ while *Flóres saga konungs ok sona hans* (*The Saga of King Flóres and His Sons*) ends by stating that one of its protagonists' grandsons was Herburt "who abducted Falborg, the daughter of King Arthur of Britain, as it says in Þiðreks saga."¹²⁴ Like several *riddarasögur*, this saga closes with an apology for not providing more information about the protagonists' descendants, suggesting an awareness that audiences expected *fræði* from sagas' closing sequences: "Because these people are distant from our lands, we have not heard what these people achieved."¹²⁵

Revisers sometimes tried to fill these information gaps. The first recension of *Konráðs saga keisarasonar* (*The Saga of Konráðr, the Emperor's Son*) ends by tracing Konráðr's line down to his grandson Kirialax, "and there are many noteworthy sagas about him, but we have not set them out in this short account." The second recension condenses the main storyline but expands its postlude to cover another generation and subsequent lineages, removing the apology in the process.¹²⁶ This genealogical extension was taken to an extreme in some versions of *Mágus saga jarls* (*The Saga of Earl Mágus*). These double the length of the oldest recension with sequel-episodes spanning four generations, making this saga, in Kalinke's words, "a genealogical

---

122 *Late Medieval Icelandic Romances*, ed. Loth, 2:97–100, 259.
123 Ibid., 3:250.
124 Ibid.
125 *Drei Lygisǫgur*, ed. Åke Lagerholm (Halle: Niemeyer, 1927), 177: "er burt tók Falborg, dóttur Artús konungs af Brettaníá, sem segir í Þiðreks sǫgu […]. En fyri því at þessir menn eru fjarlægt várum lǫndum, þá hǫfum vér eigi spurt, hver afdrif orðit hafa þessarra manna." For similar apologies for *fáfræði* (lack of learning), see *Late Medieval Icelandic Romances*, ed. Loth, 1:185; 5:36, and *Dínus saga*, ed. Jóhannesson, 94.
126 *Konráðs saga keisarasonar*, ed. Otto Zitzselsberger (New York: Peter Lang, 1987), 123: "ok erv tra honvm margar sogvr merkil<i>gar þo at ver greiðim þer eigi i þessv skommo mali."

romance, not unlike the cyclical *chansons de geste* of France."[127] A later, even longer reworking made this implicitly historical stance explicit in a new prelude and postlude which frame the saga's chronology within summaries of information from other historical sources: books (*bækr*), royal biographies (*ævi keisaranna*, lives of the emperors), and annals (*annálar*).[128] The postlude is particularly ostentatious. Synchronisms align the saga's events with defining moments in Norwegian and Icelandic history, a backdrop associated more with family sagas:

> It is shown in annals that Karl took the kingship in Saxony when Haraldr Fairhair divided the realm between his sons. At that time Stephen, seventh of that name, was Pope. Karl ruled for twenty-seven years before he was betrayed and imprisoned by Herbert. Three nights after his fall, Úlfljótr came with the law to Iceland, and at that time Eiríkr Bloodaxe became overking over his brothers. Three years later Haraldr Fairhair died. One year previously, Hrafn Hængsson had become Lawspeaker in Iceland.[129]

This postlude's seriousness may seem undercut by the equivocating epilogue which follows in this manuscript, beginning with a cautionary remark about the saga's reliability. Yet this epilogue goes on to insist that such *riddarasögur* should not be treated as lies, since much of what seems unlikely may be true.[130]

---

127 Kalinke, *Stories Set Forth*, 79.
128 Reykjavik, Stofnun Árna Magnússonar, AM 152 fol., fol. 159v. Published editions of this manuscript text alter its wording, so I here cite the manuscript itself.
129 Ibid., fol. 196r: "[E]n suo uijsar aa ij annal · at Karl tok riki ij Saxlande þaa Haralldur hinn harfagre skipti riki med sonum sijnum · enn þaa war Stefanus paue hinn ·uij med þuij nafnne styrde Karl uij aar oc xx· adr hann war svikinn oc kastadr inn af Herberto · oc iij nottum eptir fraafall hans kęme Ulfliotr med lǫg til Ijslandz oc þaa war Eirekr blodox ordinn yfirkonungr brædra sinna · Þrim uetrum sijdar andadizt Haraldr harfagre einum uetri adr tok Hrafn Hęngssonn logsogn aa Islande."
130 Ibid., fols. 196r–v. I discuss this passage more fully in a forthcoming publication.

We have seen similar juxtapositions of historical contextualizing with defenses of veracity in other *fornaldarsögur* and *riddarasögur* above. Some post-medieval redactors buttressed *Mágus saga*'s historical claims by removing the equivocating remarks and adding dates to the last three events in the synchronisms: "in the year 927," "in the year 931," and "in the year 930."[131] As the later recensions of *Dínus saga* and *Konráðs saga* have shown, the reworking of *riddarasögur* often involved strengthening their historical claims rather than the retreat from historicity which standard accounts of romance would suggest.

What are we to make of these elaborate historical frameworks erected around sagas that no modern historian would credit for a moment? The ubiquity of their historical cross-references was noted long ago by Margaret Schlauch, in her still-unrivaled survey of Icelandic romance. For Schlauch, these preludes displayed a "desire to make *lygisögur* masquerade as history"; they probably "deceived no one, but were considered effective in winning attention" by "pretending to be connected with a tale already popular."[132] But the attention they demanded in their openings, and validated in their conclusions, was precisely that which encouraged its audience to respond to the story as history. And, to judge from the numerous manuscripts preserving these sagas between 1400 and 1920, whose witness deserves a full analysis in its own right, they earned more than just a "modicum of esteem."[133] Of course, with these sagas there was less at stake for Icelandic audiences in terms of how closely, if at all, the saga's narration corresponded to real past events, compared to sagas about saints venerated in the audience's own time or sagas about audience-members' own ancestors. As with the more overtly exemplary sagas discussed earlier in this section, there were ways of enjoying and learning from these sagas without any strong investment in their veracity. But there is no

---

131 Reykjavik, National Library of Iceland, Lbs 1680 4to (c. 1789), page 410: "Anno 927 […] Anno 931 […] Anno 930."
132 Margaret Schlauch, *Romance in Iceland* (Princeton: Princeton University Press, 1934), 47, 37.
133 Ibid.

evidence that they were generally assumed to be made up. Indeed, an underlying assumption that the story's events were or might be true could equally have added to an audience's enjoyment, as with modern films or novels "based on a true story" or ghost-stories swapped around campfires.[134] We must allow for diverse attitudes and preferences within any audience. One reason why the indigenous *riddarasögur* survived so long is that they were composed to satisfy multiple expectations. And, as Barnes has shown so effectively, some not only claim to be history, but embody sophisticated reflections on history's shape and significance within their main storylines.[135] Historicity was not always mere window-dressing.

These sagas' formulaic and implausible nature, with their dastardly raiders, knowledgeable princesses and shape-shifting wizards, is often invoked as if it proved these sagas' fictionality. But these features are part of the stories' claim to be believable accounts of distant times and places. Characters conform to type, as in Cicero's vision of history worthy of credence (*probabilis*), of history as filled-out *argumentum*.[136] Tyrants behave like tyrants, heroes like heroes, troll-wives like troll-wives, deviating only in subtle ways to maintain interest. These formulaic elements are deliberately exaggerated for dramatic effect, as Mathias Kruse has shown in detail. But even the most outlandish or humorous episodes are rarely pure fantasy, but replicate, extend or otherwise work with then-current ethnographic, geographical, and natural-historical learning.[137] The same blend of replica-

---

134 For helpful discussion, see Mathias Kruse, *Literatur als Spektakel: hyperbolische und komische Inszenierung des Körpers in isländischen Ritter- und Abenteuersagas* (Berlin: Utz, 2017), 611–76.
135 Barnes, *Bookish Riddarasögur*, 66–112.
136 On these conceptions of history, see this volume's Introduction; Lake's chapter in this volume and "Truth, Plausibility, and the Virtues of Narrative at the Millennium," *Journal of Medieval History* 35, no. 3 (2009): 221–38; Morse, *Truth and Convention*; and Matthew Kempshall, *Rhetoric and the Writing of History, 400–1500* (Manchester: Manchester University Press, 2011), 265–427.
137 Rudolf Simek, *Altnordische Kosmographie: Studien und Quellen zu Weltbild und Weltbeschreibung in Norwegen und Island vom 12. bis zum 14. Jahrhun-*

tion and variation may apply to the historical and genealogical frameworks discussed in this chapter.

Conclusion

My survey raises more questions than it answers. I have been emphasizing continuity of practices across several centuries and across an extremely diverse corpus. I have not had space to explore fully how these practices changed over time, between saga groups or in different manuscripts, or whether the composition of new sagas posed different challenges from the reworking of old ones. The differing priorities of secular and ecclesiastical patrons, too, would deserve their own study. Short shrift has been given to the relationship between the truth-claims of hagiography and secular histories, including romances, and to the playfulness of experiments with new narrative modes — a playfulness which could, upon occasion, approach fictionality in its own way. Generalizations are dangerous; yet, where continuity does exist, it deserves underlining as a basis for finer-grained distinctions. Whether their subject matter was close at hand or far away, whether its audience found it of burning personal significance or merely general interest, the attitude that a saga was expected at some level[138] to communicate true stories about the past seems to have remained surprisingly constant, despite considerable variation in its expression.

The conventional model of literary narrative moving from a historical starting point up an escalator of fictionality does not work for the sagas. For their authors, increasing inventiveness did not presuppose decreasing veracity. How these observations affect our picture of medieval European narrative overall, especially romance, remains to be seen. The case of the sagas sug-

---

dert (Berlin: de Gruyter, 1990), and Florian Schreck, "Science in Medieval Fiction: The Reception of Learned Writing on Natural History in Old Icelandic Romance 1300–1550" (PhD diss., University of Bergen, 2018).

138 Compare O'Connor, "History or Fiction?" 117: the italicized qualifier is important.

gests that medieval writers could revel in entertaining invention within a framework of implicit veracity. In many of the texts discussed, invention was not limited to flights of fancy or anecdotal interludes within a solidly "historical" main narrative but rather dominates the whole story. It may be time to lengthen the list of genres we include within medieval "historiography," and to stop excluding romance *a priori* from this domain, however out of place it may look to us.

Bibliography

Primary

Arngrímur Jónsson. *Opera latine conscripta.* Edited by Jakob Benediktsson. 4 volumes. Bibliotheca Arnamagnæanæ 9–12. Copenhagen: Munksgaard, 1950–1957.
Austfirðinga sǫgur. Edited by Jón Jóhannesson. Íslenzk fornrit 11. Reykjavik: Hið íslenzka fornritafélag, 1950.
Chrestien de Troyes. *Yvain (Le Chevalier au lion).* Edited by Wendelin Foerster and Thomas B.W. Reid. Manchester: Manchester University Press, 1974.
Corpus genealogiarum Hiberniae. Edited by Michael A. O'Brien. Dublin: Dublin Institute for Advanced Studies, 1976.
Die "Bósa-saga" in zwei Fassungen. Edited by Otto Luitpold Jiriczek. Strassburg: Trübner, 1893.
Dínus saga drambláta. Edited by Jón Jóhannesson. Reykjavik: Háskóli Íslands, 1960.
Drei Lygisǫgur. Edited by Åke Lagerholm. Halle: Niemeyer, 1927.
Egils saga Skalla-Grímssonar: Bind I, A-redaktionen. Edited by Bjarni Einarsson. Editiones Arnamagnæanæ A 19. Copenhagen: Reitzel, 2001.
Eyfirðinga sǫgur. Edited by Jónas Kristjánsson. Íslenzk fornrit 9. Reykjavik: Hið íslenzka fornritafélag, 1956.
Fornaldar sögur Norðurlanda. Edited by Guðni Jónsson. 4 volumes. Reykjavik: Íslendingasagnaútgáfan, 1950.
Grettis saga. Edited by Guðni Jónsson. Íslenzk fornrit 7. Reykjavik: Hið íslenzka fornritafélag, 1936.
Hálfdanar saga Eysteinssonar. Edited by Franz Rolf Schröder. Halle: Niemeyer, 1917.
Hallfreðar saga. Edited by Bjarni Einarsson. Reykjavik: Stofnun Árna Magnússonar, 1977.
Harðar saga. Edited by Þórhallur Vilmundarson and Bjarni Vilhjálmsson. Íslenzk fornrit 13. Reykjavik: Hið íslenzka fornritafélag, 1991.
Islandske annaler indtil 1578. Edited by Gustav Storm. Christiania: Grøndahl, 1888.

Íslendingabók, Landnámabók. Edited by Jakob Benediktsson. Íslenzk fornrit 1. Reykjavik: Hið íslenzka fornritafélag, 1986–1988.

Kjalnesinga saga. Edited by Jóhannes Halldórsson. Íslenzk fornrit 14. Reykjavik: Hið íslenzka fornritafélag, 1959.

Konráðs saga keisarasonar. Edited by Otto Zitzselsberger. New York: Peter Lang, 1987.

Late Medieval Icelandic Romances. Edited by Agnete Loth. 5 volumes. Editiones Arnamagnæanæ B 20-4. Copenhagen: Munksgaard, 1962–5.

Marie de France. *Lais*. Edited by Alfred Ewert. Bristol: Bristol Classical Press, 1995.

Membrana Regia Deperdita. Edited by Agnete Loth. Editiones Arnamagnæanæ A 5. Copenhagen: Munksgaard, 1960.

Norse Romance II: Knights of the Round Table. Edited and translated by Marianne E. Kalinke. Cambridge: Brewer, 1999.

Óláfs saga Tryggvasonar en mesta. Edited by Ólafur Halldórsson. 3 volumes. Copenhagen: Munksgaard and Reitzel, 1958–2000.

Saga Heiðreks konungs ins vitra. Edited and translated by Christopher Tolkien. London: Thomas Nelson, 1960.

Samsons saga fagra. Edited by John Wilson. Copenhagen: Jörgensen, 1953.

Saxo Grammaticus. *Gesta Danorum: The History of the Danes*. Edited by Karsten Friis-Jensen, translated by Peter Fisher. 2 volumes. Oxford: Clarendon Press, 2015.

Strengleikar: An Old Norse Translation of Twenty-One Old French Lais. Edited and translated by Robert Cook and Mattias Tveitane. Oslo: NHKI, 1979.

Þorgils saga ok Hafliða. Edited by Ursula Brown. London: Oxford University Press, 1952.

Vestfirðinga sǫgur. Edited by Björn K. Þórólfsson and Guðni Jónsson. Íslenzk fornrit 6. Reykjavik: Hið íslenzka fornritafélag, 1943.

Vǫlsunga saga ok Ragnars saga loðbrókar. Edited by Magnus Olsen. Copenhagen: Møller, 1906–1908.

Vǫlsunga saga: The Saga of the Volsungs. Edited and translated by Kaaren Grimstad. Saarbrücken: AQ-Verlag, 2000.

Secondary

Ainsworth, Peter. "Legendary History: *historia* and *fabula*." In *Historiography in the Middle Ages*, edited by Deborah Mauskopf Deliyannis, 387–416. Boston and Leiden: Brill, 2003.

Ármann Jakobsson. *A Sense of Belonging: Morkinskinna and Icelandic Identity, c. 1220*. Translated by Fredrik Heinemann. Odense: University Press of Southern Denmark, 2014.

———. "History of the Trolls? *Bárðar saga* as an Historical Narrative." *Saga Book of the Viking Society* 25 (1998): 53–71.

———. "The Earliest Legendary Saga Manuscripts." In *The Legendary Sagas: Origins and Development*, edited by Ármann Jakobsson, Annette Lassen, and Agneta Ney, 21–32. Reykjavik: University of Iceland Press, 2012.

Barnes, Geraldine. "Authors, Dead and Alive, in Old Norse Fiction." *Parergon, New Series* 8, no. 2 (1990): 5–22. DOI: 10.1353/pgn.1990.0023.

———. "Romance in Iceland." In *Old Icelandic Literature and Society*, edited by Margaret Clunies Ross, 266–86. Cambridge: Cambridge University Press, 2000. DOI: 10.1017/CBO9780511552922.012.

———. *The Bookish Riddarasögur: Writing Romance in Late Medieval Iceland*. Odense: University Press of Southern Denmark, 2014.

Baumgartner, Emmanuèle. *De l'histoire de Troie au livre du Graal: Le temps, le récit (XIIe–XIIIe siècles)*. Orléans: Paradigme, 1994.

Bibire, Paul. "From *riddarasaga* to *lygisaga*: The Norse Response to Romance." In *Les Sagas de chevaliers (Riddarasögur)*, edited by Régis Boyer, 55–74. Serie Civilisations 10. Toulon: Sorbonne, 1985.

Bloch, R. Howard. *The Anonymous Marie de France*. Chicago: University of Chicago Press, 2003. DOI: 10.7208/chicago/9780226059693.001.0001.

Burgess, Glyn S. "Introduction." In Marie de France, *Lais*, edited by Alfred Ewert, vii–xxxvi. Bristol: Bristol Classical Press, 1995.

Clunies Ross, Margaret. *Prolonged Echoes: Old Norse Myths in Medieval Northern Society*, Volume 2: *The Reception of Norse Myths in Medieval Iceland*. Odense: Odense University Press, 1998.

Glauser, Jürg. *Isländische Märchensagas: Studien zur Prosaliteratur im spätmittelalterlichen Island*. Beiträge zur nordischen Philologie 12. Basel: Helbing and Lichtenhahn, 1983.

———. "Staging the Text: On the Development of a Consciousness of Writing in the Norwegian and Icelandic Literature of the Middle Ages." In *Along the Oral-Written Continuum: Types of Texts, Relations and Their Implications*, edited by Leidulf Melve, Else Mundal, and Slavica Ranković, 311–34. Turnhout: Brepols, 2010.

Green, D.H. *The Beginnings of Medieval Romance: Fact and Fiction, 1150–1220*. Cambridge: Cambridge University Press, 2002. DOI: 10.1017/CBO9780511485787.

Hall, Alaric. "Changing Style and Changing Meaning: Icelandic Historiography and the Medieval Redactions of *Heiðreks saga*." *Scandinavian Studies* 77 (2005): 1–30.

Hufnagel, Silvia. "Sörla saga sterka and Rafn's Edition." In *Á austrvega: Saga and East Scandinavia: Preprint Papers of the 14th International Saga Conference*, edited by Marco Bianchi, Fredrik Charpentier Ljungqvist, Agneta Ney, and Henrik Williams, 398–404. Gävle: Gävle University Press, 2009.

———. "*Sörla saga sterka*: Studies in the Transmission of a *fornaldarsaga*." PhD diss., University of Copenhagen, 2012.

Hughes, Shaun F.D. "The Old Norse Exempla as Arbiters of Gender Roles in Medieval Iceland." In *New Norse Studies: Essays on the Literature and Culture of Medieval Scandinavia*, edited by Jeffrey Turco, 255–300. Islandica 58. Ithaca: Cornell University Press, 2015.

Hume, Kathryn. "Beginnings and Endings in the Icelandic Family Sagas." *Modern Language Review* 68, no. 3 (1973): 593–606. DOI: 10.2307/3724996.

———. "From Saga to Romance: The Use of Monsters in Old Norse Literature." *Studies in Philology* 77 (1980): 1–25. https://www.jstor.org/stable/4174026.

Johansson, Karl G. "Narratives and Narrators on the Move: Some Examples of Change and Continuity in the Tradition of Fantastic Fiction." In *The Legendary Sagas: Origins and Development*, edited by Ármann Jakobsson, Annette Lassen, and Agneta Ney, 351–71. Reykjavik: University of Iceland Press, 2012.

Kalinke, Marianne E. "*Ectors saga*: An Arthurian Pastiche in Classical Guise." *Arthuriana* 22, no. 1 (2012): 64–90. DOI: 10.1353/art.2012.0014.

———. *Stories Set Forth with Fair Words: The Evolution of Medieval Romance in Iceland*. Cardiff: University of Wales Press, 2017.

Kempshall, Matthew. *Rhetoric and the Writing of History, 400–1500*. Manchester: Manchester University Press, 2011.

Kruse, Mathias. *Literatur als Spektakel: hyperbolische und komische Inszenierung des Körpers in isländischen Ritter- und Abenteuersagas*. Berlin: Utz, 2017.

Lake, Justin. "Truth, Plausibility, and the Virtues of Narrative at the Millennium." *Journal of Medieval History* 35, no. 3 (2009): 221–38. DOI: 10.1016/j.jmedhist.2009.05.003.

Lassen, Annette. "*Origines Gentium* and the Learned Origin of Fornaldarsögur Norðurlanda." In *The Legendary Sagas: Origins and Development*, edited by Ármann Jakobsson, Annette Lassen, and Agneta Ney, 35–58. Reykjavik: University of Iceland Press, 2012.

———. "The Old Norse Contextuality of *Bárðar saga Snæfellsáss*: A Synoptic Reading with *Óláfs saga Tryggvasonar en mesta*." In *Folklore in Old Norse—Old Norse in Folklore*, edited by Daniel Sävborg and Karen Bek-Pedersen, 102–19. Tartu: University of Tartu Press, 2014.

Liberman, Anatoly. *The Saga Mind and the Beginnings of Icelandic Prose*. Lewiston: Edwin Mellen, 2018.

Manhire, William. "The Narrative Functions of Source-References in the Sagas of Icelanders." *Saga-Book of the Viking Society* 19 (1974–1977): 170–90.

McTurk, Rory, ed. *A Companion to Old Norse-Icelandic Literature and Culture*. London: Blackwell, 2005. DOI: 10.1111/b.978 0631235026.2004.00002.x.

Meulengracht Sørensen, Preben. *Fortælling og ære: studier i islændingesagaerne*. Aarhus: Aarhus Universitetsforlag, 1993.

———. *Saga and Society: An Introduction to Old Norse Literature*. Translated by John Tucker. Odense: Odense University Press, 1993.

Mitchell, Stephen A. *Heroic Sagas and Ballads*. Ithaca: Cornell University Press, 1991. DOI: 10.7591/9781501735974.

Morse, Ruth. *Truth and Convention in the Middle Ages: Rhetoric, Representation, and Reality*. Cambridge: Cambridge University Press, 1991.

Mortensen, Lars Boje. "The Status of the 'Mythical' Past in Nordic Latin Historiography (c. 1170–1220)." In *Medieval Narratives between History and Fiction: From the Centre to the Periphery of Europe, c. 1100–1400*, edited by Panagiotis A. Agapitos and Lars Boje Mortensen, 103–40. Copenhagen: Museum Tusculanum, 2012.

O'Connor, Ralph. "History and Fiction." In *The Routledge Research Companion to the Medieval Icelandic Sagas*, edited by Ármann Jakobsson and Sverrir Jakobsson, 88–110. London: Routledge, 2017. DOI: 10.4324/9781315613628-8.

———. "History or Fiction? Truth-Claims and Defensive Narrators in Icelandic Romance-Sagas." *Mediaeval Scandinavia* 15 (2005): 1–69.

Ó Corráin, Donnchadh. "Irish Origin Legends and Genealogy: Recurrent Aetiologies." In *History and Heroic Tale: A Symposium*, edited by Preben Meulengracht Sørensen, Tore Nyberg, Iorn Pio, and Aage Trommer, 51–96. Odense: Odense University Press, 1985.

Partner, Nancy F. *Serious Entertainments: The Writing of History in Twelfth-Century England*. Chicago: University of Chicago Press, 1977.

Poppe, Erich. "Narrative History and Cultural Memory in Medieval Ireland: Some Preliminary Thoughts." In *Medieval Irish Perspectives on Cultural Memory*, edited by Jan Erik Rekdal and Erich Poppe, 135–76. Münster: Nodus, 2014.

———. *Of Cycles and Other Critical Matters: Some Issues in Medieval Irish Literary History and Criticism*. E.C. Quiggin Memorial Lectures 9. Cambridge: Department of Anglo-Saxon, Norse and Celtic, 2008.

Pulsiano, Phillip, and Kirsten Wolf, eds. *Medieval Scandinavia: An Encyclopedia*. New York: Garland, 1993.

Ranković, Slavica. "Authentication and Authenticity in the Sagas of Icelanders and Serbian Epic Poetry." In *Medieval Narratives between History and Fiction: From the Centre to the Periphery of Europe, c. 1100–1400*, edited by Panagiotis A. Agapitos and Lars Boje Mortensen, 199–234. Copenhagen: Museum Tusculanum, 2012.

Righter-Gould, Ruth. "The 'Fornaldar sögur Norðurlanda': A Structural Analysis." *Scandinavian Studies* 52 (1980): 423–41.

Rowe, Elizabeth Ashman. "*Quid Sigvardus cum Christo?* Moral Interpretations of Sigurðr Fáfnisbani in Old Norse Literature." *Viking and Medieval Scandinavia* 2 (2006): 167–200. DOI: 10.1484/J.VMS.2.302023.

———. *The Development of* Flateyjarbók: *Iceland and the Norwegian Dynastic Crisis of 1389*. Odense: University Press of Southern Denmark, 2005. ———. *Vikings in the West: The Legend of Ragnarr Loðbrók and His Sons*. Vienna: Fassbaender, 2012.

Sanders, Christopher. "*Bevers saga* in the Context of Old Norse Historical Prose." In *Sir Bevis of Hampton in Literary Tradition*, edited by Jennifer Fellows and Ivana Djordjević, 51–66. Cambridge: Brewer, 2008.

Sävborg, Daniel. "Den 'efterklassiska' islänningasagan och dess ålder." *Journal of English and Germanic Philology* 127 (2012): 19–57.

Sävborg, Daniel, and Karen Bek-Pedersen, eds. *Folklore in Old Norse — Old Norse in Folklore*. Tartu: University of Tartu Press, 2014.

Schlauch, Margaret. *Romance in Iceland*. Princeton: Princeton University Press, 1934.

Schreck, Florian. "Science in Medieval Fiction: The Reception of Learned Writing on Natural History in Old Icelandic Romance 1300–1550." PhD diss., University of Bergen, 2018.

See, Klaus von. *Europa und der Norden im Mittelalter*. Heidelberg: Winter, 1999.

Shepherd, G.T. "The Emancipation of Story in the Twelfth Century." In *Medieval Narrative: A Symposium,* edited by Hans Bekker-Nielsen, Peter Foote, Andreas Haarder, and Preben Meulengracht Sørensen, 44–57. Odense: Odense University Press, 1979.

Simek, Rudolf. *Altnordische Kosmographie: Studien und Quellen zu Weltbild und Weltbeschreibung in Norwegen und Island vom 12. bis zum 14. Jahrhundert*. Berlin: de Gruyter, 1990. DOI: 10.1515/9783110887570.

Svanhildur Óskarsdóttir. "Writing Universal History in Ultima Thule: The Case of AM 764 4to." *Mediaeval Scandinavia* 14 (2004): 185–94.

Sverrir Tómasson. "The 'fræðisaga' of Adonias." In *Structure and Meaning in Old Norse Literature: New Approaches to Textual Analysis and Literary Criticism,* edited by John Lindow, Lars Lönnroth, and Gerd Wolfgang Weber, 378–93. Odense: Odense University Press, 1986.

———. "The Middle Ages: Old Icelandic Prose." In *A History of Icelandic Literature,* edited by Daisy Neijmann, 64–173. Lincoln: University of Nebraska Press, 2006.

Taranu, Catalin. *The Bard and the Rag-Picker: Vernacular Verse Histories in Early Medieval England and Francia*. London: Routledge, 2021.

Vésteinn Ólason. *Dialogues with the Viking Age: Narration and Representation in the Sagas of the Icelanders*. Translated by Andrew Wawn. Reykjavik: Heimskringla, 1998.

———. "The Fantastic Element in Fourteenth Century Íslendingasögur: A Survey." *Gripla* 18 (2007): 7–22.

———. "The Icelandic Saga as a Kind of Literature with Special Reference to Its Representation of Reality." In *Learning and*

Understanding in the Old Norse World: Essays in Honour of Margaret Clunies Ross, edited by Kate Heslop, Judy Quinn, and Tarrin Wills, 27–48. Turnhout: Brepols, 2007.

———. "The Marvellous North and Authorial Presence in the Icelandic Fornaldarsaga." In *Contexts of Pre-Novel Narrative: The European Tradition,* edited by Roy Eriksen, 103–34. Berlin: de Gruyter, 1994.

Wiley, Dan M., ed. *Essays on the Early Irish King Tales.* Dublin: Four Courts, 2008.

Würth, Stefanie. "Historiography and Pseudo-History." In *A Companion to Old Norse-Icelandic Literature and Culture,* edited by Rory McTurk, 155–72. London: Blackwell, 2005. DOI: 10.1111/b.9780631235026.2004.00012.x.

———. "The Common Transmission of Trójumanna saga and Breta sögur." In *Beatus Vir: Studies in Early English and Norse Manuscripts in Memory of Phillip Pulsiano,* edited by A.N. Doane and Kirsten Wolf, 297–328. Tempe: Arizona Center for Medieval and Renaissance Studies, 2006.

7

"Truth is the Trickiest": Vernacular Theories of Truth and Strategies of Truth-making in Old English Verse

Catalin Taranu

One day in the early ninth century in the kingdom of Mercia, a learned individual from the king's entourage sat down and inserted Julius Caesar into the genealogy of the royal line of East Anglia as the son of the pagan god Woden. This piece of knowledge was then spread to other centers of power in early medieval England through authoritative channels of information.[1] Judging by the cultural-political context and prestige of manuscripts containing this piece of information, this act of creative history-writing was by no means singular in early medieval England. Nor can we assume it was a mere slip of the quill, or a fanciful instance of private creativity.

---

1 "Caser Wodning/Uodning" is found in MS London, British Library, Cotton Vespasian B. vi, 109v (probably written in Mercia in the early ninth century), MS London BL, Cotton Tiberius B. v, 23r (Sussex, the second quarter of the eleventh century), and MS Cambridge, Corpus Christi College 183, 66v (Wessex, the first half of the tenth century). Documented in David Dumville, "The Anglian Collection of Royal Genealogies and Regnal Lists," *Anglo-Saxon England* 5 (1976): 23–50: for provenance and dating, 24–26; for genealogies: 31, 34, 37.

While for Bede, Woden was the starting point for the genealogy of many English royal dynasties, by the late eighth century, competitive genealogists in the service of the different royal houses had begun to extend the pedigrees back into time beyond Woden.[2] The pedigrees of Deira, Bernicia, Mercia, Kent and East Anglia were all pushed a step beyond Woden to Frealaf. The Lindsey genealogy was the first to trace its dynasty back five generations beyond Woden to Geat: Woden — Frealaf — Friodulf — Finn — Godulf — Geat, and soon the other genealogists followed suit, eager to imbue their patrons with the cultural capital afforded by these ancestral back-formations.[3] The insertion of Caesar was thus no giant leap for a royal genealogist, but only an additional small step in a tradition of creative, and sometimes competing, history-writing.

It is unclear who exactly all these mythistorical figures were (the name Geat, for instance, is particularly mysterious) or rather who the early English writers and readers of such information believed they were.[4] Still, we are quite confident of what their addition to the genealogies was meant to achieve: previous research on early English royal genealogies and regnal lists has copiously shown that such fanciful rewritings of the past were deliberate political acts meant to bestow prestige and cultural capital on the kings who commissioned them.[5] In Craig Davis's

---

2   Craig R. Davis, "Cultural Assimilation in the Anglo-Saxon Royal Genealogies," *Anglo-Saxon England* 21 (1992): 23–36, at 28. *Bede's Ecclesiastical History of the English People* I.xv, ed. Bertram Colgrave and R.A.B. Mynors, Oxford Medieval Texts (Oxford: Oxford University Press, 1969), 73.

3   Davis, "Cultural Assimilation," 28.

4   For Geat, see Catalin Taranu, "Goths, Geatas, Gaut: The Invention of an Anglo-Saxon Tradition," in *Transforming the Early Medieval World: Studies in Honour of Ian N. Wood*, ed. Kivilcim Yavuz and Ricky Broome (Leeds: Kismet Press, forthcoming). For mythistory as the playful commingling of myth and history, see John D. Niles, "Myth and History," in *A Beowulf Handbook*, ed. Robert E. Bjork and John D. Niles (Lincoln: University of Nebraska Press, 1998), 213–33, at 218.

5   Dumville called these the "Anglian collection" as opposed to Wessex traditions associated with the *Anglo-Saxon Chronicle*. The classical account is in David Dumville, "Kingship, Genealogies, and Regnal Lists," in *Early*

words, royal pedigrees were "an ideological workshop," a place to assemble and reconstruct the different traditions important to the culture of early English courts.[6]

Yet nobody ever asks what these people believed they were doing. How did the early medieval people involved in the making and reception of such repeated acts of obvious fabrication regard the truth of the fictions they were producing, consuming, and perpetuating with no obvious qualms? The question of whether serious-minded, Christian, early medieval English intellectuals believed that Julius Caesar was truly the son of Woden and that both of them were indeed the ancestors of their kings has never been asked, despite the wealth of scholarship revealing the complex socio-cultural and political work such fictions fulfilled. A negative response is by no means obvious. And, as argued in the introduction to this volume, explaining the functions of these narratives in no way solves the issue of their truth status. Were such claims meant to be believed literally? Were they some sort of figure of speech whose meaning and rhetorical mechanics we have lost?

Indeed, scholars of early England, and medievalists more generally, virtually never discuss whether, for instance, the writers and readers of the *Anglo-Saxon Chronicle* really believed that "fiery dragons were seen flying in the air" in Northumbria in 793, or whether the people reading or listening to *Beowulf* believed and were expected to believe by the poet — these are two separate, though related, issues — that the protagonist existed as a historical figure and truly killed all those monsters, let alone whether reports of dog-headed saints, monstrous people in the Orient, or supernatural beings like elves were really believed.

Such questions might appear as either imperceptive: one might say that it does not matter whether they believed these things, only what they did with them. Or, they may be read as veiled Gibbonesque indictments of medieval credulity. We

---

Medieval Kingship, ed. Peter H. Sawyer and Ian N. Wood (Leeds: University of Leeds, 1977), 72–104, and Dumville, "The Anglian Collection."

6 Davis, "Cultural Assimilation," 28.

medievalists are fond of the real people we sense behind the sources we study and thus would rather not address the cognitive dissonance between our view of reality and their belief in things and events that appear impossible to us.

Yet these questions are pertinent if we are to understand why these features are present in many sources alongside more everyday occurrences which require no suspension of disbelief on our part. The texts I mentioned — the royal genealogies, the *Anglo-Saxon Chronicle*, *Beowulf* — never seem to signal in any way that their most outlandish claims are no more than tall tales. Their authors never wink at their reader, Pynchon-style, to draw attention to their story's fictionality. On the contrary, these texts are thoroughly invested in presenting their narratives as true: as explained above, the genealogies were seriously political acts, while the *Chronicle* includes the dragon episode in a series of *forebeacna* (foretelling signs) of the disasters that would befall Northumbria. As such, the dragons are *tacnum* (omens) mentioned in relation to their very palpable historical fulfillment in the guise of a severe famine and the Viking depredation of Lindisfarne.[7] Meanwhile, *Beowulf*'s dragon and the Grendelkin are recounted in the same narrative breath as verifiably historical events such as Hygelac's raid on Frisia or the Yngling Swedish royal dynasty. There is no sign that the dragons in the Northumbrian or Geatish skies and Caesar as the son of Woden are to be taken figuratively.

Indeed, *Beowulf* is much less fantastic than it may seem. It gives Grendel and his mother human characteristics, and "a his-

---

7 The 793 entry in Manuscript E of the *Anglo-Saxon Chronicle* (though not, for instance, in Manuscript C) reads: "Her wæron reðe forebecna cumene ofer Norþanhymbra land 7 þet folc earmlice (26r) bregdon: þet wæron ormete ligræscas, 7 wæron geseowene fyrene dracan on þam lyfte fleogende. Þam tacnum sona fyligde mycel hunger, 7 litel æfter þam þæs ilcan geares on .vi. idus Ianuarii earmlice heðenra manna hergung adiligode Godes cyrican in Lindisfarenaee þurh reaflac 7 mansleht." *The Anglo-Saxon Chronicle: A Collaborative Edition, Vol. 7: MS. E*, ed. Susan Irvine (Cambridge: D.S. Brewer, 2004), 42.

torical human plausibility, hence their descent from Cain."⁸ The "digressions" of the poem into dynastic history serve to embed these "monsters" — our terms, not the poet's — into a historical context. In a nutshell, the poem was more likely read as a type of history than as a fantastic tale by at least some of its early audiences. I have spent much of my first book to make this argument, and am in full agreement with Andrew Scheil's contention that, rather than a *liber monstrorum* (*pace* Andy Orchard), Cotton Vitellius A.xv (the *Beowulf* manuscript) was more likely read as a *liber de diversis historiis, anglice,* echoing Kenneth Sisam's original formulation.⁹ The division of the poem into "'historical' and 'fabulous' elements is […] based on a simplified assumption about 'what people really believe,'" as Derek Pearsall remarked, "one that we can hardly make even about the materials of our own experience, in a sceptical and empirical age."¹⁰

Indeed, it is one of the arguments of this chapter, and one of the theoretical starting points of this volume, that such narratives are shaped according to truth-making strategies precisely so that they may be believed. The concept of truth-making strategy is meant to encapsulate the means by which a narrative invites and compels its audience's belief in its truth, while taking into account both the larger social acts which the narration is part of, as well as the even larger cultural web of meaning in which are inscribed both the signals towards veracity within the

---

8   Andrew Scheil, "The Historiographic Dimensions of Beowulf," *The Journal of English and Germanic Philology* 107, no. 3 (2008): 281–302, at 285. Grendel is called *rinc* (man, 720b), *healdegn* (hall-thane, 142a), *wonsceli wer* (unhappy man, 105a), *gromheort guma* (hostile-hearted man, 1682a), *feasceaft guma* (wretched man, 973a), and he walks on *weres wæstmum* (in the shape of a man, 1352a). Grendel's mother is a *wifunhyre* (monstrous woman, 2120b) bearing *idese onlicnces* (the shape of a woman, 1351a).

9   Catalin Taranu, *The Bard and the Rag-Picker: Vernacular Verse Histories in Early Medieval England and Francia* (London: Routledge, 2021). Scheil, "The Historiographic Dimensions," 302. Pace Andy Orchard, *Pride and Prodigies: Studies in the Monsters of the Beowulf Manuscript* (Toronto: University of Toronto Press, 2003), 1, and Kenneth Sisam, *Studies in the History of Old English Literature* (Oxford: Clarendon Press, 1953), 96.

10 Derek Pearsall, *Old English and Middle English Poetry,* Routledge History of English Poetry 1 (London: Routledge, 1977), 8–9.

story and the story's social life. Since these signals are not cultural universals and are often implicit, buried in the texture of the account, they must be excavated, abstracted, made explicit from the narrative, poetic, rhetorical, and emotional traces they leave in the text.

These strategies can vary so significantly that the narrative truth they conjure becomes unrecognizable across socio-cultural/textual communities. Thus, a particular type of truth may become identified as a blatant lie when encountered by a community that abides by different truth-making standards, hence the denunciation of myths and fables as sinful by Christian theologians, or of Christian theology as fabulous by Enlightenment apologists. More to the point, I argue that the narratives arising in early medieval England explored here were constructed and taken by at least some part of their audiences as true. But, the even more fruitful part of this argument lies in making explicit the strategies of truth-making that describe the implicit contract between narrators of apparently impossible events and their audiences.

For this remains a dead angle in many otherwise perceptive and highly valuable scholarly discussions of the fictionality of otherwise factually oriented medieval historical writings.[11] For instance, Elizabeth Tyler's groundbreaking work on historical narrative in early medieval England rightfully destabilizes received notions of fiction and history by pointing out that medieval narratives worked in milieux which did not recognize our category of "fiction."[12] Yet her account of the invented status

---

11 For general surveys, see Nancy Partner, *Serious Entertainments: The Writing of History in Twelfth-Century England* (Chicago: University of Chicago Press, 1977); Monika Otter, *"Inventiones": Fiction and Referentiality in Twelfth-Century English Historical Writing* (Chapel Hill: University of North Carolina Press, 1996); and Matthew S. Kempshall, *Rhetoric and the Writing of History: 400–1500* (Manchester: Manchester University Press, 2011).

12 For narrative traditions of early medieval England, Elizabeth M. Tyler is the foremost authority — among others, see Tyler and Ross Balzaretti, "Introduction," in *Narrative and History in the Early Medieval West*, ed. Ross Balzaretti and Elizabeth M. Tyler (Turnhout: Brepols, 2006), 1–9; Elizabeth

of certain parts of the historical narrative woven by the author of *Encomium Emmae* is based on the implicit assumption that these made-up stories were recognized as untrue by both their authors and audiences; that is, it is simply that they held such texts to different standards of factuality, wherein *inventio,* fictional narrative, was not rejected as improper for history-writing but savored as part of a tacit contract between the author and his audience that was based on a very particular notion of *historia.*[13]

This may well be the case for the Encomiast and his audience, but one cannot assume this very particular understanding of fiction to be representative for other texts narrating to other audiences things that we understand to be fictional. As suggested in the introduction to this volume, I aim to go one step further from investigating the various ways in which medieval narratives play with fictionality and historicity to exploring the strategies of truth-making that enabled certain medieval narratives of, to us, impossible events to be actually believed. For, as I argue there, much of the scholarship on medieval fictionality of the past decades still works within, and thus reinforces, the post-Enlightenment logic of truth familiar to us (i.e., that truth is a correspondence between an utterance or narrative and a state of facts of the external world), despite providing much needed correctives to previous assumptions of credulity, confusion, or unsophistication as explanations for the bewildering multiplicity of configurations of fact and fiction in medieval history-writing.

In a nutshell, then, this chapter is concerned with how such strategies of truth-making come to be, as processes both cognitive and socio-cultural by which truth is legitimized, enjoined, and sanctioned — as explained in the introduction, and also how they differ from what we, post-Enlightenment, understand by "truth." My preoccupation lies specifically with vernacular

---

M. Tyler, "Poetics and the Past: Making History with Old English Poetry," in *Narrative and History,* ed. Balzaretti and Tyler, 225–50; and, Elizabeth M. Tyler, *England in Europe: English Royal Women and Literary Patronage, c.1000–c.1150* (Toronto: University of Toronto Press, 2017).

13 Tyler, *England in Europe,* esp. 51–134, and 105.

theories of narrative truth—the heuristic reconstructions of the conceptualizations of truth produced via such truth-making strategies—as they are implicitly present in Old English poetic sources. This is not because I take them to be somehow unique to the loosely related set of cultural and political contexts that scholarship usually, and unhelpfully, describes as "Anglo-Saxon England" or as a manifestation of some particular *Geist* of early medieval English culture "as if Culture were a Platonic form that occasionally took terrestrial shape in oral or written communication."[14] Rather, this corpus preserves strategies of truth-making that are widely encountered in other socio-cultural settings that are non-Western, pre-modern, or both (and that sometimes manifest themselves even in Western, modern, industrialized milieux) and are distinct from the one prevalent in most early medieval narrative or historiographical sources rooted in the Latinate Christian or Classical narrative tradition. Still, as we shall see, these strategies did not exist in separate socio-cultural spheres but can often be found at work within the same texts.

The peculiarity of configurations of truth in early medieval England has not gone unnoticed by previous scholars, and I will refer to their work throughout this essay—here, I only briefly review their approaches and outline how my aims are different. Jeremy Downes is the first scholar of Old English attempting to tease out the peculiar nature of truth in *Beowulf* via the concepts of verisimilar and legisimilar truth: the former born out of an impulse to account for every detail and accidental fact of a state of facts, the latter aiming to provide coherence and conformity to the laws of the speaker's universe.[15] John Niles's insightful musings on the essentially social and personal nature of truth in early medieval English society are based on his work on storytelling and myth in oral traditions, which he sees as rooted in a

---

14 Stephen Harris, *Race and Ethnicity in Anglo-Saxon Literature* (London: Routledge, 2003), 31ff.
15 Jeremy Downes, "Or(e)ality: The Nature of Truth in Oral Settings," in *Oral Tradition in the Middle Ages*, ed. W.F.H. Nicolaisen (Binghamton: Medieval & Renaissance Texts & Studies, 1995), 129–44, at 130.

particularly counterfactual notion of truth related to "thinking in the subjunctive mood" that is very different from the objective, calculating, evidence-based path to truth we moderns like to think we pursue.[16]

Carolingianist Geoffrey Koziol eloquently opposes the pluralistic and context-dependent meaning of the Old English term *soð* (usually translated as "truth," but nowhere near what we understand by the word) to the Carolingian absolute faith in the possibility, indeed necessity, of separating true from false, orthodoxy from heresy, theology from idle fable.[17] In a thought-provoking study of Carolingian myth, or rather of the reasons for its inexistence, Koziol argues that, in distinction to the language used by Carolingian intellectuals — who were obsessed with issues of truth, authenticity, and orthodoxy, which they framed as dependent on their correspondence to Scriptural truth and its various ecclesiastical forms of institutionalization — Old English had no word for what we understand by "truth."[18]

The cognates of "truth" in all early Germanic languages (Old Saxon *trûên*, OHG *trôsten*, OE *truwian*), in fact denoted "loyalty, uprightness, and trustworthiness."[19] While OE *soð* did come to mean "truth" when used to translate Latin *veritas*, it was mainly used in contexts of speaking oaths, citing customs and proverbs, telling the future, and telling stories.[20] Indeed, like ON *saga*, OE *soð* basically means "saying, something said" and

---

16 John D. Niles, "True Stories and Other Lies" in *Old English Heroic Poems and the Social Life of Texts*, ed. John D. Niles (Turnhout: Brepols, 2007), 279–307, at 298.
17 Geoffrey Koziol, "Truth and Its Consequences: Why Carolingianists Don't Speak of Myth," in *Myth in Early Northwest Europe*, ed. Stephen Glosecki (Tempe: Arizona Center for Medieval and Renaissance Studies, 2007), 71–103, at 86, n. 39. See also Patrick Wormald, *The Making of English Law: King Alfred to the Twelfth Century* (Oxford: Blackwell, 1999), 122, 280, 283, and 316.
18 Koziol, "Truth," 84.
19 Ibid. Dwight Herbert Green, *The Carolingian Lord: Semantic Studies on Four Old High German Words: Balder, Frô, Truhtin, Hêrro* (Cambridge: Cambridge University Press, 1965), 117–26.
20 Ibid., 85.

is closely related to *secgan* "to say."[21] In Koziol's formulation of the implicit theory of truth in the word, "*soð* was less a veridical proposition about the world than a capacity adhering to the man deemed credible to speak it or a quality of the truth being spoken."[22] As such, it is deeply rooted in a social context dominated by the spoken word and personal bonds, based on values such as "trustworthiness, wisdom, standing, cunning," in which oath was a common means of judicial proof, "where interpreting dreams and healing illnesses needed canniness and command of lore; where truths were expressed by maxims, similes, riddles, and tales."[23] Koziol in fact suggests that the increasing appearance of *soð* in tenth-century early medieval English law codes and sermons and its gradual semantic evolution towards a closer correspondence with *veritas* is a result of trying to absorb Carolingian innovations in law and pastoral writing.[24]

Tom Shippey and Craig Williamson have made valuable contributions, particularly regarding what they call the riddling nature of truth in Old English sources. Particularly Shippey focuses on the socio-cultural context of speaking truth in early medieval England where both audience and speaker are part of tightly knit communities in which loss of face is catastrophic, in which it was crucial to master the art of saying what you mean without really saying anything by using riddles, proverbs and references to a corpus of verse and sayings encoded in highly

---

21 See the second chapter of Taranu, *The Bard and the Rag-Picker*; Jan de Vries, *Altnordisches etymologisches Wörterbuch*, 2nd edn. (Boston and Leiden: Brill, 1962), s.v. "sanna"; Ferdinand Holthausen, *Altenglisches etymologisches Wörterbuch*, 2nd edn. (Heidelberg: Carl Winter, 1963), s.v. "soð"; Jane Robert and Christian Kay, with Lynne Grundy, *A Thesaurus of Old English*, 2 vols. (London: King's College London, Centre for Late Antique and Medieval Studies, 1995), 1.372–73; and *Die Gesetze der Angelsachsen*, ed. Felix Liebermann, 2 vols. (Halle: Max Niemeyer, 1903), vol. 2, s.v. "soð," "soðfæst," esp. references to: Alfred, "Einleitung," 45, p. 40 ("Soðfæstne man 7 unscyldigne"); IV Edgar 14, p. 214, ("mid his soðe"), all quoted in Koziol, "Truth," 85.

22 Koziol, "Truth," 85.

23 Ibid.

24 Ibid., 86, n. 39. See also Wormald, *The Making of English Law*, 122, 280, 283, 316.

traditional genres via tactful implications that may or may not be understood by the concerned party.

These studies, however perceptive and inspiring, tend to explore one characteristic of the multifarious ways in which truth is claimed, assessed, and legitimized in early medieval England (all three aspects are different, though inextricably linked to each other), and tacitly assume it describes *the* early medieval English concept of truth, or even one specific to medieval or traditional oral cultures: Niles focuses on its social-embeddedness, Koziol on its pluralism, Downes on its oral-cultural context, Williamson on the endlessly refractive and playful mechanics of truth. The only exception, which is also the most recent study and the most direct inspiration for the present investigation, errs in the opposite direction. Tom Shippey's superb account of the multiplicity of truth sources identifies a potentially infinite number, though he stops at seven, of what he calls "polymorhps of truth" that can be reducible, I suggest, to only three to four strategies of truth-making, which I aim to prove in the following.[25]

Shippey puts to work Kurt Vonnegut's concept of Ice-Nine from his novel *Cat's Cradle,* where it is a form of water that turns everything into ice. He does this in order to make explicit some of the underlying concepts of truth lying implicit in Old English verse, of which there are many, just as there are many polymorphs of water. To provide a brief rehearsal of his model: Truth One is used to label the biblical truth not open to debate; Truth Two, the metaphorically playful and potentially misleading truth of riddles; Truth Three, maxims expressing "cultural imperatives even in the face of a history or a reality which denies them"; Truth Four, proverbs, ranging from the banal to the oracular; Truth Five is that of promises, vows, boasts, and other pronouncements that are in abeyance until they become true by being fulfilled through actions; Truth Six is the performative

---

25 Tom Shippey, "Introduction," in *The Complete Old English Poems,* trans. Craig Williamson (Philadelphia: University of Pennsylvania Press, 2017), xv–li (esp. xxvi–xxxv).

truth of charms; Truth Seven is that of allegories. And the series could go on indefinitely if Shippey didn't abandon it for fear of making "one of the characteristic errors of the literate mind confronting the preliterate," namely, "to fix boundaries, make distinctions, reduce reality to bullet points."[26]

This is a fair point, yet this is what Shippey accomplishes with nuance and gusto, and we are left much the wiser for it, and while his model was one of the starting points for this chapter, I suggest that what he reveals are not so much different theories of truth as context-dependent uses of strategies of truth-making. Thus, what he calls Truths Two, Three, and Four can be envisaged as different genre-dependent manifestations of the same theory of truth based on a participative, or rather constellative, strategy of truth-making that provides disparate or cryptic utterances that express a truth awaiting an audience to piece it together based on cultural patterns of meaning and personal experience. At the same time, Truth Five, while very different in its social embeddedness and performative dimension, could be understood as being rooted in the very same theory of truth not as a quality already present in an utterance but as something to be established *post factum*, a virtuality that awaits fulfillment which is conceptually the same as the truth of a riddle or maxim that awaits to be brought to light by an audience or by its members making the truth lying in the maxim or riddle their own. The strategy of truth-making is thus conceptually the same, being based in each case on a performance that fulfills the truth of the oath, of the proverb, or of the riddle — performances that differ only in their socio-cultural and genre shapes — a heroic action in the former case, a mental piecing together in the latter two.

This chapter, then, aims to provide pathways to describe the several processes by which truth is identified, enjoined, and authorized in a variety of discourses from early medieval England without assuming they are particular to this time and space. My focus is on the multi-level (i.e., cognitive, rhetorical, aesthetic, socio-cultural, political) processes of generating truth and not

---

26 Ibid.

on any one early medieval English, or even vernacular medieval, concept of truth.

In order to make these strategies of truth-making explicit, I will survey a number of different types of sources (i.e., individual words and glosses, proverbs, genealogies, as above), but as will become apparent, instances of story-telling and poetic composition in *Beowulf* are particularly rich venues for investigating implicit theories of truth. Indeed, I am not the first to notice *Beowulf*'s preoccupation with epistemology, with how knowledge of the truth is possible, though troublesome.[27] Thus, I will focus on a number of scenes where the poem itself brings to the fore issues related to how the truth of a narrative is constructed, which includes but is not limited to correct and incorrect ways of recounting events and contradicting versions of the same events: the disputation with Unferth, verse-making in Heorot, the protagonist retelling his own adventures, and his adventures being made into verse inside the poem. But I leave these close readings of *Beowulf* scenes for the second half of the essay, because in them the different strategies of truth-making are closely entangled, allowed to contend with each other or taken to breaking point. My first aim is to make these strategies explicit as they are encountered more straightforwardly in other Old English sources and only then read the *Beowulf* poet's sophisticated use of truth procedures in light of this preliminary work of reconstruction.

But before getting even there, I first need to defamiliarize the theory of truth widely current in the cultural horizon most readers of this piece probably share in order to open a space for alternative conceptions. For one cannot become aware of how truth is constructed via different strategies until one realizes that one's own implicit theory of truth is neither natural, nor self-evident, but simply one among many. For this purpose, I will only briefly rehearse my arguments in the introduction, which have sought to play the same role with regard to the volume as a whole.

---

27 Michael Lapidge, "*Beowulf* and Perception," *Proceedings of the British Academy* 111 (2001): 61–97, at 88.

First, the usual methodological operation of focusing on the cultural, social, or political functions fulfilled by narratives of impossible events rather than on their truth status prevents us from understanding the variety of processes by which truth is judged, recognized, and legitimized as truth. Some of these processes (i.e., truth-making strategies) may appear wildly dissonant to the researchers working with pre-modern or non-Western sources overwhelmingly belonging to WEIRD (Western, Educated, Industrialized, Rich, and Democratic) societies.[28]

Even the theories of truth elaborated by present-day academic philosophers are multifarious, though they can be roughly categorized in five families of theories: correspondence-based (i.e., truth is the correspondence between an utterance and a real fact in the world), pragmatist (i.e., truth is whatever is socially or psychologically useful to believe, a function of the "practices people engage in, and the commitments people make"), deflationary (i.e., only tautologies can be said to be true, that is, to assert that a statement is true is just to assert the statement itself), pluralist ("different statements can be all true without being true in the same way"), and coherence-based (i.e., the truth of an utterance derives from its coherence with the other utterances within a system of beliefs or representations).[29]

---

28 For the landmark critique of the bias of most sociological research towards individuals from WEIRD societies who are the majority of its subjects, see Joseph Henrich, Steven J. Heine, and Ara Norenzayan, "The Weirdest People in the World?," *Behavioral and Brain Sciences* 33, nos. 2–3 (2010): 61–83.

29 Brief introductions in the following articles from the *Stanford Encyclopedia of Philosophy*: Marian David, "The Correspondence Theory of Truth," in *The Stanford Encyclopedia of Philosophy* (Fall 2016 Edition), ed. Edward N. Zalta, https://plato.stanford.edu/archives/fall2016/entries/truth-correspondence; John Capps, "The Pragmatic Theory of Truth," in *The Stanford Encyclopedia of Philosophy* (Summer 2019 Edition), ed. Edward N. Zalta, https://plato.stanford.edu/archives/sum2019/entries/truth-pragmatic; Nikolaj Jang Lee Linding Pedersen and Cory Wright, "Pluralist Theories of Truth," in *The Stanford Encyclopedia of Philosophy* (Winter 2018 Edition), ed. Edward N. Zalta, https://plato.stanford.edu/archives/win2018/entries/truth-pluralist; Daniel Stoljar and Nic Damnjanovic, "The Deflationary Theory of Truth," in *The Stanford Encyclopedia of Philosophy* (Fall 2014 Edition), ed. Edward N. Zalta, https://plato.stanford.edu/archives/fall2014/entries/

The implicit theories of truth I discover at work in Old English sources will be shown to be more in tune with pragmatist, pluralist, and coherence theories of truth than with the correspondence-based one which is the default for most highly educated, present-day people. In these alternative theories of truth, which may well appear counterintuitive to habits of the mind that consider an utterance as either true or false and nothing in between, truth is not a relationship existing *a priori* between things in the world and things in the mind; rather, it is something made true by its being embedded in a narrative and poetic tradition formally and stylistically, or an assessment reached *post factum*, a virtuality left in abeyance until a commitment is fulfilled or until a collective judgment is made.

To see some of these truth-making strategies in action, I briefly rehearse here my argument in the introduction, where, together with Ralph O'Connor, I unpacked the two truth-making strategies at work in Bede's *Historia Ecclesiastica* that cause the author some uneasiness evident in his preface. On the one hand, what Bede sees as the superior truth of theology or the authority of written sources (in both cases, a truth only discernible to a minority of elite readers), and, on the other hand *vera lex historiae*, by which, as both Roger Ray and Walter Goffart point out, Bede did not mean any definitive and universal "law of history" in an anachronistic Hegelian or even Rankean sense. He meant, instead, a grudging concession to the role of *fama vulgans* (public opinion), however wrong, when writing a certain type of historical truth.[30] These two strategies are *auctoritas* (i.e., spiritual or simply factual truth via Scripture or other trustworthy written sources such as canonical authors) and, in my formulation, *traditio* (i.e., community-dependent and socially useful truth expressed and transmitted via oral tradition). Clearly,

---

truth-deflationary; and James Young, "The Coherence Theory of Truth," in *The Stanford Encyclopedia of Philosophy* (Fall 2018 Edition), ed. Edward N. Zalta, https://plato.stanford.edu/archives/fall2018/entries/truth-coherence.

30 Roger Ray, "Bede's *Vera Lex Historiae*," *Speculum* 55, no. 1 (1980): 1–21, at 11. Walter Goffart, "Bede's *uera lex historiae* Explained," *Anglo-Saxon England* 34 (2005): 111–16, at 114.

neither of them is based on a correspondence theory of truth but on different flavors of pragmatic truth, where the former is legitimized by divine or institutional authority, the latter by the judgment of a community as to the true narrative of events.

Bede clearly prefers the former theory of truth and is only compelled to use *traditio* by the scarcity of written reports and primarily by his writing a history meant for a secular elite audience, rather than a hagiography or private letter aimed at a theologically trained audience, for which the version of events known to public opinion was what mattered.

Yet if we focus on Bede, we run the risk of forgetting that he was by no means representative of the large majority of people living at all times in early medieval England, and indeed in other places of the world. His intimate knowledge of Latin Classical and Christian authors and consequently of the theories of truth with which they operated had little in common not only with the way common folk understood truth, but also with the certainly elite communities from which texts like *Beowulf* emerged, monastic though they may have been.[31] And as I have striven to show elsewhere, Bede and *Beowulf* do not belong to two separate worlds. They were both part of "the living Anglo-Saxon world, dominated by talk and not texts, gossip not parchment."[32]

And, as Alaric Hall reminds us, "[t]he way we write and think now is less radically different from people in highly oral medi-

---

[31] For the ground-breaking and compelling argument against usual assumptions of how representative or well-known Augustinian psychology was for the vast majority of people in early medieval England or Europe, which entertained very different conceptualizations regarding the soul, mind, and body, see Leslie Lockett, *Anglo-Saxon Psychologies in the Vernacular and Latin Traditions* (Toronto: University of Toronto Press, 2011). For the classical argument that *Beowulf* probably originated in an aristocratic monastic foundation (*Eigenkirche*), see Patrick Wormald, "Bede, *Beowulf* and the Conversion of the Anglo-Saxon Aristocracy," in *The Times of Bede: Studies in Early English Christian Society and its Historian*, ed. Stephen Baxter (Cambridge: Wiley, 2006), 30–105.

[32] See the second chapter of Taranu, *The Bard and the Rag-Picker*, and Catherine Cubitt, "Folklore and Historiography: Oral Stories and the Writing of Anglo-Saxon History," in *Narrative and History*, ed. Balzaretti and Tyler, 189–221, at 221.

eval societies than the prevailing discourse in medieval studies would suggest," a discourse that tells us more about our own need to construe ourselves as moderns than about premodern or non-Western rationality.[33] Indeed, I completely agree with Hall's point that the configurations of truth I discover in early medieval texts are not fundamentally different from those at work in our culture. I am not suggesting *traditio* is characteristic of "oral culture" and *auctoritas* of "literate culture" as if any meaningful distinction can be made between them — and Hall argues convincingly against the usefulness of these concepts. Yet there are significant differences between how truth is understood and practiced, and my task here is to delineate these differences and provide a model that accounts for them.

Indeed, not just the *Historia Ecclesiastica*, but *Beowulf*, too, uses both *traditio* and *auctoritas*. Indeed, the *Historia Ecclesiastica* also employs other truth-making strategies, too. Once we can recognize their similar mechanics beneath the variety of genre, narrative, and poetic conventions they underlie, we can see one or both of these two truth-making strategies at work in any text or discourse. It is *traditio*, for instance, that enables one's grandfather's wartime stories or conspiracy theories circulating on social media, both of which adhere to particular traditional patterns of narrative expectation to be regarded as true, and it is *auctoritas* that allows us to see the work of a present-day, professional historian writing on the same war as equally, though differently, true.

While *Beowulf* predominantly relies on truth procedures other than *auctoritas*, the latter is indeed present in its inclusion of Christian narratives which many early scholars found so incongruous. The Grendelkin as descendants of Cain, the poetic commentary on the Danes' slip into idolatry, the song of

---

[33] Alaric Hall, "The Orality of a Silent Age: The Place of Orality in Medieval Studies," in *Methods and the Medievalist: Current Approaches in Medieval Studies*, ed. Marko Lamberg, Jesse Keskiaho, Elina Räsänen, and Olga Timofeeva, with Leila Virtanen (Newcastle upon Tyne: Cambridge Scholars Publishing, 2008), 270–90, at 285. I am deeply grateful to Alaric for his thoughtful comments on this chapter.

creation in Heorot using recognizable Genesis tropes, the story of the Flood — all these are meant for an audience not just acquainted with Christian lore but also implicitly with the truth procedure on which it is based, namely *auctoritas,* the divine authority legitimizing Scriptural truth that the poem's audience certainly recognized and abided by. But the suspicious readings of these passages as later "interpolations" — though wrong, as has been thoroughly demonstrated — attest to the tension existing between not simply different story worlds but primarily between different truth-making strategies at work in these different narrative traditions.[34]

For it is *traditio* that is the main truth-making strategy in *Beowulf,* as it is in many cultures that are predominantly oral (as is the heroic society imagined in the poem) or in which orality still informs the way people tell stories, relate to each other, or write verse, as was the case with many communities in early medieval England. The many instances of poetic composition in the poem give us valuable insight not just into oral poetic craft (at least at the time the poem was composed), but into the truth procedure underlying it, which is different from that underlying scriptural culture. And though we should beware of assuming these scenes are anything more than fictional representations of purely oral composition imagined by early medieval English poets composing in a textual mode of discourse constructing "a pastoral of pre-textuality," there is much to be learned about this textually expressed but orally informed culture of which the latter were part.[35]

Unlike with *auctoritas,* with *traditio* it is not the voice of "authors" (poets) that makes the story true but rather their ability to remember and expand on the tradition they not only bear with-

---

[34] The best survey of the historiography on the poem's essential unity remains Tom Shippey, "Structure and Unity," in *A Beowulf Handbook,* ed. Robert E. Bjork and John D. Niles (Lincoln: University of Nebraska Press, 1998), 149–74.

[35] Roy M. Liuzza, "*Beowulf*: Monuments, Memory, History," in *Readings in Medieval Texts,* ed. David Johnson and Elaine Treharne (Oxford: Oxford University Press, 2005), 91–108, at 105.

in themselves but in which they are also active participants. It is the process (of transmission and (re)production using culturally sanctioned forms), not the person that authorizes the story. This is not only a function of orality, but, as Carol Braun Pasternack has demonstrated, also of the orally informed textuality of Old English poetry, which "does not employ an idea of the author but rather an idea of tradition," and in which "the virtual absence of poets' names signifies the author's insignificance."[36] Yet this tradition is not envisioned as a reservoir of stories and linguistic patterns, but rather as something which exists as part of a process in which "inscribed verse lays itself open to recomposition by subsequent poets and [...] in certain respects, scribes and readers could function as poets themselves."[37]

I explore this collaborative nature of *traditio* at greater length below, indeed, its agonistic nature too, since narrators often contend with the tradition or with one another. For now, I only wish to point out the peculiarity of Old English verse, whose orally derived nature (open to recomposition and reworking by future scribes and readers) has been thoroughly explored and demonstrated.[38] For there is a very different truth-making strategy underlying what Thomas Bredehoft regards as the productive, as opposed to the reproductive, ideology on which much of vernacular early medieval English textual culture is based (wherein an originary text is merely the raw material for subsequent reworkings rather than an archetype of which all subsequent reproductions aim to be faithful copies).[39] While the con-

---

36 Carol Braun Pasternack, "The Textuality of Old English Poetry," in *The Postmodern Beowulf: A Critical Casebook*, ed. Eileen A. Joy and Mary K. Ramsey (Morgantown: West Virginia University Press, 2006), 519–46, at 531.
37 Pasternack, "Textuality," 525.
38 Ibid.; Katherine O'Brien O'Keeffe, *Visible Song: Transitional Literacy in Old English Verse* (New York: Cambridge University Press, 1990); Mark Amodio, *Writing the Oral Tradition: Oral Poetics and Literate Culture in Medieval England* (Notre Dame: University of Notre Dame Press, 2004); and Thomas A. Bredehoft, *The Visible Text: Textual Production and Reproduction from Beowulf to Maus* (Oxford: Oxford University Press, 2014).
39 Bredehoft, *The Visible Text*, 29.

struction of truth in a reproductive logic of textuality is based on *auctoritas*, in a productive mindset, *traditio* reigns.

Much of the power of *traditio* in legitimizing truth is based on the stability of its formal features and of the linguistic patterns it employs. We can see the power to claim truth that a living, oral-verse tradition can deploy in Scandinavia and Iceland, which had a living formalized oral verse tradition late into the Middle Ages, enacted by skaldic poets for whose politically powerful audiences they constructed "a flattering and definitive version of the life and works of the king or chieftain being praised, securely enmeshed in the strict and complex forms of *dróttkvætt* which would ensure its enduring testimony."[40] Like so many times in the Old English poetic corpus, skaldic poets, too, refer to hearsay (or, what Bede called *fama vulgans*, the narrative of events as known to public opinion) as the main source for their poetic presentation of the praise-worthy deeds of their addressees via "I have heard" formulae (ON *frák*, OE *we gefrunon*). Yet, as Judith Jesch argues, skaldic verse does not merely "allude" to "oral discourse and oral tradition," but "is still very much a part of them"; for unlike the fictional early medieval English oral poets who "cannot assume the kind of stability in discourse and in the matter of discourse which the literate poet can," skaldic poets legitimate the truth of their narrative through the strict forms of *dróttkvætt*, "designed precisely to ensure as much fixity in the text as possible in an oral culture, and which also ensured that the texts survived reasonably intact until they were written down."[41]

The faithfulness to the formal features of the tradition (i.e., epithets, oral formulae, verse patterns) and its productive logic, infinitely amenable to generating new truths are inseparable, for as Elizabeth Tonkin's work on active epic traditions dem-

---

40 Judith Jesch, "The 'Meaning of the Narrative Moment': Poets and History in the Late Viking Age," in *Narrative and History*, ed. Balzaretti and Tyler, 251–65, at 264.

41 Ward Parks, "The Traditional Narrator and the 'I Heard' Formula in Old English Poetry," *Anglo-Saxon England* 16 (1987): 45–66, at 47 and 51, quoted in Jesch, "Meaning of the Narrative Moment," 259.

onstrates, tradition "offered a means of evoking genuine emotions," though "it would use an existing rhetoric to reformulate [...] unique, subjective responses."[42] With *traditio,* the teller "'codes' memories or reports of remembered events into existent stereot[y]pic forms," though sometimes even members of WEIRD cultures feel that they can represent their experience "more truthfully by working through a well-standardised genre — and one that in many ways seems formulaic, and inimical to individual autobiography."[43] Thus, when the participants in such *traditio*-based cultures "try to proffer this experience into words, they will turn to known formulations, modes and genres to do so. This may mean that deeply-felt experiences appear cliché-ridden, but even the most 'original' experience has to be represented through accepted rules of language and narrative production."[44] It is the "presence and recognition of familiar plot structures" that make stories "true" to the participants in a tradition, and it is the intertexts, the formal features of versification or formulae, that "label the text as part of the community's traditions in that it expresses similar thoughts in similar language, and thereby sanction it as 'true.'"[45]

New truths (e.g., novel experiences, events, insights) have to be made understandable in the extant cultural horizon, hence they have to be formulated in extant poetic or narrative forms; rather than signifying stagnation, it is this insistence on faithfulness to traditional forms that ensures that new truths are understandable within mental frameworks already in place. In Katherine O'Brien O'Keeffe's formulation, it is because "formulaic language appears in many places instead of being specific to one context" that "people hearing the echoes may bring to their

---

42 Elizabeth Tonkin, *Narrating Our Pasts: The Social Construction of Oral History* (Cambridge: Cambridge University Press, 1990), 60.
43 Ibid.
44 Ibid., 87.
45 Craig R. Davis, "Theories of History in Traditional Plots," in *Myth in Early Northwest Europe,* ed. Stephen O. Glosecki (Tempe: Arizona Center for Medieval and Renaissance Studies, 2007), 31–45, at 34, and O'Brien O'Keeffe, *Visible Song,* 20–21.

experiences diverse intertexts," so that "though the language announces the conservativeness of the text, it does not require the reader to conform to a certain interpretation" but rather through "its multiplicity of possible associations, [it] opens the text to varieties of interpretation."[46] Underlying the "aesthetics of familiarity" that characterizes, as Elizabeth Tyler argues, much Old English verse, whereby the impression of its belonging to an atemporal tradition masks its ability to express sharp political and social commentary, *traditio* as truth-making strategy is based on a theory of truth that is coherence-based (i.e., truth as what is formally coherent with a corpus of knowledge).

This understanding of truth pervades many of the scenes of poetic production and storytelling in Beowulf. Here is the poet at Heorot turning *Beowulf*'s recent adventure (the defeat of Grendel) into song:

> At times the king's thane,
> a man laden with heroic boasts, mindful of songs,
> he who very many of the old stories,
> remembered heaps, found new words
> bound in truth; the man began then
> Beowulf's trial reciting cleverly
> and with skill telling a right tale
> weaving his words.[47]

This court poet's authority (he is "the king's retainer") is established by his description as *gilphlæden* ("full of grand stories") and *gidda gemyndig* (mindful of songs/remembering songs) sig-

---

[46] O'Brien O'Keeffe, *Visible Song*, 20–21.
[47] Beowulf, ll. 867b–874a: "Hwilum cyninges þegn | guma gilphlæden gidda gemyndig | se ðe ealfela ealdgesegena | worn gemunde word oþer fand | soðe gebunden secg eft ongan | síð Beowulfes snyttrum styrian | ond on sped wrecan spel gerade, | wordum wrixlan." All quotations from *Beowulf* are from *Klaeber's Beowulf and The Fight at Finnsburg*, ed. Robert E. Bjork, Robert Dennis Fulk, Friedrich Klaeber, and John D. Niles (Toronto: University of Toronto Press, 2008). All translations are mine, unless stated otherwise.

nifying not just the quality of his memory also praised below ("he remembered much, many of the old stories" [*se ðe ealfela ealdgesegena | worn gemunde*]), but also his formal fidelity to the tradition. The other side of his skill lies in "finding other words," or perhaps more idiomatically, "finding new words" (*word oþer fand*). This is not a question of stylistic innovation but of appropriateness: the words need to be *soðe gebunden* (bound in truth), which testifies to the song being true while primarily referring to the technical skill of proper alliteration so that the phrase could be better translated as "rightly strung together." The point is that formal appropriateness and moral truthfulness are equivalent here. There is no doubt about his poetic ability, which legitimates his ability to convey the truth. He "recites with skill" (*snyttrum styrian*) and "adeptly tells an apt tale" (*on sped wrecan spel gerade*) while "interweaving his words" (*wordum wrixlan*).

Much has been made of the latter phrase, and after many decades Leyerle's argument about poetic interlace still stands. Indeed, this is what the poet does here on a narrative level, interweaving Beowulf's tale with Sigemund's and indeed with the entire tradition to which the latter belongs, as well as on the verse level, where syntactic dislocation and interlace seems to have been a prized skill of poets composing Old English verse.[48] The point is that this technical poetic skill ensures the truthfulness of the new story. On the one hand, one has to keep in mind a tradition, which is both a canon of stories and themes and a style characterized by particular technique of composition. Words and verses have to alliterate properly, but more generally, they (as well as the narrative they build) have to be woven together with skill. On the other hand, the tradition exists so that new events (such as Beowulf's exploit) can become part of the community's cultural memory and used in their turn.

In light of the nature of *traditio* explained above, these two aspects are interconnected. The truth of the new narrative is guaranteed by its being interwoven with a canon of narratives

---

48 John Leyerle, "The Interlace Structure of *Beowulf*," *University of Toronto Quarterly* 37, no. 1 (1967): 1–17.

about heroes like Heremod or Sigemund, which in its turn requires a strict adherence to the stylistic and technical specificities of this poetic mode of narrative. Thus, the tale of Beowulf is accepted as true because it is so skillfully told that it comes to resemble the stories about events that had happened many generations before him and that make up the tradition. In a sense, the narrative about current events has to be transported into the story-world of Sigemund or at least made formally homogeneous with the latter for it to become true.[49]

The epithet *gilphlæden* may signify the "lofty speech" characteristic of *gilp* (often translated as "heroic boast"), though its usual association with heroic action may appear slightly incongruent when attributed to a poet. Yet, as Nolan and Bloomfield argue, the epithet points to the task of "the official story-teller" of "determin[ing] that the hero's *gilp* has been properly fulfilled and that his performance does indeed fit an a priori pattern of heroism," and of "maintain[ing] the long tradition [...] and reiterating anew the moral values which distinguish every hero from his fellows."[50]

Another passage of oral composition that also evinces this truth-making strategy comes later in the poem, when Beowulf provides a lengthy account of his adventures to Hygelac, from which he omits many action-oriented details but in which he dedicates a full sixteen lines (2101–2117a) to describe and assess the verse-making going on at the feast in honor of his defeating Grendel. Interestingly, it is the same event that occasions these two meditations on poetic craft and its ability to encapsulate and convey truth: the previous one by the *Beowulf* poet, this one by Beowulf himself. These are rare occasions throughout the Old English poetic corpus where anything resembling a theory of truth, story-telling, and poetic composition, implicit throughout the corpus, is put into quasi-explicit terms.

---

49 Catalin Taranu, "Who Was the Original Dragon-slayer of the Nibelung Cycle?," *Viator* 46, no. 2 (2015): 23–40.

50 Barbara Nolan and Morton Bloomfield, "*Beotword, gilpcwidas,* and the *gilphlædan scop* of Beowulf," *Journal of English and Germanic Philology* 79, no. 4 (1980): 499–516, at 510.

What are the conditions of an authoritative narrator of the past and implicitly, of a truthful account in the protagonist's view? The old Scylding making verse, whether Hrothgar or not, had "heard tell of many things, from long ago narrated," or possibly it was he who "told of far-off times" (*felafricgende feorran rehte*, l. 2106). In either case, we encounter again the need for a tradition whose meeting point with the present revival of the past is the poet's live verse-making. This characterization is reinforced further below when it is unequivocally the king himself who remembers much (*worn gemunde*, l. 2114b), and can thus tell many tales: "at times, he would make song true and sorrowful, at other times strange tales rightly recounted" (*hwilum gyd awræc | soð ond sarlic hwilum syllic spell | rehte æfter rihte*, ll. 2108b–2110a).

There are two types of composition discussed here: a song "true and tragic," or "true and sorrowful" (*soð ond sarlic*), and "strange tales" (*syllic spell*), which are "recounted rightly" (*rehte æfter rihte*). The former seem to describe quasi-historical or heroic-themed poems, such as the Finnsburg narrative whose popularity is indicated by its presence inside the poem as well independently of *Beowulf*, while the latter might be something more akin to a "Wonders-of-the-East"-type of tale, telling of strange far-away lands or perhaps more fantastical tales of supernatural beings. In either case, much is made of their truth. In the former case, the tragic theme and mood of the poem is coupled with its truth, and in the latter we encounter again the insistence on correctness of form, which ensures their truth.[51] The strangeness of the tales does not lead them to be considered any less true than the songs from the former category. Rather, it is the rightness of the telling that makes them true or not. We can envisage strange stories not being narrated correctly from a formal point of view, in terms of poetic craft or what Craig Davis calls culturally determined "patterns of narrative even-

---

51 For an insightful comment on *rihte* as it appears here and in Hrothgar "reading" the magic sword hilt, see Seth Lerer, "Hrothgar's Hilt and the Reader in Beowulf," in *The Postmodern Beowulf*, ed. Joy and Ramsey, 587–628.

tuality," and thus rejected by the audience, which Davis argues happened with *Beowulf* itself.⁵²

It is true that the songs from the former category do not seem to need an authorizing strategy. They are already "true and sad," yet the poet does dwell on the truth strategies involved in embedding Beowulf's recent exploits into the tradition that includes Sigemund and Heremod. It is not that the mood and theme (*sarlic*) guarantees their truth but that the mood and theme involve their being composed in a certain mode which guarantees their truth. Thus, *sarlic* is shorthand for the correct poetic technique, which is correct because it evokes the sorrow (*sar*) that is one of the emotion schemas characteristic of such songs, as I argued elsewhere.⁵³ This sorrow describes the emotional schema embedded in a certain genre of verse which thus constitutes its truth; although the range of emotional nuance and their textual expressions subsumed under the rather vague *sar* varied greatly from nostalgia through anxiety to sheer grief. This understanding is corroborated by the poet of another "sorrowful song," the Exeter Book elegy *The Seafarer*, whose claim that he is "telling a true story" (*soðgied wrecan*) — even though the story of course does not correspond to any factual reality, and is in any case, "less a story than a song built around an extended metaphor" — can be understood in light of its belonging to a tradition which validates its moral and existential content, which makes it, in Geoffrey Koziol's formulation, "a fragmentary utterance that speaks to the truth of the world."⁵⁴

These passages not only show us how the textual community from which *Beowulf* emerged imagined a poet of the preliterate world within the poem to have composed, but also how this community may have envisaged *Beowulf* itself as a composition aiming to be read as belonging to the tradition into which the Heorot poet inserted Beowulf's recent exploits. If Beowulf was indeed a new hero, invented or magnified by the poet to the sta-

---

52 Davis, "Theories of History in Traditional Plots," 31–45, at 32.
53 See Taranu, *The Bard and the Rag-Picker*, chapter 2.
54 Koziol, "Truth," 85.

tus of protagonist with no pre-existing stories such as the ones Ingeld or Sigemund had, as Larry Benson and Roberta Frank have argued, then passages such as these may be read as this new narrative being anchored into this Germanic story-world as a claim to its truthfulness.[55] The Heorot poet's skill in making Beowulf's story true for his audience may echo the Beowulf poet's desire for his own larger story about *Beowulf* to be perceived as "bound in truth."

But what happens when two or more narratives purporting to be true come to clash? And how does the collaborative and sometimes adversarial nature of producing truth work in the world of early medieval England? As we shall see, *traditio* and *auctoritas* only partly cover the complexities of truth in *Beowulf.* As at least some early medieval people recognized, truth gets trickier still. I now move to other regions of the Old English spectrum of discourses. In the wisdom poem *Cotton Maxims II*, among other pithy utterances about appropriate or typical states of facts in the world (e.g., "a king shall rule his kingdom," "a dragon shall lie on his hoard"), we find the statement "truth is the trickiest" (*soð bið swicolost*, l. 10). In some editions and translations, this is emended to "clearest" (*switolost*), although the manuscript itself (BL Cotton Tiberius B.i, fol. 115r) clearly displays a "c," not a "t."[56] Underlying this emendation might be a need felt by modern editors to correct the original so that it corresponds to the more expected dignified rhetoric of a wisdom poem — a certain clarity as to what exactly truth is and how one can find it. This is what, after all, one expects to find in a wisdom

---

55 Scheil, "The Historiographic Dimensions of Beowulf," 287; Roberta Frank, "Germanic Legend in Old English Literature," in *The Cambridge Companion to Old English Literature*, ed. Malcolm Godden and Michael Lapidge (Cambridge: Cambridge University Press, 1991), 88–106, at 98, 100–101; and Larry Benson, "The Originality of *Beowulf*," in *The Interpretation of Narrative: Theory and Practice*, ed. Morton W. Bloomfield, Harvard English Studies 1 (Cambridge: Harvard University Press, 1970), 1–43, at 43.

56 *The Exeter Anthology of Old English Poetry: An Edition of Exeter Dean and Chapter MS 3501*, ed. Bernard J. Muir, 2 vols. (Exeter: University of Exeter Press, 2000).

poem: wisdom, not further confusion. Or at least this is the expectation set by a post-Enlightenment theory of truth.

However, as Craig Williamson deftly demonstrates, in the context of *Maxims II*, this statement makes perfect sense.[57] This wisdom poem, as many other riddles and proverbs in the vernacular tradition of early medieval England (and indeed in many oral, trust-based, *Gemeinschaft*-type societies across the world and through time), is not meant to provide an uncomplicated image of "reality as the early medieval English saw it."[58] Take the first line of the poem: the apparently banal "Cyning sceal rice healdan." Greenfield and Evert list the following possible translations, including the implications of each of them: "a king ought to rule/preserve a kingdom" (i.e., a king ought to rule it rather than abuse or neglect it) or "a king shall rule a kingdom" (i.e., it is in the nature of a king to rule a kingdom) or "a king must rule a kingdom" (i.e., each kingdom must be ruled by some king rather than by an upstart or an usurper).[59] Each of the maxims could be thus exploded into a variety of different meanings that are mutually contradictory when considered at once. This shows that the poem is not simply meant to be a static reservoir of wisdom and that in it the maxims are not simply quilted together but placed "against one another — colluding, colliding" in a pattern that, as Williamson shows, "raises

---

57 Craig Williamson, *Beowulf and Other Old English Poems* (Philadelphia: University of Pennsylvania Press, 2011), 178–81.
58 For the origin of the concepts of *Gemeinschaft* ("community" based on personal social interactions) vs. *Gesellschaft* ("society," constructed via indirect interactions, impersonal roles, formal values), see Ferdinand Tönnies, *Community and Association*, trans. Charles P. Loomis (London: Routledge and Kegan Paul, 1955). For a recent appraisal of the concepts, see Michael Hardt and Kathi Weeks, eds., *The Jameson Reader* (New York: Wiley-Blackwell, 2000), 145.
59 Williamson, *Beowulf*, 179, and Stanley B. Greenfield and Richard Evert, "*Maxims II*: Gnome and Poem," in *Anglo-Saxon Poetry: Essays in Appreciation for John C. McGalliard*, ed. Lewis E. Nicholson and Dolores Warwick Frese (Notre Dame: University of Notre Dame Press, 1975), 337–54, at 342.

the question of perception" and "defamiliarizes and deepens reality."[60]

At any rate, any culture's corpus of proverbs and maxims, despite (once again) modern expectations, is not meant to provide so much a coherent canon of axioms on the way the world works and on rules of proper behavior — a vernacular *Physics* and *Ethics* — as a toolkit of culturally validated truths fitting for different occasions from which members of said culture can pick and choose depending on the message they want to convey and on the social context in which they do so. The truth espoused by such maxims is not unitary and non-contradictory but rather a testament to an underlying belief that reality is not so much an external entity separate from its observer, as "a mosaic of man's perception" that can be apprehended only when the audience of a riddle or of such a riddling weave of proverbs restructures their perceptual categories when confronted with a constellation of possible objects to be perceived.[61] In the case of the king proverb, "beneath the apparently straightforward gnomic half-lines, the poem points to a variety of possible kingly behaviours" so that "what is slides into what should or might be [and] the possibility of 'might not' always lurks beneath the surface [so that] the ideal is haunted by the shadow of real-world kingly faults and failures."[62]

Still, I suggest that even Shippey's and Williamson's profoundly perceptive comments cast the underlying theory of truth in modern correspondence-truth terms: it is not "reality" that the maxims and riddles are aimed at conveying, but truth. We cannot assume that the people involved in the production and consumption of these discourses found the source of truth in any modern notion of realism. In other words, that they had a conception of reality as separable from the thinking subject. In

---

60 Williamson, *Beowulf*, 181.
61 Craig Williamson, *The Old English Riddles of the Exeter Book* (Chapel Hill: University of North Carolina Press, 1977), 25, quoted in Tom Shippey, "Introduction," in *The Complete Old English Poems*, trans. Williamson, xv–li, at xxvii.
62 Williamson, *Beowulf*, 179–80.

the statement "truth is the trickiest," the very action of uttering the truth is called into question and, in the genres of riddle and riddling maxims, but on a grander level in *Beowulf*, as we shall see, is reconceptualized as a participative experience by an audience tasked with recasting the shards of language into a truth that is culturally and also personally relevant.

This activity of co-generating truth is often profoundly social and communal in the Old English corpus, as we can see in two poems in the Exeter Book that provide us with a glimpse into one possible social context in which such riddling-proverbial truths were exchanged and generated together by a community of speakers.[63] *Vainglory* (15–18a) presents a scene in which warriors "sit at feast, pronouncing true sayings, exchanging words, seeking to find out which battlefield might still dwell among men within the hall" (*sittaþ æt symble, soðgied wrecað | wordum wrixlað, witan fundiaþ | hwylc æscstede inne in ræcede | mid werum wunige*). As Emily Thornbury argues, "the verb *wrixlan* 'to interchange' and the creation of *gied*—here *soðgied*, doubly true sayings—links this passage with the challenge of *Maxims I* (1–4a)':[64]

> Question me with wise words. Do not keep your mind concealed, leaving hidden that which you know most deeply. I will not tell you my secrets if you hide from me your mind's power and the intentions of your heart. Wise men ought to exchange sayings.

But rather than simply dialogue, *Vainglory* depicts a "many-sided conversation focused on shared memories," while "the generic scope of *gied* allows for the possibility that some of

---

63 As quoted, punctuated, translated, and interpreted in Emily Thornbury, *Becoming a Poet in Anglo-Saxon England* (Cambridge: Cambridge University Press, 2016), 101.

64 Ibid: "Frige mec frodum wordum! ne læt þinne ferð onhælne, degol þæt þu deopost cunne! Nelle ic þe min dyrne gesecgan, gif þu me þinne hygecræft hylest ond þine heortan geþohtas. Gleawe men sceolon gieddum wrixlan." Thornbury's translation.

these speeches took the form of poems," which did not exclude "a competitive edge — later in the poem, arrogant words lead to bloodshed," though at this point "the exchange of words is chiefly a medium of social solidarity."[65] These passages imply a society where conversation and disputation are taken seriously, whether via the ritualized exchange of wisdom in the *Exeter Maxims* or the emphasis on *soð* in the warriors' debate in *Vainglory*.[66]

We can see the competitive, agonistic side of this truth-making strategy in another Old English source often characterized as a "wisdom poem," the second of the dialogues of Solomon and Saturn, found in MSS Corpus Christi College Cambridge 422 and 41, which are some of the most complex Old English texts to survive.[67] Here, Saturn is a "wandering scholar" who seeks out Solomon to be taught wisdom and for "a contest of wits": in *Solomon and Saturn I*, he wishes to understand the truth about the Pater Noster, while in *Solomon and Saturn II* the two are presented as "sages engaging in a contest of wisdom," wherein they "test one another by asking riddles with mysterious, legendary answers — a four-headed lamenting bird, a Beowulf-like hero — or simple, quotidian solutions, like a book or deep water."[68] This is a prime example of truth-finding via dispute, and this social function of the truth procedure is present throughout the poems, especially in the latter, which shows "knowledge [...] gained and displayed" in the "agonistic verbal performance characteristic of oral cultures":[69]

---

65 Ibid.
66 Ibid.
67 The latest edition is *The Old English Dialogues of Solomon and Saturn*, trans. and ed. Daniel Anlezark (Cambridge: D.S. Brewer, 2009). See also Elaine Tuttle Hansen, *The Solomon Complex: Reading Wisdom in Old English Poetry* (Toronto: University of Toronto Press, 1988).
68 Irina A. Dumitrescu, "Solomon and Saturn," in *The Encyclopedia of Medieval Literature in Britain* (Oxford: Wiley-Blackwell, 2017).
69 O'Brien O'Keeffe, *Visible Song*, 52–59, 54. See also Robin Waugh, "Competitive Narrators in the Homecoming Scene of *Beowulf*," *The Journal of Narrative Technique* 25 (1995): 202–22, at 218, and John P. Hermann, *Allegories of*

> Lo! I have learned through disputation in days of old | mind-sharp men, counselors of the world | working about their wisdom.[70]

and

> [...] the Philistine wise men, when we sat at disputation | spreading out books and laying them on our laps | mingling sayings.[71]

But despite the appearances, these are not judicial proceedings but congenial disputations generating truth by exchanging items of wisdom but also allowing them to contend with each other. As in *Maxims I*, where wise men should *gieddum wrixlan* (which in this context can be translated as "exchange sayings," though in a more Beowulfian context "interweaving songs" would be more appropriate), this interweaving of truths is at once agonistic and collaborative, pointing to the tension between these separate individual truths which generate truth when allowed to compete. The ultimate judgment often belongs to the audience. More importantly, this competitive collaboration is not seen as a zero-sum game, for even the defeated parties come out of it with a renewed sense of truth:

> Then that wise man, the son of David, had overcome | and rebuked the earl of Chaldea. | Still he was joyful, he who had come | on that journey, traveling from afar: | never before had his soul laughed out.[72]

War: Language and Violence in Old English Poetry (Ann Arbor: The University of Michigan Press, 1989), 36.

70 *Solomon and Saturn II*, ll. 185a–87a: "Hwæt! Ic flitan gefrægn, on fyrndagum, modgleawe men, middangeardes ræswan, gewesan ymbe hira wisdom."

71 *Solomon and Saturn II*, ll. 471a–73b: "Filistina witan, ðonne we on geflitum sæton, bocum tobræddon, and on bearm legdon, meðelcwidas mengdon."

72 *Solomon and Saturn II*, ll. 181–84: "Hæfde ða se snotra, sunu Dauides, forcumen and forcyðed Caldea eorl. Hwæðre was on sælum, se ðe of siðe cwom, feorran gefered; næfre ær his ferhð ahlog."

What is remarkable about these passages is the co-existence of both an agonistic and a socially cohesive function to such exchanges, whose purpose is finding, observing, or arriving at truth. The strategy of truth-making at work in such contexts can be thus conceptualized as both a battle between opposing narratives and a communal exercise out of which truth can emerge, without the competitive side drowning out its collaborative basis; truth seen as a relational, intersubjective practice rather than a quality already dwelling in conceptual objects of perception. I suggest there is an overarching truth-making strategy at work in these texts, which I label *collaboratio* — an essentially constellative truth procedure, the result of a collective judgment of a community which can be either in-dwelling in the text or can be identified with the audience of a text. This type of truth can coagulate into a definitive sentence on a state of facts presented as such in the text after a community's deliberation (as in *Solomon and Saturn II*) can be presented in a process-oriented fashion (as in the passage of collegial competition in *Maxims I*), or finally, it can be opened up towards the audience for a final extratextual assessment, as I will argue with relation to *Beowulf*. In the latter embodiment of this truth strategy especially, truth can remain pluralistic, indeterminate, in abeyance, in which case the audience is expected to piece together the truth of the matter depending on their personal experience and immediate needs.

These characteristics define *collaboratio* as essentially constellative, which is consonant with Renee Trilling's argument that much of Old English poetry represents history in a constellative mode as distinct from the teleological ideology underlying salvation history. Trilling uses Walter Benjamin's notion of the constellation to great effect in accounting for the peculiar nature of the vernacular theory of history present in the Old English poetic corpus: "a constellation takes shape from the relative position of the stars that form it, and is thus a function of the position of the stargazer, who sees a pattern and names it, thus giving it meaning, which the stars in themselves do not of course have," which is a very apt figure for grasping the way in which "concepts […] appear to the critic in such a way that their relative arrangement is suddenly perceived as meaningful and becomes an image, or idea."[73]

This understanding of constellative arrangements of concepts and narrative elements whose meaning is left open to the audience builds on the insights of scholars like Carol Braun Pasternack and Katherine O'Brien O'Keeffe, who argue that Old English poetry is a collaborative phenomenon, and that scribes and readers play an active and creative role in textual production, which throws into question the issue of "authorial intention" and thereby our "accustomed goals of interpretation."[74] In light of these practices of textuality, composition, and reading, *collaboratio* is merely a scholarly label describing a way of generating truth that must have appeared as natural to at least some audiences of Old English verse.

In other words, at least some communities of readers and listeners of texts like *Beowulf* would have been expected and felt invited to deliberate, judge, and apply their own wits and experiences and thus find *their* truth in what modern readers have often regarded as a fundamentally inconclusive string of narrative moments and cryptic statements. As Elizabeth Tyler insists, medieval texts, as products of a world in which orality remained primary, are completed by a web of social and textual relations which call into question modern expectations that coherence relies on a single author's vision, or that closure must be woven into the text rather than, for example, supplied by a shared understanding of the progress of time within salvation history, or by the social ritual in which a text played a part, or by the place of a poem within poetic tradition.[75]

---

[73] Renée Trilling, *The Aesthetics of Nostalgia: Historical Representation in Old English Verse* (Toronto: University of Toronto Press, 2009), 31. The origin of the image of the constellation is Walter Benjamin's "Epistemo-Critical Prologue," in *The Origin of German Tragic Drama*, trans. John Osborne (London: Verso, 1998).

[74] Pasternack, "The Textuality of Old English Poetry," 519–46, at 522. O'Brien O'Keeffe, *Visible Song*, 193

[75] Balzaretti and Tyler, "Introduction," in *Narrative and History*, ed. Balzaretti and Tyler, 1–9, at 2.

In this light, apparently confusing passages such as the Unferth–Beowulf battle of narratives or the meta-narrative juxtaposition of the first roughly 2000 lines of the poem with Beowulf recounting his own adventures appear strikingly different. These scenes have received the attention of generations of scholars, so I will neither recount them at length nor attempt to rehearse all the arguments that have been made about them. I am strictly focusing on the truth-making strategies that come to light in these clashes of diverging narratives.

Shortly after Beowulf arrives at the Danish court and meets Hrothgar, he is challenged abruptly by Unferth the *þyle* (variously translated as anything from "jester" to "court spokesman"), concerning a swimming match between Beowulf and his friend Breca. In Unferth's account of the events (ll. 506–28), Breca won the contest because, after a week in the water, he was washed up among the Heatho-Ræmas, from where he made it back home, thus apparently obtaining victory. In his reply (ll. 530–606), Beowulf gives us a different version of the events: after five days' swimming together, he and Breca did indeed become separated, after which Beowulf was busy killing sea monsters before being washed up in Lapland.[76]

A common interpretation of the episode is to take Beowulf's story at face value, including his implicit devaluation of Unferth's story by his assessment of the latter as drunk or sinister hints at his being a murderer of his kin. Unferth is often made out to be a malignant opponent of the protagonist, jealous of the latter's heroic virtue.[77] Yet, as Michael Lapidge remarks, "neither of these accounts is wholly true or demonstrably false: they simply report the incidents from differing perspectives," and while "it is usually assumed that Beowulf 'won' the contest because

---

76 Lapidge, "*Beowulf* and Perception," 68. The discrepancies between the two accounts of the swimming match are discussed by Fred C. Robinson, "Elements of the Marvellous in the Characterization of Beowulf: A Reconsideration of the Textual Evidence," in *The Beowulf Reader*, ed. Peter S. Baker (New York: Routledge, 2000), 79–96, at 86–92.

77 See for instance Downes, "Or(e)ality: The Nature of Truth in Oral Settings," 129–44, at 130.

he presented a truer account of the events" or demonstrated finer rhetorical skills, "there is nothing in the text to support this assumption."[78]

Indeed, as Scott Gwara has demonstrated, there is much in the text to support a very different attitude towards the protagonist, detectable in what he calls "subaltern" characters in the poem, such as Unferth, Wulfgar, the guard on the beach, voicing doubts about the consequences of Beowulf's cavalier heroism.[79] Gwara makes a powerful argument that there is an essential ambivalence built in the poem about the heroic ethic that is usually assumed to lie at its heart, embodied in the figure of the *wrecca*, a foreign or exiled warrior of superior strength and courage but also overconfident and reckless. Beowulf is implicitly characterized as one of them, being placed in a gallery of figures both heroic and sinister alongside Sigemund and Heremod. Reading the poem with eyes unclouded by a hypermasculine ideal of heroism that is more Victorian than medieval, it is clear that people in "subaltern" positions in the heroic society at whose apex are both generous kings and arrogant *wreccan* express serious anxieties about Beowulf, who appears to be more the latter than the former.

Read in this light, then, Unferth is not the heel to Beowulf's babyface but a voice of reason at Heorot, expressing doubts that both some of Hrothgar's retainers and some of the poem's audience members may initially have had towards this newly arrived *wrecca*, who by all signs may be no more than an individualistic seeker of glory at all costs, potentially at the expense of the lives of men under his command. As Gwara argues, Unferth's accusation against Beowulf has seemed "'mean-spirited' to many, but it highlights a common anxiety of the warband," and indeed he "expresses a majority opinion — not the view of cowards or

---

78 Lapidge, "*Beowulf* and Perception," 69.
79 Scott Gwara, *Heroic Identity in the World of Beowulf* (Boston and Leiden: Brill, 2008), 2.

rogues but of Hroðgar's fighting men — that engaging Grendel is foolhardy."⁸⁰

While Beowulf mocks Unferth as "drunk with beer" (*beore druncen*, l. 531a), the text makes it clear that Unferth is a highly respected member of Hrothgar's household. He is not just a foolish drunkard but an esteemed Dane sitting at the feet of Hrothgar (l. 500), whose "spirit everyone trusted" (ll. 1165b–68a), who was known to have great courage, (l. 1465), and even Beowulf concedes that his "wit is clever" (l. 589b). Michael J. Enright has challenged views of a negative Unferth by arguing that the *þyle* holds an important warband position as the king's official spokesman.⁸¹ It is not clear that Beowulf's attempts at discrediting Unferth are as well-received by either the intra- or extra-textual audiences as usually thought, including his accusation of kin-slaying (ll. 587–89) as deserving of "punishment in hell" or "in the hall," according to Mitchell and Robinson's more probable reading. The fact that he has yet to face any punishment may point to the fact that at least Hrothgar does not think Unferth deserves any such thing.

Beowulf's next accusation is purely counterfactual and, rather than involving Unferth's worth, could be read as more of a faux pas, the newcomer casting aspersion on the entire court, if not on all the Danes: Grendel could not have wreaked such havoc had Unferth's heart been more battle-fierce, indeed the monster found that the "Victory-Shieldings" did not give him any trouble at all (ll. 591–97). The use of *Sige-Scyldinga* in this particularly un-victorious context may have come across as an irony. As Gwara notes, neither the Danes nor any other audience of the poem may have been too impressed with Beowulf's boastful and rather arrogant attitude, at least at this point in the poem.

Throughout his *flyting* with Unferth, Beowulf seems preoccupied with being perceived as telling the truth. He repeatedly

---

80 Ibid., 129, 131.
81 Michael J. Enright, "The Warband Context of the Unferth Episode," *Speculum* 73, no. 2 (1998): 297–337, at 310, quoted by Gwara, *Heroic Identity*, 129.

declares, "I tell the truth" (*soð ic talige*, l. 532b), and "I say to you truly" (*secge ic þe to soðe*, l. 590), which may be interpreted as no more than rhetorical markers or speech tics. On the other hand, this repeated reference to truth can be read as a more substantial proof of either the protagonist's trustworthiness, or, on the contrary, as testifying to an anxiety over that which his story might be lacking most: truth. Both readings are possible, but my point is that Beowulf's truth was not necessarily *the* truth for all audiences of the poem, some of whom may have been much more sympathetic to Unferth's truth. The intra-textual subalterns' anxieties about his motivations and "the potential for immoderation that he seems to express" may have been echoed by at least some of the audience's members, even while for others the protagonist may have been "an enigmatic figure whose incommensurate power they admire and fear."[82] It is not improbable, then, that some people reading or listening to the episode would have had misgivings about Beowulf's claim to truth, without necessarily taking Unferth's at face value. For them, truth was thus left in abeyance, or both narratives may have been seen as potentially true in different contexts.

Beowulf's pre-emptive truth-claims are different from most other instances of *soð* or *soðe* in the poem (ll. 524, 533, 590, 700). They refer neither to a boast or promise that can be fulfilled with deeds nor to an eternal truth such as "that mighty God has always ruled humankind" (*soð is gecyþed | þæt mihtig god manna cynnes | weold wídeferhð*, ll. 700b–702a). So, his pronouncements of speaking truth, while not necessarily coming across as dubious, call into question the very issue of the truth of these clashing accounts. At the end of the episode, the truth of the matter is left suspended, unresolved, for the audiences (both the Danes in the poem and the early medieval English hearing or reading it) to ruminate on and judge for themselves or collectively as in the more collegial and wisdom-seeking *flytings* in *Maxims I* or *Solomon and Saturn*.

---

82 Gwara, *Heroic Identity*, 13.

The peculiar semantic valences of *soð*, based on interpersonal trust and moral worthiness rather than on correspondence to an abstract "reality," evinced by Koziol and mentioned at the start of this essay parallel many of the aspects of the procedures of generating truth discussed so far — their social dimension, their collaborative and agonistic logic, in which the audience and the tradition-bearer are involved in the production of truth and meaning.

In his study of the "subjunctive mood" type of truth encountered in myth and story-telling, John Niles poignantly corroborates Koziol's argument through an account of early medieval English judicial proceedings in which "what mattered was not exactly the answer to the question 'What happened?', for the people of that time did not necessarily assume the possibility of direct access to the truth," but those that were rather determined by the implicit question "Which of the two parties has the power of speaking a 'true' story?"[83] The procedure of arriving at the truth of a case was not forensic and evidence-based but entirely socially-determined, a matter of "trustworthiness and [...] powerful connections"; the defendant was legally "oath-worthy" (*aþwurþe*) if recognized as someone for which "enough people of high rank were willing to offer [...] *mundbyrd* 'personal protection', thereby serving as sureties for his word."[84]

The judicial clash of narratives was thus decided in the favor of the one with a higher degree of "oath-worthiness," measured by the number or rank of such "sureties," which were not exactly witnesses in the sense of being able to corroborate the narrative put forth by one side as much as attesting to the social standing of the narrator. Far from being relegated to the realm of storytelling, this pragmatic conception of truth as whatever produces social cohesion and as the judgment of a community held wide cultural currency in early medieval England. As Elizabeth Tonkin notes, not all legal systems "are geared to finding 'the truth', or to making 'an impartial' decision," but rather to

---

83 Niles, "True Stories," 282.
84 Ibid.

generating "social solutions to perceived social breakdowns, and support therefore the litigant who has mobilised the strongest support, which may be an equally rational (and honourably considered) decision."[85]

With this understanding, scholars may surmise what many early medieval audiences of *Beowulf* would have thought when hearing both the *flyting* and the protagonist's protestations of *soð*. Since Beowulf's dispute with Unferth was not a judicial proceeding but a contest of truths, there was no need for Hrothgar, or the poet, to intervene or pronounce a final judgment. Preserving the social cohesion of the Danes was the foremost duty, and when expedient, this need requires a collaborative and pluralistic theory of truth, whereby truth is left in abeyance or the possibility of more than one truth is entertained. Read in the light of the workings of *collaboratio*, such clashes of perspectives or narratives appear as not simply verbal contests with one clear victor, for they still generate truth according to the same constellative strategy as the more congenial exercises of collaboration analyzed above. Rather, I would characterize them as points of inflection for truth procedures, where the issues of truth and of how it generated, authorized, and assessed are brought to the fore to an extent not encountered in other early medieval texts.

This willingness to allow divergent narratives to exist, the issue of their ultimate truth being left unresolved, can be seen also on an even grander scale in the scene of Beowulf's homecoming, in which he provides a "critical retelling of the poem to this point, the hero becom[ing] his own poet," as Seth Lerer remarks.[86] The episode has received close scrutiny from, among others, Lerer and Michael Lapidge, whose astute investigations provide a range of dazzling insights into the poem's highly sophisticated, even experimental, play with narrative authority and interpretative possibilities.[87]

---

85 Tonkin, *Narrating Our Pasts*, 114.
86 Seth Lerer, "Hrothgar's Hilt and the Reader in *Beowulf*," in *The Postmodern Beowulf*, ed. Joy and Ramsey, 587–628, at 589.
87 Lerer, "Hrothgar's Hilt," and Lapidge, "*Beowulf* and Perception."

Lapidge explains the striking discrepancies between Beowulf's retelling of his adventures to Hygelac (2000–2151) and the roughly 1700 lines of the poem preceding it as a point at which "the poet clearly expected the audience retroactively to compare" his own account with the protagonist's perception of events.[88] Meanwhile, Lapidge explains the tension between these different narratives of the same events as "a humorous critique of tale-telling, and another reassessment of the nature of narrative authority."[89] Both scholars poignantly bring home the point that this tension between the accounts is absolutely intentional and allows us a glimpse into a very different way of conceiving perception (Lapidge) and constructing narrative (Lerer). However, at the same time, this is another point of inflection for truth procedures, one in which *collaboratio* is opened up to an even more radical extent toward the audience with Beowulf's insistence on declaring that he speaks the truth in the Unferth episode, echoed here in the way he is "carefully manipulating" his re-creation of his own past in his account to Hygelac through "his emphases on the precision of detail and the correctness of his own and of the scop's earlier performances," discussed with *traditio*.[90] This savvy manufacturing of consensus around his narrative, this seduction towards his own truth, may have worked in this episode (more than in the Unferth *flyting* at least) in establishing "the audience's trust in Beowulf's narrative authority" through both "his imposing bearing" and "from the pervasive associations between the hero and the *scop*."[91]

Yet, as in the case of the Unferth episode, it is not clear that all members of all audiences of Beowulf would have seen Beowulf's account as true. Indeed, the poet's juxtaposing it with his own points to the problematic nature of assessing the truth. In both of these cases, the lack of commentary on the poet's part may well confuse any audience, modern or medieval. What are

---

88 Lapidge, "*Beowulf* and Perception," 70.
89 Lerer, "Hrothgar's Hilt," 608.
90 Ibid., 617.
91 Ibid.

we to make of these accounts? Which one are we to believe? The lack of overt, explicit commentary does not exclude more subtle cues, though, which different audience members can piece together in different ways. Lapidge sees this feature of the poem as intentional, and indeed "unprecedented": his argument is that "the *Beowulf*-poet's mental orientation was philosophical and epistemological," which explains the poem's "eccentric" narrative structure.[92] At moments of repetition such as these two (although they are not the only ones — indeed, the battle with Grendel is retold three times), the poet fully "intended the audience of the poem to reflect, retroactively, on the narrated events and their relationships, during the course of the telling."[93] In these inflection points, the audience is fully brought into the truth-making strategy of *collaboratio*, though this also happens to a lesser or greater extent in wisdom poems such as the ones explored above, indeed the entire tradition of Old English riddling verse and gnomic discourse prepared Beowulf for this unprecedented *flyting* of the poem with its audience, understood as both collegial weaving together and clash of narrative with traditional and personal truths.

It is not that these people belonging to an otherwise highly traditional society were ambivalent about truth like some postmodernists *avant la lettre*, or, rather, like the vulgarized understanding of the latter. My point is that these texts show us that they understood very well that truth claims are often adversative — one person's truth is another one's lie — but that for society to work, the final judgment must often be open-ended, the truth always awaiting an audience to piece it together via exchanges of wisdom, stories, and perspectives veering more towards the agonistic or the collaborative but at no point turning into either a zero-sum game or, at the other end of the spectrum, a choir singing in unison. Hence Beowulf vs. Unferth is not a trial, but a momentary clash of narratives, whose ultimate truth the Danes in the poem or the early medieval English audience

---

92 Lapidge, "*Beowulf* and Perception," 88.
93 Ibid.

outside it have to establish for themselves. The poem is interested not in establishing but in allowing the procedures of generating truth to unfold, intermingle, contend with each other, and sometimes fail. In the Unferth-Beowulf *flyting* and Beowulf's account of his adventures, we see *collaboratio* and that socially embedded notion of *soð* turn competitive and shrill, while also being opened up to the audience. In the scenes of verse composition, we see *traditio* at work restating old truths and producing new truths out of recent events, and through its uses we can glimpse at what the *Beowulf* poet is trying to achieve in telling these sad and strange tales.

In Koziol's assessment, in a cultural horizon such as that of early medieval England, dominated by such vernacular theories of truth, a tradition, both as a story-world and as a set of formal requirements, can be the bearer of truth via *traditio* as truth procedure. This is not because the events it conveys are factual, since in it "there might be good stories and bad stories, useful stories and not-so-useful ones, stories that conformed to and supported tradition and ones that did not" but because their adherence to the tradition enabled the criteria according to which their truth was assessed to be "highly specific to particular needs in particular situations (just as a particular god was good and useful in one situation but not another)"; in any case, "the idea that a story was simply 'true' as an abstract absolute—this is something we do not find [in early medieval England]."[94] Here is where *collaboratio* comes into play: the task of finding truth rests upon the audience or in a more adversarial context, on each other's narrative antagonist. Several truths can coexist depending on the different needs of members or groups of the audience, but when there is a need for one truth, as in a judicial debate, that truth is as much a function of the social standing of the narrative protagonists (in its turn a function of the performative truth an individual has enacted) as of the social cohesion that the better truth can foment (in its turn at least

---

94 Koziol, "Truth," 86.

partly a function of the cultural and narrative-patterning coherence it can elicit).

Recast as based on a concept of truth that combined *collaboratio* and *traditio,* then, the Caesar-Woden additions to the early medieval English genealogies I discussed at the beginning of this essay open up a space for narrating the past ruled equally by cultural-political symbolism and playful riddling, not by factual truth as representing a historical reality. The self-conscious insertion of such figures as Geat, Woden, or Caesar in the line of East Anglian kings can be understood only when considered from outside the paradigm set by correspondence-based truth and understood rather as a puzzle to be pondered by a highly educated audience who has the necessary background knowledge for its solution. Its truth exists not so much in the piece of information conveyed as in the negative space of the audience's act of reading it and mulling it over — a narrative truth that dwells in virtuality, becoming actual insofar as this audience can piece it together from the names strung together by the genealogist. In the truth of genealogical tradition and the story-worlds it subtends, the constellative dynamics of *collaboratio* which awaits an audience to cause it to emerge are married to the conventionality of *traditio* underlying the traditional form of the genealogy that alone can be made to express new cultural-political truth, namely, the insertion of both the Roman past and the Germanic pre-Christian past into the newly national ideology of *Angelcynn*.[95] Both of these functions of the genealogy are based on underlying pragmatist theories of truth: in the former case, the truth is constellative, in abeyance, waiting to be fulfilled, pieced together, by the narrative's audience; in the latter, the truth of the line of descent, however improbable, is legitimized by the authority of the form of the genealogical tradition and, narratively, of the story-worlds of Roman history and of Germanic pagan gods (however euhemerized).

---

95 See Taranu, *The Bard and the Rag-Picker,* ch. 4.

Bibliography

Primary

Bede's "Ecclesiastical History of the English People". Edited by Bertram Colgrave and R.A.B. Mynors. Oxford Medieval Texts. Oxford: Oxford University Press, 1969.

Die Gesetze der Angelsachsen. Edited by Felix Liebermann. 2 Volumes. Halle: Max Niemeyer, 1903.

Klaeber's Beowulf and The Fight at Finnsburg. Edited by Robert E. Bjork, Robert Dennis Fulk, Friedrich Klaeber, and John D. Niles. Toronto: University of Toronto Press, 2008.

The Anglo-Saxon Chronicle: A Collaborative Edition. Volume 7: MS E. Edited by Susan Irvine. Cambridge: D.S. Brewer, 2004.

The Exeter Anthology of Old English Poetry: An Edition of Exeter Dean and Chapter MS 3501. Edited by Bernard J. Muir. 2 Volumes. Exeter: University of Exeter Press, 2000.

The Old English Dialogues of Solomon and Saturn. Translated and edited by Daniel Anlezark. Cambridge: D.S. Brewer, 2009.

The Complete Old English Poems. Translated by Craig Williamson. Philadelphia: University of Pennsylvania Press, 2017.

Robert, Jane, and Christian Kay, with Lynne Grundy. *A Thesaurus of Old English*. 2 Volumes. London: King's College London, Centre for Late Antique and Medieval Studies, 1995.

Secondary

Balzaretti, Ross, and Elizabeth M. Tyler, eds. *Narrative and History in the Early Medieval West*. Turnhout: Brepols, 2006.

Benjamin, Walter. *The Origin of German Tragic Drama*. Translated by John Osborne. London: Verso, 1998.

Benson, Larry. "The Originality of Beowulf." In *The Interpretation of Narrative: Theory and Practice,* edited by Morton W. Bloomfield, 1–43. Harvard English Studies 1. Cambridge: Harvard University Press, 1970. DOI: 10.4159/harvard.9780674733183.c1.

Bredehoft, Thomas A. *The Visible Text: Textual Production and Reproduction from Beowulf to Maus.* Oxford: Oxford University Press, 2014.

Cubitt, Catherine. "Folklore and Historiography: Oral Stories and the Writing of Anglo-Saxon History." In *Narrative and History in the Early Medieval West,* edited by Ross Balzaretti and Elizabeth M. Tyler, 189–221. Turnhout: Brepols, 2006. DOI: 10.1484/M.SEM-EB.3.3768.

Davis, Craig R. "Cultural Assimilation in the Anglo-Saxon Royal Genealogies." *Anglo-Saxon England* 21 (1992): 23–36. DOI: 10.1017/S0263675100004166.

———. "Theories of History in Traditional Plots." In *Myth in Early Northwest Europe,* edited by Stephen O. Glosecki, 31–45. Tempe: Arizona Center for Medieval and Renaissance Studies, 2007.

De Vries, Jan. *Altnordisches etymologisches Wörterbuch.* 2nd edition. Boston and Leiden: Brill, 1962.

Downes, Jeremy. "Or(e)ality: The Nature of Truth in Oral Settings." In *Oral Tradition in the Middle Ages,* edited by W.F.H. Nicolaisen, 129–44. Binghamton: Medieval & Renaissance Texts & Studies, 1995), 129–44.

Dumitrescu, Irina A. "Solomon and Saturn." In *The Encyclopedia of Medieval Literature in Britain.* Oxford: Wiley-Blackwell, 2017. DOI: 10.1002/9781118396957.wbemlb043.

Dumville, David. "Kingship, Genealogies, and Regnal Lists." In *Early Medieval Kingship,* edited by Peter H. Sawyer and Ian N. Wood, 72–104. Leeds: University of Leeds, 1977.

———. "The Anglian Collection of Royal Genealogies and Regnal Lists." *Anglo-Saxon England* 5 (1976): 23–50. DOI: 10.1017/S0263675100000764.

Enright, Michael J. "The Warband Context of the Unferth Episode." *Speculum* 73, no. 2 (1998): 297–337. DOI: 10.2307/2887155.

Frank, Roberta. "Germanic Legend in Old English Literature." In *The Cambridge Companion to Old English Literature,* edited by Malcolm Godden and Michael Lapidge, 88–106.

Cambridge: Cambridge University Press, 1991. DOI: 10.1017/CCOL0521374383.005.

Greenfield, Stanley B., and Richard Evert. "*Maxims II*: Gnome and Poem." In *Anglo-Saxon Poetry: Essays in Appreciation for John C. McGalliard,* edited by Lewis E. Nicholson and Dolores Warwick Frese, 337–54. Notre Dame: University of Notre Dame Press, 1975.

Goffart, Walter. "Bede's *uera lex historiae* Explained." *Anglo-Saxon England* 34 (2005): 111–16. DOI: 10.1017/S0263675105000049.

Green, Dwight Herbert. *The Carolingian Lord: Semantic Studies on Four Old High German Words: Balder, Frô, Truhtin, Hêrro.* Cambridge: Cambridge University Press, 1965.

Gwara, Scott. *Heroic Identity in the World of Beowulf.* Boston and Leiden: Brill, 2008. DOI: 10.1163/ej.9789004171701.i-420.

Hall, Alaric. "The Orality of a Silent Age: The Place of Orality in Medieval Studies." In *Methods and the Medievalist: Current Approaches in Medieval Studies,* edited by Marko Lamberg, Jesse Keskiaho, Elina Räsänen, and Olga Timofeeva, with Leila Virtanen, 270–90. Newcastle upon Tyne: Cambridge Scholars Publishing, 2008.

Hansen, Elaine Tuttle. *The Solomon Complex: Reading Wisdom in Old English Poetry.* Toronto: University of Toronto Press, 1988.

Hardt, Michael, and Kathi Weeks, eds. *The Jameson Reader.* New York: Wiley-Blackwell, 2000.

Harris, Stephen. *Race and Ethnicity in Anglo-Saxon Literature.* London: Routledge, 2003. DOI: 10.4324/9780203497999.

Henrich, Joseph, Steven J. Heine, and Ara Norenzayan. "The Weirdest People in the World?" *Behavioral and Brain Sciences* 33, nos. 2-3 (2010): 61–83. DOI: 10.1017/S0140525X0999152X.

Hermann, John P. *Allegories of War: Language and Violence in Old English Poetry.* Ann Arbor: The University of Michigan Press, 1989.

Holthausen, Ferdinand. *Altenglisches etymologisches Wörterbuch.* 2nd Edition. Heidelberg: Carl Winter, 1963.

Jesch, Judith. "The 'Meaning of the Narrative Moment': Poets and History in the Late Viking Age." In *Narrative and His-*

tory in the Early Medieval West, edited by Ross Balzaretti and Elizabeth M. Tyler, 251–65. Turnhout: Brepols, 2006. DOI: 10.1484/M.SEM-EB.3.3770.

Kempshall, Matthew S. *Rhetoric and the Writing of History: 400–1500.* Manchester: Manchester University Press, 2011.

Koziol, Geoffrey. "Truth and Its Consequences: Why Carolingianists Don't Speak of Myth." In *Myth in Early Northwest Europe,* edited by Stephen Glosecki, 71–103. Tempe: Arizona Center for Medieval and Renaissance Studies, 2007.

Lapidge, Michael. "*Beowulf* and Perception." *Proceedings of the British Academy* 111 (2001): 61–97.

Lerer, Seth. "Hrothgar's Hilt and the Reader in *Beowulf.*" In *The Postmodern Beowulf: A Critical Casebook,* edited by Eileen A. Joy and Mary K. Ramsey, 587–628. Morgantown: West Virginia University Press, 2006.

Leyerle, John. "The Interlace Structure of *Beowulf.*" *University of Toronto Quarterly* 37, no. 1 (1967): 1–17. DOI: 10.3138/utq.37.1.1.

Liuzza, Roy M. "*Beowulf*: Monuments, Memory, History." In *Readings in Medieval Texts,* edited by David Johnson and Elaine Treharne, 91–108. Oxford: Oxford University Press, 2005.

Niles, John D. "Myth and History." In *A Beowulf Handbook,* edited by Robert E. Bjork and John D. Niles, 213–33. Lincoln: University of Nebraska Press, 1998.

———. "True Stories and Other Lies." In *Old English Heroic Poems and the Social Life of Texts,* edited by John D. Niles, 279–307. Turnhout: Brepols, 2007. DOI: 10.1484/M.SEM-EB.4.00073.

Nolan, Barbara, and Morton Bloomfield, "*Beotword, gilpcwidas,* and the *gilphlædan scop* of *Beowulf.*" *Journal of English and Germanic Philology* 79, no. 4 (1980): 499–516. https://www.jstor.org/stable/27708719.

O'Brien O'Keefe, Katherine. *Visible Song: Transitional Literacy in Old English Verse.* Cambridge: Cambridge University Press, 2006.

Orchard, Andy. *Pride and Prodigies: Studies in the Monsters of the Beowulf Manuscript*. Toronto: University of Toronto Press, 2003.

Otter, Monika. *"Inventiones": Fiction and Referentiality in Twelfth-Century English Historical Writing*. Chapel Hill: University of North Carolina Press, 1996.

Parks, Ward. "The Traditional Narrator and the 'I Heard' Formula in Old English Poetry." *Anglo-Saxon England* 16 (1987): 45–66. DOI: 10.1017/S0263675100003859.

Partner, Nancy. *Serious Entertainments: The Writing of History in Twelfth-Century England*. Chicago: University of Chicago Press, 1977.

Pasternack, Carol Braun. "The Textuality of Old English Poetry." In *The Postmodern Beowulf: A Critical Casebook*, edited by Eileen A. Joy and Mary K. Ramsey, 519–46. Morgantown: West Virginia University Press, 2006.

Pearsall, Derek. *Old English and Middle English Poetry*. Routledge History of English Poetry 1. London: Routledge, 1977.

Ray, Roger. "Bede's *Vera Lex Historiae*." *Speculum* 55, no. 1 (1980): 1–21. DOI: 10.2307/2855707.

Robinson, Fred C. "Elements of the Marvellous in the Characterization of Beowulf: A Reconsideration of the Textual Evidence." In *The Beowulf Reader*, edited Peter S. Baker, 79–96. New York: Routledge, 2000.

Scheil, Andrew. "The Historiographic Dimensions of Beowulf." *The Journal of English and Germanic Philology* 107, no. 3 (2008): 281–302. https://www.jstor.org/stable/20722635.

Shippey, Tom. "Introduction." In *The Complete Old English Poems*. Translated by Craig Williamson, xv–li. Philadelphia: University of Pennsylvania Press, 2017.

———. "Structure and Unity." In *A Beowulf Handbook*, edited by Robert E. Bjork and John D. Niles, 149–74. Lincoln: University of Nebraska Press, 1998.

Sisam, Kenneth. *Studies in the History of Old English Literature*. Oxford: Clarendon Press, 1953.

Taranu, Catalin. "Goths, Geatas, Gaut: The Invention of an Anglo-Saxon Tradition." In *Transforming the Early Medieval*

World: Studies in Honour of Ian N. Wood, edited by Kivilcim Yavuz and Ricky Broome. Leeds: Kismet Press, forthcoming.

———. *The Bard and the Rag-Picker: Vernacular Verse Histories in Early Medieval England and Francia.* London: Routledge, 2021.

———. "Who Was the Original Dragon-slayer of the Nibelung Cycle?" *Viator* 46, no. 2 (2015): 23–40. DOI: 10.1484/J.VIATOR.5.105360.

Thornbury, Emily. *Becoming a Poet in Anglo-Saxon England.* Cambridge: Cambridge University Press, 2016.

Tonkin, Elizabeth. *Narrating our Pasts: The Social Construction of Oral History.* Cambridge: Cambridge University Press, 1990.

Tönnies, Ferdinand. *Community and Association.* Translated by Charles P. Loomis. London: Routledge and Kegan Paul, 1955.

Tyler, Elizabeth M. *England in Europe: English Royal Women and Literary Patronage, c.1000–c.1150.* Toronto: University of Toronto Press, 2017. DOI: 10.3138/9781442685956.

Tyler, Elizabeth M. and Ross Balzaretti, eds. *Narrative and History in the Early Medieval West.* Turnhout: Brepols, 2006.

Waugh, Robin. "Competitive Narrators in the Homecoming Scene of *Beowulf*." *The Journal of Narrative Technique* 25 (1995): 202–22. https://www.jstor.org/stable/30225967.

Williamson, Craig. *Beowulf and Other Old English Poems.* Philadelphia: University of Pennsylvania Press, 2011.

———. *The Old English Riddles of the Exeter Book.* Chapel Hill: University of North Carolina Press, 1977.

Wormald, Patrick. "Bede, *Beowulf* and the Conversion of the Anglo-Saxon Aristocracy." In *The Times of Bede: Studies in Early English Christian Society and its Historian,* edited by Stephen Baxter, 30–105. Cambridge: Wiley, 2006.

———. *The Making of English Law: King Alfred to the Twelfth Century.* Oxford: Blackwell, 1999.

Contributors

Kim Bergqvist is a doctoral candidate in medieval history in the Department of History at Stockholm University. He is currently completing a dissertation on aristocratic insurrections, resistance, and political values in Castile-León and Sweden, c. 1250–1370. Bergqvist specializes in medieval political and comparative history, history writing, genre and fictionality, and the history of gender and emotions. He is the co-editor of *Conflict and Collaboration in Medieval Iberia* (Cambridge Scholars Publishing, 2020). Other recent publications include: "The Vindication of Sancho II in the Crónica de Castilla: Political Identity and Historiographical Reinvention in Medieval Castilian Chronicles," *The Medieval Chronicle* 11 (2018); "Performing Chivalric Masculinity: Morality, Restraint, and Emotional Norms in *El Libro del cavallero Zifar*," in *Affective and Emotional Economies in Medieval and Early Modern Europe* (New York: Palgrave Macmillan, 2018); and "Kings and Nobles on the Fringes of Christendom: A Comparative Perspective on Monarchy and Aristocracy in the European Middle Ages," in *The Routledge History of Monarchy*, ed. Elena Woodacre at al. (London: Routledge, 2019).

Cynthia Turner Camp is Associate Professor of English at the University of Georgia, publishing on hagiography, historiography, and monastic culture. She is the author of *Anglo-Saxon*

Saints' Lives as History Writing in Late Medieval England (Cambridge: D.S. Brewer, 2015) and with Emily Kelley, co-editor of *Saints as Intercessors between the Wealthy and the Divine: Art and Hagiography among the Medieval Merchant Classes* (London: Routledge, 2019).

Catherine Karkov is Chair of Art History in the School of Fine Art, History of Art and Cultural Studies at the University of Leeds. She has written and edited numerous books and articles on early medieval English Art, including *The Art of Anglo-Saxon England* (Rochester: Boydell Press, 2011) and, most recently, *Imagining Anglo-Saxon: Utopia, Heterotopia, Dystopia* (Rochester: Boydell Press, 2020). She is currently completing a book on Form and Image in Early Medieval England.

Michael J. Kelly lectures history, critical theory, and the philosophy of history at Binghamton University (SUNY) and is Director of Networks and Neighbours and Gracchi Books. His publications include *Isidore of Seville and the "Liber Iudiciorum": The Struggle for the Past in the Visigothic Kingdom,* The Medieval and Early Modern Iberian World 80 (Boston and Leiden: Brill, 2021) and the volume *Theories of History: History Read Across the Humanities* (London: Bloomsbury, 2018). Funded by a Fulbright Fellowship and a Senior Research Fellowship from the RomanIslam Center, University of Hamburg, he is currently preparing a monograph on the concept of "human nature" in early medieval theology.

Justin Lake is Associate Professor of Classics at Texas A&M University. He studies Medieval Latin historiography, medieval rhetoric, and the Classical Tradition. His most recent book is *Confronting Crisis in the Carolingian Empire: Paschasius Radbertus's funeral oration for Wala of Corbie,* an annotated translation of Paschasius Radbertus's *Epitaphium Arsenii,* undertaken together with Mayke de Jong, Professor Emerita of History at the University of Utrecht. Current projects include a study of the rewriting of Aimoin of Fleury's *Gesta Francorum* in the *Grandes Chroniques de France* and the comparative study of Byzantine and Medieval Latin historical prologues.

Ingela Nilsson is Professor of Greek and Byzantine Studies at Uppsala University and Director of the Swedish Research Institute in Istanbul (2019–21). She is a specialist in Byzantine literature with a particular focus on issues of literary adaptation, often from a narratological perspective. Her most recent publications include the co-edited volumes *Storytelling in Byzantium: Narratological Approaches to Byzantine Texts and Images* (Princeton: Princeton University Press, 2018); *Reading the Late Byzantine Romance: A Handbook* (Cambridge: Cambridge University Press, 2019); and the monograph *Writer and Occasion in Twelfth-Century Byzantium: The Authorial Voice of Constantien Manasses* (Cambridge: Cambridge University Press, 2021). In 2018 Nilsson was elected a member of the Royal Swedish Academy of Letters, History and Antiquity, and in 2019 she was awarded the Thureus award from The Royal Society of Sciences at Uppsala. She is editor of the series Studia Byzantina Upsaliensia, associate editor of Brill's Narratological Commentaries to Ancient Texts, and Byzantine Studies editor of Byzantine and Modern Greek Studies.

Ralph O'Connor is Professor in the Literature and Culture of Britain, Ireland and Iceland at the University of Aberdeen, where he teaches in the departments of Celtic & Anglo-Saxon Studies, History, and English. He has published widely on fictional and factual writing about the distant past in the medieval and early modern Gaelic and Norse-Icelandic cultural zones and in the English-speaking world since 1800.

Catalin Taranu is a literary-historical scholar working on the vernacular poems and cultures of early medieval England and Francia. He has taught medieval literature and Old English and has shared his research on Beowulf, medieval rhizomes of narratives, and vernacular theories of truth and history in talks and publications. Catalin is currently a postdoctoral researcher at New Europe College, Bucharest, where he studies the socio-emotional economy of shame and honor in medieval heroic poetry. His first book, titled *The Bard and the Rag-Picker: Vernacular Verse Histories in Early Medieval England and Francia* (London: Routledge, 2021), explores alternative modes of early medieval historical representation.

Index

Adalbero of Laon, bishop – 194
Adeliza, abbess – 126, 128, 129
Ælfgifu, abbess – 119, 121, 123–26, 128, 129, 131
Æthelthryth, queen – 66, 67
agency – 27, 70, 115, 116, 121, 126, 127, 129, 142, 144, 149, 152, 157, 239
Aimoin of Fleury, incl. *Gesta Francorum* – 194, 196, 197
Alfonso X, king – 86, 92, 93, 97; *Siete Partidas* – 92
Alfonso XI, king – 99
Anti-History – 13, 15–17, 27, 30
archive – 20, 65, 71, 74, 101, 113–15, 122, 126, 128, 132, 141, 142
Arthur, king – 44, 274, 282, 283, 290, 291, 292
auctoritas – 17, 29, 47, 51, 53–56, 65–68, 74, 93, 121, 162, 181, 261, 268, 273, 279, 288, 290, 307, 318, 321–25, 331–33, 346, 347, 350
Badiou, Alain – 15–17, 19, 21, 23, 25, 26, 30
Barking *Ordinal* – 20, 116, 120–130
Bede, incl. *Historia Ecclesiastica* – 35, 36, 50, 52, 62–69, 118, 121, 142, 148, 150, 160, 161, 168–70, 186, 308, 321, 322, 323, 326
Beowulf – 28–30, 46, 149, 170, 308–11, 314, 319, 322–25, 328–34, 340–50
Bernardus Silvestris – 88
Bewcastle, Bewcastle Cross – 152–60, 162, 168–70 et passim
biography – 222, 224, 229, 240, 263, 272

Bobbio, monastery – 189
Boniface VIII, pope – 85
Caracalla – 222, 223, 228
Cassiodorus – 185
Chanson de Roland (*Song of Roland*) – 18, 95
Cicero, incl. *De inventione* and *De oratore* – 23, 24, 49, 50, 72, 177–83, 186–91, 193, 196, 201, 202, 295
collaboratio – 29, 54, 74, 318, 325, 333–40, 346–50
community – 35, 38, 54, 56, 65, 67, 70, 116, 118, 119, 122, 126, 128, 130, 131, 168, 288, 312, 318, 336–39, 345, 347–49
Constantine Manasses – 24, 26, 27, 72, 218–35, 237–42
Cnut, king – 200, 201
Croft, Alice, abbess – 129
Crokesley, Richard, abbot – 127
Crónica abreviada (*Abridged Chronicle*) – 86, 100, 101
de Felton, Sybil, abbess – 120
de Sutton, Katherine – 129
de Veer, Ann, abbess – 126
Domesday – 118
Dudo of Saint-Quentin, incl. *Gesta Normannorum* – 187, 191
Ecgfrith of Northumbria – 169
Edith, nun – 121
Edgar, king – 125
Einhard – 186–87
El Conde Lucanor (*Tales of Count Lucanor*) – 86, 93–103
Erkenwald, bishop – 118, 125
Emma, queen, incl. *Encomium Emmae* – 23, 199–201, 313
Estoria de Hispania (*History of Spain*) – 86, 100
Ethelberg, abbess – 118, 120
fama vulgans – 62–65, 68, 321, 326
fabula (incl. fable) – 14, 49, 53, 67, 86, 89, 92, 97–100, 178, 254, 257, 287, 290, 312, 315
fabliau – 67, 254, 281, 283, 291
fantasy (also fantastical, fabulous) – 14, 51, 53, 56, 60, 73, 88, 104, 161, 264, 266, 272, 279, 280, 295, 310–12, 331
Fanum Cocidii   152–53, 161

Fernando III, king – 86, 99
Felix of Crowland, incl. *Life of Guthlac* – 149, 159, 169, 170
Flete, John – 127, 129
Flodoard of Rheims – 188
folklore (also fairytale) – 45, 51, 84, 85, 102, 254, 274, 265, 286, 294, 311, 316, 322
falsehood (also falsify, false, forged) – 19, 26, 29, 41, 50, 52, 57, 60, 62, 90, 98, 181, 188, 197–202, 263, 281, 315, 321, 341
formula (also formulaic) – 27, 29, 295, 326–28
Franks Casket – 150, 152, 166
Frechulf of Lisieux – 187
genealogy (also lineage) – 39, 102, 115, 121, 197, 201, 259–63, 266–72, 276–81, 288, 291, 292, 296, 307–10, 319, 350
Geoffrey of Monmouth – 38, 39, 44, 48, 51, 53, 202, 258, 283, 288, 290, 291
Gildas – 148, 160, 170
Goscelin of Saint-Bertin – 119–21
Gonzalo García (Pérez) Gudiel, archbishop – 85
Gregory of Tours – 185
Hadrian's Wall – 143, 148, 151, 153, 168–69
hagiography (also saint's life) – 42, 64–66, 149, 159, 169, 252, 254, 296, 322,
Hagiotheodorites, Michael – 233–35
heterotopia – 147, 148, 165–67
Hildelith, abbess – 119–21
India – 71, 142, 146–47
Inkan Andes, Inka, Andes – 142–46, 156, 167
Isidore of Seville, incl. *Etymologies* – 14, 49–51, 89, 141–43, 149, 157, 185, 257, 285
Iurminburh, queen – 169
Jaume II, king – 84
judicial process (incl. trial) – 59, 67, 74, 84, 190, 315–19, 337–39, 341–49
Komnene, Anna – 236
lai – 43, 45, 46, 253, 281, 284–86
legend (also myth) – 38, 39, 51, 54, 85, 97, 100, 191, 252–56, 265, 269, 271–73, 276–78, 280, 286, 292, 337

Libro de la caza (*Book on Hunting*) – 86
Libro de las tres razones (*Book of the Three Reasons*) – 83, 101
Libro del cauallero Zifar (*Book of the Knight Zifar*) – 85
Liturgy and liturgical rites (incl. mass) – 19, 20, 71, 116–23, 126–31, 157
Livy, incl. *Ab urbe condita* – 184
Lupus of Ferrières – 186
Manuel I Komnenos, emperor – 219, 221, 224, 225, 232
Manuel, Don Juan, incl. *Libro de los estados* (*Book of the Estates*) – 17–20, 26, 70, 84, 86, 97–104
Marius Victorinus – 177–79, 186, 189, 193–97, 203
Martianus Capella – 185
Martínez, Ferrand, archbishop – 185
memory (also memorial, commemoration, forget) – 19–21, 41, 46, 65, 71, 101, 113–17, 120–32, 141, 142, 145, 149, 150, 152, 157, 160, 167, 226, 251, 255, 262, 266, 272, 280, 282, 284, 285, 290, 322, 324, 327–29, 331, 336
narratology – 36, 40, 98, 102, 103, 215, 217, 218, 222
Norman (incl. Anglo-Norman) – 113, 128, 130, 153, 191, 193, 198, 200, 201, 219
Notker Labeo of St. Gall – 196
oath – 190, 315–18, 345
Oppian – 223–24, 228, 229, 238–40
orality (also oral) – 35, 46, 57, 64–69, 74, 185, 186, 251, 252, 265, 273, 314, 316, 317, 321–26, 330, 334, 337, 340
Otto II, king – 189
patronage – 22, 25, 26, 40, 46, 72, 122, 125, 127, 214, 216, 218, 220, 226–34, 238–41, 267, 268, 308, 326
Paul the Deacon – 187
Plantagenet, Matilda – 128, 131
Pliny – 143
Polybius – 182, 184
Priscian – 89
Quintilian – 189
reader response (also audience) – 15, 18, 25–28, 36–38, 41–49, 52, 54, 58, 59, 62, 69, 73, 74, 84, 90, 91, 92–99, 102–4, 183, 188,

194, 197, 200, 201, 203, 213, 217–21, 224, 229, 238, 239, 252, 255, 257, 259, 261–63, 268, 269, 278, 279–84, 287, 288, 289, 292, 294–96, 309, 310–13, 316, 319–22, 324–26, 328, 333, 335–38, 340–50

Rhetorica ad Herennium – 49, 177–79, 187, 191

Richer of Saint-Remi – 187

riddle – 14, 316–18, 335–37, 348, 350

ruins – 22, 144, 150–56, 159, 160, 169, 170

Saxo Grammaticus, incl. *Gesta Danorum* (*The History of the Danes*) – 44, 53, 252, 265, 273

Septimius Severus – 222

supernatural – 57–60, 280, 309, 310, 331

Sylvester II (Gerbert of Aurillac), pope – 188–90

Tondberct, king – 66

Tortgyth – 121

traditio – 24, 29, 36, 40, 42, 50, 52, 53, 64–74, 98, 103, 146, 185–87, 214, 217, 219, 222, 234, 251, 252, 255, 259, 262–64, 270, 273, 276–81, 284, 286, 291, 308, 309, 314, 321–34, 345–50

vera lex historiae – 15, 16, 50, 62, 64. 65

Vikings – 118, 253, 274, 281, 310

von Zirclaere, Thomasin – 90, 91

Ware, Richard, abbot – 127

White, Hayden – 40, 41, 47, 69, 115, 213, 217

Wilfrid, bishop – 66, 162–68

William I, king – 125

William of Jumièges – 197

William of Malmsbury – 169, 198, 201

William of Tyre – 201

Wroxall Abbey, "Leiger Book" – 125, 129

Wulfhild, abbess – 120, 121

www.ingramcontent.com/pod-product-compliance
Lightning Source LLC
Chambersburg PA
CBHW070835160426
43192CB00012B/2197